INTERFERENCE PATTERNS

INTERFERENCE PATTERNS

Literary Study, Scientific Knowledge, and Disciplinary Autonomy

Jon Adams

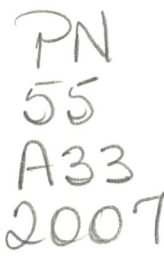

Lewisburg
Bucknell University Press

© 2007 by Rosemont Publishing & Printing Corp.

All rights reserved. Authorization to photocopy items for internal or personal use, or the internal or personal use of specific clients, is granted by the copyright owner, provided that a base fee of $10.00, plus eight cents per page, per copy is paid directly to the Copyright Clearance Center, 222 Rosewood Drive, Danvers, Massachusetts 01923. [978-0-8387-5681-2/07 $10.00 + 8¢ pp, pc.]

Associated University Presses
2010 Eastpark Boulevard
Cranbury, NJ 08512

The paper used in this publication meets the requirements of the American National Standard for Permanence of Paper for Printed Library Materials Z39.48-1984.

Library of Congress Cataloging-in-Publication Data

Adams, Jon, 1977–
  Interference patterns : literary study, scientific knowledge, and disciplinary autonomy / Jon Adams.
     p. cm.
  Includes bibliographical references and index.
  ISBN-13: 978-0-8387-5681-2 (alk. paper)
  ISBN-10: 0-8387-5681-6 (alk. paper)
    1. Literature and science. 2. Literature—History and criticism—Theory, etc. I. Title.
  PN55.A33 2007
  809'.93356—dc22   2006039232

PRINTED IN THE UNITED STATES OF AMERICA

Contents

Acknowledgments	7
Introduction: Interference Patterns	11
1: Scientism and the Unity of Knowledge	23
2: Making a Science of Criticism	39
3: Evolutionary Psychology	77
4: Relativism and the Unity of Culture	100
5: Relativism and the Commonsense Realists	127
6: Centralities of Language and Matter	157
Conclusion: Tessellation Patterns	199
Notes	208
Works Cited	247
Index	257

Acknowledgments

Much of this book was written while I was the recipient of an A.H.R.B. (now A.H.R.C.) award between 2000–2002 at the University of Durham, Department of English Studies. Further work has been carried out at the Department of Economic History, London School of Economics and Political Science, as part of the Leverhulme Trust/E.S.R.C. funded project called "The Nature of Evidence: How Well do 'Facts' Travel?"

Many thanks to Professors Patricia Waugh, Stephen J. Burn, Julie Sanders, David Amigoni, Mary Morgan, and to Mr Dickinson and Ms. Dickson. The people at Bucknell and AUP and especially my copyeditor have been vital in making this happen. Also to my parents, family, and friends. Thanks to Maria for holding me up while I was letting myself down.

Permission to reproduce material from the following sources is greatly appreciated:

From *THE INFORMATION*, by MARTIN AMIS
Reprinted by permission of HarperCollins Publishers Ltd.
© Martin Amis, 1995.

From *EINSTEIN'S MONSTERS* by Martin Amis (© 1987), published by Jonathan Cape. Reprinted by permission of The Random House Group Ltd.

From *THE ADAPTED MIND: EVOLUTIONARY PSYCHOLOGY AND THE GENERATION OF CULTURE*, edited by Jerome H. Barkow, Leda Cosmides, and John Tooby (1992) used by permission of Oxford University Press, Inc.

From *EVOLUTION AND LITERARY THEORY* by Joseph Carroll, by permission of the University of Missouri Press. Copyright © 1994 by the Curators of the University of Missouri.

From *THE SELFISH GENE*, by Richard Dawkins (© 1989) used by permission of Oxford University Press, Inc.

From *UNWEAVING THE RAINBOW: SCIENCE, DELUSION AND THE APPETITE FOR WONDER* by Richard Dawkins. Copyright © 1998 by Richard Dawkins. Reprinted by permission of Houghton Mifflin Company. All rights reserved.

From *DARWIN'S DANGEROUS IDEA: EVOLUTION AND THE MEANINGS OF LIFE* by Daniel C. Dennett. Reprinted with the permission of Simon & Schuster Adult Publishing Group. © 1995 by Daniel C. Dennett.

From *PROFESSIONAL CORRECTNESS: LITERARY STUDIES AND POLITICAL CHANGE,* by Stanley Fish (© 1995) used by permission of Oxford University Press, Inc.

From *ANATOMY OF CRITICISM: FOUR ESSAYS,* by Northrop Frye ©1957 Princeton University Press, 1985 renewed Princeton University Press, 2000 paperback edition. Reprinted by permission of Princeton University Press.

From *LANGUAGE AND LITERATURE,* by Roman Jakobson, edited by Krystyna Pomorska and Stephen Rudy (© 1987) by permission of The Roman Jakobson Trust and Harvard University Press.

From *CREATED FROM ANIMALS: THE MORAL IMPLICATIONS OF DARWINISM,* by James Rachels (© 1990) used by permission of Oxford University Press, Inc.

From *CONSILIENCE: THE UNITY OF KNOWLEDGE* by Edward O. Wilson, copyright © 1998 by Edward O. Wilson. Used by permission of Alfred A. Knopf, a division of Random House, Inc.

INTERFERENCE PATTERNS

Introduction: Interference Patterns

LITERARY CRITICS SHARE AN ANXIETY THAT IS GROUNDED NOT IN doubts about the worth of the novels, poems, and plays that they study, but about the manner in which those studies are conducted. This anxiety arises because of the sciences. It is thought to be no coincidence that while the sciences have enjoyed an unprecedented level of demonstrable success in achieving their aims, they have simultaneously conducted their studies according to methods quite different from those employed within the humanities. My purpose is not to dispute that success, nor to question the applicability of those methods employed by the various scientific disciplines in the pursuit of their aims. My purpose is rather to address the anxiety of literary critics regarding the epistemological status of their work. There is a perception that the type of knowledge scientists possess about natural phenomena is superior to the type of knowledge possessed by literary critics. This insecurity is felt across the humanities and exacerbated by those scientists who, emboldened by the achievements of their colleagues, would seek to convert all knowledge into scientific knowledge. They allege that the intellectual demands of the humanities, and the consequent epistemological value of their productions, are grossly inferior to those of the sciences. There is no shortage of voices from within the humanities willing to corroborate those claims. This, for example, is the philosopher of science Bas van Fraassen: "There is a reason why metaphysics sounds so passé, so *vieux jeu* today; for intellectually challenging perplexities and paradoxes it has been far surpassed by theoretical science. Do the concepts of the Trinity, the soul, haecceity, universals, prime matter, and potentiality baffle you? They pale beside the unimaginable otherness of closed space-times, event-horizons, EPR correlations, and bootstrap models."[1] Those problems that have traditionally exercised the humanities have come to seem not only elementary but—what is perhaps worse—artificial and unnecessary. Literary study looks weak, easy, and, above all, parochial beside the technologies and universal truths of science.

Consequently, literary critics will either admit defeat and accept a subservient role beside science (a sense of inferiority before scientists that Auden compared to feeling like "a shabby curate in a drawing-room full of dukes,"[2]) or else challenge the claims of scientists to epistemological superiority. This challenge often manifests in a defensiveness that seeks not to answer directly the complaints of the scientists, but to deny the validity of those complaints. The philosophical positions most suitable for supporting such a denial are those that seek to establish a relativism of human knowledge with respect to culture. Recognizing that their own work is bounded by cultural norms and true only within the culture from which it arises, thinkers within the humanities often choose to demand that scientists impose similar constraints on their knowledge claims (constraints that strategically abduct most all of science's validity and affect literary study not at all). Largely because such positions are adopted solely for defensive purposes, rather than out of any genuine conviction that knowledge is indeed limited in this sense, this strategy all too often results in literary critics embracing crude forms of cultural relativism that fare poorly under scrutiny and lead to absurd positions that attempt to deny the effectiveness of scientific knowledge and its technologies. Such positions are all too easily overturned by such simple responses as Richard Dawkins's "knock-down" airplane argument, "Show me a cultural relativist at thirty thousand feet and I'll show you a hypocrite."[3] Unwilling or unable to confront the technical difficulties involved with arguing against scientists on their own ground, literary critics often adopt relativistic positions only instrumentally, expediently diverting criticisms to better continue the real task at hand: the analysis of novels, poems, and plays. I contend that such a retreat is unnecessary and that literary study need not deny the validity of scientific knowledge to preserve its place in the academy.

How then to defend literary study in anything like its present form without ceding to some version of scientization? Not all literary critics agree that such scientization is entirely undesirable. Following the path of such disciplines as linguistics or psychology, attempts have been made to introduce into literary study some of the empirical methods and conceptual organization that characterize scientific thinking. In the second half of the twentieth century, both linguistics and psychology have achieved (partial) recognition as scientific disciplines, and in the crossover study of psycholinguistics, they find a degree of mutual reinforcement for this status.[4] Both adhere to a scientific materialism that seeks to root the phenomena they study in evolved biological structures, and although they still possess their unscientific elements (for example, the remnants of psychoanalysis in psychology and pragmatics in linguistics), these are not necessarily inconsistent with the sciences, simply less theoretically dependent on them. (This is especially true of pragmatics.) Crucially, what both linguistics and psychology have achieved is a methodological alignment with the sciences, and it is this sort of methodological alignment that literary study conspicuously lacks. The twentieth century saw attempts to forge links with both linguistics and psychology, but these coalitions were for the most part unsuccessful. The hopes triggered by thinkers like Roman Jakobson for a linguistic base for literary study proved short on content and unable to discriminate value, and the influence of Freudian theories of interpretation and Jungian theories of origin, while popular, ultimately proved to be a damaging alliance when these same theories were shed from academic psychology precisely because they lacked scientific credibility.

In the last decade of the twentieth century, however, a new possibility for scientific integration arose through evolutionary psychology, a discipline branching from psychology and ethology that seeks to understand human behavior through an understanding of the adaptive benefits of a particular behavior or cognitive trait to Stone Age man. Evolutionary psychology takes as its starting point the claim from William James that humans have more instincts than the other animals, not fewer, and the claim from Noam Chomsky that the human mind is modular—not a general-purpose processor, but one equipped with task-specific (and genetically inherited) mechanisms. As part of their ongoing project to comprehensively understand and explain human behavior through Darwinian theory, evolutionary psychologists began to turn their attention to art and literature, which, as species-typical behaviors, must be accounted for. (The conceptual foundations of evolutionary psychology and its particular interest in literature are explored in the second chapter.)[5]

Although it is not the explicit intention of evolutionary psychology to subsume literary study, the threat of elimination is very real. What evolutionary psychology apparently offers is a means of drawing literary study into the sciences, legitimizing it in the same way that linguistics and psychology have become legitimate. What this threatens is to render obsolete the current practices. Couple this with the imperialistic claims of those reductionists who would see all explanations given in scientifically digestible terms, and it becomes clear that modest calls for "conceptual integration" translate to calls for the excision of literary study from the academy. So there is some hesitation among literary critics to accept the evolutionary account of literature. While there are relativistic positions of considerable sophistication, resisting the explanatory power of evolutionary thinking need not involve the denial of evolutionary theory. The core argument against the adoption of an exclusively evolutionary view is put succinctly by

Hilary Putnam. "What is wrong with evolutionary epistemology is not that the scientific facts are wrong, but that they don't answer the philosophical questions."[6] Putnam's arguments (explored in the first chapter and reintroduced in the third through Richard Rorty) trade on defining *explanation* in terms of answering the questions asked. In this study, I contend that a discipline is defined not by its subject matter but by the questions it answers regarding that subject matter (and this is discussed in the sixth chapter, with reference to Stanley Fish's arguments about disciplinary identity). That said, evolutionary psychology has its adherents even among the literary critics. Joseph Carroll was quick to adopt wholeheartedly the idea that literary study could profit from a closer relationship with the sciences. Under scrutiny, however, it becomes apparent that Carroll's argument for the relevance of evolutionary theory to literary study has as much to do with what an evolutionary psychological perspective would exclude as what it would facilitate. (This idea is discussed in the second and sixth chapters.)

So the relationship between literary study and the sciences is more muddled than the idea of mutual-incomprehension-tending-toward-hostility that Charles Percy Snow first detected in 1959. In 1964, the same year that Snow published the second edition of his "Two Cultures" lectures, physicist Richard Feynman was still able to claim that, in the West, "We respect the arts more than the sciences."[7] Despite the persistent feeling among scientists that this situation still obtains,[8] the position is increasingly implausible. Seen from outside the universities, literary study has come to seem one of the weaker academic disciplines. Unlike science, it is without technologies and it is sharply limited in its scope. By contrast, the public appetite for science, sustained by popularizations and regularly (and sensationally) reported in news stories, is huge.[9] Because it has such wide application, science assumes and maintains a relevance and a cultural importance that literary study cannot hope to challenge. Our immersion in and dependence on its technologies is able demonstration of the success of the sciences over the past two or three hundred years. Even without the prodding of imperialists like E. O. Wilson, that success alone is apt to make the unscientific disciplines feel somewhat inadequate.

With no technologies or practical applications beyond unwanted and increasingly perverse interpretations of texts, literary study remains bound up with the universities, unable to be more than an academic exercise. Meanwhile, *scientific* has become a synonym for precision in much the same way as *academic* has become a synonym for unnecessary, joining *sophistry* as a pejorative tag for learned debate. Technological application is what stops the work of scientists being merely academic. When it matters, we turn to science to maintain our health, as in medicine, or to settle disputes, as in the courts of law. (That the relations between science and technology are more complex than this sketch suggests is something discussed in the fifth chapter.)

So literary study sits uncomfortably in the modern academy. Its failure to adopt a research program and methodology consonant with the sciences is seen by some scientists as a stubborn and willful rejection of what has been an indisputably successful approach to their own subject of study. In what follows, I aim to show that methods applicable to one discipline are often not applicable to another, and that it is not stubbornness, but necessity, that has left literary study floating outside the sciences. Integration cuts off too much of what we want to say. It is not that we cannot talk about books scientifically, just that the type of answers that science can offer us about fiction are inapplicable to the questions we had been asking. Of course, this is not to say literary study is not also stubborn and backward looking, and there are many ways in which the sciences and the arts can be interesting to one another, but these should not demand the collapse of existing practices in the weaker discipline. In terms of disciplinary autonomy, that is what is meant by imperialism, and what looks like interdisciplinarity is very often this sort of negative interference, a cancelling out of methods.

Interference Patterns, the title of this study, refers to just such disturbance. The two cultures do not exist entirely harmoniously, neither has one simply brushed the other aside. The relations and interactions between literary study and the sciences are complex. The term *interference patterns* is a reference to Thomas Young's famous two-slit experiment (first conducted in the early nineteenth century) that physicists use to demonstrate that light travels in waves. The experiment involves two boards—the first with one slit, the second with two—and a third surface at a sufficient distance behind the boards. A light source is shone at the first board, and it passes through the single slit. A narrower beam of light is cast onto the two slits of the second board. While it might have been expected that the light subsequently cast from these two slits would simply project two discrete beams onto the wall beyond, Young discovered that the actual result was a complex pattern of dark and light bands, like a barcode. These patterns are caused by what is called constructive and destructive interference. So my choice of title is intended to suggest that a similar interference occurs between the sciences and the humanities. The interference is both complex and unexpected.

Given that this book is about science and literature, a conspicuous omission from what follows is fiction. Although I discuss fiction indirectly throughout, I address it directly only in the latter part of the final chapter, with reference to Kurt Vonnegut's *Slaughterhouse-Five* and two novels by Martin Amis: *Time's Arrow* and *The Information*. Even then, it is not the fiction of Vonnegut and Amis that is being discussed so much as the philosophical and theoretical content of their work, and their perspective on the issue under discussion (namely, how science offers new ways of thinking about time and mankind's place in the universe). That the ideas appeared in works of fiction becomes incidental. (In Amis's case, those ideas had already been touched on in his literary criticism before they were discussed by characters in his novel.) Much has already been written about the interactions between science and literature—how authors have been scientifically alert, how they have been influenced by the science of their day, and even the extent to which science borrows ideas from literature. The majority of literature and science criticism takes as its foundation the shared ground of language and very often concentrates on the use of metaphor.[10] The metaphor-based approach is avoided here for two reasons. First, it is inconsistent with my particular interests. Second, I am unsure of the effectiveness of the metaphor approach.

Talking about the exchange of metaphors between science and literature is complicated. One of the reasons it is complicated is that what literary critics call a metaphor is often nothing of the sort for a scientist. New language spills out from the sciences (novelist Don DeLillo calls science "a source of new names"[11]), and as it seems that you need an (at least putative) object or phenomenon before you can have a noun, it is obvious why: science catalogs the world. It gives us names for physical entities and processes that can subsequently be used metaphorically.[12] Poets are not a source of new names; their particular skill has always been importing words metaphorically. It is the scientists who offer the neologisms. When a certain scientist says "the mind is a machine," that is not a metaphor. She is trying to explain to us that she really thinks that the mind should be understood as machines like typewriters and steam engines and computers are understood (in terms of the causal relations that hold between components, and so on). She will argue that it is a very complex machine, but that this does not mean it is not a machine.

While much interesting work has been written about the cross-pollination of metaphor between science and literature, the tendency among literary critics taking this approach is to overstate the metaphorical content of scientific writing, to assume that everything that might be metaphorical probably is. By looking for metaphorical language within a scientific text, the critic has found a means of treating scientific writing as if it were literary writing. In other words, the critic is able to draw scientific writing into the rhetorical domain, effectively removing it from the jurisdiction of the science. Literary critics are trained to detect and account for metaphorical language, but they are also conditioned to expect metaphorical language. This, in turn, leads to an oversensitivity to the presence of language that might have been legitimately read as figurative had it occurred in a literary text. It is not, of course, either impossible or invalid to read a scientific text as if it were a literary text. But to do so is to deliberately ignore all but the aesthetic features, and it is surely invalid to infer from this possibility that the scientific text is, therefore, of the same epistemological status as a literary text. A technical illustration (such as a map or a zoological plate) may possess aesthetic merit, but it is an error to assume that an appreciation of its aesthetic qualities is sufficient to exhaust its purpose (that is, a map is not only an abstract composition; with the addition of a key, it is also a map). By apparently failing to recognize this distinction, such approaches often miss something important about the limitations of the literary approach to scientific writing. The following extract from Gillian Beer underlines my concerns here:

> The excitement generated among non-scientists by chaos theory is an instance: chaos theory calls attention to observed but excluded irregularity, asymmetry and flux. That it has developed alongside deconstruction, with its refusal of parameters of interpretation, its obdurate relativism, is as intriguing as is the rediscovery of plate-tectonics at the height of the fashion for Derridean epistemology, with its emphasis on un-grounding. Are such analogies just a play of words? I do not believe so.[13]

Her answer to that last question is where we should begin to stop listening. What Beer is doing is bringing the type of interpretive skills quite valid within her own discipline of literary study and treating scientific work as if it could be evaluated or even sensibly discussed in such terms. "Un-grounding" means quite different things in each case. Tectonic plate movement is not a metaphor. Geophysicists call the sections of crust "plates" because they are flat sheets (dinner plates being, of course, only an instance of this broader definition of a plate). The movement is because the plates move. This is not a metaphor. There is no language play here. There are plates, albeit big ones, and they are moving around, albeit only very slowly and very slightly. These are matters of empirical fact. Why, then, do we have Gillian Beer pondering the metaphorical content of plate tectonics? In a sense, she is looking at the map without the key. Even if the revival of plate tectonics had been brought about by a geophysicist reading Derrida, the influence of Derrida's thinking on plate-tectonics *insofar as that is a science* would have been nil.¹⁴ No causality exists between these two events; the only link is linguistic. If you only perform a literary-critical or linguistic reading, then it starts to look as if there might be something in it because these readings recognize an intriguing verbal echo, but that is not substantive. It is true insofar as the echo exists, but it says nothing about the validity of either theory in light of the coincidence of terms (and would, in any case, probably not be true in other languages).

Another anxiety with analyzing fiction through literature-science criticism involves the risk of layering scientific ideas over artworks that can be adequately explained without reference to those ideas. This type of overdetermination leaves its culprits looking too eager to have scientific ideas meaningfully active within literary texts or paintings in order to allow their favored authors or artists to share in the prestige of science. This approach creates an intellectual climate where consonance with *scientific* ideas scores an *aesthetic* point for the artist. As John Limon has it, "One finds oneself at slide shows aching with good intentions to see special relativity in the *Demoiselles d'Avignon*."¹⁵ This is both needless and, insofar as it implicitly acknowledges a superior status for scientific ideas, pernicious.

Limon's comment reminds us that the metaphor approach has been particularly popular with scholars interested in exploring the similarities between modernist art and what was often called "the new science"—quantum mechanics and relativity. The appeal here is understandable: in the early decades of the twentieth century, both art and science made radical breaks from their histories. Rumors emerged from within the sciences that suggested the world was far stranger than Newton had expected; there was talk of the observer affecting the observed, of human consciousness being inseparably enmeshed with the process of measurement, and, most tantalizing of all, the German physicist Werner Heisenberg had spoken of *uncertainty*. The word suggested that the Laplacean complacency of the physical sciences was unfounded, that the universe was unpredictable at every level. The so-called Copenhagen Interpretation of quantum physics (endorsed by Niels Bohr and resisted by Einstein) seemingly placed categorical limits on the knowable, introducing randomness as a feature of reality. Self-destructively, the scientists themselves seemed to have proved that the omniscience and precision of physics were only façades behind which their work was as subjective as the arts. At more or less the same time as Einstein was publishing his Special Theory of Relativity, Picasso had parted ways with the realist tradition. All appearances were unstable, representational depiction was just another convention, no closer to how things were than his own dislocated images where surfaces were relative to the viewer and not one another. In fact, in light of the new science, Picasso's paintings themselves came to seem more accurate accounts of reality than the outmoded photorealism of Vermeer. As e. e. cummings (who had consciously tried to do to poetry what the cubists had done to painting) had it, "you hew form truly."[16] But the disruption of realism in the arts was a very different thing than the disruption of reality implied by the new physics. The hoped-for affinities between *uncertainty* in science and uncertainty in painting, music, and literature are as shallow and as incidental as the link between Derridean epistemological ungrounding and the revival of plate tectonics.

While a good case can be made for the influence of imaginative popularizations of science having an effect on the way writers, musicians, and painters create their art, the case for a central cultural ferment or *Zeitgeist* from which both emerge is less strong. Some of the confusion can be traced back to the use of *uncertainty*—a word often preferably translated as *indeterminacy* or even *undecidability*.[17] (Einstein, similarly misread, had favored *invariance* over *relativity*.) The Uncertainty Principle—much like the also ever-popular Incompleteness Theorem of Kurt Gödel—attracts thinkers from the humanities who fail to realize that these are specialist terms with strictly limited application. (In crude terms, Heisenberg's principle is about the measurement of position and velocity of particles, and Gödel's theorem is a mathematical version of the epimenidean liar-paradox for formal systems in set theory.) As with "chaos" or "the selfish gene," the tag is attractive for all the wrong reasons (although, since these same reasons are deliberately exploited by the popularizers to attract attention, there is an extent to which nonscientists are understandably confused).

While my title is taken from physics, in discussing the relations between literary study and science, I concentrate almost exclusively on the biological sciences. I took this approach in part for the reasons given above regarding the vacuity of much that is said within art criticism regarding the parallels between uncertainty in quantum physics and uncertainty in the interpretation of texts, but also because writing in any meaningful way about quantum physics would require acquiring a level of learning that I suspect would have been prohibitively time-consuming, not to mention beyond my capacities as a mathematician. The biological sciences are less committed to and dependent on mathematics. Nor does an upheaval within atomic physics necessarily affect the truth of biological statements. Linnaean taxa and Darwinian evolution are, as it were, functional accounts, and their truth or falsity remains unaffected by the shift from a Newtonian to an Einsteinian universe. (To the extent they are functional descriptions, they can be said to supervene on the physical structures in which they are instantiated.) Furthermore, the biological sciences—through evolutionary theory and, to some extent, neurobiology—seek to explain human behavior directly *as* behavior; whereas the sense in which physics might be said to explain human behavior is an incidental consequence of humans being made of atoms. Chief among those biologies of behavior are evolutionary psychology and cognitive science. Although both have influenced literature-science criticism,[18] my attention is asymmetric. Evolutionary psychology is referenced throughout this study and looked at in some detail in the third chapter, while cognitive science is almost wholly excluded—largely for reasons of space, but also to try to introduce some focus to an increasingly generalist project. Most of the conclusions about evolutionary psychology can also be applied to cognitive science.

On a related note, and as something of a disclaimer, interdisciplinarity also opens problems for communication that revolve around a discipline's characteristic (and, some will argue, constitutive) vocabulary: its particular approach to its subject matter, the questions it seeks to answer, and the (often technical, discipline-specific) language in which it offers those answers. Since so much of this study is devoted to the problems of interdisciplinary exchanges created by the specificity of disciplinary vocabularies, it is an issue of some considerable importance here.

A crucial problem for the dissemination of scientific knowledge to non-specialists is effecting a suitable compromise between the preservation of the distinctive vocabulary of the science under discussion and the requirement that this material be accessible to an untrained readership—that is, the extent to which the translation of that vocabulary involves a dilution of the concepts being discussed. This is, of course, the central problem confronted by popularizers of science (discussed at length in chapter five). But while the sincere popularizer will aim to minimize (as much as is possible) the deleterious effects of what Aldous Huxley called the necessary evil of abbreviation,[19] a risk remains that this potential for confusion can be more cynically exploited by those seeking to avoid the direct questions of specialist interrogation. Mary Midgely calls this tactic "Chinese metaphysics": the idea being that we talk metaphysics to the Chinese and Chinese to the metaphysicians, so leaving both parties unsure as to whether they have the relevant authority to question the point being made. "Real interdisciplinary work," Midgely contends, "includes some of the hardest thinking in the trade, though the substitute activity that sometimes passes under its name includes some of the easiest."[20]

Although this work is (at least nominally) addressed to literary critics, to make my arguments, I have drawn on the work of philosophers and scientists whose specialist vocabularies and deployment of terms such as *begging the question* and *fitness* are often at odds with their use outside those disciplines. In so doing, I have sought as much as possible to avoid falling into Chinese metaphysics. Consequently, sections here explain at some length such topics as evolutionary theory and neopragmatist philosophy that, while crucial to my arguments, may be unfamiliar to those trained exclusively in literary study. The issue of audience is a central problem for any interdisciplinary or multidisciplinary work, and the absence of a common language is still the major obstacle standing between the two cultures (indeed, plausible claims have been made to the effect that such a common language is impossible, and these are discussed in the fifth chapter). The tension here is between the demands of specialism and the necessity of generalism. The anxiety here is falling into a trap highlighted by the American novelist David Foster Wallace. Reviewing two fictionalized accounts of mathematical discoveries, Wallace found what he considered to be a "paradoxical-looking problem": "the type of audience most likely to appreciate the novels' lofty . . . view of pure math is also the audience most apt to be disappointed by the . . . vague . . . or inconsistent ways the novels handle the actual mathematics they're concerned with." In other words, by trying to include fairly complex material in what is marketed as a popular novel, the author creates a work that is at once too technical and not technical enough—a situation, as Wallace puts it, where "necessary conditions for liking the novel are also sufficient conditions for disliking it."[21] The lengthy explanations in this study, when they occur, are intended only to make clear the foundations of the positions of their proponents or to offer some context to the points discussed and are obviously not intended as substitute for scientific training.

Related to this issue is a further problem intrinsic to this work: I am a nonscientist proposing to discuss in nontrivial terms certain scientific ideas while running a parallel argument to the effect that only scientists can discuss scientific ideas in a meaningful fashion. Consequently, I apparently leave myself vulnerable to the charge that any sections seeking to discredit particular claims of scientists involve an error of logic: either my argument about the insularity of specialist vocabularies is false or my critiques of scientific ideas are meaningless. Hence, I appear to be a victim of my own arguments. Obviously, I do not think that this is the case. Preempting what will be discussed at more length in the fifth chapter, my arguments about the accessibility of scientific ideas to the non-specialist are intended to challenge directly the inconsistency at the heart of the twin claims made by hostile advocates of science that scientific ignorance is unforgivable (there are, after all, plenty of popular accounts) and that scientific knowledge is difficult to acquire (and that popular science cannot teach real scientific knowledge). With the majority of scientific information rendered inaccessible to the nonspecialist, knowledge of scientific ideas comes largely from popular accounts. It is a condition of my case here that if my knowledge of the science is inadequate and any critiques of scientific ideas are invalid on account of my distance from the specialism, then my arguments about the invalidity of the criticisms regarding the scientific ignorance of literary scholars made by advocates of science still hold. To be criticized by scientists for ignorance is for them to implicitly concede the educational redundancy of popular science and to reveal the accusation of "you haven't tried to learn about scientific ideas" to be the far sharper accusation of "you are not a scientist." That is, it turns an argument about epistemological superiority into a territorial issue, which is irresolvable beyond the ablation of literary study from the academy.

1
Scientism and the Unity of Knowledge

C. P. SNOW'S "TWO CULTURES" LECTURE DREW THE BORDERS CLEARLY. "Literary intellectuals at one pole—at the other scientists, and as the most representative, the physical scientists. Between the two a gulf of mutual incomprehension—sometimes (particularly among the young), hostility and dislike."[1] The thrust of the argument was a call to unity, to knit together a separation that Snow saw as "sheer loss to us all."[2] To those optimistic about the possibilities of cultural synthesis, Snow's was a welcome contribution to a history of such attempts that stretched back through the ideals of the Enlightenment to Francis Bacon and before and that finds voice today in the likes of E. O. Wilson, whose 1998 book *Consilience* marked another step in an on-going project to understand human behavior through an understanding of human evolutionary biology. Wilson began his scientific career as an entomologist and secured his professional reputation through his work with ants—organisms with a tightly regimented society and very little intelligence. It was, however, 1975's *Sociobiology* that made his name outside the scientific community. Because it makes little sense to talk of the cultural transmission of social structure in ants, the explanation for the manifest complexity of their societies must come from innate biological mechanisms. Entomologists, therefore, assume that any ant behaviors they observe are preprogrammed, mechanical performances. The central premise of *Sociobiology*—the book and the science that it spawned—consisted in the transferral of that perspective to the animal kingdom as a whole. A simplistic way to describe Wilson's work is that he sees all animal behavior in the way he saw ant behavior. Each section of *Sociobiology* examined behavior (in terms of evolutionary biology) in the societies of progressively more complex animals. The last chapter focused on human society, and this caused a good deal of controversy because, with barely a pause, Wilson had begun talking about humans with the same vocabulary he had been using to talk about animals just a few pages before. The evolutionary perspective of sociobiology put humans back among the animals; it implied that anthropology was just another ethology. So, having united the animal kingdom with *Sociobiology*, *Consilience* is Wilson's attempt to unite the disciplines by urging, once again, that we can use the same tools.

That the goal (and subtitle) of *Consilience*, "the unity of knowledge," is a worthwhile end is held to be axiomatic: all true beliefs will cohere, and the "sheer loss" of polarization can be turned to intellectual profit. So Snow bemoaned "our fanatical belief in educational specialisation"[3] as a block to "the clashing point of two subjects," which "ought to produce creative chances."[4] Similarly, Wilson complains that, "It is the custom of scholars when addressing behaviour and culture to speak variously of anthropological explanations, psychological explanations, biological explanations, and other explanations appropriate to the perspectives of individual disciplines."[5]

But there is a loss in unity, too, for unity also implies homogenization—less a true synthesis and more an incorporation of one worldview into the parameters of what will become the dominant other. Wilson is quite clear on what the dominant other will be. "I have argued that there is intrinsically only one class of explanation. It traverses the scales of space, time, and complexity to unite the disparate facts of the disciplines by consilience, the perception of a seamless web of cause and effect."[6] More explicitly he states, "The central idea of the consilience world view is that all tangible phenomena, from the birth of stars to workings of social institutions, are based on material processes that are ultimately reducible, however long and tortuous the sequences, to the laws of physics."[7]

Wilson's decision to ground his reductionism in physics is a deliberate return to the principles of logical positivism and the Vienna Circle. Like the logical positivists, Wilson believes that every complex system is explicable in terms of the simpler rules governing the component parts of that system. For the positivists, this method demonstrates the unity of the sciences; the thinking being that in this manner, all the various disciplines can be collapsed back into or analyzed in terms of causally more basic physical laws and thereby shown to be unified in this respect (and, accordingly, dependent on the physical sciences). The issue of reductionism has also featured in debates within the philosophy of mind where mental properties—what Descartes called *res cogitans*—are explained in terms of the physical properties of the brain. No longer need we posit two kinds of things, mind and matter, because all that needs to be explained can be explained by matter alone. As materialism (or physicalism) has become orthodoxy, resistance to a reduction of this kind leads to accusations of what Kathleen Lennon has called "closet Cartesianism."[8] To some extent, Wilson trades on the same threat. Either everything is made of matter and thus explicable in terms of that matter, or you are trying to insert into the explanation something other than matter—something like the soul, the spirit, or the *res cogitans* of Descartes. "Belief in the intrinsic unity of knowledge," Wilson writes, "rides ultimately on the hypothesis that every mental process has a physical grounding and is consistent with the natural sciences."[9] Wilson presents it as a choice between accepting both materialism and consilience or rejecting consilience and accepting some form of dualism. It is as if Wilson is using dualism to bully us into agreeing with him.

The motivation for such reductionism is usually parsimony or conservation of information. Demonstrating that different phenomena can be explained by reference to the same causes stems the ontological spread. This is how Paul Oppenheim and Hilary Putnam explain the appeal in their 1958 paper "Unity of Science as a Working Hypothesis": "the meta-scientific study of major aspects of science, is the natural means for counterbalancing specialization by promoting the integration of scientific knowledge."[10] The threat from specialization is incommunicability, where without some sort of organizing principle, the various specialisms would collectively amount to what biologist Erwin Chargaff called the "Tower of Babble." Chargaff's fear is that the sheer volume of data necessary to participate in any one scientific specialism would preclude meaningful exchanges between those specialisms, and individual scientists would increasingly find they were unable to "know more than an ever smaller portion of what they must know in order to function properly."[11] The fear is echoed by Joshua Lederberg when he complains that "[b]iology is already so fact laden that it is in danger of being bogged down awaiting advances in logic and linguistics to ease the integration of the particulars."[12] It seems that, in every sense, the end of science is data. Snow was also wary of the multiplicity of subdisciplines and feared this fragmentation, believing that the educational system in the United Kingdom encouraged specialization too early, and saw this as a wedge keeping the two cultures apart. So the positive dimension of Wilson's *Consilience* is the drawing up of a method by which specialists might find a common language so as to ease the difficulty of communication and in so doing to bridge the divisions between the various disciplines.

Wilson's approach for achieving this is modeled on Oppenheim and Putnam's. They proposed a six-tier hierarchy of "natural" reductive levels, where each thing of each level (except of course the lowest) is composed solely of things from the level immediately below it, and so "[i]n this sense each level will be as it were a 'common denominator' for the level immediately above it."[13] The six levels they list are (from the top): Social Groups, (multicellular) Living Things, Cells, Molecules, Atoms, and the Elementary Particles.[14] So, cell biology can be explained in terms of molecular biology, molecular biology in terms of organic chemistry, chemistry to molecular and then atomic physics, and atomic physics by reference to the elementary particles. These incremental, "cumulative micro-reductions" as Oppenheim and Putnam call them are seductively simple, and no less so when they scale up rather than down: from cell biology to zoology to evolutionary biology to behavioral science or perhaps to neuroscience, to psychology and to sociology—each step shading into the next. As should be apparent, the so-called bottom-up approach is divergent, aiming for a specific discipline (here, sociology via behavioral science or psychology). This differs from the top-down approach, which always converges on physics. Scaling up and subsuming disciplines as you go makes dependency on the physical laws less obvious. Without a fairly painstaking series of reductions, it's hard to see how sociology can be explained in mathematico-physical terms. This is one reason why the extension of the (relatively uncontroversial) unity of science to include a reductive account of sociology, psychology, or the humanities is often resisted. Wilson's belief is that this is just a temporary obstacle, a symptom of working with an incomplete scientific ontology.

Sixty years before, in their *International Encyclopaedia of Unified Sciences*, the positivists of the Vienna Circle had expressed similar hopes. Rudolf Carnap assured followers that although "it is obvious that, at the present time [1937], laws of psychology and social science cannot be derived from those of biology and physics . . . no scientific reason is known for the assumption that such a derivation should be in principle and forever impossible."[15] Oppenheim and Putnam agree:

> It is not absurd to suppose that psychological laws may eventually be explained in terms of the behaviour of individual neurons in the brain; that the behaviour of individual cells—including neurons—may eventually be explained in terms of their biological constitution; and that the behaviour of molecules—including the macro-molecules that make up living cells—may eventually be explained in terms of atomic physics. If this is achieved, then psychological laws will have, in principle, been reduced to the laws of atomic physics.[16]

However, they are quick to stress the limits of such an approach, adding that "it would nevertheless be hopelessly impractical to try and derive the behaviour of a single human being directly from his constitution in terms of elementary particles."[17] Like Carnap, Wilson admits that the type of unification he is aiming for is not yet possible: "The belief in the possibility of consilience beyond science and across the great branches of learning [the sciences and the arts] is not yet science. It is a metaphysical world view.... It cannot be proved with logic from first principles or grounded in any definitive set of empirical tests, at least not by any yet conceived."[18]

But unlike Oppenheim and Putnam, he doesn't seem to think the effort "hopelessly impractical." Wilson believes that scientific unity is as good as achieved and is confident that the linkage of the humanities and the sciences (what he calls "the greatest enterprise of the mind"[19]) will be possible in time. But his phrasing here is telling, clearly giving preference to the scientific over the metaphysical and implying that consilience, while not yet a science, eventually will be. That is to say, while only a belief or a hope, consilience is philosophy; but completed, it is a science, and all the better for it. Moves such as this make real the uneasy feelings many hold about the power and influence of science. While reconciliation will always entail some form of compromise, what is being proposed here is closer to a rewriting than an edit, a subsumption of the humanities into the sciences. The fuzzy thinking and lack of methodological rigor seen in the humanities can be brought into line with the empirical clarity enjoyed by science— which, of course, loses nothing in the bargain. The advantages for Wilson are clear: what Snow called the "sheer loss" of polarization is no longer a loss to us all.

This idea is liable to engender a certain unease with the project of consilience, and Wilson does little to allay the concerns of those who might question the desirability of such a unity when he reveals his view of philosophy as a filler for everything science hasn't managed to achieve yet. We are encouraged to view philosophy as a temporary measure, a sort of heuristic scaffolding to be done away with as soon as possible. "Philosophy," he writes, "the contemplation of the unknown, is a shrinking dominion. We have the common goal of turning as much philosophy as possible into science."[20] It is unclear whether the inclusive pronoun refers to all humanity or just the scientists. It is difficult to believe that many philosophers (except maybe the later Wittgenstein) would be interested in achieving a unity of knowledge if that unity rendered philosophy obsolete. The implication seems to be that if a field of study can be reduced to underlying scientific principles then that study becomes a science itself. This raises important questions about the ontological status of those theories and subject matter that have been successfully reduced in this manner, but they are questions that Wilson seems reluctant to entertain. As might be expected given his opinion of the relative merits of philosophy and physics, Wilson seems to see philosophical inquiry as something of an impediment to progress, an academic concern that the commonsense realist can simply step over. He writes, "The unification agenda does not sit well with a few professional philosophers. The subject I address they consider their own, to be expressed in their language, their framework of formal thought. They will draw this indictment: *conflation, simplism, ontological reductionism, scientism*, and other sins made official by the hissing suffix. To which I plead guilty, guilty, guilty. Now let us move on...."[21]

This attitude is unfortunate. What Wilson fails to address when he talks about consilience and the reduction to physics is the question of what he intends to happen to the objects, properties, and disciplines when they have been collapsed into or explained in terms of physics. The threat here is from overdetermination and its corollary, elimination: if the contents of one theory can be wholly explained by the contents of a causally more basic theory, then the first theory can be trimmed away as superfluous. As Kathleen Lennon and David Charles explain, "Where we thought we had two sets of concepts, entities, laws, explanations, or properties, we in fact have only one, which is most perspicuously characterised in terms of the reducing vocabulary."[22]

Eliminativism has caused much controversy in the philosophy of mind, where it is the name for a radical form of physicalism that effectively denies the existence of the mental as described in terms of propositional attitudes (such as beliefs, desires, and intentions) as real properties of the mind (and thus the world). Eliminativists are materialists who hold with a form of the identity theory of mind,[23] but who are pessimistic about the chances of finding identities between our existing propositional attitudes and particular structures at the neuronal level. Beliefs and desires, say the eliminativist, are the wrong things to be looking for; they won't be found because they don't exist. Paul Churchland, an advocate of eliminativism, believes that "we cannot expect a truly adequate neuroscientific account of our inner lives to provide theoretic categories that match up nicely with the categories of our common-sense framework."[24] The thinking here is that beliefs and desires are prescientific notions, part of what is called "folk psychology" (or less derisively, "commonsense psychology"), and that this account has consistently failed to describe accurately the causes of behavior and enjoyed no significant revision in thousands of years (with the possible exception of the Freudian subconscious as a motivator). In the wake of cognitive neuroscience, we should be prepared to reevaluate folk psychology as we have since reevaluated folk astronomy (the stars are in one plane stretched over a dome surrounding the earth, the sky and sun turn around the earth, and so on) in the wake of scientific astronomy.

The eliminativists concede that it is bound to be difficult at first to reject the folk-psychological, commonsense view, but argue that this is not a good enough reason to maintain it. They argue that there have been too many occasions in the history of science when an apparently necessary causal property has turned out to be no more than a convenient fiction. One example they often give is of phlogiston which at the turn of the eighteenth century, was commonly assumed by learned men to cause combustion in wood or rusting in iron. The idea was that the combustible material possessed a quantity of phlogiston that was released during burning, and that once all the phlogiston had been released, the material would no longer be combustible. Phlogiston certainly seems to explain combustion; it fits all the facts available to the naked eye. But modern chemistry tells us that combustion can be explained more accurately and comprehensively by oxidation and reduction—an exchange of electrons between the material and the surrounding environment. As oxidization also explains a broad range of other phenomena,[25] we can do away with phlogiston as an unnecessary postulate. Eliminativists claim that beliefs and desires, the propositional attitudes commonly used to explain the causes of behavior, are just such convenient fictions, and that as we gave up belief in phlogiston (and in witches, demonic possession, vital forces for explaining animate matter, and so on) so too must we be prepared to give up our folk-psychological account of the mind as neuroscience gradually corrects our assumptions.[26]

Eliminativism problematizes the ontological status of those subject matters picked out by the reduced theory, but it does not imply that all reducible theories (and their subject matter) can and should be eliminated. Recall that the eliminative materialist seeks to do away with folk psychology only because he is skeptical about the possibility of a complete reduction into neuroscience. As Churchland sees it, "The one-to-one match-ups [demanded by the identity theory] will not be found, and our common-sense psychological framework will not enjoy an intertheoretic reduction, *because our common-sense psychological framework is a false and radically misleading conception of the causes of human behaviour and the nature of cognitive activity.* . . . Accordingly, we must expect that the older framework will simply be eliminated, rather than be reduced, by a matured neuroscience."[27] So the eliminativist only scraps the old theory because that theory is (or is expected to be) incommensurable with the new theory. Reduction does not imply elimination. If a smooth and complete (or near complete) reduction of the framework of the old theory into the framework of the new theory can be achieved, then the old theory can be preserved, should that be wanted—which is to say, if it is still useful as a heuristic tool. A popular example of a reduction of this type can be found in the reconciliation of "folk inheritance" with molecular biology. Gregor Mendel's work on inherited characteristics tessellates fairly comfortably with our commonsense beliefs that a child often resembles its parents or that two strong horses will produce a similarly strong foal. It augments these assumptions with statistical patterns—the genetic theory of inherited characteristics. But as Peter Smith points out, "If this theory isn't to invoke embarrassingly magical powers then genes need in some way to be realized in the biological materials involved in reproduction."[28] Fortunately for the genetic theory, just such a physical location was discovered as DNA in the chromosomes present in the gametes, the ova, and the sperm. The functional explanation—genes—was grounded in a structural explanation—DNA. Genes, then, can still be used to explain the inheritance of particular characteristics and (for those currently named and mapped) also pointed to as a real, physical feature of the world with a real (and more or less precise) location.[29]

The genetic theory is said to reduce smoothly because (almost) all the predictions of the genetic theory are accounted for by the molecular biological theory. The ontological status of genes is ensured by the success of the reduction. Baldly, physical instantiation is proof of existence, and much faith is invested in this. As Jennifer Hornsby points out, "If a subject-matter is shown to be reducible to physics, its metaphysical status is revealed, and, presumably (supposing that the reduction carries conviction), rendered unproblematic."[30] So the reality of the postulated entity or property is ensured only if it will reduce to "whatever-physicists-will-countenance," as Richard Rorty puts it.[31] Everything that does reduce is real, everything that doesn't, isn't. (By the examples given above, our folk psychology will, like phlogiston, be eliminated if the propositional attitudes it proposes cannot be shown to reduce to neuronal arrangements, whereas genes, because they can be explained with reference to chromosomes and DNA,[32] can be authenticated as real.)

Being told that everything real is made of matter seems to be so obvious as to be trivially true; it is perhaps our folk ontology.[33] And this is presumably what Wilson has in mind when he talks about "turning as much philosophy as possible into science."[34] From "what isn't science isn't real," it isn't a big leap to "outside science there is no knowledge,"[35] and this seems to be Wilson's stance. His argument seems to be of the form that

(1) Only science can properly explain physical matter.
(2) Everything real is made of physical matter.
(3) Therefore, science can explain everything real.
(4) This can be extended (somewhat tenuously) to argue that if the subject matter isn't covered by science, it therefore isn't real.
(5) If not real, it cannot be known, and therefore isn't knowledge.

Consequently, science is the only way to know. By privileging the ground of matter and reducing all knowledge to scientific knowledge, the relatively modest call for a unity of science becomes the unity of knowledge by default.

If this answers some of the concerns about the ontological status of the higher levels in a hierarchic reductive scale, it still leaves open the question of how best to talk about them. Would a reductionist like Wilson want to argue that the best way to talk about biology is in terms of chemistry (in virtue of the causal primacy of chemistry to biology)?[36] Ultimately, all discourse would properly take the form of talk of the interaction of fundamental particles, exchanges, and transformations of energy at the subatomic level. This is plainly absurd, and the applicable escape route seems to be Oppenheim and Putnam's notion of "proper levels." To stem the reduction, they add the clause that although "each level includes all higher levels . . . the highest level to which a thing belongs will be considered the 'proper' level of that thing."[37] The idea is that not every account qualifies as an explanation, but rather that explanations are always interest-relative. Unlike Wilson, who argues that "there is intrinsically only one class of explanation,"[38] Oppenheim and Putnam want to retain the separate levels for their explanatory power and because different levels address different aspects of the subject matter under study.

Just as they considered it "hopelessly impractical" to try and describe one man's behavior from an analysis of his constituent atoms, they also point out that "a physicist, when he talks of 'all physical objects,' is also speaking about living things—but not qua living things."[39] So there is a trivial sense in which the strong materialist claims are true. If the explanation refers to a phenomenon that is instantiated within a physical system (and, if we include minds, then it is hard to think of phenomena that do not), then it is "explained" by physics, if only because, at the level of the atoms, electrons, photons, and so on of which the phenomenon is composed, physical laws will apply. But what is questionable here is the extent to which reference to *only* those physical laws counts as an explanation. Displaying the same sort of threatening imperialism that Wilson often falls back on, particle physicist Steven Weinberg writes:

> Almost any physicist would say that chemistry is explained by quantum mechanics and the simple properties of electrons and atomic nuclei. But chemical phenomena will never be entirely explained in this way, and so chemistry persists as a separate discipline. Chemists do not call themselves physicists; they have different skills and different journals from physicists. It's difficult to deal with complicated molecules by the methods of quantum mechanics, but still we know that physics explains why chemicals are the way they are. The explanation is not in our books, it's not in our scientific articles, it's in nature; it is that the laws of physics require chemicals to behave the way they do.[40]

The imperialism is carried in the condescension. It is worth noting that it is the physicist, and not the chemist, who is happy to agree that physics explains chemistry, and that it is chemistry (and not physics) that stubbornly "persists." What Weinberg does touch on here, however, is the idea that although physics could account for all the phenomena chemistry covers, to use physics to talk about chemistry is undesirable because the replacement of vocabularies would be inefficient (and possibly prohibitively so). That there seems to be a difference between "accounting for" and (in a satisfactory sense) "explaining," was an idea Putnam was to expand on and is wedded to his functionalist theory of mind.[41]

Putnam makes a distinction between a deduction and an explanation. Anticipating Wilson's mode of materialism, Putnam says that "[v]ery often we are told that if something is made of matter (and we make a lot of assumptions), then there should be a deduction of its behaviour from its material structure."[42] But he does not consider that deduction to be the same thing as an explanation. Using the simple example of a square peg not fitting through a round hole, Putnam argues that the explanation of why this is will not be found in talk of a latticework or cloud of atoms, but in terms of geometry: the hole is too small. For the purposes of explaining why the peg doesn't fit, "*the ultimate constituents don't matter, . . . only the higher level structure matters,*" and that this is "a correct explanation whether the peg consists of molecules, or continuous rigid substance, or whatever."[43] Putnam stresses the relevance of an explanation to what we are interested in and (following John Stuart Mill) separates the everyday use of "cause" from "total cause," pointing out that "we regard certain parts of the total cause as 'background', and refer only to the part of interest as 'the' cause."[44] He goes on to add that "one man's . . . 'background condition' can easily be another man's 'cause'. What is and is not a 'cause' or an 'explanation' depends on background knowledge and our reasons for asking the question."[45] Explanations, then, are interest-relative; to qualify as (successful) explanations[46] they have to explain something to someone, and they must address the salient features of the situation in terms of the questions asked. Hence, the deduction of why the square peg will not fit through the round hole by reference to the respective atomic structures of the peg and the board fails, in part, because these features are not relevant and can even be misleading. "The explanation at the higher level brings out the relevant geometrical relationships. The lower level explanation conceals those laws."[47]

It might be argued that Putnam is separating aspects of the same thing and treating those aspects as if they were two different things; that is, he is talking of two aspects of the same thing as if they were caused by two separate objects. When Putnam talks about separating the structure or the organization of the material from the material in itself, he is adhering to a sort of property dualism, insofar as he thinks there ought to be separate vocabularies to discuss organization on the one hand and substrate on the other. Putnam's position on this[48] leans on Saul Kripke's argument that a statue is not the same thing as the clay it is made from. Descriptively speaking, there are *two* objects present, one defined (or named) by its shape and one defined by its substance. The clay will still be the same piece of clay even if it is rolled into a ball, but it will no longer be the statue. Likewise, the statue will still be recognizable if a mold is made of it and it is then cast in bronze or latex. But nowhere is the claim made that there are two *physical* objects, "clay" and "statue," respectively; there is only one. As Putnam explains, "the difference between the objects lies in the different statements that are true of them, not in their physical distinctness."[49] As should be obvious, there is a proper level for talking about the clay as a statue and a proper level for talking about the clay as a substance. Talk of the clay as a substance needn't involve any mention of macrostructure, just as talk of the statue needn't make any reference to the medium and its microstructure.

Returning to the notion of total cause, causes are said to be proximal or distal depending on their position in a causal chain. So, as Elliott Sober explains, in a causal chain A to B to C, the content of B accounts for C, but A accounts for both B and C, and so is more comprehensive. B is said to be the proximal cause of C, and A the distal cause.[50] The question Putnam inserts here is deciding which is the more useful as an explanation. To lift this out of the algebraic, we might talk about how an organism's behavior was proximally caused by an environmental stimulus, but seek a more distal cause in an understanding of the organism's biology. Evolutionary theory posits distal causes for biological behavior.[51] Wilson sees this as the strength of the Darwinian explanation: using this conceptual apparatus we can explain a vast range of biological phenomena. As seen with Putnam before, the objection is usually not that the evolutionary explanation is wrong, just that it is hopelessly general. This threatens to collapse to a *reductio ad absurdum*, where the ultimate distal cause is the Big Bang. This is what Mary Midgely objects to in the Wilsonian account of culture. While not disputing that the "account we give of culture must indeed be *compatible* with its evolutionary history," she nonetheless feels that "the remoteness of causes by no means increases their explanatory force": "If it did, the original big bang would be the only true explanation of everything, and we all ought to be doing astro-physics, not evolutionary biology. The concepts of cause and explanation, which are essential tools of Wilson's argument, are far subtler and trickier to use than he supposes. He thinks he is quite at home in handling them—but he is wrong."[52] In his enthusiasm for a unified academy, it does indeed seem as if Wilson has willfully simplified the complexity of causal relations.

The introduction of interest-relative explanations and the condition that there are proper levels for entities shores up the ontological hierarchy. As long as we are interested in different features of objects, we will need different vocabularies to talk about them. This also seems to refute Wilson's assertion that "there is intrinsically only one class of explanation"[53]—assuming that by this he intends that "one class" to be explanation in terms of the laws of physics. (His dismissal of the idea of "appropriate levels" of explanation as "misguided" would seem to suggest that he does.) But does Wilson really want to talk about everything in terms of physical structure? Apparently, he doesn't. For although he argues for there being only the one class of explanation, his own explanations come in several different classes—none of them only physical. In *Consilience*, we are given a pheromonal account of ant behavior, a neurochemical account of sleep, and an account of art in terms of evolutionary biology.[54] Surely, Wilson's use of various levels, types, and strategies of explanation suggests that he implicitly acknowledges that appropriate levels exist. He might retort that the levels he uses are there only to better guide the reader toward understanding how everything is reducible to physics. But even so, to do this he finds it necessary to employ different perspectives; which is to say, perspectives appropriate to the subjects (zoology, sociology, religion, ethics, and so on) he is addressing—surely the very thinking he wanted to undercut. One thing common to all Wilson's explanations, however, is that they consistently entail the conversion of nonscientific explanations into scientific or at least scientifically digestible terms. The thesis turns out to be a negative one, less concerned with the one true class of explanation than with the rejection of all nonscientific explanations. What matters here is not whether the explanation is particularly appropriate to neuroscience, biology, chemistry, or physics, but that it is *not* appropriate to sociology, anthropology, philosophy, or literary criticism.

This is the point that the neopragmatist philosopher Richard Rorty picks up on in his response to *Consilience*, "Against Unity."[55] Rorty's position on the relationship between the arts and the sciences emerges from a complex account of disciplinary boundaries and the status of scientific knowledge. How "Against Unity" fits into that will become more clear when situated within the context of his philosophical work, which is given a fuller treatment later. But his comments here, coming as they do in a direct reply to Wilson, deserve a brief mention.

Rorty sees nothing attractive about what he considers as a scientistic homogenization of knowledge, and he questions the basic desirability of dissolving the current boundary lines between subjects that consilience demands: "The various things that people build and repair with tools are, to be sure, parts of a seamless causal web. But that seems no reason to impugn the plumber-carpenter or the carpenter-electrician distinction.... What strikes me as a reasonable and necessary division of cultural labour strikes Wilson as fragmentation.... But contemporary knowledge does not seem to me to be fragmented, any more than does the home repair industry."[56] What Rorty rejects and what Wilson embraces is the claim that scientific knowledge is the best and possibly the only type of knowledge available, and that everything else is conjecture and assumption. This drift toward an all-out scientism leaves the humanities seeming methodologically inadequate. Behind this drift is the assumed hierarchy of hard and soft science and the "physics envy" that drives much of the reductionist program, which Lynn Margulis describes as "a syndrome in which scientists in other disciplines yearn for the mathematically explicit models of physics."[57] But with the scientization of all knowledge a credible proposition, physics envy has become an issue for nonscientists, too. The absence of a mathematical base to a discipline creates an anxiety in its practitioners that their work lacks rigor—that it is "soft" thinking. The scale is fairly simple, as Niles Eldredge and Ian Tattersall explain. "We get farther away from 'hard' science the farther we go from physics,"[58] but its impact on how we think of what it means to be rigorous (or any of its synonyms) has been quite dramatic. As Rorty has it: "For more than two centuries, up through the heyday of logical positivism, practitioners of many disciplines had wondered if they were being 'sufficiently scientific'—a term they used almost interchangeably with 'sufficiently rational' and 'sufficiently objective.' The 'hard' sciences—physics in particular—were viewed as models which other disciplines should imitate."[59] But Rorty does not agree that everything is best addressed scientifically. Taking an analogy from Hilary Putnam's arguments for functionalism and Daniel Dennett's talk of adopting the appropriate stance,[60] he argues that while it might be possible to explain and predict the behavior of a computer in terms of its circuitry, "we do not use this vocabulary if we can help it: it is much easier to predict and explain what the computer is going to do by reference to the program it is running."[61] In a move similar to F. R. Leavis's rebuttal of Snow and Matthew Arnold's response to Thomas Huxley, Rorty argues that Wilson's *Consilience*, and reductive accounts like it, fail to give an account of meaning and value because they insist on using a hardware language, which is the wrong type of language for describing how the software works.[62] As such, a scientific account of the world will always be an incomplete account. Rorty is not arguing that these are grounds for ignoring science, but he does call for a recognition that science addresses some issues better than others, and that what Wilson sees as the fragmentation of knowledge across different disciplines using different explanatory frameworks is better seen as a constructive pluralism that more effectively addresses the types of questions we ask and things we do. "Reality is one but descriptions of it are many. They *ought* to be many, for human beings have, and ought to have, many different purposes."[63] Rorty's insistence on maintaining separate levels of explanation reflects his belief that science is not the only way to know, that it "provides us with a spectacularly useful and astonishingly beautiful set of tools, but only one such set among many others."[64] What he doesn't want to see is the elimination of "soft" thinking or the wholesale shift into exclusive use of hardware language. Rorty holds that knowledge about the workings of the brain will not help us decide what to do with our lives, that science can offer explanation but not justification.[65] So: "when we know what we want but don't know how to get it, we look to the natural sciences for help. We look to the humanities and arts when we are not sure what we should want. This traditional division of labor has worked pretty well. So it is not clear why we need the further consilience which is Wilson's goal."[66] For Rorty, consilience is both undesirable (because of the types of thinking it excludes) and inadequate (because it fails to offer satisfactory replacement accounts for the values and meanings provided by the arts and humanities). He feels that the hardware language of science, occupied as it is with mechanism and not meaning, is simply inapplicable to discussions involving value, and he fails to see how "our answers to such moral or practical questions will be improved by better knowledge of how things work."[67]

This division, that sees the humanities addressing meaning and the sciences addressing mechanism, is crucial in keeping the two cultures separate. It also creates a situation where discussions of meaning and value are inherently unscientific discussions. With all the pejorative connotations this carries, those seeking scientific credibility will consequently limit their talk to mechanism. But in an age where scientific credibility is enthusiastically sought by many other disciplines—psychology, economics, linguistics—literary study seems to remain stubbornly outside the sciences, both in terms of its subject matter and, more importantly, in the approach it takes toward that subject matter. This failure to integrate is partly because novels and poems don't seem the type of things that could be understood by the quantitative analyses that often characterize the scientific disciplines (and are the first things that disciplines bidding for scientific status will construct for their own subject). It is also because it seems difficult to imagine a science that could talk about meaning and value.

When Wilson talks about making literary interpretation more scientific, he is well aware that his is not the first such attempt. Calls for the scientization of literary study have long been made, and often from within the discipline (for example, from I. A. Richards and Northrop Frye). So it is clear that elimination, however likely a consequence it seems under a system like Wilson's, is not the goal of effecting such a shift. What Wilson wants to impose in the service of his consilience program is a system of thought and analysis across the disciplinary spectrum that translates all knowledge into scientific knowledge. This approach is grounded in his central belief that, if minds are only brains, then all thoughts have material bases and so are best characterized in terms of those bases and best analyzed with the empirical methods of the sciences. What this threatens to exclude is a space where meaning and value can be discussed. That is, this approach would lead to an end to such disciplines as philosophy and literary criticism (or at least an end to their individual approaches and traditional, existent methods of addressing these issues). It demands that we look always to the hardware to explain ourselves.

This is not, however, as crude a method as it may first appear. Among the various approaches open to the materialist, recent developments in evolutionary psychology promise to offer comprehensive accounts of many aspects of human behavior, cultural practices, and values within an ostensibly scientific, materialist framework. The response to these accounts is divided, and not always along the strict and familiar boundaries of science and the humanities. That some scientists (such as Stephen Jay Gould) offer a degree of resistance to aspects of evolutionary psychology, while some philosophers (such as Daniel Dennett) offer enthusiastic support, suggests that here is a domain of scientifically acceptable thinking where value—or at least a functional analogue of value—can be reintroduced and stably situated within the materialist ontology.

Wilson is only one of several thinkers, either actually working within the sciences or just desirous of their prestige, who have explicitly called for the implementation of a literary criticism founded on the principles of evolutionary psychology. Before analyzing in some depth evolutionary psychology's claim to be a suitable replacement for the current vocabulary and methodology, it is worth exploring the general motivation for and rationale behind the scientization of literary study. The following section analyzes some previous attempts, both in terms of their approaches and in how they can be seen as preparatory for the evolutionary psychology route currently in favor.

2
Making a Science of Criticism

IN THE WAKE OF THE SYSTEMATIC STUDY OF LINGUISTICS ENABLED by cognitive science and the Chomskyan revolution, Steven Pinker happily salutes a new age, "Language is beginning to submit to that uniquely satisfying kind of understanding that we call science."[1] That shift, as far as Pinker is concerned, from social study into natural science began in the 1950s with Noam Chomsky's suggestion that human languages are underpinned by a human grammar: that is, that all human languages share sufficient characteristics to be collectively considered as self-similar. As with Wilson's consilience program, Chomsky's work takes off from absorbing the materialist collapse of mind into matter.[2] With this distinction out of the way, it becomes possible to ask, as Chomsky does, "Why, then, should we not study the acquisition of a cognitive structure such as language more or less as we study some complex bodily organ?" He recognizes that this seems, at first blush, an absurd suggestion—language is simply too various, and the attempted analogy with bodily organs surely cannot hold.[3] But linguists studying world languages had already found evidence for the existence of "linguistic universals"—regularities of grammar that made it reasonable for Chomsky to make the counterintuitive claim that while the words change between locations, humans everywhere speak approximately the same language. In other words, what was common to human languages was greater than what was different between them. That root commonality, Chomsky suggested, was a "universal grammar," such that "[e]ach human language will conform to U[niversal] G[rammar]; languages will differ in other, accidental properties."[4] The "accidental" properties here are the specific words of any given natural language, organized by the "highly restrictive principles that guide the construction" of this universal grammar. And since "human beings are obviously not designed to learn one human language rather than another; the system of principles must be a species property."[5] Linguistics thus transcends the merely cultural (and accidental) to root itself in the more inclusive categories of the biological (and essential).

In perhaps much the same way as we struggle, even with the assurances of disinterested chemists, to see both diamond and coal as allotropes of carbon, our initial resistance to these claims for grammatical similarity is grounded in our first-hand experience of the manifest differences between the spoken languages, most of which are indecipherable to us. Sympathetic to this, Chomsky recognizes that "[i]t is natural in our daily life we should concern ourselves only with differences among people, ignoring uniformities of structure." But he adds to this an important and telling qualifier, "But different intellectual demands arise when we seek to understand what kind of organism a human really is."[6] By making this scalar shift from the semantic surface to the underlying structure, linguistics announced its intention to move away from what was simply "natural in our daily life." There is little ambiguity about how the "intellectual demands" of this new approach will differ: linguistics intends to find out how humans *really* are.

Seen now as patterned and structured by a universal grammar, hard-wired into known regions of the human brain, the study of linguistics matriculated to a science, and as a science, shed itself of the methodological sloppiness and hazy speculation that had marked it out as one of the "soft" disciplines before. This association of "scientific" with something like "methodologically sound" recalls Rorty's frustration with the influence of the positivist program, and Eldredge and Tattersall's account of how the center of all things rigorous was physics: the "harder," the more rigorous, the better. Would this "uniquely satisfying" understanding be as welcome in literary criticism, and is it even conceivable? Critics of the current state of literary studies often cite as its weakness a lack of rigor and a tendency to settle for what Raymond Tallis has called "evidence-free generalisations"[7]—the type of loose theorizing that the sciences claim to have driven out. Linguistics became scientific by the slow accumulation of data and by specifying and searching for certain recurring patterns within its domain of study (and, as importantly, by finding them). In this respect, what criticism lacks is a taxonomical system capable of subdividing and categorizing literature. This, in turn, assumes that literature is the type of thing that might be so categorized. Several candidates exist for what such a system might look like, although they tend to be, as John Ellis has argued, "more admired for [their] ambition than [their] accomplishment."[8] The issue, then, is whether literary criticism could be formalized along these lines, and whether such a system is ultimately desirable.

In his *Anatomy of Criticism* (1957),[9] Northrop Frye asked, "What if criticism is a science as well as an art?"[10] What would a science of criticism look like, and is it either a possible or desirable goal? The question is a methodological one: are the approaches science takes to its study of natural phenomena applicable or transferable to the study of literature? Frye points out that, to some extent, we already recognize a scientific element to literary criticism, at least insofar as we acknowledge that "previous authorities are used scientifically; fields are investigated scientifically; texts are edited scientifically. . . . [So,] Either literary criticism is scientific, or all these highly trained and intelligent scholars are wasting their time on some kind of pseudo-science like phrenology."[11] Philology and prosody look more like specific branches of linguistics than of literary criticism, but Frye—unlike Roman Jakobson and those Structuralists who would also attempt to scientize literary studies—is not interested in pursuing the linguistics of literature. Instead, Frye locates literary criticism somewhere between philosophy and history,[12] although in the notes to *Anatomy*, he also wonders if it would be possible to set up a more complex relationship: "The arts might be more clearly understood if they were thought of as forming a circle, stretching from music through literature, painting and sculpture to architecture, with mathematics, the missing art, occupying the vacant place between architecture and music. The feeling that mathematics belongs to science rather than art is largely due to the fact that mathematics is an art that we know how to use."[13] This move to draw mathematics sideways into the arts (and claim that inclusion in the sciences turns on an only-contingent instrumental usefulness) is a clear attempt to borrow prestige from mathematics, a discipline that—over the distinction between pure and applied—is, like literary studies, prey to charges of being merely an intellectual sport. But the internal consistency of mathematics grants it a unique independence from the sciences that rely on it,[14] and it is precisely this type of insular self-sufficiency that Frye is looking to establish within literature when he talks about the "the possibility of a self-contained literary universe."[15] That such an internally consistent, world-independent model eludes him is why the attempted analogy with mathematics is only a footnote in a book that owes more to Carl Jung than David Hilbert. In the end, despite Frye's eagerness to make a science of criticism, the result fell short, and M. H. Abrams is typical in underlining the limitations of Frye's approach when he notes that "a thoroughgoing archetypal theory of literature does not resemble physics, chemistry, or biology nearly so much as it resembles alchemy."[16] Abrams's comment here underlines the common feeling that where the *Anatomy* fails is not in a lack of data, but in the absence of a means of organizing those data. The graduation from alchemy to science awaits an advance in theoretical sophistication.

Among the quotations attributed to him, Einstein is supposed to have remarked, "The most incomprehensible fact about the universe is that it is comprehensible."[17] In other words, there's no reason natural phenomena should make sense to us, and pattern is something we have no right to expect. When James Watson and Francis Crick suggested the first successful model for the structure of the DNA molecule, they were among many teams all working toward the same goal. But while competing theories existed as to what shape the molecule would take, everyone involved agreed that there would be some shape or other and that the search for structure was not misdirected. In searching for mechanism and pattern, the natural sciences proceed from the belief that those mechanisms and patterns exist to be discovered and that (relatively) simple rules underlie the manifest complexity of natural phenomena.

Unfortunately, literary fiction has no such security. We can talk of literature being patterned in two senses. At the small scale is the question of whether individual works can be thought of as internally patterned. Obviously, this is something the author is in a good position to control—although a reader faced with an overtly complex text like Pound's *Cantos* or Joyce's *Finnegans Wake* has no guarantee that there is sense to be made of it. Surface complexity may shield a profound and subtle architecture, or the work may be as unstructured, fragmentary, and chaotic as it appears to be. Wayne C. Booth draws attention to the problems for interpretation of complexity without structure: "One can't be sure that *Finnegans Wake* is *not* a great novel; perhaps someday readers will discover that the complex structure they now dream of and quarrel about is a realizable structure, an experienced structure. I doubt it, but it may happen. Until then, each new intricacy discovered . . . reveals precisely nothing more than that: a new intricacy."[18] What's missing is the "skeleton key," the conceptual center around which overall coherence might be achieved from what had seemed to be unconnected parts. If this sort of center cannot be found in the individual work, it may yet obtain between works. There is the example Borges uses of how Kafka's work retrospectively conveys a familial similarity to previously unconnected works. The quality of being "Kafka-esque" is the only thing common to the pieces, but it was not apparent (or rather—the paradox that excites Borges—did not exist) prior to Kafka's writing.[19] This example brings us to the second sense in which literature might be thought of as patterned—not within works, but across them. On the larger scale, is it possible that literature as a whole could be understood as patterned? Frye believed that the assumed existence of a pattern mapped between works was a prerequisite to a science of criticism: "It is clear that criticism cannot be a systematic study unless there is a quality in literature which enables it to be so. We have to adopt the hypothesis, then, that just as there is an order of nature behind the natural sciences, so literature is not a piled aggregate of "works," but an order of words."[20] Frye's "order of words" is an order in the sense that the Linnaean system of classification in biology reveals (or imposes) an order; it is a system that assumes the existence of "natural kinds." Natural kinds mark the boundaries between nouns; the lines along which the world can be sensibly cut up into discrete classes of objects and types, which can then be grouped accordingly, like with like. (That this essentialism is something that many philosophers have found problematic is discussed later.)

The Linnaean system in biology splits living things into six kingdoms and those kingdoms into phyla, phyla into families, families into genera, and genera into species. Frye's system sifts literature into similarly concentric sets. The model he develops rejects the linear, historical view that sorts writers only by such external factors as the name of the monarch under whose reign they lived and wrote. He attempts instead to record the internal patterns suggested by a survey of the works themselves. His model is like the distinction cartographers make between a political and a topographical map—Frye is looking for something like a natural order beneath the arbitrary boundaries. Again, we might think of Chomsky's division between the essential and the accidental features of a language correlating with, respectively, the biological and the cultural. To be scientific, Frye's taxa must be found and not made.

The *Anatomy* is subdivided into four essays:

The Theory of Modes (by which works are allocated to modes calibrated against the power of the protagonist)
The Theory of Symbols (which seeks to organize around a coherent structure the various universally recognized archetypes)
The Theory of Myths (which seeks to locate the meanings of those archetypes)
The Theory of Genres (by which the four seasons are used as an index for the four main genres).

These form a confusing matrix of categories and subcategories, into which works can be slotted and against which they can be cross-referenced. Despite this complexity, it is possible to call the basic pattern Linnaean, insofar as there exist groups within groups, and, like the Linnaean system, the *Anatomy* is prey to debates about the appropriate level of specificity. Classification can look arbitrary, and the exact specifications in Frye's schema are often quite unclear. His system is not always hierarchical, and some of his categories appear all the more arbitrary for their apparent instability. For example, in 1951 Frye links the genre of romance with Spring, and comedy with Summer.[21] By the publication of the *Anatomy* six years later, these had been inverted. That said, Frye admits that the exact interrelations of his system are tentative—"not only elementary but grossly over-simplified."[22] The point is not that the scheme fits this or that particular account, the point is that there is believed to be a scheme at all.[23] What matters is approach, the aim here is to lay foundations.

Frye's structuring is spurred by the belief that "primitive formulas" can be found, a series of familiar story lines and narrative events that recur across world literature. This suggests that literature may be organized not just across time, but also "in conceptual space from some kind of center that criticism could locate." He thinks that this center will be "a group of universal symbols," but stresses, "I do not mean by this that there is any universal archetypal code book which has been memorized by all human societies without exception. I mean that some symbols are images of things common to all men."[24] *Anatomy of Criticism* was Frye's attempt to locate that center, and to organize satellite myths around it. In search of the type of internal coherence that biology had achieved with the addition of Darwinian theory to the existing taxonomy of speciation, Frye believed that "what is at present missing from literary criticism is a co-ordinating principle, a central hypothesis which, like the theory of evolution in biology, will see the phenomena it deals with as parts of a whole."[25]

Cézanne claimed that his painting was guided by the belief that all shapes were combinations of the cube and the sphere. Frye believes that in literature, a similar atomism applies, with the "primitive formulas"—the myths and the archetypes—taking the place of the sphere and the cube. "The structural principles of literature are as closely related to mythology and comparative religion as those of painting are to geometry." In another analogy with painting, he argues that close readings and rhetorical analyses are akin to an examination of brushwork, but that by moving away from the painting we can see first the figures in the picture and, subsequently, the organizing structure of the painting.[26] Frye believes that if we "stand back far enough" from literature—that is, if we think about it in sufficiently abstract, general terms—then similar regularities and patterns emerge, both within and between works. What those patterns reveal are the common cultural origins of Western literature, Frye suggesting that "the symbolism of the Bible, and to a lesser extent Classical mythology" will offer "a grammar of literary archetypes."[27] Here and elsewhere, the language of the *Anatomy* shows some telling similarities with the manner in which linguists talk of the language instinct. Although Frye doesn't draw on it explicitly—the theory was new and not yet popularized[28]—there are many ways in which his work is similar to the Chomskyan account of a universal grammar. Just as linguists stress that the language instinct worked only on grammar—on the rules for organization and not the contingent, accidental details—so Frye talks about aiming to discover "the grammatical rudiments of literary expression."[29]

As it threatens to do with language, codification in this manner seems like a type of natural constraint, a cap on possibility. Just as advocates of the language instinct (and proponents of any theory that posits the existence of innate mechanism) are wary of sounding repressive with respect to freedom of agency, so Frye is cautious when suggesting "that the resources of verbal expression are limited, if that is the word, by the literary equivalents of rhythm and key," and is quick to qualify this: "though that does not mean, any more than it means in music, that its resources are artistically exhaustible."[30] This inexhaustibility is one of the key differences Frye finds between art and science. He believes that a mature and completed science would have nothing more to say about the world; that the total description of the system would be the end of science. He does not, however, think that this holds for literary criticism, arguing that literature "is, so far as we know, an inexhaustible source of new critical discoveries, and would be even if new works of literature ceased to be written."[31] It is not clear if Frye's confidence on this point is well founded; "so far as we know," science is also inexhaustible. There seems little evidence for projecting from the current wealth of new criticism a continuation of that productivity. Indeed, the force of opinion against the obscurity of much of that new criticism (see, for example, John Ellis's *Literature Lost*) might suggest that limits are already being reached.

Like Pinker with linguistics, Frye seems to want to reinforce the scientific elements of literary criticism to inaugurate the study into science's "uniquely satisfying kind of understanding." And he clearly reserves much respect for science. "The presence of science in any subject changes its character from the casual to the causal, from the random and intuitive to the systematic, as well as safeguarding it against external invasions."[32] Part of Frye's motivation for drawing up the scientized, taxonomical system that is laid out in *Anatomy* was his frustration at seeing literary criticism submit to the confines of another perspective—such as Marxism, feminism, phenomenological criticism, and so on—that he saw as deeply flawed because such approaches take for their conceptual framework something outside of literature. This is the external invasion Frye feared. Literary criticism would be formless without internal structure, and so would have to take its structuring principles from outside of literature: from Marxist thinking, feminist thinking, phenomenological thinking, and so on. But give literature its own structure, one drawn out from and built around the "order of words," and the discipline can be self-contained, it can be a science of criticism. As Frye has it: "To subordinate criticism to an eternally derived critical attitude is to exaggerate the values in literature that can be related to the external source, whatever it is. It is all too easy to impose on literature an extra-literary schematism, a sort of religio-political color-filter which makes some poets leap into prominence and others show up as dark and faulty."[33]

This, then, is the negative aspect of the work. Frye's hope is that the systematization he proposes will remove the myopia of critical attitude to allow literature to be judged by the standards of literature, whatever that may turn out to mean, and not by the standards of any external ideology. But the system he sets out is as much at risk from critical myopia as any other. The framework may well be designed specifically for literature, but its application requires just as much selective inclusion as a system borrowed from politics. One of the criticisms leveled at Frye's *Anatomy* is that the subordination to taxa is just as forced as the subordination to political ideologies. The problem is one of inclusion, and it is a recurrent problem for all taxonomical systems. It is difficult, too, to see how Frye's work is meant to be applied in practical terms—or what follows from the fact that literature might be so organized. In other words, the *Anatomy of Criticism* is just that: a metatheoretical analysis of the conditions necessary for a science of literature and not in itself a prescriptive guide for how to study texts scientifically. Wayne C. Booth finds Frye's classification "of limited use . . . since they give us groups of works still unmanageably large and heterogeneous, groups distinguished from each other less by an induction from their common effects than by a deductive classification of the materials represented."[34] Booth's criticism is in part a criticism that Frye's categories are simply too big to be of any use. They are phyla and genera, but they are not species.

At times, it does seem as if Frye is willing to break down his system into smaller parts. Inviting comparisons with what Claude Lévi-Strauss would later develop into his structural theories of mythology, he explicitly appeals to the parallels between his formulations and the work of anthropology, considering "The possibility of seeing literature as a complication of a relatively restricted and simple group of formulas that can be studied in primitive culture. If so, then the search for literary archetypes is a kind of literary anthropology, concerned with the way that literature is informed by pre-literary categories such as ritual, myth and folktale."[35] From here, "We may next proceed inductively from structural analysis, associating the data we collect and trying to see larger patterns in them." This approach is more atomistic, less concerned with the coherence he sought in locating the conceptual center of literature and closer to the simple cataloging of the primitive formulas of which literature is a complication. This feeds out of and appeals to the long-held popular suspicion that there exist only a finite number of plots from which all stories are formed. The level of detail varies. It is sometimes said there are just seven stories (usually, but not absolutely, Orpheus, Achilles, Cinderella, Tristan and Isolde, Circe, Romeo and Juliet, Faust) of which all other stories are versions. Although this seems too reductive and the categories too broad, the notion that atomic plots exist is a seductive one that has attracted much attention. One of the more thorough attempts to identify and catalog these and to arrange them into a taxonomy was carried out by Georges Polti. Polti's scheme is not especially well known (or useful), but it is exemplary of the urge to reduce and categorize. If Frye's *Anatomy* had tried to map a Linnaean order over literature, then Polti's attempt was closer to the construction of a periodic table. But where Frye's taxa labored under their lack of specificity, Polti's enumerations tend toward absurdity in their arbitrary precision.

Taking as his inspiration a comment by Goethe that there were said (by Gozzi) to be only thirty-six dramatic situations, Polti began charting the parallels between narratives, isolating recurrent story lines and sorting them into groups according to shared features. Polti claimed to have condensed the whole range of available story lines down to only a few dozen, and these he collected and published as *The Thirty-Six Dramatic Situations*.[36] Unlike Frye, whose systematization was designed as an aid to criticism, Polti's work was addressed chiefly to playwrights and scriptwriters, intended to act as an a compositional aid, allowing writers to concentrate on theme and dialogue by removing the burden of fashioning a plot (something which, if Polti's scheme is correct, is never original anyway).

Polti sees himself as resurrecting a lost line of inquiry—much as Frye did when he bemoaned the paucity of literary criticism's technical vocabulary, complaining that it had not moved on since Aristotle's *Poetics*.[37] Polti finds few precedents to his project, complaining that only one other writer "had grasped and presented briefly the ensemble of all dramatic production," yet he finds the basis of this scheme—"the outworn classification of the seven capital sins"—"far from satisfactory." He maintains that "no one has treated, in [a] genuinely technical manner, of the secrets of invention." The failure to treat creativity in a technical (which is to say, scientific) manner is diagnosed as typical of the intellectual attitude of the day; such aims being "ill comprehended by an age that dreads didacticism—that is to say, dreads any serious reflection upon art."[38] A precursor to Frye's belief that a more analytical, empirical approach would change the character of literary studies "from the casual to the causal,"[39] Polti felt that this type of taxonomy was long overdue. Unfortunately, Polti is far from rigorous in his own methodology. Although he criticized the basis of previous attempts, he gives scant description of his own basis, nor any indication of the criteria by which situations are to be considered either similar or separate. His account of how the thirty-six situations were derived is almost comically abrupt. "Finally, in brief, I rediscovered the thirty-six situations, as Gozzi doubtless possessed them . . . for there were indeed, as he had indicated, thirty-six categories."[40] Once again, the scheme is essentialist, with the emphasis on these categories being found rather than made, consistent with the act of scientific discovery.

Since the number of possible narrative events is grossly underdetermined by the thirty-six subheadings in the scheme, Polit allows an inevitable flexibility for determining the appropriate situation for any given story and, under his cryptic formulations, what qualifies as meeting those criteria. He notes, "Murder, for instance, may be reduced to a wound, a blow, . . . a too-hasty word, an intention not carried out, . . . a thought, a wish, an injustice" and so on.[41] Polti also permits free-combination, considering this a strength of his system. "There is . . . no Situation which may not be combined with any one of its neighbors, nay, with two, three, four, five, six of them and more!"[42] Later on the same page, Polti seems to imply that there are constraints on these possibilities, that is, combinatory rules. But he is unwilling to explore these as yet, leaving their explication to a never-to-be-written future work called *The Laws of Literary Invention*. "I cannot here elaborate the system by which this study of the Thirty-Six Situations may be continued, and by means of which they may be endlessly multiplied; that is a separate work upon the 'Laws of Literary Invention'."[43] One of the constraints he does include is purely arithmetical. With his characteristic manner of making the absurd sound obvious, Polti realizes that the combination of situations "will not go very far, however, since we cannot . . . receive from the drama, or from life, more than one thousand three hundred and thirty-two surprises. . . . Perform the multiplication; result, one thousand, three hundred and thirty-two."[44]

Polti's bluntly empirical tone reflects his belief that what he has done is not devise a new formulation, but simply discover an underlying and preexisting structure. He is fully assured that these situations are not arbitrary, but concrete and given,[45] and this confidence spills over into the remarkable claim that "to this declared fact that there are only thirty-six dramatic situations, is attached a single corollary, the discovery that in life there are but thirty-six emotions." And so "It is with these thirty-six emotions—no more—that we color, nay, we comprehend cosmic mechanism, and since it is from them that our theogonies and our metaphysics are, and ever will be constructed; all our dear and fanciful 'beyonds;'—thirty-six situations, thirty-six emotions, and no more."[46] Polti's writing here slips into the mystic—the inference from a catalog of popular narratives to an exhaustive catalog of human emotion is surely not a valid one, and he offers no explanation of how the purported matchup between the number of situations and the number of emotions was discovered. But in this respect, Polti's bold pronouncements chime with much of what evolutionary psychology and human ethology has since begun to say about the numerous similarities between, and the limits or constraints on, human behavior in different cultures (the concepts of similarity and constraint here running together). It also chimes with the stronger claim, recently made first by sociobiologists like Wilson and now reiterated by evolutionary psychologists, that human nature is everywhere the same. Polti's moral atomism is less well supported but certainly not inimical in principle to the type of limitations that ethologists like Irenäus Eibl-Eibesfeldt, following psychologist Paul Ekman, have cataloged since.[47] Crucially, in evolutionary psychology and ethology, the inference runs the other way. If there is any correlation between the type and number of emotions and the type and number of (consistently entertaining) plots, then the theorist would expect the latter to derive from the former; that is, new plots derive from much older emotions and not, as Polti seems to suggest, the other way around.

The value of Polti's work is not in the exact specifications of his taxonomy, but in the way he approaches creativity (which is to say, he believes that there is logic and pattern behind the inspiration) and in his belief that we would benefit from a more structured theory of literary creation and appreciation. Amid the make-it-new-Modernism of the early 1920s, Polti had perhaps good reason to feel that the artists shared his desire for systematization. "It is," he writes, "toward an art purely logical, purely technical, and of infinitely varied creations, that all our literary tendencies seem to me to be converging. In that direction proceed . . . all writers deliberately unmindful of their libraries."[48] Like Frye, Polti's schema is designed not to subsume art under a scientized framework, but by the construction of such a framework, to secure for art a place safe from what Frye would call the "external invasions" of politics and religion. To this end, Polti sees "A whole new generation springing up, futurists, 'loups,' cubists, [who] seem to me to be seeking the same goal, the final abolition of absolute authority, even that of Nature and of our sciences her interpreters; and the erection upon its debris of simple logic, of an art solely technical, and thus capable of revealing an unknown system of harmony; in brief, an artists' art."[49]

If the assumption that plot is finitely bounded in anything like the manner Polti suggests is correct, then any praise for originality of plot would seem to be misdirected. At best, we could applaud writers for their originality in combining certain situations (according to the unwritten Laws of Literary Invention), although presumably even such combinations would be subject to a further set of injunctions, another level of organization. With every writer held to rehearsing the same plots, the interest and emphasis for criticism will be placed not on narrative event but on what variables remain: if not narrative sequence and event, then narrative style, dialogue, and poetic or rhetorical accomplishment. These constraints and this necessity to work within given limits (maintains Polti) would gradually increase the quality of the writing being produced, as it did for the dramatic works of the ancient Greeks: "We are not unaware of the importance, in the perfecting of Greek art, of the fact that it was circumscribed and restricted to a small number of legends . . . , which each poet had in his turn to treat, thus being unable to escape comparison, step by step, with each of his predecessors."[50] (To a certain extent, directors of plays or translators are already judged by this system.) Polti hopes that once we stop praising plot, we might start to tease great art out of writers currently preoccupied with trying to surprise us with novel story lines. And so the "artists' art," an autonomous art uninterested in making profit or political statements, emerges.

Despite Polti's certainty, it is hard to understand how a system as tightly knit as this could be reached. His bizarre claims for finitude in all directions seem baseless and, despite his denials, cabalistic (and this is at odds with the "genuinely technical manner"[51] he aims at). *The Thirty-Six Dramatic Situations* lacks a larger coherence and reasoning. Most of the situations are so vague as to admit almost any plotline (and certainly too many plotlines as to successfully serve as boundaries), and given that Polti allows them to be used in combination, almost like an alphabet, it is not clear how these can be considered usefully elementary: knowing the limits of the alphabet is not the same thing as knowing which are the best words to make with it. Stopping at thirty-six situations seems arbitrary—a number chosen for convenience (and to agree with Goethe) that seemingly fits on a continuum of available detail passing from just four or seven situations to a taxonomy so accurate as to count each and every production as an original type. This far end of the detail scale, the chaos of irreducibility, is the stance taken by those resistant to classification, those who abhor what Polti called "didacticism." At this end of the scale we cannot classify at all. The argument here is that there are not "types" in literature, or that if types do exist then canonical classics are not simply tokens of those types. Joseph Carroll calls this the "traditional humanistic belief in the irreducible singularity of all artistic productions."[52] This irreducibility is pointedly limited to *artistic* productions, tacitly excepting mere entertainment. It is no coincidence that genre fiction struggles to merit literary status. A book obedient to the conventions of a particular genre is no longer irreducibly singular and no longer literary; genre labeling can be a method of suppression, a convenient means of dismissing by type. A system like Polti's threatens to turn all literary output into genre fiction of one kind or another. Those seeking to preserve a distance between the literary and the subliterary will argue that, as opposed to a formulaic romance or horror novel, a work of literature is a token not of a type of dramatic situation, but only a token of the type "literature," which is a separate and somehow special class of writing. Not enough internal similarity exists beyond this broad category to successfully impose either an atomistic or a Linnaean taxonomy. The imposition of genres, types, and "species" of literature cuts into the cherished belief in (or fallacy of) absolute creativity. If *King Lear* or *Crime and Punishment* are only tokens of types, instances of particular and ready-made dramatic situations, they lose something in the classification.

Frye recognized this as a latent difficulty within any taxonomical account of literature. He admired the systematic manner in which the sciences go about their business, and it is this rigor that he wanted to introduce into literary study through the taxa of the *Anatomy*. But science is also essentially disinterested toward its subject of study, and so Frye's problem is squaring the need to organize the knowledge with the value judgments implicit in maintaining a distinction between literary and popular fiction. Accordingly, he insisted on the difference between value-judgment ranking and organization around nonevaluative principles: "There is a place for classification in criticism, as in any other discipline which is more than an elegant mandarin caste. The strong emotional repugnance felt by many critics towards any form of schematization in poetics is again the result of a failure to distinguish criticism as a body of knowledge from the direct experience of literature, where every act is unique, and classification has no place."[53] Note how the "unique" aspect of the work of literature is shifted from the work itself to the reader's experience of that work.

Frye is at pains to stress that his scheme cannot offer a means of discriminating between good and bad literature, and that value ranking is something quite separate from the "order of words" he is looking to map out. This enables him to maintain that the structure exists, while effectively disposing of the need to account for value. What we are left with are more problems: Where do the patterns come from? And why—if value is something external to the works—is there any consensus at all about what constitutes good and bad literature?

Beyond locating their roots in the Bible and Classical mythology, neither Frye nor Polti went into an account of why the taxa they proposed existed or offered any detail as to where and how the patterns and commonalities they detect originated. But while their work was largely concerned with the interpretation of Western literature, anthropologists studying the wider field of world narratives have found similar patterning in geographically isolated cultures, suggesting that some mechanism exists below the level of straightforward cultural transmission. Joseph Campbell traced a recognition of cultural universals—what he calls "the archetypes of mythology"[54]—back to at least the sixteenth century, when Spanish conquistadors mistook Mexican images and myths for corruptions of Catholicism. James Frazer was to find similar evidence in the transubstantiation of body-into-bread rites practiced independently by Aztecs and Catholics, noting that "the ancient Mexicans, even before the arrival of Christian missionaries, were fully acquainted with the theological doctrine of transubstantiation. . . . They believed that by consecrating bread their priests could turn it into the very body of their god."[55] In the mid-nineteenth century, German scholar Adolf Bastian noticed recurrent beliefs and narratives across civilizations in China, Japan, India, Africa, and South America. These he called "Elementary" or "Folk" ideas,[56] and tentatively suggested that research into geographical and climatic conditions might point toward common causes for the observed similarities.[57] Almost twenty years later, Frazer, shifting his attention from psychology to anthropology—from "the nature of human thought" to its history—noticed that "the human mind, across a variety of cultures and times, and especially when trained upon the religious and the magical, showed certain constancies." Frazer set out "to examine the refinements of such universal thought processes and their different ways of expressing themselves in a variety of places and periods" and cataloged them in *The Golden Bough*, which sprawled from two volumes in 1890 to an encyclopedic thirteen volumes (including an index and a supplement) by the final edition in 1936.[58] Where *The Golden Bough* focused more on religion and magic than mythology, in the 1920s, the so-called Cambridge Ritualists, Gilbert Murray, F. M. Cornford, and Jane Harrison,[59] set out specifically to catalog and locate the origins of myths. Like Bastian and Frazer before them, they found that even in diverse and geographically distant cultures, the same types of stories were told again and again. Here there were continuities between cultures that had been isolated from each other since long before even the earliest serious estimates would have in place a common cultural document, such as the Bible or Classical mythology, that might explain any regularities in Western literature. So Bastian's loosely formulated "Elementary Ideas" and the continuities in ritual, religion, and myth documented by Frazer and the Cambridge Ritualists have quite profound implications, as Wendell Harris points out, "If these commonalities cannot be explained by transmission from one culture to another, the alternative appears to be that the human mind (or human experience as processed by the mind) is so constructed that certain modes of thought and correlative narratives are produced by all peoples."[60] That similarities across world narratives exist is relatively uncontroversial. What is needed is some means of grounding these patterns, and (as Harris points out) if there are similarities in the works that cannot be explained with reference to cultural transmission alone, then the similarities must be in the people who collectively produce and consume those narratives.

One early attempt—in many ways influential on the direction of Frye's work—was Carl Jung's appeal to the existence of a panhuman "collective unconscious." Maud Bodkin, in her 1934 work *Archetypal Patterns in Poetry*, takes an explicitly Jungian approach to the study and interpretation of literature. Her claims for the special quality of great literature turn on that quality being indefinable and recognizable only intuitively through the Jungian collective unconscious. Resisting the sort of reductionism seen in a scheme like Polti's and the abduction of creativity it effects, Bodkin attempts to retain a theory of archetypes, but within a framework that preserves literature as a type of writing that is immune to simple formulation.

Bodkin is attempting to expand on Jung's already flawed premise that the "special emotional significance possessed by certain poems" is the result of the poem "stirring in the reader's mind . . . 'primordial images,' or archetypes," which Jung describes as "psychic residua of numberless experiences of the same type." Bodkin explains that these experiences "have happened not to the individual but to his ancestors, and of which the results are inherited in the structure of the brain."[61] Such themes and images are recognized by our "racial memory" and are already known intuitively in the collective unconscious. Bodkin tries to encourage us to rely on these intuitions when reading poetry to experience poems on an emotional level, as opposed to a wholly analytical or intellectual level, and so to dredge the collective unconscious for a fuller appreciation of the poem. She aligns her approach with a comment by Keats that a poem should rest on the mind to be savored: "let him on any day read a certain Page of full Poesy or distilled Prose let him wander with it, and muse upon it, and reflect upon it, . . . and dream upon it."[62] Bodkin admits that "[t]he inquiry here is plainly of a subtlety and complexity apt to discourage at the outset those who prefer to avoid all questions that cannot be investigated in strict accordance with a strict technique."[63] The background belief here is that analysis is an impediment to emotion, and that it is the emotional response that deserves priority.

A detailed examination of Bodkin's work is unnecessary here, but it is important to outline the problems with trying to employ "race memories" or a collective unconscious as the basis of observed similarities in narrative or motif (not least because these problems are sufficient reason for the rejection of such accounts). Theories that talk of a psychic unity of mankind possess considerable intuitive appeal, and Bodkin urges us to content ourselves with intuition as reason enough to follow her. Rather than attempt to address the question of how racial memories are supposed to work, she sidesteps the issue, claiming, "It is not necessary for our purpose to determine exactly the method of this 'biological inheritance' from our ancestors."[64] But attractive as the idea of archetypes emerging from a collective unconscious might be, the theory is difficult to accept. The main problem—a problem Bodkin inherits from Jung—is the nature of the racial memory proposed and the method of transmission. Any account of race memory, if we are to assume it is anything like memory in the usual sense of the word, will rely on the transmission of acquired characteristics or —what is often called Lamarckian inheritance.[65] There is almost nothing in contemporary biology to recommend such a theory, nor was the state of the Darwinian version of inheritance so misunderstood when either Jung or Bodkin were writing that their theory here can be excused on historical grounds. The problems are manifold. The experiences that supposedly feed into the collective unconscious are not the experiences of the individual, but of the individual's ancestors—ancestors who were themselves individuals, and so presumably equally unable to "store" memories in the fashion that the collective unconscious demands. That the experiences are "numberless" is also irrelevant, as there is no reason to suppose that the frequency of the experiences of our descendants would increase the likelihood of those experiences being indelibly imprinted on the structure of the mind (as the theory seems to suggest) anymore than one experience of one individual would be stored for genetic transmission to the next generation. (This is, in part, because memory is what is called by some philosophers a success term, which means that you can't truly remember something unless it actually happened while you were there.) A memory is an acquired characteristic. The notion of inheriting memory assumes that an experience of a descendant was somehow stored in a form transferable to successive generations. If we are not to abandon the genetic theory entirely, this basically assumes that an experience was transferred within an individual's lifetime from his or her memory to his or her gametes—gametes that, in the case of females, are in place and fixed in the ovaries from before birth. So even if we do allow for sperm (which, unlike ova, are synthesized throughout adult life) to carry memories somehow, there is still only a race memory for half the race—something which, as a woman, Bodkin might be expected to resist.[66]

So, the notion of a collective unconscious is no more viable than the standard examples of the inheritance of acquired characteristics (giraffes' necks growing longer as each generation stretches a little more, mice whose tails are amputated at birth eventually splitting off into a subspecies of tailless mice, and so on), but it is perhaps easier to believe. With the mechanics of acquisition now concealed in mental processes, talk of inherited memories appeals to lingering Cartesian intuitions about the normal rules of biology not applying to *res cogitans*. The only method of transmission that could conceivably work is cultural; that is, transmission through language, dance, or art. But this is a much weaker version of "race memory" and hardly the type of mechanism that would satisfy the Jungian account Bodkin wants to use. In the interests of consistency, to accept Jung and Bodkin we have to reject Darwin, and the appeal of the collective unconscious seems insufficient to justify this.

Although this biological refutation of Bodkin's project may seem a little too literal-minded, it is intended to underline quite how distant much of literary studies is from criteria used in the sciences for the evaluation of theories. That Jung's theories could go as far as they have in literary studies highlights a more serious incompatibility: the easy acceptance and stubborn retention of implausible ideas like the collective unconscious widen the rift between literary studies and the sciences. The implications are quite broad, as Joseph Carroll says, "This kind of scholasticism isolates literary study from the forces of progressive understanding within the larger intellectual community, and it eliminates the methodological constraints with which other disciplines establish their intellectual validity."[67]

Few other subjects make it acceptable to shrug off the demand for a feasible mechanism as Bodkin does when she says "[i]t is not necessary for our purpose to determine exactly the method of this 'biological inheritance' from our ancestors."[68] Carroll wants to argue that accounts like this, which lack empirical footing and so fail to integrate conceptually with the sciences, have encouraged literary criticism's affiliation with relativistic, often antiscientific philosophies; principally those lumped under poststructuralism. But not all critics of the poststructuralist movement are so sure of the relationship. For John M. Ellis, who shares many of Carroll's concerns, it is not a lack of objectivity in literary criticism that has led to the shift toward relativism, but rather, that the proliferation of pseudo-objective accounts inevitably provoked a relativist-driven backlash. According to Ellis, who is strongly opposed to the presence of theory in the literary academy (and in particular the often subjective, antiestablishment criticism found in what he brands "race-gender-class" criticism), the real invasion does not come from the external threat of Marxist and feminist perspectives that Frye spoke of; it comes from within literary studies and spreads outward, even as a response to the formalization. As Ellis has it in *Literature Lost*, "the overambitious systematizing tendencies of Frye and of French structuralism provoked a reaction, and by the 1960s the newest version of anti-objectivism had appeared. It is this latest swing of the pendulum that race-gender-class scholars are part of. Another manifestation of this reactive development is reader-response theory. . . . Still another is the strain of deconstructionism that stresses the infinite deferral of meaning in language."[69]

The systematizing of Frye and the structuralists is apparently not the type of "objectivism" that Ellis sees as appropriate for literary studies, and his argument here is a little weak. When he talks of "the mood swings of the field, from attraction to controlled scientific methods to distaste for them and back again,"[70] he seems to be implying that the pendulum would swing anyway, as a matter of rhythmic historical necessity, and Frye is blamed simply because he was at the end of the last swing. Taxonomic systems of the type Frye and Polti suggest will always meet with resistance, with the principal objection grounded in accusations of reductionism. As detailed above, what systems like Polti's threaten is a reduction of literature to expressions of formulae—formulae that precede the individual creative act and that underpin literary texts in ways that seem to erode the creativity of the author. The formulae remove the conscious authorial element and replace it with an unconscious, automatic one. This is not the death of the author that Barthes spoke of, but something closer to the death of creativity, or at least the death of the Romantic notion of creativity.

The central question here is whether a materialist, scientific theory of literary creation demands the rejection of anything like the traditional notion of creativity. Certainly, a materialist account will be sure to reject any conception of artistic creativity that defined it with reference to an immaterial source. That the Romantic (and vernacular) conception of creativity does just this goes some way to explaining the familiar hostility directed toward the project (or threat) of codifying and categorizing imagination. Polti complained, "I hear myself accused, with much violence, of an intent to 'kill imagination'."[71] It is as if creativity is something of a Golden Goose—it will work as long as we don't try to find out the mechanism. It is quite possible to read the story of the Golden Goose as concealing a moral deeply opposed to scientific investigation. This is the lot of those greedy for knowledge, impatient, and ungrateful to providence. This is the scientist who, as Wordsworth had it, murders to dissect, and who cummings saw as paying too much attention to the "syntax of things"; their "naughty thumb[s]" rudely probing nature's beauty.[72] Here again, analysis impedes (and even precludes) both the experience of the artwork and the act of creation itself. Scientific understanding threatens to demystify and mechanize creativity. In the introduction to his *Consciousness Explained*, Daniel Dennett writes of how such demystification might be regrettable: "It might be like the loss of childhood innocence, which is definitely a loss, even if it is well recompensed."[73]

The critic keen to share in the prestige of scientific recognition and willing to offer literature up to empirical scrutiny must be willing to accept that the analysis may yield an undesirable result. It is not guaranteed that creativity will survive the operation and even less certain that an empirical account of literary creativity could support an evaluative distinction between high and low art. The following section looks in some detail at two attempts to analyze literary creativity in highly reductive (and at least proto-scientific) terms through linguistics and through computer simulations of creativity. Just as linguistics served as the springboard and model for structuralism, which sought to understand the mind through systems more or less analogous with language, so computer simulations attempt to understand and integrate creativity into a computational model of the mind/brain. Both accounts assume creativity to be explicable in atomistic terms.

Applying the methods of linguistics to literary analysis apparently offers a means of grounding criticism's evaluative claims in something more substantial than a traditional consensus and so provides a response to accusations of unfounded elitism. Sometimes called stylistics, the approach is, as Stanley Fish has it, at least "an attempt to put criticism on a scientific basis."[74] The hope is that linguistics will disclose some difference between the literary and the nonliterary text. However, it is not at all clear that any such linguistic distinction exists to be found. A. L. Binns sounds a cautionary note: "it is entirely possible that the many objective differences which would be revealed by a complete linguistic description of Shakespeare's Sonnets and of a theatre programme would not of themselves permit us to distinguish between the similarly complete descriptions of two other texts and say with confidence that one was literature and one was not."[75] A linguistic analysis might exhaust the text and still not find anything like "literary quality" as it is spoken of within conventional evaluative criticism. Of course, this doesn't necessarily mean it isn't there; it might be that a linguistic vocabulary is the wrong sort with which to talk about literary quality. As Binns goes on to point out, "[the linguistic] method becomes dangerous only when it assumes that it has, by completing a dissection and finding no soul, disproved the existence of any soul."[76]

One of the first and most influential attempts to analyze literature linguistically was conducted by the Czech linguist Roman Jakobson. Jakobson's aim was to disclose what he eventually called the "literariness" of literary texts. His approach relied heavily on analyzing a text's internal structure, and so discovering, by the performance of a meticulous linguistic analysis, patterns of opposition and repetition that would normally be invisible to even the most sensitive reader. Jakobson's work, building on that of Saussure,[77] was seminal to structural linguistics, which promised "scientific" analyses of texts, revealing a depth in literary productions absent in other writing. Just as microscopy had reinvigorated the biological sciences, the specialized tools of linguistics were to disclose hidden structures and regularities that might explain in a technical manner the more familiar properties and qualities apparent at the surface. Tzvetan Todorov, writing in 1969 (by which time the project was as good as bankrupt), sums up the hopes invested in the method. "The structural analysis of literature is a kind of propaedeutic for a future science of literature."[78]

In a series of essays, including "Linguistics and Poetics" and "Poetry of Grammar and Grammar of Poetry,"[79] Jakobson set forth a program for the linguistic analysis of literary texts. He believed that poetics—understood as asking, "What makes a verbal message a work of art?"—was "entitled to the leading place in literary studies." The rationale for this comes by way of an appealingly tight (and curiously familiar) syllogism. Jakobson argues, "Poetics deals with problems of verbal structure, just as the analysis of painting is concerned with pictorial structure. Since linguistics is the global science of verbal structure, poetics may be regarded as an integral part of linguistics."[80] He draws poetics into the field of linguistics in the same way that materialists like Wilson draw the other disciplines into physics. The logic is that of the reductionist who claims that since everything is made of matter, and physics is the study of matter, everything can be studied by physics. Since literature was made of language, it followed that an analysis of the language would be an analysis of the whole work, with no remainder. Equipped with these new tools, Jakobson went on to conduct detailed and exhaustive linguistic analyses of poems.[81]

In his analysis of Baudelaire's "Les Chats" co-authored with Lévi-Strauss, Jakobson spent nearly 7,000 words on an exclusively linguistic analysis of a fourteen-line poem. The discussion avoids all digressions into biography, literary allusion, or thematic concerns. Consequently, to readers unacquainted with linguistic terminology, it is only occasionally cogent, displaying interest in very different features than conventional criticism. For example, ". . . the cats manage to identify themselves with the *grands sphinx*. A chain of paranomasias, linked to these key words and combining nasal vowels with continuant dentals and labials, reinforces the metamorphosis."[82] While Jakobson's interest in the relationship between linguistic texture and semantic content is familiar in literary criticism (as when rhythm is said to modify tone, for example), the detail of his technical vocabulary when discussing linguistic features ("continuant dentals," and so on) far outstrips that usually found in literary criticism (particularly in an academy where even rudimentary prosody is usually avoided in scholarly analyses of poems). In short, Jakobson's are readings for a specialist audience, unashamedly employing the vocabulary of that specialism. Although his subject matter—poems—may be unfamiliar to fellow linguists more accustomed to the analysis of transcribed conversation, the approach toward that subject matter is not. Conversely, although the literary critic may feel at home with the subject matter, he or she is liable to be alienated by the approach.

Through this sort of analysis, Jakobson seemingly finds ingenuity in every syllable of the poem. Baudelaire is not the only poet able to be profitably unpacked in this way: Jakobson goes on to produce another detailed reading, this time of Shakespeare's Sonnet 129, "Th' Expense of Spirit." Once again, the analysis is both extraordinarily thorough and almost entirely avoids digression into semantic content and the broader thematic issues typical of conventional literary criticism. Reinforcing the similarities to a science paper, Jakobson breaks his essay into such subsections as "Rhymes," "Strophes," "Lines," "Spelling," and "Punctuation." By the end of the 6,000 words of the essay, Jakobson seems to have exhausted the 110 words of the sonnet. He adds a tenth section somewhat cautiously entitled "Anagrams?"[83] where, picking up on a clue from Sonnet 76—"every word doth almost tell my name"—Jakobson scours Sonnet 129 for support. Predictably, the evidence is found, but now even Jakobson seems a little skeptical:

"Since in wordplays Shakespeare was prone to equate the vocables *will* and *well*, the entire concluding couplet could—perhaps!—conceal a second, facetious autobiographical reading: 'All this [is] the world Will knows, yet none knows Will to shun the heaven that leads men to this hell.'"[84] It is as if even Jakobson is beginning to doubt the validity of his findings. Part of his motivation for conducting this particular analysis was a reaction against what he called "forced, oversimplified, and diluting interpretations." He also wanted to offer a corrective to those critics (he names Laura Riding and Robert Graves and their essay "William Shakespeare and E. E. Cummings") who would offer, in the place of a simplified reading, one that simply goes too far: "there is a far-reaching distance from [Shakespeare's] puns and double meanings to the surmise of the free and infinite multiplicity of semantic load attributed to Sonnet 129 by [Riding and Graves]." What Jakobson sees himself as doing is replacing this free interpretation (notably a semantic rather than syntactic or phonetic interpretation) with "an objective scrutiny of Shakespeare's language and verbal art" to reveal "the cogent and mandatory unity of its thematic and compositional framework."[85] Riding and Graves's complexities are made, Jakobson's are found.

Impressive though these readings are, they invite us to commit a version of Wimsatt and Beardsley's intentional fallacy and wonder if Baudelaire or Shakespeare had any idea of the linguistic complexity—the manifold oppositions, the contrasting strophes and rhymes—that Jakobson finds. Frye recognized this as a common objection. "Critics of Shakespeare are often supposed to be ridiculed by the assertion that if Shakespeare were to come back from the dead he would not be able to appreciate or even understand their criticism."[86] And it seems Jakobson, too, was alert to this potential for skepticism: "Whenever and wherever I discuss the phonological and grammatical texture of poetry, and whatever the language and epoch of the poems examined, one question constantly arises among the readers or listeners: are the designs disclosed by linguistic analysis deliberately and rationally planned in the creative work of the poet, and is he really aware of them?" The answer comes in the affirmative:

> A calculus of probability as well as an accurate comparison of poetic texts with other kinds of verbal messages demonstrates that the striking particularities in the poetic selection, accumulation, juxtaposition, distribution, and exclusion of diverse phonological and grammatical classes cannot be viewed as negligible accidentals governed by the rule of chance. Any significant poetic composition, whether it is an improvisation or the fruit of long and painstaking labour, implies a goal-orientated choice of verbal material.[87]

The first claim in this answer—that an "accurate comparison" of poetic and non-poetic texts reveals distinctive features—is worth clarifying in light of the type of features Jakobson is interested in. Given the criteria suggested for examination ("juxtaposition, distribution, and exclusion of diverse phonological and grammatical classes"), it seems safe to assume that by "accurate comparison," he is thinking of a specifically linguistic analysis and comparison. The second claim—that the choice of verbal material is "goal orientated"—is relatively uncontroversial. But it also slips past the question: no one doubts that poets usually have goals in mind when they write.[88] We assume and accept that the poet is trying to evoke pity or wonder or whatever by a choice of certain words, but this is largely a semantic operation, and Jakobson is describing not a level of semantic sophistication, but a syntactic one. The skepticism about Jakobson's analyses arises from a sense of incredulity at the extent of the "choices" he thinks a writer makes. It is one thing to carefully choose words to bring to mind a certain image and to some extent to find echoes such as assonance or rhyme. It is quite another thing to simultaneously control, with the level of detail Jakobson retrieves, "the phonemic, morphological, and syntactic framework"[89] into which those words will fit, particularly when it is unlikely that anyone but a trained linguist would even recognize the available complexity. Yet it gradually becomes apparent that Jakobson doesn't think that the authors are consciously controlling these things, and that they are consequently not fully aware of the rich texture of their own writings, thus complicating an issue of authorial decision making that he had made seem quite straightforward.

This complication becomes clear when the poet under analysis is, unlike Shakespeare or Baudelaire, available to respond. Jakobson records how the Russian Velimir Xlebnikov,[90] looking back at his poem "The Grasshopper," realized that "throughout its first, crucial sentence . . . each of the sounds k, r, l, and u occurs five times" and this, adds Xlebnikov, "without any wish of the one who wrote this nonsense."[91] He is thus added to "all those poets who acknowledged that a complex verbal design may be inherent in their work irrespective of their apprehension and volition."[92] This is far from the "goal-orientated choice of verbal material" at the root of poetry that was supposed to ensure the reality of Jakobson's discoveries. Whatever is informing Xlebnikov's poetry on this level, it isn't choice (unless Jakobson has in mind some sort of "unconscious choice," which doesn't seem to be a particularly coherent notion). Presumably recognizing this, Jakobson does include a modification, a clause that allows for "the relevance of the phonemic . . . framework" to "remain outside of [the author's] awareness, but . . . the poet and his receptive reader nevertheless spontaneously apprehend the artistic advantage of a context embedded with those components over a similar one devoid of them."[93] Quite how these recognitions are made is not explained. (Neither does he address the somewhat question-begging introduction of "sensitive readers"—sensitive to what?—surely the very property under analysis.) It seems clear, however, that what Jakobson is outlining here is a theory of authorship that credits the poet with more than just the achievements he was aware of. (Something like crediting a person with being unusually tall, this is a reward for an achievement you had no choice in making or didn't know you had made.)

The ingenuity, however, apparently does not stop here. "Xlebnikov failed to recognize the much wider range of those regular phonological recurrences."[94] Jakobson rather audaciously goes on to detail the full linguistic depth that Xlebnikov himself had not noticed and, it follows, that he had certainly not consciously intended. The reason given for this is a discrepancy between the poet's ability as a poet and his ability as a critic, and a corollary that these two abilities are not linked: "The poet's metalanguage may lag far behind his poetic language, and Xlebnikov proves it."[95] Frye had said something similar more than a decade before, "Criticism can talk, and all the arts are dumb."[96] He makes few concessions to the artist:

> The poet may of course have some critical ability of his own, and so be able to talk about his work. But the Dante who writes a commentary on the first canto of the *Paradiso* is merely one more of Dante's critics. What he says has a peculiar interest, but not a peculiar authority. It is generally accepted that a critic is a better judge of the *value* of a poem than its creator, but there is a still a lingering notion that it is somehow ridiculous to regard the critic as the final judge of its meaning, even though in practice it is clear that he must be.[97]

The motivation for such a stance, one that seems to leave the poet as something of an awkward but necessary stage on the way to criticism, is strategic. It is a way of getting criticism clear from accusations of parasitism: "The notion that the poet necessarily is or could be the definitive interpreter of himself or the theory of literature belongs to the conception of the critic as parasite or jackal."[98] Note that Frye conflates two different points here: (1) the writer would be a poor interpreter of the theory of literature, and (2) the writer would be a poor interpreter of himself. The first of these arguments does seem plausible (there is, after all, no reason why the poet need be well-read or even interested in other people's books; he or she may have no concept of literature in its totality). The second is a little more puzzling.

While Jakobson's work with Xlebnikov seems to give support to Frye's argument, it is difficult to see how the author might not have access to the meaning of his own work.

What Frye's formulation does is to invert the "folk-theory" of literary criticism, what he calls "the absurd quantum formula," whereby "a critic should confine himself to 'getting out' of a poem exactly what the poet may vaguely assumed to have been aware of 'putting in'."[99] This doesn't seem so absurd while we still have an interest in the poet's abilities as distinct from those of the critic. Frye's opinion that the poet has no special claims to understand his own work is consonant with his analogy between physics and poetry: "Physics is an organized body of knowledge about nature, and a student of it says that he is learning physics, not nature. Art, like nature, has to be distinguished from the systematic study of it, which is criticism. It is therefore impossible to 'learn literature': one learns about it in a certain way, but what one learns, transitively, is the criticism of literature."[100] For Frye, to achieve a systematic criticism demands we recognize that literature is an object of study, rather than a subject, and that as a completed object, the circumstances of creation are not an issue: "Criticism, rather, is to art what history is to action and philosophy to wisdom: a verbal imitation of a human productive power which in itself does not speak."[101] The way Frye describes it, the poet doesn't just seem dumb in the (presumably intended) sense of "mute," but also a little dumb in the sense of "stupid," or at the least, unaware and incongruously inarticulate. When Frye and Jakobson write about poets, it is as if the poets had no real grasp of what they were doing, as if they were just flailing and helpless, waiting to made great by the superior critical skills of others. For Frye, this seems especially true: "Whatever popularity Shakespeare and Keats have now is . . . the result of the publicity of criticism."[102]

In trying to enable writers to escape from what he calls this theory of authorial ignorance, E. D. Hirsch makes a distinction here between an understanding of the meaning and an understanding of the subject matter.[103] It may be, he claims, that the interpreter knows more about, or has a clearer conception of, the subject matter than the author, and so finds himself able to draw from the author's text details that the author was unaware of having included. But while this fits the example Hirsch uses of Kant's reading of Plato, it doesn't seem to be the case when Frye is claiming that, although the author supplies the words, it is the reader that brings the meaning. Hirsch allows that there may be features of a text that seem to contribute to the meaning, but of which the author is unaware. In a case very similar to Jakobson's exchange with Xlebnikov, he uses the example of a linguist subjecting casual conversation to stylistic analysis. "Did you know that those last two sentences of yours had parallel constructions which emphasized their similarity of meaning?" To which the speaker replies, "No! How clever of me! I suppose I really did want to emphasize the similarity, though I wasn't aware of that, and I had no idea I was using rhetorical devices to do it."[104] Here, the author appears to have unintentionally inserted meaning, but as Hirsch points out, "How can an author mean something that he did not mean?" "The answer to that question is simple. It is not possible to mean what one does not mean, though it is very possible to mean what one is not conscious of meaning. That is the entire issue in the argument based on authorial ignorance. That a man may not be conscious of all that he means is no more remarkable than that he may not be conscious of all that he does. There is a difference between meaning and consciousness of meaning."[105] He goes on to make a distinction between "attended" and "unattended" meanings by analogy with consciousness and self-consciousness. This allows the author in a self-congratulatory mood to claim any "meanings" thus revealed as evidence of his cleverness, but throws up a problem with intention that affects how we allocate praise.

The poets in Frye and Jakobson are intellectually inert, almost animalistic or autistic in their ability to write well and seemingly fail to fully realize what they have done. This opens a telling analogy between how Frye and Jakobson treat poets and how physicists treat athletes. Neuroscientist William Calvin investigated how hunters and sportsmen threw spears and balls with such accuracy, calculating the "launch window" for when a swinging arm must release a missile: too late and the missile hits the floor, too early and it sails off into the sky.[106] For what he calls "a reasonable beginner's throw"—hitting a rabbit-sized target approximately four meters away (a task that most able-bodied persons could perform)—he found the launch window was about 11 milliseconds wide. The launch window shrinks rapidly, as Calvin underlines, "Hitting the same target from twice the distance with equal reliability [8 out of 10] means releasing within a launch window about eight times narrower, 1.4 msec."[107] He adds, "An eightfold decrease in total launch window occurs when the distance doubles, a 27-fold decrease when distance triples." This assumes a stationary target and a stationary thrower. Needless to say, the physics behind a sprinting cricketer catching and almost immediately throwing a ball while running all the while (and still successfully striking the stumps from twenty meters) is significantly more complex.[108] A parallel can be found in most ball sports. Clearly, the athlete involved is not consciously making the calculations necessary—not, at least, on the level the physicists recognize of working out trajectory, velocity, and direction and taking into account wind speed, release time, and the force necessary relative to the mass of the projectile. On paper, the task seems impossibly difficult and certainly beyond what we would credit the mind with being capable of within the time available. Yet it palpably is possible, forcing us to recognize that there is a level of sophistication here far beyond the conscious intention of the person doing the action. Or rather, because the intention is quite clear—make the missile connect with the target—it is more correct to say that these actions are beyond the conscious *calculation* of the actor. The calculations and the physics behind realizing this intention are where the actor's purpose and the mechanics of execution part ways. In light of the physicists' analysis, we gain a renewed respect for the achievement of the sportsman as a biological organism or machine, but not for the sportsman as a conscious agent.

The way physicists treat sportsmen is comparable to the way literary critics treat creative writers. Is this what Jakobson and Frye have in mind when they call the writer dumb, unable to articulate or even recognize his own brilliance? Inasmuch as Frye thinks we need critics to fully appreciate art, it is apparent that just such an analogy is being made, albeit implicitly. If this is the case, then our respect for the literacy of writers must be analogous to our respect for the mathematics of sportsmen; which is to say, it will be tempered by a realization that their achievements are on the whole unconscious and that the cleverness is quite beyond their reckoning or volition. This conclusion seems to be an unavoidable consequence of adopting what Hirsch calls the doctrine of "semantic autonomy."[109] What is being admired is no longer someone's achievement, but the intricacy of nature, and this has important ramifications for how literary critics want to talk of great writers. If Dante and Wordsworth don't know what they are doing (at least to the same extent that the critic knows what they are doing[110]), then it becomes difficult to maintain an intentional vocabulary with regard to literary merit. With the text as object, we should no longer talk of "who" is being admired, but "what."

This abduction of conscious intention is certainly in keeping with the analyses Jakobson conducts. Having discussed the linguistic depth present (and largely expected) in canonical literature, he begins to take examples from outside literature. Recall that Jakobson allows for sophistication not only in the fruits of "painstaking labor" but also in "improvisation."[111] To illustrate the potential complexity even in improvisation, Jakobson finds in an off-the-cuff comment by Turgenev (a seven-word list, rattled off at a dinner) all the phonetic richness and poetic texture that he had found in Baudelaire and Shakespeare.[112] And not only here, but in political slogans. Dwight Eisenhower's apparently simple "I like Ike" campaign concealing an unrecognized complexity in the pairing of "-ike" and "Ike."[113] Jakobson seems to find this structure and poetic texture in all places equally, like some background hum that emanates from all writing, undermining his belief that "an accurate comparison of poetic texts with other kinds of verbal messages demonstrates . . . striking particularities in the poetic selection."[114] That the magic is everywhere he looks suggests that the magic is all Jakobson's and exists not in the text but in the analyst. (Or, at least, if it does exist in the text, it exists below the level of conscious decision and so throws into question the extent to which we might want to credit the writer for it.) This only brings us right back to where we started: the lack of a linguistic basis on which to found an ontological distinction between literature outwith fiction.

It was always part of Jakobson's project to define rationally and rigorously the unique features of specifically literary texts, prompting his famous comment that "the subject of literary scholarship is not literature but literariness, that is, that which makes of a given work a work of literature."[115] But Jakobson's conviction here that "literariness" exists as a property that could be teased out of a text, isolated, and described by linguistics has proved to be more problematic than at first hoped. At its most mechanical, this is what Binns called the Fermat theorem of literature: "a formula in linguistic terms which will generate literature and only literature," an approach which for Binns "reflects a computer age at its worst." The problem, once again, is related to the difference held to exist between literature, which is ideally irreducible, and generic fiction, which is likely to be formulaic. The Fermat theorem of literature, Binns explains, "seems to assume that the study of language in the art of literature is the establishment of a formula of lowest common multiples, similar to that evidently used in the production of much successful entertainment, a repetition of previously successful elements to achieve an even greater success." It further assumes, "It is possible to prescribe in linguistic terms alone the sufficient and necessary conditions for the production of all the sentences of the literature of the past, as well as those . . . of the future."[116] It is obvious that Jakobson holds nothing so crude in mind when he is talking about "literariness." It is likely that, in fact, no one seriously holds such a mechanistic view of literature and that the Fermat theorist is just a straw man. But as a thought experiment, the results are illustrative of the background beliefs about the differences between literature and generic fiction. Even if an algorithm for creating fiction could be found, it would stretch only to the creation of "successful entertainment" (that is, popular or sub-literary fiction). As it would not also produce literature (could not, in fact, produce literature), it maintains the qualitative difference between genre fiction (which can be formulaic) and literary fiction (which resists such formulation). Literature begins to seem by definition to be just that kind of writing that is impossible to formulate.[117]

In addition, these linguistic analyses, though rigorous, seem to fall short of what we might hope literary criticism will achieve. They include no talk of the text's subject matter or semantic content. With this comes the complaint that stylistics is contentless and that its readings, for all their technical sophistication, fail to explain anything to us. Fish sees this as deep problem for the approach: "The machinery of categorization and classification merely provides momentary pigeonholes for the constituents of a text, constituents which are then retrieved and reassembled into exactly the form they previously had. There is in short no gain in understanding; the procedure has been executed but it hasn't gotten you anywhere."[118] Of course, there is no requirement to conduct exclusively linguistic readings, and a stylistic analysis could simply be supplemented with sections that discussed thematic matters. We could still have a rigorous analysis in the linguistic mold, but one that was supplemented by the type of emotional response or thematic reading typical of much conventional interpretive criticism. But the conventional sections, being the only bits we were actually interested in, would remain as unsupported as before. The linguistic method offers no foundations whatsoever for evaluative criticism.[119] Whatever implications the method has for literary texts are an incidental feature of its having implications for all texts.

Aware of these limitations, but reluctant to concede that a rigorous methodology was wholly inapplicable to the analysis of literary texts, Tzvetan Todorov argued that to bring to bear directly the methods of linguistic analysis is to be taken in by the "too-obvious relationship" between language and literature that says that as literature is made of language, an analysis of the language would be an analysis of the whole work. This is to be overly concerned with "language as material," when the more interesting relation is "rather with language as model."[120] While Todorov would probably hold with Jakobson in saying that "poetics may be regarded as an integral part of linguistics,"[121] as Jonathan Culler explains, Todorov's poetics "is based on linguistics but is not simply an application of linguistic categories to the language of literature."[122] Although Todorov makes a distinction between his poetics and straightforward linguistic readings, his early criticism is remarkably similar to linguistic readings insofar as it seeks to remove itself from interpretation altogether. Todorov limits his discussion to the same type of systematically describable features of the text that Jakobson was looking at. According to James Bennett, this is because

Todorov, like Frye (and in a recurrent motive for those trying to scientize the discipline), wants to eliminate from literary study "the 'external'—history, culture, biography, psychoanalysis, Marxism."[123] In Todorov's words, it "reduces literature to the status of mere material which illustrates a subject other than itself."[124] What emerges from this is a method at once rigorous but limited, and in similar ways to Jakobson's. For Bennett, this is unduly restrictive: "We discern here Todorov's persistent effort to delimit 'literature' as an autonomous object for scientific study, and to that extent we can follow him. But his rejection of the 'world' and the whole concrete text as elements of the proper study of literature raises issues so fundamental to the whole enterprise of literature that we can wish Todorov had examined his postulates more thoroughly."[125] Todorov's refusal to assimilate content with context—that is, the removal of historical and cultural relevance for the text—is the price paid for his rigor. For Bennett, it is too much. Rather than ground literary value in unassailable empirical facts, Todorov's restricted approach instead only "contributes to the continued diminution of the importance of literature to life."[126]

This is much the same problem that faces any technical treatment of literature and seems to be a direct consequence of adopting such an approach. Faced with charges of elitism and arbitrary value codes, the promise of a rigorous and empirically defensible method of analysis seems to offer a means of supporting the established system by demonstrating its compatibility with scientific rationalism. But the irony is that such systems are indifferent to value and, if successfully implemented, may not support the canon but dissolve it. Rather than ground claims for literary value, an approach like Jakobson's instead makes it not matter what type of texts you examine. If Shakespeare can yield as good a result as an advertising slogan, that is, if all types of writing are inexhaustible in the sense Frye spoke of, then the linguistic approach cannot support an account of literature that seeks to preserve an ontological distinction between the literary and the subliterary.

So it becomes apparent that the merit of literary productions lies below the radar of linguistics. The linguistic approach offers neither an explanation for creativity nor any support for evaluative claims. The difficulty is that with the promise of rigor comes a loss of value. Scientists are ideally disinterested in their object of study. Scientific inquiry is at least partially characterized by this disinterest: the cleverness is all in the method of analysis. Linguistics, insofar as it is scientific, shares this indifference toward its subject matter, and this is something Jakobson stresses, believing that "scientific poetics will become possible only when it refuses to offer value judgments. Wouldn't it be absurd for a linguist to ascribe values to dialects according to their relative merits?"[127] Biologists are not considered to be any the poorer as scientists for studying bacteria rather than mammals. In the sciences, what counts is how the analysis is conducted, and there is (ideally, at least) little question of the status of the subject matter. If the tools of literary analysis are anything like the tools of scientific analysis in this crucial respect, then what matters should not be the status of the subject matter but the skill of the analyst in how well these tools are employed. Distinctions of value between literature and subliterary fiction would be irrelevant.

That just such a value system is paramount to the survival of literary studies as an autonomous discipline within the academy has been the central claim of many scholars who see the relativizing of value as signaling the end of literary study in its present form. Books such as Harold Bloom's *The Western Canon*, Sven Birkett's *The Gutenberg Elegies*, and Alvin Kernan's *The Death of Literature*,[128] their authors pessimistic in an age where the book is an anachronism, see literary study as being an historical contingency, now gradually marginalized or subsumed under the variety of electronic distractions available. Thinkers such as I. A. Richards, Frye, or Jakobson had all in their own ways tried to secure a place for literary study in an academic environment increasingly receptive only to the empirical methods of the sciences. Their consistent failure to shore up value within these accounts leaves the canon as exposed and unstable as ever, insofar as whatever the empirical methods could support didn't include the value gradient necessary for the maintenance of a canonical order. In reaction to that failure, and in common with the traditional basis for a division between the arts and sciences, humanities scholars have widely rejected the validity of the empirical method, siding against those sciences that reject them.

In *The Death of Literature* (1990), Alvin Kernan is worried about this tendency. He sees a deep hostility to scientific modes of investigation of the arts expressed in a tendency for the arts to set themselves methodologically in opposition to the sciences:

> Scientific rationalism has been the official mode of knowledge in modern society, but the artist has inevitably been distinguished by the possession of its mirror opposite, an intuitive power to create art and literature out of the creative imagination. . . . [W]hatever the poetry-making power has been called, romanticism has constantly made it the essential energy of creative literature, making lovelier and truer things than the rational mind can discover in its laboratories and with its computers.[129]

Once again, here is the idea that rational analysis impedes or excludes emotion. This thinking supports an antagonistic relationship between the arts and sciences, one that, in Kernan's view, literature cannot afford to maintain. By claiming for its own the intuitive faculties and creative wellspring of poetry (knowledge that science rationally cannot and ideologically will not touch), literature does not so much capitalize on a gap in the market as drive itself further from scientific rationalism. When appeals to intuitive capacities are embraced, what is being tacitly resisted is the idea that creativity is analyzable in the same way that natural phenomena are analyzable.

In the sciences, simulation is a type of understanding.[130] If a simulation obedient to a theory reproduces the expected natural conditions, then this counts as good evidence that the theory is correct. Biologists can demonstrate, using relatively simple computer simulations, that populations of predators and prey obey the expectations of their theories when the results of those simulations tally with conditions found in natural populations. Richard Dawkins's "Blind Watchmaker" program used simulation to demonstrate that the Darwinian theory of descent with modification could account for phenotypic variation across species. An extreme case occurs in cosmology, where many of the phenomena studied occur in time scales and at such great distances so as to prohibit direct observation. What the cosmologist has is often only a series of snapshots of a celestial event. A good example is the galactic collision. Because there is no feasible way to observe the whole event unfolding in real time, a complex simulation is constructed using powerful computers. As a mark of how much trust the cosmologists put in the accuracy of their simulations, the simulation is studied rather than the phenomenon itself.[131] Talk of there being a Fermat theorem of literature was intended to capture the idea that somewhere there exists an elusive algorithm capable of producing literary fictions. Recall that Binns derided the idea of such an algorithm as the reflection of a computer age at its worst. The imagination, it is felt, simply isn't like animal populations or star clusters. But research with artificial intelligence (AI) systems is producing increasingly sophisticated simulations of creativity, simulations suggesting that there are algorithms for the process.

If a computer simulation of creativity yielded similar enough productions to what might be expected of a human, then the scientists would be in a position to better claim to understand creativity, without reference to intuition or a creative wellspring and entirely within the materialist framework. Margaret Boden, in her survey of the field *The Creative Mind: Myths and Mechanisms*,[132] collects many incidents of what appears to be creativity emerging from AI programs: computers drawing original pictures or composing original stories. These are simplistic, crudely formulaic works for the main part, a reassembly of preprogrammed elements according to certain rules. But they are perhaps different only in degree and not in kind from the creative acts they are designed to mimic.

Boden cites examples of children's stories produced by a program called TALE-SPIN. Not all the stories are successful. Some fall into loops of infinite repetition, which often sound as if they might have occupied Zeno or Borges (as when one character offers to find another a worm, but only if he will tell him where a worm is), although, obviously, this occurs without the self-awareness of Zeno or Borges. At other times, characters act with a brutality inappropriate to children's fiction, something the computer fails to appreciate ("Joe threatened to hit Irving if he didn't tell him where some honey was."[133]). Others suffer merciless fates, and the ruthless logic of the computer has no place for compassion. The following is typical of TALE-SPIN's oeuvre: "Henry Ant was thirsty. He walked over to the river bank where his good friend Bill Bird was sitting. Henry slipped and fell in the river. He was unable to call for help. He drowned. THE END."[134] Here the programmers had included the rule "being underwater prevents speech," but failed to incorporate a rule that made Bill Bird aware of his environment. What these examples (and their failures) demonstrate is the immensity of world knowledge necessary to compose or comprehend even the simplest stories. Of course, no one is claiming that the computers (in any usual sense of the word) "comprehend" or understand what is happening in the stories, just as the resident in John Searle's Chinese room didn't understand Chinese.[135] But, unlike the Chinese room, it is not important to these experiments that the computer understands the concepts it is using or what it means to feel jealous or angry. As Boden points out, "Our prime interest is in what [the program] can teach us about human minds, which *can* make sense of these words. A program may embody psychological hypotheses about how concepts are used by people, without understanding those concepts itself."[136] The difficulty for the programmers is that all the simple and seemingly endless connections and causal laws that make up our common sense (solid objects to fall to earth, water is fluid, creatures can suffer, and so on) must be explicitly prescribed. This is an enormous and difficult task. But while our commonsense background knowledge is "certainly much more powerful, and much more subtle, than any current program," Boden believes that the outputs of human and computer are at least "broadly comparable,"[137] and this is the crucial point. She is hoping we will look past the simplicity of the TALE-SPIN narratives to recognize these similarities.

One of Boden's central claims is that what it means to be creative is closely tied up with our ignorance of the creative process. This idea is consistent with the belief that rational analysis impairs aesthetic appreciation. Creativity is defined, at least in part, in opposition to known rhythms: mechanical, formulaic, plodding. The creative process is one that cannot be replicated by labor and effort; it comes spontaneously or not at all. What research like that described by Boden does is to erode the idea that the creative process is unknowable and so outside of what can be simulated. If creativity can be simulated (and Boden's examples strongly suggest that it can), then it can be understood. The mystique evaporates as creativity, like combustion, genetic transmission, and language acquisition, cedes to what Pinker called the "uniquely satisfying type of understanding we call science."[138] Those who insist that creativity is a somehow-special and uniquely human characteristic must explain how the AI simulacrum differs from the man-made original. (Perhaps one way would be to dispute that the nature of the intelligence behind the creations was the same. We might, for example, argue that the human mind just doesn't work like the computers, however superficially similar the results. That is, it doesn't use multiple goal-directed programs, but instead its productions are the result of a more general problem-solving capacity that resists easy formalization.[139] Of course, as a counterargument this collapses if it turns out that creativity really is constrained in the way that Boden's talk of "creativity algorithms" suggests: the process needn't be simple to be algorithmic.)

One interesting consequence of the work Boden looks at is that it presents problems about authorship and intentionality similar to those seen with critics who insist on the autonomy of the text. Maintaining a doctrine of authorial irrelevance with regard to Dante or Wordsworth was a strategic move, enabling the critic to escape charges of parasitism. In the case of a narrative produced by a computer, the problem would not now be ignoring, but rather *locating* the author. When chess grand master Gary Kasparov was defeated by a computer called Deep Blue in 1999, no one seriously assumed that what the name Deep Blue pointed to was the sort of being to whom we should accordingly direct our admiration (and this despite the reports that claimed "Deep Blue beats Kasparov"). Instead, Deep Blue stood for the collective achievement of the team of technicians and software engineers who had built and programmed the computer. In the parallel case, if a computer wrote a story, who would be the author, and how would that story be received if it was known to be the product of an algorithmic code? Of course, if Boden is correct, then we are already in a situation where all stories are the products of algorithms; it is simply that those algorithms appear impossibly complex to us, for the time being. With the translation of mind into machine, our interest seems drawn toward the mechanism as the better of the available explanations. This is because we think the mechanical explanation trumps the intentional one or, as Dennett puts it, "*the mechanistic displaces the purposive.*"[140] If there are algorithms for the generation of narratives, then on the reductionist account, they will take causal primacy over the claims of the author.[141] Once more, like Calvin's athlete, we find the more comprehensive explanation of the act is given in terms of the unconscious processes, and that the more we learn about the mechanics of production the less we care about the intention of the writer. Within the materialist worldview, every subject matter is (at least professionally) treated as an object.

Because creativity, as mentioned above, seems to be at least partly defined in opposition to the formulaic, this reduction into algorithmic code, if successful, looks likely to eliminate creativity in its current sense. Yet it seems impossible to reserve a special and distinct place for creativity within the limits of a coherent materialist framework. (This was the fulcrum of Wilson's argument for the plausibility of consilience across the arts and sciences.) At best we might want to argue that creativity operates on a higher level of complexity than could be eventually (which is to say, in principle) simulated by the as-yet-too-crude tools of the computer scientist. But this reduces the problem of modeling creativity to a problem of insufficient computational power and reduces its solution to a matter of time. It does not mean that creativity is qualitatively distinct from the relatively easy-to-simulate (and "lower" or simpler) brain functions such as motor control and stimulus response.

Although they differ on when it will happen, most people have little trouble believing that science might one day produce an intelligent robot or computer, one quite capable of passing the Turing test. The proliferation of such robots in science fiction attests to this.[142] However, science-fiction robots conspicuously lack creative powers; typically, they are emotionless automata. Creativity and empathy are not seen simply as properties emergent from sufficiently intelligent minds, but as specifically (and uniquely) *human* traits. Creativity is assumed to be different from other brain functions. The lesson from cognitive science and Boden's research is that this is not the case or is true only in terms of quantitative and not qualitative difference. One of the points Boden tries to stress is that creative ability is on a continuum with TALE-SPIN at one end and Shakespeare at the other; their respective methods are (at least) "broadly comparable."[143] But, as with holding on to the collective unconscious because it seemed intuitively easy to believe, there is an inversely similar resistance to accepting the strong materialism that says creativity, like the rest of mental life, is algorithmic and mechanical. Joseph Carroll calls this resistance "a quasi-religious desire to preserve an area of human subjectivity that is somehow, mystically, distinct from the objective world that can be known by science."[144] The notion that the source of poetry could be coded algorithmically, that inspiration is only a series of analogical connections, jars with the standard Romantic account of poetic composition. Whether or not the parallels between how computer programs produce narratives and how the human mind does it are strongly analogous in the way Boden suspects they may be matters less than the more general point that here is a plausible suggestion for one way in which creativity might be understood in terms acceptable to the materialist.

Those projects described in *The Creative Mind* are ongoing and expected to bring more impressive results as the technology develops and computational power increases. Unfortunately, despite the hopes invested in the method during the 1960s, the linguistic approach to literature looks less promising. There is, however, an important sense in which the structuralist movement that Jakobson spawned has had an impact on the method and direction of subsequent work, making possible such projects as Wilson's *Consilience*.

Structuralist thinking was soon applied more broadly than just to linguistics, expanding rapidly to become a philosophical position that held that we must look to the underlying structure to properly understand a system, be that system a text, a government, a society, or whatever. This expansion was something anticipated by Saussure and actively encouraged by Jakobson. "Semiology" (as Saussure called it) or, more commonly "semiotics" is the application of structuralist ideas to systems other than language: it proposes a science of signs. Semiotics is where the evolutionary psychology advocated by Wilson and linguistic structuralism find common ground. The pervasiveness of semiotics and its application in fields as diverse as social organization and the patterns of world myths (most famously by Lévi-Strauss) are testaments to the power of the structuralist insight—so much so that linguistic structuralism now seems to be an offshoot of the wider study of semiotics.

Jakobson himself felt that the structuralist method was able to account for more than just literary art, as Krystyna Pomorska explains: "Even if language, in some cases, is not directly involved in the act of creation, it still remains a model for such an act. Consequently, the methods of modern linguistics, elaborated by Jakobson and his fellow scholars in the Moscow and Prague Linguistic Circles, serve as a basis for the scientific analysis of any language or artistic code."[145] Even this broad claim is understating the case, for Jakobson felt that the relations that held between terms in a language were analogous to a greater or lesser degree with the relations within any system. In light of this, David Robey argues that by 1970, structuralism had acquired two quite distinct meanings and had come to mean something far removed from its origins as a way of looking at the interrelations of terms in a language. In its broader sense (the sense largely taken up by semiotics), structuralism is simply a "method of inquiry based upon the concepts of totality, self-regulation, and transformation, common not only to anthropology and linguistics, but to mathematics, physics, biology, psychology, and philosophy as well."[146] Which is to say, the analogy with structure in linguistics is weak and incidental. But in the sense that Jakobson seems to endorse, and the sense that Lévi-Strauss and literary criticism embraced, structuralism remains closely tied to its origins in linguistics and projects from linguistic principles outward to make broad statements about the parallels between linguistic structure and societal and psychological organization. As Robey notes, "This new science (as it claims to be) has grown out of the supposition that the theories and methods of structural linguistics are directly or indirectly applicable to the analysis of all aspects of human culture, in so far as all of these, like language, may be interpreted as systems of signs."[147]

Here, the analogy with linguistics is strong, and the parallels between the structures of language and the structures of human cultural practices are not incidental but linked and possibly even causally related. The first interpretation is relatively uncontroversial, making only general claims for the existence of structure in disparate fields, whereas the second apparently suggests that it is legitimate and fruitful to project outward from linguistic structuralism and analyze nonverbal systems in the same terms as verbal systems.

It is as if linguistics might offer the basis for another sort of consilience—the various disciplines now organized, not by a shared material base in the laws of physics, but in a shared epistemological base in language. The assumption here is that all knowledge is locked into language, and therefore the study of language would be the study of knowledge. As Christopher Norris explains, by this route, the structural linguist can make claims comparable to the imperialism of Wilson's physics. "For if language was indeed the key to all understanding then structural linguistics was the pilot science that alone provided an adequate grasp of the various discourses (narratives, paradigms, modes of representation, etc.) which comprised the entirety of knowledge at any given time."[148] Structuralism seemed to offer a means of uniting knowledge, and a clear case is made for the claim that the role once played by structuralism is now occupied by evolutionary psychology.

Both claim to be global sciences, and inasmuch as structuralism seems to offer a scientific way of thinking about subjects not usually covered by science, it can be seen as a propaedeutic not just, as Todorov predicted, for a science of literature (directly), but also for evolutionary psychology (indirectly). The appeal of each is similar, both assuming that diverse behaviors and phenomena might be explicable in a common vocabulary, and both projecting outward, ultimately seeking to systematically relate the way the mind works with how texts, societies, and so on are organized. Although structuralism is now widely rejected within the disciplines from which it emerged (linguistics, literary criticism, and anthropology),[149] much of the work carried out in the name of structuralism by thinkers like Lévi-Strauss has been employed by adherents of evolutionary psychology, such as Wilson, who recognizes the intuitive appeal of structuralism as salvageable if redirected: "The structuralist approach is potentially consistent with the picture emerging from natural sciences and biological anthropology. . . . Their problem is not the basic conception, . . . but its lack of a realistic connection to biology and cognitive psychology. That may yet be achieved, with potentially fruitful results."[150]

3
Evolutionary Psychology

IN THEIR INTRODUCTION TO *THE ADAPTED MIND*, JEROME BARKOW, John Tooby, and Leda Cosmides call for a "conceptual integration" of the behavioral and social sciences with the natural sciences. Like Wilson, they believe that "[t]he natural sciences are already mutually consistent" but mean by this that "the laws of chemistry are compatible with the laws of physics, even though they are not reducible to them. . . . A conceptually integrated theory is one framed so that it is compatible with data and theory from other relevant fields. Chemists do not propose theories that violate the elementary physics principle of conservation of energy."[1] Their claim that conceptual integration is not the same as reductionism rings a little hollow: it is unclear how chemists could lay down rules that physicists were prohibited from violating. Conceptual integration is still reductionism in as much as every concept must "integrate" with physics if it is to integrate successfully. Reciprocal integration between, for example, sociology and anthropology[2] would not be considered sufficient. But the wider concern of Barkow, Tooby, and Cosmides is a methodological alignment: "The behavioural and social sciences borrowed the idea of hypothesis testing and quantitative methodology from the natural sciences, but unfortunately not the idea of conceptual integration."[3]

What the authors want to impose is a unity similar to Wilson's consilience, but one that preserves current disciplinary boundaries while dissolving autonomous disciplinary methodologies. (This is problematic in itself, as it assumes that methods are transferable. This issue is discussed at more length below.) As they see it, that the claims of anthropology and sociology are not checked against the more primary claims of biology and the natural sciences constitutes a violation of the hierarchy whereby, under the rubric of conceptual integration, everything must square with the level immediately below and consonance with the claims of the natural sciences becomes a necessary condition for all knowledge claims. Because evolutionary psychology can claim a filial bond to the natural sciences in a way that anthropology, for example, cannot, it is accordingly better placed in the hierarchy. So evolutionary biology trumps anthropology. Because of this priority, Tooby and Cosmides hold that for anyone "to propose a psychological concept that is incompatible with evolutionary biology is as problematic as proposing a chemical reaction that violates the laws of physics."[4]

As evolutionary psychologists, their starting point for cultural analysis is, like Wilson's, a claim for the universality of human nature, regardless of surface cultural differences. That this sounds like a return to an essentialist account marks a sharp break with what Tooby and Cosmides call the Standard Social Science Model (SSSM) typified by Clifford Geertz when he writes "humanity is as various in its essence as in its expression."[5] The evolutionary psychologist argues that psychological mechanisms are in place that shape behaviors but do not define their particulars. These are the "epigenetic rules" described by Wilson as "the neural pathways and regularities in cognitive development by which the individual mind assembles itself."[6] They are the rules prescribing what Martin Seligman called "prepared learning," the idea that an organism is born with an evolved set of innate preferences and aversions toward certain stimuli and behaviors, tending to steer development along what become species-typical directions.[7] According to Wilson, epigenetic rules not only govern prepared learning but also "comprise the full range of inherited regularities of development in anatomy, physiology, cognition and behaviour. They are the algorithms of growth and differentiation that create a fully functioning organism."[8] It is important to note here that the epigenetic rules are not only rules for psychological development, but for all development, the view from here being that physiological and psychological development are equally subject to genetic constraint. That little or no distinction is made between the somatic and the psychological reflects the materialists' collapse of mind into matter, which is an ideological foundation of evolutionary psychology.

As inherited mechanisms, the epigenetic rules for behavior are thus also evolved mechanisms—adaptations developed to solve a problem. The evolutionary account of how such adaptations arise is numbingly familiar, but worth reiterating for clarity. Without any protective environment, a savannah grazer like the gnu that is born knowing how to walk and run is more likely to survive than an infant gnu that spends weeks struggling to stand upright. Likewise, a gnu drawn to seek out lions will not normally live long enough to pass on the genes that code for predator affinity. Accordingly, those otherwise normal gnus predisposed to avoid predators will be more likely to survive, reproduce, and so increase the chances of their offspring and descendants also possessing predator avoidance mechanisms. The account is a negative one insofar as selections for are just deselections elsewhere; predator avoidance isn't really chosen (and certainly not consciously so). Rather, any behavior that does not include predator avoidance will be eventually bred out of the population; alternatives are eliminated. Blindly, the species as a whole eventually becomes wary of lions. But while predator avoidance or infant motor coordination have clear adaptive advantages to gnus, what of the epigenetic rules that supposedly guide human behavior? How comprehensive an account does evolutionary psychology want to offer?

It is hard to see how the sheer massive diversity of human behavior could be explained in terms of adaptive advantage, but according to the evolutionary psychologists, this is only a problem because too many behavioral and social scientists are working with faulty conceptions both of the limits of human diversity and the genesis and function of adaptations. The diversity of human behavior is indeed amazing, but (argue the evolutionary psychologists) so is the frequency with which behavioral patterns recur. No two human societies are so different that they cannot be recognized from a catalog of behaviors as human societies (rather than ant colonies or whale pods). In their essay "The Psychological Foundations of Culture," where the authors lay out something of a manifesto for evolutionary psychology,[9] Tooby and Cosmides draw on this self-similarity between geographically diverse cultures to better facilitate the analogy between adaptively evolved physiology and adaptively evolved cognitive architecture: "Empirically, of course, the fact that any given page out of *Gray's Anatomy* describes in precise anatomical detail individual humans from around the world demonstrates the pronounced monomorphism present in complex physiological adaptations. Although we cannot directly 'see' psychological adaptations (except as described neuroanatomically), no less could be true of them. Human nature is everywhere the same."[10] Here is Steven Pinker in *The Language Instinct* using the same example with less of the specialist vocabulary: "you can open up any page of *Gray's Anatomy* and expect to find a depiction of organs and their parts and arrangements that will be true of any normal person."[11] In even less technical language, Matt Ridley makes more of the same point in the opening pages of *The Red Queen:* "When a surgeon cuts into a body, he knows what he will find inside. . . . All people have stomachs, all human stomachs are roughly the same shape and all are found in the same place. There are differences. . . . [b]ut the differences are tiny compared to the similarities. . . . There is, it is safe to say, such a thing as the typical human stomach and it is very different from a non-human stomach. It is the assumption of this book that there is also, in the same way, a typical human nature."[12] What Ridley is doing is walking us through his case gradually, progressing quietly from uncontroversial claims about physiological similarity to far more controversial claims about psychological similarity. This is a strategy common to many advocates of evolutionary psychology. It is easy to persuade someone to agree that physiology is relatively similar in all humans and relatively easy to persuade someone to agree that the mind is a product of the brain. The brain is part of the physiology—which we have already agreed is similar in all humans—therefore, the mind is similar (and "in the same way") in all humans. So now we all agree that the psychological divergence between individuals is no more dramatic than the divergence between individuals in the physiology of the stomach.

This argument has lots of problems, the most obvious being the willingness to hand psychology over to physiology. What is trivially different about anatomically similar human stomachs is their content. What the analogy encourages us to overlook is that, in brains, this difference is not so trivial. However, a universal human nature is essential if evolutionary psychology or human sociobiology (the two being, for these purposes, indistinguishable[13]) are to proceed; without it, they cannot make the species-wide generalizations necessary for their causes. If generalizations can only be made within geographically or ethnically bounded groups, then those generalizations will indeed look more like the products of culture than the products of an evolved psychology. If a psychological foundation for culture exists, it must be the foundation for all cultures and be panhuman or specieswide (and usually species-specific) or else it would suggest that each culture was independently evolved, that is to say, that each culture was as another species. If there are innate behavioral patterns, they are specieswide and of probable adaptive advantage.

Much of the work of evolutionary psychology involves "reverse engineering" manifest behavioral patterns to their often unclear adaptive origins. They are unclear, claim Barkow, Tooby, and Cosmides, because "the evolved structure of the human mind is adapted to the way of life of Pleistocene hunter-gatherers and not necessarily to our modern circumstances."[14] Civilization—and certainly modern civilization as we know it—has simply not been around long enough for adaptations to civilization to have had time to arise. (This is [at least partly] why we do not seem to have useful modifications to civilisation and do seem to have plenty of redundant features, such as the vestigial appendix.[15]) Because the bulk of human evolutionary history was spent as hunter-gatherers, any adaptations will be adaptations to hunter-gatherer life, rather than to city or town life. As Denis Dutton explains: "While there is no denying the importance of culture in creating the character of modern homo sapiens, civilisation, and with it modern culture, only goes back 10,000 years, to the invention of agriculture and the establishment of cities. That's less than one percent of our hunter-gatherer history as humans and near proto-human ancestors."[16] As Barkow, Tooby, and Cosmides have it, "this means that in relating the design of the mechanisms of the mind to the task demands posed by the world, 'the world' means the Pleistocene world of hunter-gatherers."[17] Consequently, the types of stories that the evolutionary biologists[18] tell about how and why we evolved our spots are linked to circumstances that do not necessarily obtain in modern life. What were beneficial adaptations for our ancestors may prove to be vestigial or even positively cumbersome to twenty-first-century humans. These stories vary in credibility; some seem efficient and satisfying explanations, others are simply spurious. For example, morning sickness in pregnant women is explained as a mechanism to reduce the ingestion of toxins that may harm the fetus by increasing the body's sensitivity to unusual foods;[19] human hairlessness save for the patch on the top of the head is explained as a sunshield for the bipedal posture; our love of certain landscapes featuring water, vegetation, and shelter (rural idylls, choice locations for property, Constable's *Haywain*) is explained by these being the ideal habitats for survival;[20] and acne in teenagers (and our repulsion to it) is "nature's way" of preventing youths below the optimum breeding age from reproducing by making them unattractive to the opposite sex.[21]

Few people who accept the Darwinian theory of evolution doubt the power of adaptationist thinking, and some adaptations (for example, an eye to see things with and a stomach to digest food) have such an obvious function that they do not seem to need an explanation at all.[22] What is criticized is the sheer untestability of many of the hypotheses, the accusation being that these are just Kiplingesque "just-so stories." As Daniel Dennett cautions, "since *some story or other* must be true, we must not conclude we have found *the* story just because we have come up with *a* story that seems to fit all the facts."[23] Steven Pinker admits that "there is no shortage of bad evolutionary 'explanations'," but it is unclear how to distinguish the "glib and lame"[24] from the successful. Clifford Geertz's warning to credulous anthropologists seems especially pertinent: "there is nothing so coherent as a paranoid's delusion or a swindler's story. The force of our interpretations cannot rest, as they are now so often made to do, on the tightness with which they hold together."[25]

The other criticism is that, in some cases, perhaps no story is true. This was the position Stephen Jay Gould and Richard Lewontin famously took in their critique of the adaptationist program "The

Spandrels of San Marco and The Panglossian Paradigm." Gould and Lewontin do not oppose adaptationism so much as panadaptationism: the idea that every feature of an organism must have (or have had) a good reason for developing. They argue that some characteristics may be non-adaptive side effects, so-called "spandrels" (after the name given to the curved triangular spaces left over when a dome is mounted on a junction of arches[26]). The spandrels are often decorated (as they are in Venice's San Marco church, hence the title) and sometimes so ingeniously they even appear to be designed for just this purpose. But what they really are is wasted space, a necessary compromise opportunistically co-opted into the design of the dome. Gould and Lewontin claim that, as with architecture, so it is with organisms: some features are just leftover spaces, with any "current utility as an epiphenomenon of non-adaptive structures."[27]

Gould and Lewontin's point about spandrels is that not everything that is used by an organism for some purpose necessarily evolved for that purpose; some features are opportunistically co-opted by the organism, giving the appearance of having evolved for that purpose.[28] Gould calls such features "exaptations." Their concern about seeking purpose where there was none is mounted on top of the wider question of how specific adaptations are, and how much flexibility is allowed within the adaptive framework: must everything have a use? Gould and Lewontin's criticism is that the adaptationists seemingly want to explain every feature of an organism (that is, both physiological and psychological) in adaptive terms.[29]

More worrying for some is that this treatment contributes to the dissolution of the boundary between biology and psychology. As Dennett has it, "If human minds are nonmiraculous products of evolution, then they are, in the requisite sense, artifacts, and all their powers must have an ultimately 'mechanical' explanation."[30] This is the same line of reasoning Wilson followed through *Consilience*. If our minds are just our brains, then what explains our brains explains our minds, and, because our brains are physical organs, the best answer to that seems likely to come from evolutionary biology. The materialist evolutionary view can be quite sobering, as Dennett realizes: "If this is right, then all the achievements of human culture—language, art, religion, ethics, science itself—are themselves artifacts (of artifacts of artifacts . . .) of the same fundamental process that developed the bacteria, the mammals, and *Homo sapiens*. There is no special creation of language, and neither art nor religion has a literally divine inspiration. If there are no skyhooks needed to make a skylark, there are also no skyhooks needed to make an ode to a nightingale."[31] The implication of this is that the products of the mind are also (on some level) artifacts of evolution. Consequently, the adaptationist program can be stretched to explain in functional terms not just the disappearance of body hair or the appearance of eyelids, but also—through such frameworks as Seligman's notion of prepared learning—the structure of the mind and the types of things (and thoughts) it is likely to produce or contain.

What is the character of the evolved mechanisms that control prepared learning? Are they so specific as to prescribe the foundations of religion, mathematics, art, and storytelling? How much are we prepared to learn? There is much debate as to the level of specificity, how much is prescribed and how much is (socially or culturally) acquired. At the skeptical end are those proponents of the SSSM who believe that man is born everywhere the same and everywhere as a blank slate, the idea (here polemically simplified by Tooby and Cosmides) that "human nature is an empty vessel, waiting to be filled by social processes."[32] Opposing this view are the advocates of prepared learning, who vary in the degree of "hardwiring" they believe exists in the mind. As very few people really believe the mind is a blank slate at birth (this is, even according to Geertz, a position "which no one of any seriousness holds"[33]), the question, as Tooby and Cosmides put it, is: "Does the mind consist of a few, general-purpose mechanisms, like operant conditioning, social learning, and trial and error induction, or does it also include a large number of specialized mechanisms, such as a language acquisition device . . . , mate preference mechanisms . . . , sexual jealousy mechanisms . . . , mother-infant emotion communication signals . . . , social contract algorithms . . . , and so on?"[34] Once again, there is more resistance to the notion that humans have mechanisms of prepared learning in place than to conceding that other animals have such mechanisms. Ethologist Irenäus Eibl-Eibesfeldt talks of blue whales swimming "with fully coordinated movements immediately after birth. A newborn gnu trots or gallops after its mother when danger threatens." He points out that in (at least nonhuman) animals, "these obviously innate propensities have long been known to behavioral scientists."[35] Importantly, these behaviors are species-specific: it is easier to believe that a beaver could learn to build a dam than it is to believe you could teach a dog (or even a chimp) the same trick.[36] Opponents tend to view the human mind as something different—a general-purpose processor—and resist thinkers like Chomsky who posit specific modules. The idea is that the mechanisms of the language instinct are different in degree but not in kind from the mechanisms that make dam building so easy for beavers (and difficult for dogs). Despite initial resistance, Chomsky's view that the brain is not empty at birth is now widely accepted by linguists and cognitive scientists and has led to enthusiastic speculation in other fields. If language (or, at least, the learning mechanism for language) is innate in this sense, what else might be? As Chomsky had it, "Why, then, should we not study the acquisition of a cognitive structure such as language more or less as we study some complex bodily organ?"[37]

Evolutionary psychologists posit innate mechanisms for increasingly specific functions that, following Chomsky's lead, suggest that much of what we had assumed to be learned may have been (in this sense) prescribed. Sometimes called the "Swiss Army knife" theory of mind, this theory sees the mind as designed to cope with a large number of relatively specific problems. Each blade or tool on the knife is a "module" or "faculty" or, in Pinker's use, an instinct. Just as there are typical behaviors for gnus and whales, there are such things as typical human behaviors, something that, as Eibl-Eibesfeldt notes, anthropologists and ethologists have seen in different cultures all over the world. People everywhere smile when happy, frown when sad.[38] This is part of the evidence supporting Tooby and Cosmides' claim that human nature is everywhere the same. But in a very important way, the human mind is not like the mind of the beaver or the gnu: whatever specific mechanisms are in place, the human mind is also (as Chomsky's opponents argued) a general problem solver. Unlike dogs, we can copy the beaver and build dams of our own. As Dennett notes, this suggests "that there are two profoundly different ways of building dams: the ways beavers do and the way we do. The differences are not necessarily in the products, but in the control structures within the brains that create them."[39] If the language instinct gives us the ability to speak, it also in some way constrains what we can say, just as the beaver can only ever build the same types of dams. As naturalists have seen the continuities in beaver dams and nests within bird species, so the linguist seeks the continuities in human languages.

As discussed above, it has become a commonplace in linguistics that universals are found across the variety of every spoken language. These regularities are symptoms of the language instinct; they do not necessarily reflect the best way or the only way to construct a language, but they are the way humans do it. Language (or at least its acquisition) is outside the domain of the general problem-solving capacities because its structure comes to us as already given, subject to what Chomsky called "highly restrictive principles."[40] This implies that in a very real sense we are not free to dictate the grammar of our languages, and that while we may invent new words, we are powerless to significantly change the structures into which they will fit.[41] It is important to realize here that the psycholinguists are not talking about schoolroom (or "prescriptive") grammar: rules such as "never use double negatives," or "never end a sentence with a preposition," or "never split infinitives." Such rules are not features of innate grammar, but are usually, like irregular verb endings, arbitrary constraints comparable to Johnsonian faux-Latin spellings (for example, debt and receipt) in both their origins and idiosyncrasies.

In the sciences, where there is regularity there is assumed to be mechanism and structure. The specieswide regularities of language strongly indicate the existence of mechanism, although, as Pinker cautions, "[n]ot everything that is universal is innate."[42] One of the concerns of those who object to seeing the general problem-solver mind constrained in this way is that it appears as a block on human freedom. Unfortunately, the emphasis of the researchers involved is indeed often weighted toward the limiting powers of innate mechanisms, rather than their enabling powers.[43] Critics consequently see themselves as defenders of human freedom, claiming that whatever constraints apply to beavers do not apply to us, that the "'biological,' or 'innate' aspects of human behavior or psychological organization are negligible," because the "evolution of the capacity for culture has led to a flexibility in human behaviour that belies any significant 'instinctual' or innate component."[44] But the evidence suggests that there are simply too many regularities for there not to be some form of innate structure to the human mind. Unsurprisingly, this area of evolutionary psychology has been an enormous boon to those looking to explain the regularities of human behavior and culture in terms digestible to science. Their thinking leads to the question: If we share a language structure, what else do we share?

In a defense of Wilson's consilience program, biologist Paul R. Gross asks the same question. "Since there are social arrangements most of the way down the phylogenetic tree, what regularities have they?"[45] Anthropologists looking for these cultural regularities find them (with a few exceptions) in such practices as monogamy, hierarchical society, and wearing clothes, and in creativity, in decoration, and in storytelling. Typically, the arts are singled out from these practices as being entirely products of culture with little or no utility. But it is this very disutility—the often heard "uselessness of art"[46]—that marks its recurrence out for study. Unlike the invention and subsequent reinventions of the wheel or the spear, we find no clear (survival) function to which the emergence of and similarities in art would converge to provide a common solution. Art is entertainment; a luxury. As Dennett points out, this means that if there are common features in different and isolated cultures, we can usually discount those that solve a problem as inevitable. It is the useless similarities that provide better evidence for common cultural descent. "Anthropologists looking for evidence of shared culture are, quite properly, more impressed by common idiosyncrasies of decorative style than by common functional shapes."[47]

Of course, this account of descent says nothing about art being innate. It still allows for a chain of cultural transmission that in no way implies that the creative urge or any specifics of art are hardwired into the human mind. But the regularity with which decoration, storytelling, music, and myth recur across cultures is, argues Ellen Dissanayake, strongly suggestive of there being some biological basis to creativity. Dissanayake underlines that art is one of the few truly universal cultural norms. "Although no one art is found in every society, or to the same degree in every society, there is found universally in every human group that exists today, or is known to have existed, the tendency to display and to respond to one or usually more of what are usually called the arts."[48]

According to Dissanayake, this ubiquity suggests that even if the details of the art are cultural, the foundations for the urge to create art at all are biological. She argues that the urge to create art is perhaps the prime characteristic that sets humanity apart from the other great apes, that creativity is innate, and that *Homo sapiens* might be better labeled *Homo aestheticus*.[49] Just as a language instinct revealed itself through regularities of grammar, so regularities in decoration and in narrative seem to suggest that a case can be made for a "creative instinct," one perhaps as enabling and as restrictive as the language instinct. Paleoanthropologist Alexander Marshack makes this link explicit, arguing for what Graham Richards describes as a "protohuman capacity for symbolic representation intimately related to the emergence of language." Marshack writes:[50] "The Rock art [of preliterate Eurasian/African/American and Australian cultures] evidences the same modes of image use, reuse, association and accumulation as are found in the earlier Eastern and Western European traditions. In this sense, the cognitive mode, involving the periodic use of image and symbol, approaches a universal *H. sapiens sapiens* capacity comparable to, but not equivalent to, the capacity for language use."[51] Marshack's proposition seems to be that art and narrative could be explained along lines similar to the explanation of the origins of language; that is, in terms of a function, an evolved adaptation. If this is the case, then it suggests that art and narrative (or at least their origins and our continued interest) might be explicable in terms of evolutionary biology, and accordingly genetics, and ultimately the laws of physics.

Averse to the pejorative connotations such words as *myth* and *archetype* have acquired, and trying to maintain the distance between Darwin and Jung, some evolutionary epistemologists have been tempted to propose a more science-friendly thought-unit. Richard Dawkins suggested these be called *memes*.[52] He explains that the meme works like the gene. "Genes are replicated, copied from parent to offspring down the generations. A meme is, by analogy, anything that replicates itself from brain to brain, via any available means of copying."[53] It is important to notice that Dawkins has a special way of talking about genes and memes. The way he writes about them gives the reader the idea that the gene or meme is isolatable, autonomous. It "replicates itself," as if it had torn free from the body or mind (the dualism here is unavoidable) in which it inhered. But for this way of thinking about evolution, the gene-centric or gene's-eye view, it is essential that the gene be separable. It must appear that it is primarily the genes that replicate, and the body is merely a vehicle for those genes. That the body replicates or exists at all is just a side effect or consequence of or means for the genes to better their chances of replicating. Dawkins asks us to think of this like a Gestalt drawing; a Necker cube where the perspective flips between the "two ways of looking at natural selection; the gene's angle and that of the individual. If properly understood they are equivalent; two views of the same truth. You can flip from one to the other and it will still be neo-Darwinism."[54] The conceptual shift effected here is repeated for the memetic theory. As the body was a vehicle for the genes on the gene-centric view, so the mind is just a vehicle for the memes. These are the terms in which Daniel Dennett, a keen advocate of both Darwin and Dawkins, lays out the analogy: "Genes are invisible; they are carried by gene vehicles (organisms) in which they tend to produce characteristic effects (phenotypic effects) by which their fates are, in the long run, determined. Memes are also invisible, and are carried by meme vehicles—pictures, books, sayings (in particular languages, oral or written, on paper or magnetically encoded, etc.)"[55] He offers a clear illustration of the consequences of this type of thinking. "A scholar is just a library's way of making another library."[56] It is not clear how seriously the evolutionary epistemologists want us to take the meme theory. When Dawkins first proposed the idea in *The Selfish Gene* in 1976, he presented the meme as little more than a thought experiment: a two-way analogy that reinforces the genetic theory and simultaneously employs the reinforced genetic theory to reinforce the memetic theory. Just as genes compete for places in a gene pool, so memes compete for places in a meme pool.[57]

The meme is introduced to demonstrate how powerful Darwinian thinking is, and Dawkins uses the meme idea to try to demonstrate that the principle of evolution is universal, and not specific to our planet or even life. "We biologists have assimilated the idea of genetic evolution so deeply that we tend to forget that it is only one of many possible kinds of evolution."[58] So, to help us to understand in non-technical terms how evolution works, Dawkins asks us to try imagining that thoughts and ideas are also competing for space. Here, the terrain is our minds. The most successful ideas are those that are passed from person to person, because they stand a better chance of being remembered. The method of transmission is not messy strips of DNA and transfer-RNA, but speech and writing, language, music, painting, and dance. The most successful ideas are not necessarily the best ideas or those closest to the truth—not, that is, insofar as there is another criterion for "best" other than "most successful," and it is unclear if there is. But if "best" is calibrated in terms of (biological) fitness, as it is for genes, then memes are not only not useful, but often actually detrimental. As they are not transmitted genetically, they do not need to help the genes to reproduce, as the "celibacy meme" or the "suicide meme" ably demonstrate. The memes are also presumably unconcerned with "truth" in the abstract; their content is less important than their proliferation.

This is something of an issue for Dawkins, who is often found railing against the "God meme," which he would later call "a virus of the mind."[59] The transmission and longevity of the God meme is assured by the twin pincers of blind faith and the threat of damnation for the unbelievers.[60] Other strengths of the God meme, at least the Christian God meme, include the command to evangelize and spread the meme further still. A text like the Bible ensures "copying-fidelity." "God exists," he writes, 'if only in the form of a meme with high survival value." Reflecting on the success of religious belief, Dawkins writes that "[i]t might almost have been deliberately planned by a machiavellian priesthood," adding (somewhat snidely), "[h]owever, I doubt if the priests were that clever."[61] (Of course, if this last bit is true, it should cancel his distaste. For if, rather than being manipulative and scheming, the priests really were victims of a "mind virus," then we might have expected a little less venom in Dawkins's criticism of them: in the spirit of blaming the meme not the messenger, he might do better to credit priests with intelligence.)

There is some debate as to what constitutes "one meme," just as there is debate about what constitutes one gene. Dawkins provides a list of things that we might want to consider memes: "tunes, ideas, catch-phrases, clothes fashions, ways of making pots or building arches."[62] Dennett calls them "distinct memorable units" and offers a list that contains, among other things, the arch, the wheel, the calendar, chess, *The Odyssey*, "Greensleeves," and deconstructionism.[63] Had he had the vocabulary, Georges Polti would probably want to say that the thirty-six dramatic situations he offers are also each memes. Some of these things are "meme complexes," and Dawkins invites comparisons with gene complexes (such as the carnivore's "[m]utually suitable teeth, claws, guts, and sense organs" that are "so tightly [linked together on the same chromosome] that they can be treated as one gene"[64]). Memes are an adaptable idea. Among other things, Dawkins uses the meme to explain the *Zeitgeist* and the pop-bubblegum song: "Some memes, like some genes, achieve brilliant short-term success in spreading rapidly, but do not last long in the meme pool."[65]

As should already be apparent, meme enthusiasts have a tendency to become tricky when talking about how the memes work. There is something self-congratulatory about meme-talk, something vapid about the inversions and a pleasure in the construction of examples disproportionate to the importance of the ideas being conveyed. Dennett takes some glee in pointing out that a "wagon with spoked wheels carries not only grain or freight from place to place; it carries the brilliant idea of a wagon with spoked wheels from mind to mind."[66] One of the most gnomic of these formulations comes from Sol Speigelman: "The nucleic acids invented human beings in order to be able to reproduce themselves even on the Moon."[67] As Dennett says, the meme is a successful meme; not only has it found a place in the lexicon of the evolutionary epistemologists, but in so doing, it has beaten down its competitors. Wilson lists some of the failed candidates: "mnemotype, idea, idene, sociogene, concept, culturgen, and culture type."[68]

Whether or not a theory of aesthetics from evolutionary psychology would want to employ talk of memes is debatable. Although he is happy to use memes in talking about cultural evolution, Wilson does not explicitly invoke them to explain his archetypal theory, and although Dennett is prepared to list Homer's *Odyssey* as a meme, he maintains that memes are not to be mistaken for archetypes. Whereas the archetype (on Wilson's account) appears spontaneously in disparate cultures through the pressure of universal epigenetic rules, the meme is only ever culturally transmitted. Following David Hull,[69] Dennett stresses that "we do not want to consider two *identical* cultural items as instances of the same *meme* unless they are related by descent."[70] This seems to confirm that the meme, useful as it may be as a means of demonstrating the universal power of Darwinian thinking, is far from being a scientific version of Jungian archetypes. So if the similarities in world narratives cannot be accounted for either by any direct, wholesale prescription hardwired into the mind (that is, a ready-made myth in natural language known from birth, such as that demanded by a collective unconscious), or as a product of cultural transmission, then they appear to be a result of convergent evolution.

Convergent evolution anywhere suggests function; a need is being answered by the repeated homing in on the same solution over and over again. Here, the convergence is on the same narratives. This provides a basis for a weak version of the collective unconscious. It does not demand that whole or even fragmentary myths float around in the mind before birth, but it does suggest that the same types of stories will always elicit the strongest responses. Which is to say, the mind is prepared to enjoy some stories more than others. Biologists talk of these preferences being steered by epigenetic rules, rather than being directly prescribed.[71] While a collective unconscious as Jung (or Yeats, with his "*spiritus mundi*") might have imagined it is too information-rich, this weaker version is acceptable to the more empirically cautious pronouncements of science. As Wilson has it: "Because of differences in strength among the underlying epigenetic rules, certain thoughts and behavior are more effective than others in the emotional responses they cause and the frequency with which they intrude on reverie and creative thought. They bias cultural evolution toward the invention of archetypes."[72] When these would-be-archetypal stories are found,[73] a strong positive response will tend to ensure that they will be remembered and repeated. This also affects the types of stories that people tell in the first place. The narrator is not a blind selector, but generates and selects according to what he wants to hear himself. So even before it reaches an audience the story is converging toward one particular form, and that form will be the same wherever the story is told because the minds that are generating, listening to, and responding to the tale will be everywhere the same (if we accept the first principles of evolutionary psychology from which accounts like Wilson's take off). Successive adjustments made in later tellings bring the story closer to an ideal, an ideal that is presumably crystallized to myth over the years. But the need being answered by the myth needn't be (either currently or originally) functional at all. It is quite possible that narrative works by tricking the same responses out of people as participating in (or viewing) the events described might bring. So stories amuse, arouse, shock, frighten, please, anger, and so on by fooling the mind into releasing the same neurochemical response reaction as "real"[74] fear, shock, or anger would produce.

This is close to the function of "escapism" often assigned to the novel, particularly the popular novel, whose plots we might expect to trade on these formulas most keenly. This also goes some way to explaining why "airport fiction," novels read only once and only for plot, is formulaic. The books are designed to hit all the pleasure buttons as quickly and as unsubtly as possible. By this account, the lack of subtlety found in the popular novel is, at root, the same thing as its being formulaic. Airport fiction does not attempt to disguise the origin of its appeal, but advertises it with more garish cover illustrations: an explosion or couples embracing. When Susan Sontag talks of the "entire volume of sub-literary fiction produced for mass taste,"[75] it is in tacit comparison with pornography: a need is being answered and answered as quickly and as unsubtly as possible. By contrast, canonical literature has typically struggled to escape formula (perhaps more so in recent years as formulas are explicitly codified and popularized). Many of today's art novels relish their absence of plot as a realization of Flaubert's intention to write a novel about nothing at all, a novel entirely of style, and presumably one that had completely transcended its origins as a stimulus-simulator. But for the evolutionary psychologists, the appeal of minimalism and abstraction, and of the rejection of traditional subjects and forms in modernist and postmodernist art, is limited. As Denis Dutton points out, citing John Cage's musical silences and Duchamp's urinal, "such modernist experiments . . . will never for long capture the attention of the vast public for art, whose abiding concerns involve the same themes they always have from the archaic Greeks to this afternoon's soap operas; love, death, adventure, and triumph over adversity."[76]

It is no coincidence that Georges Polti's dramatic situations fit more closely with blockbuster movies and best-selling popular novels than they do with contemporary literature and art-house films. Jung himself was (at least professionally) more interested in popular novels, where he believed that the archetypes he was interested in would feature unrestrained, claiming that "[l]iterary products of highly dubious merit are often of the greatest interest to the psychologist."[77] In his essay "Creative Writers and Day-Dreaming," Sigmund Freud would similarly insist on "an initial distinction": "We must separate writers who, like the ancient authors of epics and tragedies, take over their stories ready-made, from writers who seem to originate their own material. We will keep to the latter kind, and, for the purposes of our comparison, we will choose not the writers most highly esteemed by the critics, but the less pretentious authors of novels, romances and short stories, who nevertheless have the widest and most eager circle of readers of both sexes."[78] As with Jung, for Freud, it is the popular fiction, the mean reading habits of a given population, that are of most interest. In Freud's account, these popular works act as extensions of the type of "day-dreaming" that most adults engage in (albeit privately) as a furtive continuation of childhood play. Commonalities are drawn between popular fiction and the daydream. Characteristic of both is the heroic behavior of the protagonist (in the daydream, the daydreamer), their invulnerability, and the simplistic morality of the imagined world: "the other characters in the story are sharply divided into good and bad, in defiance of the variety of human characters that are to be observed in real life."[79] Freud recognizes that this sort of moral simplism—the defiance of reality—is by no means a feature of all fiction and that the difference between popular fiction and great literature often lies in just such a variance in complexity. But, unwilling to sever the link between the playing child, the daydreaming adult, and the creative writer, Freud does not see canonical literature as a special case. "We are perfectly aware that very many imaginative writings are far removed from the model of the naïve day-dream; and yet I cannot suppress the suspicion that even the most extreme deviations from that model could be linked with it through an uninterrupted series of transitional cases."[80] As with Boden and her creativity simulations, the emphasis here is on establishing a continuum between the simple stories and the great works of literature, dissolving the grounds for an ontological distinction between literary and subliterary fiction. With a continuum established, all that needs to be explained is the simplest case, and all other cases can be explained as complications thereof.

In a professional capacity, the psychologist may well be expected to be more interested in popular fiction than specifically literary fiction. What makes some literature worthy of further study also makes it less typical of fiction generally and so less interesting as data for the psychologist or scientist looking to formulate general patterns. To some extent this is because the psychologist looks to fiction not for the story it tells the reader, but for the story it tells about the reader: what, for example, do the choices that readers make reflect of their goals and interests? The literary critic is not the mean reader, and the psychologist (in any professional capacity, that is, qua psychologist) is not looking at art or literature for the same reasons as the critic. This complicates what we might expect evolutionary psychology to do with literature in terms of interpretation and criticism.

That there seem to be similarities across world narratives is a relatively uncontroversial (because empirically demonstrable) point. Recall that the existence of panhuman narratives was a relatively uncontroversial claim with a history co-extensive with the history of anthropological research in that area. What is disputed is more often the mechanics of how this came to be. With the possibility of direct cultural transmission disqualified by cases of prolonged geographical isolation, accounts seek instead to explain regularities in narrative fiction in terms of regularities in the minds that collectively produce such narratives. Given the apparent lack of an inheritance mechanism, the Jungian collective unconscious transpired to be a poor candidate for explaining how world narratives possess the similarities they do. A better (or rather, more scientifically credible) candidate seemed at first to be the memetic theory—but the hoped-for analogy with genes collapses when it emerges that memes demand cultural transmission and are not innate in the necessary sense. It seems just as unlikely that an innate narrative instinct would manifest as precisely as Polti's formulations suggest; but his intuition here—that there are shaping principles behind the development of plot—is key. Evolutionary psychology, with its emphasis on the task-specific modularity of mind, presents itself by analogy with the success of Chomskyan linguistics as a means of explaining the narrative regularities through hardwiring, preserving Polti's insight, but now grounding it in what seems to be a scientifically credible theory.

In linguistics, the ease and ability with which children are seen to acquire language "is hopelessly underdetermined by the fragmentary evidence available" to them.[81] Likewise, we do not need to be told what types of things will make for an interesting story; the themes that fill fiction seem given, obvious, already there. As one sociobiologist puts it, there is never likely to be a play written about filling out tax forms (or rather, if such a play was written, we would not expect it to enjoy the same level of success as a sex-and-deceit soap opera).[82] For linguists like Pinker looking for evidence of a language instinct, "[t]he crux of the argument is that complex language is universal because *children actually reinvent it*,"[83] as seen with the generational transition between pidgin and Creole. The geographically and culturally isolated recurrence of narratives, such as those recorded by Lévi-Strauss and the Cambridge Ritualists, and the regularities of worship and magic recorded by Frazer seem to constitute just such a reinvention. The independent attempts by Jung, Campbell, Frye, and others to organize an archetypal theory of literature show that there is a widespread and recurrent detection of pattern and theme, and the admiration for their ambition rather than their accomplishment that Ellis remarked on reflects a belief that their search for underlying order,[84] although unsuccessful, is not necessarily misguided. The appeal of an evolutionary account is the same as for the collective unconscious. However, unlike the collective unconscious, evolutionary psychology appears to offer a coherent scientific framework in which to insert a theory of narrative.

Evolutionary psychology offers several accounts of art and, specifically, literary fiction. These accounts vary in what they are willing to consider as art, in the importance they accord art in maintaining a healthy psychological state, and in the status and priority they accord to specific forms of art. In *Homo Aestheticus*, Ellen Dissanayake takes an ethological view. "It is time to recognise that art is normal, natural, and necessary as other things that people do, and to try to approach it ethologically, as a *behavior*."[85] She seeks to root art in the universal human impulse of "making special" our environment by decorating tools, walls, and our bodies, but Dissanayake is not specifically interested in literary art. Nor is Wilson when he turns to "The Arts and their Interpretation" in *Consilience*.[86] Wilson, interestingly, talks not only about general creativity[87] but also interpretation: that is, Wilson is proposing the application of evolutionary theories as literary criticism. In keeping with his causal view (origins explain effects), Wilson sees an understanding of the creative process as a sufficient ground for an interpretive theory. Recall that for Wilson, complexity is always explicable with reference to a reductive hierarchy. Accordingly, what he has to say about literary criticism feeds out of this strong materialist thesis. "Interpretation has multiple dimensions, namely history, biography, linguistics, and aesthetic judgements. At the foundation of them all lie the material processes of the human mind."[88] But as Richard Rorty pointed out, it is not clear that a "better knowledge of how things work"[89] (in this sense of how the hardware works) will be of any great assistance to literary criticism. As mentioned above, Wilson also holds with an archetypal theory of literature that relies on talk of epigenetic rules and convergent evolution to avoid any connection with a collective unconscious.

One of the few evolutionary accounts of art to try to deal with specifically literary fiction has been put forward by Joseph Carroll, most comprehensively in his book *Evolution and Literary Theory* (1995). Carroll has two theses: one positive, one negative. The first of these is that literary criticism would benefit from employing Darwinian evolution as a conceptual base, and second, that we should reject the theories of deconstruction, relativism, and Rortyean style pragmatics, which Carroll covers with the blanket term of poststructuralism.

For the positive thesis, Carroll is quite precise about the type of evolutionary account he wants. Although largely happy with Wilson's analysis, he criticizes what he calls the "quasi-Jungian conception of 'archetypes.'"[90] In an essay derisively titled "Steven Pinker's Cheesecake for the Mind," Carroll is found arguing with Pinker's account of the place of art in evolutionary psychology, wanting to make different (and stronger) claims for fiction. This is largely because they have different ambitions here. Carroll is principally a literary critic, and this is evident from the works he uses to support his case. His examples are drawn almost exclusively from the nineteenth-century novel. This is not simply because Carroll's background is in the nineteenth-century novel (although it is also this), but because here are realistic, character-driven narratives in contemporary (therefore, for their authors, familiar) settings, involving much social interaction and social commentary on the manners and mores of the day. This is the type of background that evolutionary psychology might be expected to better explain. However, Carroll's tight focus on literature may well be an impediment to his theory. Unlike Pinker, Wilson, and Dissanayake, who all operate with a very broad and inclusive sense of art, Carroll is trying to formulate a theory of literary appreciation that will serve the function of traditional criticism (that is, will enable canon formation and will discriminate between literary and popular fiction) but will also integrate with the wider scientific worldview via evolutionary psychology.

It might seem strange that Carroll should be hostile to the scientists he seemingly looks to for endorsement. Why attack Pinker? It seems that much of the disagreement between Carroll and Pinker turns on their different definitions of art. Pinker defines art very broadly. Art is a "pleasure technology"[91] (hence a "cheesecake for the mind"), a means of shorting the brain's pleasure circuits "without the inconvenience of wringing bona fide fitness increments from the harsh world."[92] Art also instructs through simulations of potential situations, offering people a chance to mentally rehearse responses, "so they will be prepared if they ever find themselves in similar straits."[93] "Fictional narratives," claims Pinker, "supply us with a mental catalogue of the fatal conundrums we might face someday and the outcomes of strategies we could deploy in them. . . . The cliché that life imitates art is true because the function of some kinds of art is for life to imitate it."[94] As a definition of art, this is a little vacuous and more than a little circular: art is whatever serves the function Pinker ascribes to art. Also, his definition is perhaps too inclusive; there is no distinction made between art and entertainment, both are pleasure technologies. Shakespeare is on a level with pornography (both entertain and, in their own ways, instruct). But Pinker is not concerned with developing a discriminating aesthetic theory. This is evident from the sources Pinker uses in *How the Mind Works* to support his case: Woody Allen, National Lampoon's movies (*Animal House*), pop songs (Bob Dylan and Lou Reed), and, sprinkled among them, some quotations from canonical literature (Shakespeare, Dryden, Joyce, and Kafka).[95] A clear distaste for the eclecticism of these references, which Carroll sees as vulgarity, leads him to conclude that "There is little evidence that [Pinker's] familiarity with most of the works he quotes extends very far beyond the quotations. His literary taste and judgement seem those of an undergraduate who is extraordinarily bright but who is much more sensitive to computers than to poems, plays, or novels."[96] Carroll, on the other hand, considers himself appropriately sensitive. He is (as might be expected of a literary critic rather than, as in Pinker's case, a cognitive scientist) more concerned with literary merit, with distinguishing between "great literature" and what Susan Sontag called "sub-literary fiction."[97] Carroll's interests are also more local, limited to the written word and, specifically, canonical literature. Accordingly, what Carroll is talking about when he is talking about art is art as distinct from entertainment. But given the avowedly counterintuitive, anti-mass-appeal intentions of literature and high art, can an account from evolutionary psychology ever hope to explain it?

The desire of high art not to be popular, and the fact that "popular" is pejorative and high art and the avant-garde are minority interests, suggests that the only relation high art and the avant-garde have to expected evolutionary trends is one of opposition. Perhaps then, evolutionary psychology can only take us so far: it can predict large-scale trends with relative success and can account for pornography, action movies, and romance novels. But for the type of analysis we might expect of literary criticism, it seems superfluous. If Wordsworth, Shelley, Arnold, and Henry James were all able to write the type of criticism Carroll endorses without any explicit appeal to Darwin, there seems little reason why the critic of today need invoke him to explain their reasoning. Given that Carroll's account seems to float free of his many references to evolutionary theory, it might seem puzzling that he uses it at all.

This is where the book's second thesis assumes prominence. As mentioned above, Carroll's negative account is an attempt to employ evolutionary theories to squeeze out poststructuralist theories from the literary academy. *Evolution and Literary Theory* is as much an attack on poststructuralism as it is an endorsement of evolutionary psychology. This is because it is essential for Carroll to allow no possibility of a hybrid theory here. He agrees with Wilson that, on a methodological level, a united two cultures is desirable; but he finds that to reconcile science with literary studies we must first extricate poststructuralist thinking from our critical toolbox. In part, this is because poststructuralism is often hostile to science, and so its continued popularity is an impediment to the acceptance of an evolutionary psychological theory of literary interpretation. But more than this, he believes that poststructuralism adopts assumptions that are simply incommensurable with science. We should, Carroll urges, reject the relativism of the poststructuralists and *instead* be materialists—the two being opposed positions that cannot both be sensibly held. Because Carroll holds that materialism is an essential ingredient of scientific thought, any attempt to preserve a transcendental account of literature and creativity[98] will contradict science, and so any accounts that attempt to employ ideas from both poststructuralism and science will not be simply unconventional, they will be incoherent.

Poststructuralist accounts effectively neuter any scientific ideas they incorporate. Literary critics who have used Darwinian thought in the past have often done so under the condition that science be thought of as one way of thinking among many. George Levine is typical of this type of nonscientific science in the opening pages of his study of nineteenth-century fiction, *Darwin Among the Novelists*, when he writes, "For the purposes of this volume, I, like [Michel] Serres, consider science as an unprivileged form of cultural discourse, 'a cultural formation equivalent to any other,' but one that happens to have been privileged for much of modern history."[99] For Carroll, this type of formulation is not simply different from the way scientists think of science "from the inside," it is fundamentally incompatible with scientific thought. By maintaining that science is simply another form of cultural discourse, without any special relation to the truth, poststructuralism makes scientific fact into cultural comment. So the ideas of Darwin are carried over only as ideas, and in this fashion are inert. By isolating them from their scientific context (the background beliefs of biology) they have been stripped of all that made them science. Their validity as scientific ideas was intrinsically bound up with their place in the larger scientific ontology. So, maintains Carroll, when we find poststructuralist arguments that employ incorporations of scientific thought we can be fairly sure (even from a distance) that they are wrong. Science is powerful and "spectacularly useful," as even Rorty has it,[100] but only in the hands of scientists, only when used within the limits of scientific thought. The principle here is the same as Barkow, Tooby, and Cosmides laid out in the introduction to *The Adapted Mind* as a ground rule for conceptual integration: any theories from other disciplines must be checked against what are considered to be the more primary claims of biology and the natural sciences.

Searching for ways to allow literary study to share in the prestige accorded to scientific discourse, Carroll is enthusiastic about evolutionary psychology. "The rapidly developing and increasingly integrated group of evolutionary disciplines has resulted in an ever-expanding network of reciprocally illuminating and confirming hypotheses about human nature and human society," and he believes "this information should have a direct bearing on our view of literature." However, Carroll fears that in affiliating itself with poststructuralism, literary studies risk being excluded from what should be a real opportunity for meaningful interaction with the productions of the scientific community. Poststructuralism fails woefully to conceptually integrate, its "rhetoric altogether detached from empirical study," and literary studies as a whole displays none of the "intellectual constraints through which other disciplines[101] establish their intellectual validity."[102] "For critical commentary to be susceptible to rational evaluation," he says, "critical propositions must be 'falsifiable,' that is, susceptible to being declared mistaken on grounds of logic and evidence that would be ratified by all reasonable, informed observers."[103] For Carroll, it doesn't matter whether or not we call the revised model a science, "only that we be clear about the conditions that distinguish such rational and empirical study from arbitrary rhetorical activity."[104]

Having decided to reject poststructuralism, Carroll is pessimistic about what remains to be salvaged: "A very large proportion of the work in critical theory that has been done in the past twenty years will prove to be not merely obsolete but essentially void.... It is essentially a wrong turn, a dead end, a misconceived enterprise, a repository of delusions and wasted efforts."[105] Because poststructuralism complicates the relation between author and text and, most radically, the relative causal primacy of texts and the material world, it cannot serve Carroll's Darwinian account, which insists on the importance of the relation between the author and his environment. Natural selection works on an organism's suitability to its environment. By Carroll's account, literature is equally inseparable from its environment, demanding a return to critical approaches that contextualize literature. To separate the text from the world, he argues, is both counterintuitive and deleteriously restrictive. Like Tooby and Cosmides, Carroll stresses the importance of recognizing a universal human nature. "Despite all differences of metaphysics, scientific conceptions, and cultural heritage, traditional literary theorists largely concur in the idea that literature represents or articulates human experience, and most theorists would go on to say that that experience is rooted in 'human nature.'"[106]

Carroll finds "human nature" in the writings of most "traditional critics": "in Wordsworth, Shelley, Arnold, James, and Tolstoy"[107] and in sociobiology (Wilson's *On Human Nature*[108]). He does not find it in poststructuralist critiques, "except to be repudiated."[109] By similarly holding to a belief in human nature, Carroll aligns himself with modern science and most of the literary giants and masses these forces against poststructuralism. He maintains that this "convergence of usage suggests, first, that in fundamental ways biological theory is compatible with traditional literary conceptions, and, second, that cultural constructivism is incompatible both with biological theory and with these traditional conceptions."[110]

This is the pivot of Carroll's case: you are either with science and literary history, or you reject both of these things and hold with poststructuralism instead. It is unclear, however, that this particular "convergence" between science and nineteenth-century literature is a strong enough alignment to justify the sidings he suggests. Certainly, Wordsworth and Shelley might be expected to reject the materialist claims of a creativity algorithm that Boden investigated. Important differences exist between the ways modern science talks of human nature and how Carroll's selection of nineteenth-century literary figures do.

That Carroll chooses to frame his argument in terms of a conflict between realists and relativists reflects a deeper rift between the sciences and the humanities that has largely grown up in the fallout from the two-cultures debate. The root of the incompatibility he locates between evolutionary theory and those ideas he lumps under poststructuralism is a deeper skepticism about the epistemological status of scientific claims—not those doubts that scientists like Gould or Lewontin harbored about the validity of the adaptationist program within evolutionary theory, but rather a movement questioning the fundamental claims of science to have access to privileged knowledge about the world in the first place.

4
Relativism and the Unity of Culture

WILSON'S CONCEPTION OF A PRODUCTIVE UNIFICATION BEING ONE that brings the humanities into the sciences (rather than the other way around) reflects not only his own interests as a scientist, but a belief that science is working well—working better in fact, than the other disciplines—and if unification demands eliminations, then better they occur elsewhere where nothing useful is being done. It reflects a desire to preserve the achievements of science as they stand and keep open the possibilities for future discoveries. In science, humanity has found a brilliantly successful method of exposing the mechanics of natural phenomena, and consequently, a special authority is attached to scientific validation. (This authority is employed by advertisers, who use men in white coats to endorse their products, and is seen in legal disputes, where the rhetoric of lawyers is perceived as manipulative, in contrast to the forensic scientist, who is passively channeling facts.) The consequence of all this praise and importance is the corresponding loss of status in anything not scientific. In academia, thinkers such as Freud, James Lovelock (Gaia theory), or Rupert Sheldrake (morphic resonance) are written off as unscientific and ignored for this reason. Reflecting the esteem in which science is held, the response to their work is all the more hostile for the pretense of scientific validity.

Much of the prestige of scientific knowledge comes from its impartiality: scientific knowledge, unlike other forms of knowledge, is epistemologically "pure." (As seen with Wilson, some authors question the validity of nonscientific discourses' claims to produce "knowledge" at all.) What is meant by this is that scientific knowledge is not the type of knowledge that can be corrupted by the cultural situation or the personal interests of the researchers involved: scientific knowledge is "just how things are." When talking about the epistemological security of scientific knowledge, the register is very often that of biohazard containment, and the hygiene metaphor is supposed to make us think of cleanliness without contamination, of purity, of something trustworthy. Scientific knowledge is sterile, clinical. The process of scientific data collection and the means by which it is subsequently handled ensures that few or no external concerns are allowed near. For this to be effective, the scientists themselves must appear impartial. In cultivating an image of themselves as distant from societal concerns and disinterested with respect to political or evaluative issues, the scientists often appear blunt and insensitive, allowing no room for pillowed subtleties and sensitivities, which, to the scientists, look like euphemisms. Science is defiantly against euphemism, which is the act of redescription in the interests of primness and social order. Recalling DeLillo's observation that it is a "source of new names,"[1] science redescribes in essentialist terms, providing the real words for things with no regard to the niceties and repressions of politicized culture.

Words like *sterile* and *clinical* are sometimes used pejoratively, too, when it is felt that the introduction of some personal or emotional concern might be appropriate. It can seem that science has no room for human concerns. So although this talk of "cold" and "hard" is comforting epistemologically, it is also somewhat alienating. This produces a conflict between scientific and previous modes of understanding the universe, and this conflict is reflected in a return in recent years to traditional and nonscientific solutions, exacerbating that conflict. What is often called the New Age[2] movement is willfully antiscientific—a reaction to the impartiality of a scientific universe that has apparently little or no space for human concerns. The growth in the popularity of homeopathy, for example, shows people investing more faith in the accumulated wisdom of traditional remedies than the recent discoveries of the scientifically respectable pharmaceutical industry. This resistance is tied up with a nexus of beliefs about the pharmaceutical companies and their relation to capitalist big business, but often roots itself ideologically in a defiant rejection of the superiority of scientific knowledge. This more fundamental motive appears to be a response to that same cold disinterest that the scientist cultivates in the name of impartiality. In a nonincidental contrast to the New Age movement, science has little respect for tradition and history. It erases its own past without compunction and does not care if a belief has been held for millennia; if it doesn't square with empirical results, then it will be rejected.[3]

Science becomes a civilizing force, the only thing between us and another Dark Ages. Do reactions against the dominant form of scientific rationalism (such as the New Age movement) threaten science? Andrew Ross senses an anxiety among scientists. "That a large number of North Americans today sustain a belief in creationism while living in a technologically advanced society . . . is considered a clear and present danger to civilisation."[4] Physicist and historian Gerald Holton is keen to show how this danger can materialize, and he is scathing toward what he terms anti-science. Dubious about how benign the "mass appeal of alternative forms of rationality"[5] may be, Holton cautions that "alternative sciences or parasciences by themselves may be harmless enough except as one of the opiates of the masses, but that when they are incorporated into political movements they can become a time bomb waiting to explode."[6] Holton's position is not just that nonscience is nonsense; he argues that the existence of nonscience or antiscience (because any nonscience is inimical to the principles of science), and its legitimization through the type of cultural relativism that the likes of Ross advocate, will only increase the likelihood that another Lysenko will be allowed the eminence to eventually pair up with another Stalin. The threat of alternative science and parascience lies in the power of science proper. Holton's fears here are not just a case of scientific self-importance, which Ross derides as "the myth of scientists ... standing firm against a tide of superstitions,"[7] but a reflection of the esteem in which scientific knowledge is held and the extent to which modern civilization trusts scientific pronouncements implicitly. As individuals are increasingly unable to check the veracity of a scientist's claim themselves, the truth of scientific theories is accepted on authority. The worry is that these are fertile conditions for parascientific theories to flourish. While most of these theories, such as Sheldrake's notion of morphic resonance, do indeed seem harmless, Holton believes we ought to be wary of what we are willing to countenance as scientific knowledge and is worried that parascience will erode the authority of real science. Given that parascience exhibits a willingness to exploit the authority of science (as Stalin and Lysenko did), Holton maintains that "it is prudent to regard the committed and politically ambitious parts of the antiscience phenomenon as a reminder of the Beast that slumbers below."[8]

Holton's Beast is not a metaphor for antiscience (or at least not all of it), so much as for the uglier sides of human nature. What is not clear is why the Beast should be paired only with an *anti*scientific movement. If the Beast is distinct from antiscience and is instead an evil that evil men impose on an otherwise inert (though factually wrong) thought system, then it is also equally distinct from science proper and equally able to attach itself to either. It seems to be Holton's tacit assumption that real science would never muddy its hands with something so ideologically noxious as Lysenko's neo-Lamarckism, and yet it is not clear from where the corrective would come. His complacency on this point—science could never be immoral—is perhaps an offshoot of science's self-imposed objectivity: the image that scientists deal in just the facts, and morality has nothing to do with it.

But the possibility remains that scientific fact will contradict morality, and what then? Those scientists who follow the experimental physicists' line and "trust the equation" find morality comes second to science. Robert Lange, a member of the Sociobiology Study Group, was asked what he would do if "incontrovertible facts about sex roles or, even worse, racial differences, really were to emerge?" He replied, "Then I would evidently have to become a racist, because I would have to believe in the facts."[9]

Grounding morality in science can seem intuitively jarring. A study like Richard J. Herrnstein and Charles Murray's *The Bell Curve*,[10] which examined and purported to find evidence for the heritability of intelligence across different races, might seem, as George Steiner has suggested,[11] irreconcilable with the principles of social justice. But for defenders of "free-research," this amounts to confusing the political with the strictly factual. Bernard Davis, an advocate of behavioral genetics and sociobiology, calls this confusion the "moralistic fallacy" (after G. E. Moore's naturalistic fallacy, of which it is an inversion) and defines it as "an illogical attempt to derive an 'is' from an ought'."[12] For Davis, placing limits on scientific inquiry to preserve moral norms is misguided: "Apart from the implication of a fixed rather than an adaptive concept of justice . . . this proposition seems to be blaming the messenger for the message. For science does not create the realities of nature: it only discovers them. And if it is not allowed to discover them they will still be there, determining whether or not our assumptions and our predictions turn out to be correct."[13] Davis asks instead that we "trust posterity to adapt its notions of morality to further new knowledge."[14] The implication is clearly that morality follows science and not the other way around. Seen here as just an impartial report of how things really are, science seemingly offers a route to moral immunity. The apparent naïveté of Herrnstein and Murray and other researchers like them stems from a tendency of scientists to believe their own claims for impartiality and objectivity: science produces facts, and what society chooses to do with those facts is no business of science. In assuming the stance of an apolitical, distanced researcher, the scientist is apparently able to bypass social responsibility and to retreat inside impersonality. It is these claims that many sociologists and philosophers of science choose to dispute.

Far from being an exercise in objectivity, many thinkers have argued that science is as much affected by personal opinion as any other discipline and that scientists have no warrant to claim to possess what Thomas Nagel called a "view from nowhere." Central to these claims is the belief that scientific thought and language consistently fail to escape the influence of politics, gender, and personal prejudice. In a case like *The Bell Curve*, we are left wondering quite why Herrnstein and Murray chose to investigate IQ in different racial groups. It seems highly improbable that the data were collated randomly. Rather, the researchers made a series of conscious choices: they chose to study intelligence, they chose to quantify that intelligence within certain parameters, and they chose to sort their data by race (as opposed to nationality, hair color, marital status, and so on). We imagine they held expectations for the results, too. Perhaps they were outraged at talk of stratification of intelligence across racial groups and hoped to prove once and for all that no such stratification existed. Perhaps it was only with great reservation and a strong fidelity to the principles of scientific integrity that they regretfully published their findings to the contrary (although neither Herrnstein's nor Murray's previous publications would suggest this). Even if they did begin the study with no hopes for any particular outcome, a trail of decisions leads up to the conclusion: they asked some questions rather than others, precluding certain results. As N. Katherine Hayles puts it, "*it matters what questions one asks and how one asks them.*"[15]

It is worth examining in some detail the type of evidence usually offered by those skeptical about the security of scientific knowledge to support their claims that it is as culturally contaminated as any other form of discourse. The following case is presented by N. Katherine Hayles in Andrew Ross's *Science Wars*, a collection of essays exploring the hostilities that have grown up between the humanities and the sciences. Most of the contributors to *Science Wars* subscribe to the theory of the sociology of scientific knowledge (SSK), or a variant of this, which holds that scientific beliefs are socially constructed and valid only within the limits of the social conditions and disciplinary conventions from which they emerge. Constructivists are relativists who hold that scientific knowledge is never universally applicable and that the very idea of universally applicable knowledge is nonsense.

Given that she is writing for an audience already largely convinced of the validity of her conclusions, it is instructive to follow Hayles's inferences here. She takes as her starting point the work of Donna Haraway. In *Primate Visions*,[16] Haraway wrote about the work of primatologist Clarence Ray Carpenter, pointing out ways in which data collection could be affected by what were perhaps unconscious prejudices that were being carried over from human society and mapped out onto his interpretation of the monkey societies he was studying. Carpenter's work was on group structure in rhesus macaques, and his hypothesis was that the dominant "alpha males" assured group cohesion. To test this theory, he removed and isolated the dominant males from the groups he was studying, and his hypothesis was subsequently proved correct when the structure of the group collapsed.

Haraway's objection was that Carpenter began the experiment with certain presumptions—that alpha males ensured group cohesion—and as a result, only asked certain questions—namely, those relating to males. He never thought to ask about removing females from the group, a decision, Haraway contends, reflecting the dominant ideology in human society that says males hold power and females submissively follow. The design of the experiment and the foundation of Carpenter's hypothesis then consisted in transference of this ideology onto monkey society. The intention of such a criticism is not to discredit Carpenter's findings entirely, but rather to highlight the limitations of such a study (only the males were removed), and to undercut science's general claims for objectivity by pointing to the influence of extrascientific concerns in the collection of data. It is this second move that Hayles sees as having been safely established by Haraway's analysis.

How far does a criticism like Haraway's go? As mentioned, the findings *as they stand* are no less true for the accusations of ideological contamination: the results do clearly demonstrate the importance of alpha males to rhesus macaque social groups. But the findings are also limited; if it is truth being uncovered here, then it is being uncovered selectively.[17] Furthermore, the criticisms are of limited scope. While gender prejudice might be at work in Carpenter's study, it is by no means obvious that such prejudices might contaminate other areas of scientific research. The genetic, and accordingly, phenotypic or physiological similarities between monkeys and humans open all primatology to the temptations of anthropomorphism. It is easy to see how presumptions about human behavior and social organization might be carried over to the study of rhesus monkeys, a study that perhaps has more in common with anthropology than entomology.[18]

The basic assumption behind the criticisms of Haraway and Hayles is that anthropomorphism is an attitude entirely inappropriate to scientific investigations. However, that this is the case is far from clear, and some theorists have argued that a veto on anthropomorphism is itself a sort of prejudice.[19] Even allowing limited anthropomorphic assumptions into data collection, it is not so easy to see how presumptions or prejudices concerning class or race or gender could have such influential effects on science as a whole, as Hayles at least seems to feel Haraway's work implies. Anthropomorphism is obviously a realistic worry for primatology, but it is unclear that anthropomorphism would have any effect on the findings of particle physicists or the direction of research in solar neutrino emission levels. Haraway's criticisms are interesting as far as they go, but they do little to undermine the assumed objectivity of the larger scientific project and almost nothing in terms of questioning the truth value of scientific theories. Anthony O'Hear agrees: "science does not simply read the book of nature. What it discovers, it discovers as a result of our probing into nature, and in the terms in which we probe. Science, as much as everyday perception, is the upshot of human interaction with nature." But he is quick to limit the conclusions we can sensibly draw from such a state of affairs: "The fact that much of what we discover in science we also create does not impugn the reality or objectivity of what is thus revealed. What it does is to cast doubt on a naïve view of science simply as reading off essences from what is there without us."[20] To use Haraway's study, as Hayles does, to insinuate that a possible transference of prejudice in a single experiment implies that such transferences occur regularly and across the scientific disciplines is simply invalid. Hayles wants us to see the flaws Haraway finds in Carpenter's research as falsifying science's claims for objectivity, and while readers already sympathetic to the thesis of the SSK will doubtless find Hayles's argument satisfying, the evidence is much too scant to warrant this broad inference. With no one to persuade, Hayles argues complacently.

Even given as much force as Hayles would like to grant it, Haraway's case study can only tell us about how the direction of research can be affected by the personal interests of the researchers. It does not in itself imply data fabrication. For Hayles, however, the significance of such a case is that the "assumptions implicit in the questions also helped determine what counted as an observation."[21] That is to say, plenty of phenomena will have been manifest to Carpenter, but only some—the select few things the experimental questions were designed to ask about—will have been *observed*. So studying male dominance to an extent excludes studying female nurturing, just as it excludes observations of climatic conditions, non-rhesus monkey species, or monkey behavior in relation to cloud formations. The researcher sees the types of things he or she is looking for, and that is determined by the questions asked. What is not asked is not relevant.

This would seem fairly self-evident to most scientists: observation must always be a focused activity carried out by a trained observer. Theory precedes observation insofar as you have to know what you are looking for. Although this is presented as a means by which scientific knowledge surrenders its objectivity, the claim that "it matters what questions you ask" is not something that scientists will try to deny. Heisenberg recalls Einstein's comment that "it is the theory that decides what we can observe."[22] Similarly, neurobiologist Patricia Churchland recognizes that the limited scope of any single experiment is a necessary condition for research: "It is an illusion to suppose that experimental research *can* be completely innocent of theoretical assumptions. So long as there is a reason for doing one experiment rather than another, there must be some governing hypothesis or other in virtue of which the experimental question is thought to be a good question, and some conception of why the experiment is worth the very considerable trouble."[23] To be effective, the observer must have some prior familiarity and expectations.[24] Behind allegations of theoretical "interference" in data collection, Hayles wants to argue a larger point, and one more damaging to the security of scientific knowledge.

When Hayles says that the results of an experiment are shot through with the presumptions of the researcher, she is setting up an argument that the traditional distinction between the context of discovery and the context of justification is untenable. This distinction implies that regardless of how the information was acquired—whether through a carefully constructed and informed hypothesis or simply by chance (the discovery)—what counts is how that information is then fitted into the larger scientific project, the proofs offered, and the evidence presented (the justification). So, to use a common example, the story is told of August Kekulé's dream of the snake swallowing its own tail and his subsequent (and correct) thesis about the structure of the benzene ring. Of course, the dream is just anecdotal; that part isn't science, any more than Shakespeare's diet might be a good indication of his competency as a writer. His work vindicated, Kekulé would later speak of the dream to argue the necessity of irrationality for original thought, claiming that "the waking mind does not think in leaps" and (with some theatricality) urging an audience of the German Chemical Society in 1890 to "learn to dream, gentlemen, for then, perhaps, we may find the truth." But although he goes on to insist that scientists should "publish [their] dreams, before they are put the test by waking reason," it is clear that even Kekulé holds with the two-contexts model. He recorded that, on awaking from the dream, he "spent the rest of the night working out the consequences of this hypothesis."[25] Kekulé's reputation did not rest on publishing dreams, but on having the requisite training to work out the consequences. What counts in his reputation as the founding father of organic chemistry is not the (possibly untrue) story about dreaming of a snake, but his knowledge of chemistry that enabled him to then justify that discovery through collation of experimental data.

The context of justification is like conceptual laundering, and ideology and teleology come out in the wash. In this way, the theory escapes cultural contamination. But for critics like Hayles, because the questions asked determine the *type* of answers given, what goes through that laundry or airlock to the justification stage is always already decided and tainted by its culturally contaminated genesis in the context of discovery. As Hayles has it, "Prophylactic barriers between [the context of discovery and the context of justification] cannot assure safe epistemology."[26] This was what the analysis of Carpenter's work was supposed to show, and this is why it matters what questions you ask.

As a result of the necessity of directed questions and background knowledge to the act of observing, the observations are never universally valid, but are instead limited to the extent that only *"someone who is properly enculturated and instantiated into a certain perspective* can confirm scientific knowledge claims over a wide range of sites."[27] This creates a double-edged exclusivity for scientific knowledge. We have no way of really assessing the truth value of a scientific statement unless we are already "enculturated and instantiated" into the scientific project, which means that while this knowledge is as good as incontestable outside science, it is also only true *inside* science. But if this exclusivity is true for scientific knowledge, then it is surely also true for Hayles's work and the work of writers and thinkers working within the conventions and vocabulary specific to their discipline. What Hayles, or any SSK-style constructivist, is writing is not transparent, nor is it couched in simple language. So it is not immediately clear why the exclusivity of scientific knowledge and discourse is a special case, distinct from the exclusivity of literary critical or philosophical discourse, except in who is excluded (that is, literary critics and philosophers). Presumably, science is to be considered separately because it considers itself separately, claiming universal validity and denying that the type of knowledge it produces is shaped by culture in these ways. The consequence of this line of attack is that Hayles can no longer claim a universal validity for her own argument. To succeed, the strategy has to be self-defeating, at least insofar as her criticisms can only really be applicable to those similarly enculturated as herself, which would seem to leave scientists untouched. Opening up a typical conundrum for relativists, Hayles is forced to bite the bullet and lose universal knowledge altogether, denying that it is something we should be searching for or could ever actually possess: "I want to argue, on the contrary, that culturally contingent knowledge is the only knowledge available to us as finite, embodied, culturally situated human beings. It is a fallacy, born of the objectivist tradition, to think that culturally contingent knowledge is not reliable. If we grant that knowledge is not universal, does the sky fall as a result?"[28] Here is the thrust of the criticism directed by the humanities at science (or science studies, at least): science is no more universally true or valid than any other form or mode of discourse and just as subject to cultural influence. Hence, Haylon can happily concede her own work lacks "universal truth" (although this is, in part, because it is cultural criticism) providing science is willing to do the same.

A science that lacked universal validity would not be easily recognizable, and it is unclear how far the relativist would be willing to take it. Haylon seems to see this relativizing move as an opportunity to place science and the humanities on a level plane and thus encourage the free flow of ideas and connections between the two cultures. No longer will scientific knowledge have special claims that can transcend the claims of the admittedly culturally contingent knowledge of humanities scholars. But such a conception is potentially absurd: would we then be free to contest such basic claims as "all things are made of atoms" or even "water boils at 100°C"?[29]

In the closing chapter of his 1975 work *Against Method*,[30] self-declared "anarchist philosopher" Paul Feyerabend suggests that we would, and that a "democratic science" would be better for all parties. "It is the *vote* of *everyone concerned* that decides fundamental issues such as . . . the truth of basic beliefs such as the theory of evolution, or the quantum theory, and not the authority of big-shots hiding behind a non-existing methodology."[31] As Feyerabend sees it, science is forced upon us. "Modern society is 'Copernican' not because Copernicanism has been put on a ballot, subjected to a democratic debate and then voted in with a simple majority; it is 'Copernican' because the *scientists* are Copernicans and because one accepts their cosmology as uncritically as one once accepted the cosmology of bishops and cardinals."[32]

Rather than seeing science as the civilizing force between today's world and that of the Dark Ages, Feyerabend sees the current pairing of science and state as a *continuation* of, or return to, the Dark Ages. This seems a little silly, and the implied analogy is not entirely fair inasmuch as modern society will tolerate dissenters from Copernicanism—a luxury notably not enjoyed by dissenters from the church state (as seen with Galileo's trial). Today's citizen is free to disagree with science (as relativists like Feyerabend prove) providing they are willing to be called wrong. Even if Copernicanism was put to a ballot, how would "everyone concerned" know which way to vote? Central to the democratic ideal is the informed decision. Would the evidence presented not be scientific evidence, the same evidence (and more) as that which convinced the scientists themselves in the sixteenth century?[33] It is not clear how one might go about arguing with the scientists without first becoming one. Alan Sokal and Jean Bricmont point out an apparent inconsistency in the skepticism toward scientific practice but faith in the vote. "How, after all, does one find out exactly what 'some people believe', if not by using methods analogous to the sciences (observation, polls, etc.)?"[34]

Isolated, this perhaps misrepresents Feyerabend, whose arguments are not against scientific knowledge but against scientific method, or at least the claims made for a *single* scientific method. Through case studies from Galileo onward, Feyerabend tries to demonstrate that in presuming itself to have "found a method that turns ideologically contaminated ideas into true and useful theories" science is deluded: "There is no special method that guarantees success or makes it probable. Scientists do not solve problems because they possess a magic wand—methodology, or a theory of rationality—but because they have studied the problem for a long time, because they know the situation fairly well, because they are not too dumb."[35] The consequence of what Feyerabend scornfully calls the "fairy-tale"[36] of method is the elevation and privileging of scientific knowledge.[37] Science receives special treatment because it can claim to be "not mere ideology, but an objective measure of all ideologies."[38] In opposition to methodological monism, Feyerabend proposes what he calls "an anarchistic theory of knowledge" whose credo is "*anything goes.*"[39] This turned out to be an unfortunate phrase, easily (and sometimes willfully) misread and taken to mean that any method suits any situation—a reading apparent in criticisms such as Alan Sokal and Jean Bricmont's. "There are several ways to swim, and all of them have their limitations, but it is not true that all bodily movements are equally as good."[40] It seems unlikely that Feyerabend would dispute this, as it is quite consistent with his thinking inasmuch as Sokal and Bricmont are conceding that different methods (here, for swimming) work in different situations. The criticism fails to touch Feyerabend because "anything goes" does not demand that *no* methods work, only that methodological monism is a fallacy[41] and an impediment to progress. "All methodologies have their limitations and the only 'rule' that survives is 'anything goes'."[42] The aim of *Against Method* is more to collapse what has come to be seen as a hierarchy of methods, with science at the top. By showing that scientific discovery takes any number of different (and often distinctly unempirical) approaches (such as Kekulé's famous dream of the benzene ring or Fleming's apparently chance discovery[43] of penicillin), Feyerabend wants to prove that what assures the success of a theory is not method but fit. (Added to which, it is important to recognize that *Against Method* was never intended to stand alone. Originally, the book was conceived as a joint-authored project on rationalism—*For and Against Method*[44]—with Imre Lakatos providing what would have been a useful counterbalance to some of Feyerabend's polemical excesses.

Feyerabend describes *Against Method* as a "long and rather personal *letter*"[45] to Lakatos, who died before the exchanges were completed, hence the separate publication of Feyerabend's sections.)

It seems at times as if there are two theses at work in *Against Method*. The first is the reasonable-sounding notion that scientific method is a fallacy, a myth or fairy tale, constructed to lend authority to scientific pronouncements, but one that rarely informs their discovery. The second and stronger version emerges when Feyerabend tries to show that science need not be the only way of knowing and implies that because scientific method is a fallacy so too is scientific knowledge a fallacy. The difference between these two theses turns on the dissolution of the boundary between the private and public life of science or, in other words, the two contexts of discovery and justification. If the boundary holds, then the fallacy of method is an issue only so far as the context of discovery is concerned. If the boundary is dissolved, then any problems with method carry over.

Although Feyerabend apparently rejects the distinction in *Against Method*,[46] it is not clear how committed he is to this position. He does move against it, but in a different way to Hayles. She says that the context of justification is shot through with assumptions carried over from the context of discovery, and so the justification is prejudiced from the start (hence her belief that prophylactic boundaries cannot ensure safe epistemology). But as discussed above, all the carryover implies is incompleteness or selectivity, but not falsity as such. (Selectivity, to be fair, may or may not result in a bias in the volume of data supporting one hypothesis over another, but it would not also invalidate that data.) In keeping with his insistence on methodological pluralism, Feyerabend says that a context of discovery and a context of justification are *both* very important to progress, and neither can or should be given epistemological or methodological preference. Therefore, "we are dealing with a single uniform domain of procedures all of which are equally important for the growth of science. This disposes of the distinction."[47] Note that the stress is on the progress and growth of science. Feyerabend doesn't think that science doesn't work or isn't true, he just doesn't think it works as neatly as the scientists claim it does. What is being disposed of is the idea that all the important work is done rationally. Rather than eliminate the boundary, he just gives each context equal priority. This is not the same thing as saying "one is culturally contaminated, therefore so is the other"—which is to say, this conception doesn't demand a causal relation between the two contexts. Rather, he just says that there is also a good deal of important work done in the context of discovery that should (if we embrace his anarchistic theory of knowledge) demand that it be elevated to the same status that the context of justification currently has.

What is being removed here isn't the distinction, but the privilege. Feyerabend simply thinks that the types of things that inform scientific discovery are also interesting, and he wants us to recognize that scientific ideas come from diverse sources and not just through cold, rational thought. So Feyerabend is not tied to saying that the context of justification cannot validate scientific beliefs, just that it validates them in lots of different ways. To reiterate, *Against Method* doesn't claim that the justification of scientific beliefs is impossible, it just says that there is no single special method by which information is transformed into scientific knowledge.

Unfortunately, this still leaves the problem that Hayles met: if scientific knowledge has no special privileges, is it then equal to all other forms of knowing, or just some? Where now to begin to discriminate: Must we accept/reject everything? One suspects that less-committed relativists would be tempted to respond a little like Sokal and Bricmont: there are many ways to swim but some are better than others. Without method it seems hard to preserve scientific knowledge at all. Hayles, having collapsed the prophylactic boundaries between discovery and justification, was willing to level the land to a uniformly low epistemological status, dissolving any human claims for universally valid knowledge. What Feyerabend wants us to think is less clear when he calls science a "particular superstition."[48] Unlike Hayles, he is not explicit about whether universally valid knowledge does or could exist. The rejection of methodological monism was in order to aid, not halt, scientific progress and to widen the range of possibility. "Everywhere science is enriched by unscientific methods and unscientific results."[49] He seems optimistic about science and is strongly opposed not to the content of scientific knowledge but to its didactic presentation as incontrovertible. "Almost all scientific subjects are compulsory in our schools. . . . Physics, astronomy, history *must* be learned. They cannot be replaced by magic, astronomy, or by a study of legends." He adds, "We shall not permit them to teach the fancies of science as if they were the only factual statements in existence."[50] Feyerabend has no objection to students choosing science (he studied physics himself), but he believes it must be a choice and not thrust on them as the only rational choice. (For Feyerabend, any science that insists on methodological monism is already inherently irrational because the rational method is a fairy tale.) So it is unlikely that Feyerabend wants to follow Hayles in rejecting universal knowledge altogether and unlikely that he himself really believes the myths over the science. But once again, questioning science runs into an apparently unavoidable either/or of total acceptance or rejection: if you [dis]agree with one principle you would be logically inconsistent in not [dis]agreeing with the rest. This contributes to the drift toward the idea that outside science there is no knowledge (what Feyerabend tags as *extra scientiam nulla salus*), inasmuch as we would rather have all science than no science (and therefore no technology). But it is also unduly demanding. Like Feyerabend, what we resist when we resist *extra scientiam nulla salus* is the exclusion of other forms of knowing. We do not necessarily want to be antiscience, just not exclusively scientific. There is too much to be lost either way, but where is the balance? As George Levine asks, "How then to reconcile our respect for science with our resistance to it, to recognize the need for knowledge and to sustain our sense that science is in culture, that it is never any more unpolluted by the society out of which it emerges than any other cultural product, that the power of its knowledge production requires of us more, not less, attention?"[51] Our respect for science is usually a function of our admiration for a type of knowledge that has been so successful at achieving its own ends and has managed to command almost universal assent among its adherents when in so many subjects there is such disarray. Often a practice is said to be "scientific" in character when it possesses this level of consensus.[52] Our resistance to science is largely a resistance to losing our identity under a revised vocabulary that fails to capture those aspects of our discipline that had most interested us. The worry is that the new description will allow no way to talk about these things. Pessimistic about the possibility of productive interdisciplinary exchanges, Stanley Fish puts the point succinctly as "whenever there is an apparent *rapprochement* or relationship of co-operation between projects, it will be the case either that one is anxiously trading on the prestige and vocabulary of the other or that one has swallowed the other."[53] The relativistic approach seemingly offers a means of resolving argument about epistemological superiority but, as with Hayles and Feyerabend, often to the exclusion of what we have come to think of as a powerful tool for understanding the world. We are left wondering how it is that science appears to be so effective at achieving its ends. Richard Rorty seems to offer an account that allows us to retain our respect for the achievements and power of scientific thinking while simultaneously recognizing and allowing that it is legitimate and interesting to think about subjects not covered by the scientific account. As seen with his response to Wilson's *Consilience*, Rorty's account insists that there is no foundation for the hierarchy of disciplines.

Unlike many relativists,[54] Rorty is impressed with, and careful not to deny or to understate the effectiveness of, scientific knowledge. Science, he claims, has been "spectacularly useful and astonishingly beautiful."[55] Elsewhere he writes, "I am happy to agree with C. P. Snow that modern physics is one of the most beautiful achievements of the human mind."[56] The emphasis here is on the utility and what he calls "the moral and aesthetic grandeur" of science, as distinct from its "purportedly exalted epistemico-ontological status."[57] This stress is important because for Rorty, the success of science is no reason to prioritize its field of knowledge; the job that it does it does well, but it is not the only job to be done, nor is it any more important than other jobs. He insists that "the current scientific vocabulary is one vocabulary among others, and that there is no need to give it primacy, nor to reduce other vocabularies to it."[58] Rorty wants to dispense with arguments about the relative status of various disciplines and replace them with questions about the utility of those disciplines for their different purposes.[59] Stanley Fish, a literary critic whom Rorty holds in high esteem, makes very similar noises: "The job . . . will of course always be a particular one, a job of history, or of law, or of literary criticism or whatever; and these different jobs will always be just that, *different*, and not in themselves capable of being ranked. . . . Ranking is, of course, something that happens; in our culture science is usually thought to have the job of describing reality as it really is; but its possession of the franchise, which it wrested away from religion, is a historical achievement not a natural right."[60] Rorty claims that the success of the natural sciences, and physics in particular, has created a feeling of insecurity in those subjects (including the largely non-mathematical or "higher-level" sciences such as zoology[61]) where mathematical models are inappropriate or inapplicable—a feeling the positivists encouraged and that manifests in physics envy. With "knowledge" understood as being co-extensive with "scientific knowledge," the positivists' unity of science becomes a more global claim, a way to split propositions into knowledge and nonsense. As with Wilson's scheme, what this usually means is just that all knowledge is translated into physics, into what is explicable in terms of atoms, and any proposition that will not translate is eliminated. But this simple formula, which worked so well for the Newtonian universe of the early positivists, works less well for quantum mechanics. The picture that emerged after the 1920s of the wave-particle duality, of particles that travel back in time, of properties called "spin" and "flavor," is less comprehensible and less easily substantiated to an inexpert public than a simple account of so many atoms in a stack or lattice.[62] Bas van Fraassen sees this as a conflict between the scientific image and the manifest image, which is exacerbated by "just how unimaginably different is the world we may faintly discern in the models science gives us from the world that we experientially live in. . . . once atoms had no colour; now they also have no shape, place or volume."⁶³ The consequence of this new information was not just skepticism toward the claims of physicists (although it was this, too), but rather a shift in ideas as to who could question or criticize the findings of science, "so that an ontological respect for insensate matter" was "replaced by a sociological respect for professors of physics."⁶⁴ More than ever, the physicists held the epistemological high ground. Rorty, like Fish, wants to break this ranking down, but is careful about explaining his reasoning: "I hope it is clear that I do not want to assign science a *lower* position on this pecking order. What I want to urge is that we stop using terms like 'real' and 'objective' to construct such an order. It seems to me about as silly to try to establish a hierarchy among disciplines, or cultural activities, as to establish one among the tools in a toolbox, or among the flowers in a garden."⁶⁵ This is typical of Rorty's position and his manner of speaking about the sciences. The central objection here is to using "real" and "objective" as criteria for establishing the worth of a discipline. Rorty wants to replace these terms with ways of thinking that do not insist on a background distinction of found (objective) versus made (subjective) when, in his view, all truths are made. He is also concerned with revising our definition of "objectivity" to separate it from the connotations it has picked up as a synonym for "scientific" via "rational." So instead of taking "objectivity" as a criterion, Rorty offers "unforced agreement," which, as he recognizes, is not without its ambiguities. "Unforced agreement between whom? Us? The Nazis? Any arbitrary culture or Group?"

> The answer, of course, is "us". This necessarily ethnocentric answer simply says that we must work by our own lights. Beliefs suggested by another culture must be tested by trying to weave them together with the beliefs we already have. On the other hand, we can always enlarge the scope of "us" by regarding other people, or cultures, as members of the same community of inquiry as ourselves—by treating them as part of the group among whom unforced agreement is to be sought. What we cannot do is rise above all human communities, actual and possible. We cannot find a skyhook which lifts us out of mere coherence—mere agreement—to something like "correspondence with reality as it is in itself."⁶⁶

So "objectivity" is taken as a synonym for "agreement" ("unforced" simply to remove the possibility of coercion) and, on this account, consists in the extent to which there is consensus within a discipline. Under this redescription, "we might, in an imaginary age in which consensus in these areas was almost complete, view morality, physics, and psychology as equally 'objective'."⁶⁷ For Rorty, what we have always meant when we have spoken of "objectivity" has been a recognition of this sort of consensus. "Objective" (considered properly) has never meant anything more than consensus.[68] Rorty is able to make this redefinition because he doesn't believe that truth consists in descriptions that are closer to a correspondence with "how things really are." He sees this, the correspondence theory, as untenable because he believes that truth only ever exists as a property of statements.

In trying to explain what he means when he claims to deny the correspondence theory of truth, Rorty gives the giraffe as an example.[69] We all know what he means when he says "giraffe," otherwise his example wouldn't work. But he wants us to realize that what we pick out when we say "giraffe" is not decided by the world; it is not simply given, but made—decided by conventions that emerge from our relationship with the world.[70] He says that the difference between the giraffe and the surrounding air is clear enough if you are a human hunting for meat, but not so clear if you are an amoeba or a space traveler observing earth from above.[71] There are lots of ways to describe how that particular piece of space–time occupied by a giraffe is configured, and they're all interest-relative, inasmuch as they are all valid from a different perspective.[72] This was the point Putnam was making about square pegs and round holes. You can talk in terms of atomic or geometric structures;[73] neither is more *true*, but one is considerably more useful.[74] Rorty takes this to mean that the only "truth" we'll ever have is determined by how useful the description is for our purposes. He calls this "the relativity of descriptions to purposes."[75] As Putnam said for the square peg, it might be *true* that there are these atoms here, now, in this organization, but they're always changing, they are drifting off and moving among each other. They are in this exact position only for a moment. The type of coherence and organization that we understand is a higher-level affair, and as Jerry Fodor has it, "[c]ausal powers supervene on local microstructure."[76] Certain descriptions make sense at some levels on the scale and not others. On our level of scale, they might mean "giraffe." Or else they might mean "square peg/round hole." But as Putnam says, how you choose to look at this either conceals the interesting relationships or reveals them. It makes sense for us to reveal them, so we effectively ignore the atomic structure. The atomic microstructure[77] is perhaps a more fundamental level, but Rorty's point is to ask: how is that *more* true? And his answer is that if we are talking about giraffes or square pegs in round holes, it isn't. So truth becomes always interest-relative. This is what was meant by "[r]eality is one, but descriptions of it are many. They ought to be many, for human beings have, and ought to have, many different purposes."[78]

There may at first blush seem to be an inconsistency in Rorty's refusing to grant science the privileged epistemological status it demands and yet still accepting those scientific findings (like atoms and quarks) that we cannot affirm by our own senses. However, Rorty never denies the effectiveness of science for its particular ends. By accepting that science has discovered and accurately described things like atoms and electrons, he is not tacitly agreeing that science is describing "how things really are," just accepting that we are creating for ourselves more and more descriptions from which to choose. Rorty doesn't dispute the existence of atoms, or giraffes, for that matter, saying only that these are simply there. What we choose to call them and how we choose to describe their relations and actions is where we start to decide which are relevant and which are irrelevant. A gradual increase in the effectiveness of science is not evidence of science getting "closer to the truth" or "closer to how things really are," but is instead just a case of science gradually finding better descriptions of the world, understood as more effective descriptions that enable us to do things better than the previous descriptions. The difference is not supposed to be epistemological, but there will surely always be certain descriptions that will be more effective than others, certain ways of describing their "relevance" that are more useful. (For example, it is more useful for us to use a geometric description to solve the square peg/round hole problem.) The problem here is that Rorty seems to have reintroduced something like the correspondence theory of truth. A. J. Ayer sums up the objection in a letter to the *London Review of Books*: "Professor Rorty endorses the view that 'great scientists invent descriptions of the world which are useful for purposes of prediction and controlling what happens,' and asserts that 'there is no sense in which any of these descriptions is an accurate representation of the way the world is in itself.' If the second of these sentences is true, how can one description serve the purpose of prediction more usefully than another? In what, indeed, does Professor Rorty take prediction to consist?"[79] What Ayer and critics like him want is for Rorty to admit that you cannot have a successfully predictive theory without your theory being in some way closer to how the world is, since this is what grounds prediction. Rorty's reply is that "a belief's purported 'fit' with the intrinsic nature of reality adds nothing which makes any practical difference to the fact that it is widely held to lead to successful action."[80] This is a version of William James's question: do our purported theoretical differences make any difference in practice? So by the pragmatist account, "how the world is in itself" is superfluous to our use of the theories; either they work or they don't, and either they cohere with other working beliefs or they don't. It is utility and coherence that should determine whether or not we will be persuaded to believe in one theory rather than another. There will surely always be certain descriptions that will be more effective than others, certain ways of describing their "relevance" that are more useful. The question behind this is: how do we choose between descriptions?[81] Or, given that the pragmatists hold that belief acquisition is not an issue of conscious choice but rather one of persuasion: why should one theory or account be more convincing or have more explanatory power than the other? It behooves Rorty not to answer with "one was closer to how it really was," but it is difficult to see how else we could even begin to give an answer without some reference to one description (or even some descriptions) being closer to the truth than the others. The closest Rorty comes to answering this is probably in confronting how it is that we nearly all agree that science is a good way (and even the best way) to explain how the world works. As Rorty seems to be saying that there is no important difference between science and other types of human activity, how does he account for this success? Why do we choose science? It is, he claims, nothing to do with "truth": "Our reply has to be, I think, that the benefits of modern astronomy and space travel outweigh the advantages of Christian fundamentalism. The argument between us and our medieval ancestors should not be about which of us has got the universe right. It should be about the point of holding views about the motion of heavenly bodies, the ends to be achieved by the use of certain tools. Confirming the truth of Scripture is one such aim, space travel is another."[82] Rorty never denies the existence or the solidity of the world. He agrees with common-sense materialists that the world is pushing up against us, but believes that this gives us no reason to subscribe to an essentialist account that claims we have "cut nature at the joints." This is why naming and vocabularies are so important to him. He distances himself from much of Feyerabend, whose talk of teaching witchcraft in schools[83] and placing "the views of idiosyncratic nature mystics . . . 'on a par with' the views of professors of chemistry" Rorty calls "silly relativism."[84] Nor is he an idealist: "There is such a thing as brute resistance—the pressure of light waves on Galileo's eyeball, or of the stone on Dr. Johnson's boot." But, crucially, the Rortean pragmatist insists that there is "no way of transferring this non-linguistic brutality to *facts*." Facts, on this view, "are hybrid entities; that is, the causes of the assertibility of sentences include both physical stimuli and our antecedent choice of response to such stimuli." Once again, the world is real and stable, but our interpretations of it are open to debate: "causation is not under a description, but explanation is."[85]

It is useful to note here how Rorty uses this example to indirectly reinforce his claim that there is no qualitative difference between space travel and scripture, inasmuch as both can make people happy, and no epistemological difference because neither can be said to have any more access to how the world really is (although both will claim that they do). He also enjoys making implicit comparisons between the sciences (where participation usually requires a high level of academic education) and manual work (where participation usually requires familiarity with the tools of the job, but no academic education).[86] This is not intended to be demeaning to scientists, rather, it underlines how Rorty wants us to think of them: as people skilled in using the tools (and the jargon) of their job. From the pragmatist's view, we "can see chemistry and literary criticism and paleontology and politics and philosophy all striding along together—equal comrades with diverse interests, distinguished *only* by these interests, not by cognitive status."[87] This all accords with the pragmatist view of objectivity as simply a greater amount of unforced agreement, and effecting this redefinition is how pragmatists are able to collapse the hierarchy of disciplines. One of the reasons for (or results of) collapsing the hierarchy of disciplines is an insistence that we prioritize happiness over truth. That this isn't an approach the rational realists would favor is well illustrated in a comparison with how Richard Dawkins feels about faith healers and their lack of empirical footing:

> Television is an even more powerful medium than the newspapers, and we are in the grip of a near epidemic of paranormal propaganda on television. In one of the more notorious examples of recent years in Britain, a faith healer claimed to be the receptacle for the soul of a 2,000-year dead doctor called Paul of Judea. . . . Afterwards, I clashed with the commissioning editor of this programme. . . . The editor's main defence was that the man was doing a good job healing his patients. He seemed genuinely to feel that this is all that mattered. Who cares whether reincarnation really happens, as long as the healer can bring some comfort to his patients?[88]

This last sentence is meant as an ironic appeal to our sense of robust rationality, but many people might be tempted to take it at face value, and ask: well, who does care what *really* happens? Compare this with Rorty: "Nobody knows or cares about whether a given piece of computer software represents reality accurately. What we care about is whether it is the software which will most efficiently accomplish a certain task. Analogously, pragmatists think that the question to ask about our beliefs is not whether they are about reality or merely about appearance, but simply whether they are the best habits of action for gratifying our desires."[89] For Rorty, all that really matters is whether or not the theory enables us to better cope with a situation. If the TV faith healer was not really a reincarnation, or if a particular drug was really just a sugar placebo, what would it matter so long as the desired results were achieved? Rorty holds with "the pragmatist claim that our desire for truth cannot take precedence over our desire for happiness."[90] He keeps making this distinction between utility and correctness, saying the former is the best we can hope for, and the latter may be either unobtainable or else useless. He calls it "the invidious distinction between getting it right and making it useful."[91] As regards faith healers, or whether or not we should follow a Kantian program for philosophy, this dictum seems harmless enough. But there are more controversial and difficult issues than these, where it is less than obvious that the conclusions should be dictated by the increase of happiness they would bring. Dawkins's frustration stems from the same thinking that led Bernard Davis to complain of the "moralistic fallacy," the worry that the truth will be suppressed in the interests of avoiding conflict with an existing moral scheme. Davis's point—something Dawkins would surely agree with—was that we should "trust posterity to adapt its notions of morality to further new knowledge."[92] While Rorty would probably accept that much, he would surely reject the reasoning Davis offers: in criticizing the findings of scientists, we are "blaming the messenger for the message. For science does not create the realities of nature, it only discovers them."[93] In other words, science is innocent as far as you believe scientists are simply reading off the book of nature. Their innocence is lost entirely when you claim, as Rorty does, that there is no "found" or "given" knowledge and that all knowledge is made. Does all this leave Rorty unable to discriminate between theories? Apparently not. The pragmatist who holds with a coherence theory of truth can still call creationism "*bad* science," but only insofar as it fails to cohere with other beliefs.[94] The belief has to fit with other beliefs not with "how reality really is" simply because this is not something we can ever get to.

It is important to recognize the importance of vocabularies to the pragmatist worldview. The basic argument from pragmatism says that (1) Because there is a relativity of descriptions to purposes, there is no best way to describe a situation, and (2) Because there are many different vocabularies there is no central vocabulary, so (3) Therefore, you cannot rank the vocabularies any more than you can rank the purposes. And, crucially, because each discipline is only a particular vocabulary looking at things from a certain angle for a certain purpose, (4) you cannot rank the disciplines. The conclusion is that all disciplines share an equal status. Consonant with Rortean pragmatism, Stanley Fish goes as far as to say that a discipline is exhausted by its particular vocabulary: "The vocabularies of disciplines are not external to their objects, but constitutive of them. Discard them in favour of the vocabulary of another discipline, and you will lose the object that only they call into being."[95] So a contest of disciplines is always and only ever a contest of vocabularies, and as vocabularies are always purpose-specific, any contest of disciplines is just a contest of purposes, and purpose doesn't seem to be the type of thing you could rank without a circular appeal to desires and values.

What Rorty says about what type of disciplines he likes or doesn't like is accordingly not informed by any belief in epistemological superiority, but by the extent to which he thinks their vocabularies might help us achieve our aims. He doesn't like the turn philosophy took after Descartes toward the analytic, regretting "the triumph of the quest for certainty over the quest for wisdom" that meant a concern with being rigorous or explaining the appearance of rigor in the sciences, rather than "help[ing] people achieve peace of mind. Science, rather than living, became philosophy's subject, and epistemology its centre." Rorty would replace the analytic philosophers with what he calls "edifiers." The edifier "aims at continuing a conversation rather than at discovering truth." This can be contrasted with the scientists, who would (one suspects) gladly exchange their vocation for the complete world picture they are aiming at. The scientist wants to complete and be done, whereas "the point of edifying philosophy is to keep the conversation going rather than to find objective truth." Rorty doesn't want to see the conversation end, and he thinks edifying philosophy might keep this conversation "from degenerating into inquiry, into an exchange of views."[96] From here, it is possible to see why Rorty believes that one of the best ways of keeping the conversation going is literary criticism.

For Rorty, Derrida is a shining example of what he thinks literary criticism is best for. He doesn't take Derrida seriously at all, claiming "his term 'grammatology' was evanescent whimsy, rather than a serious attempt to proclaim the discovery of a new philosophical method or strategy."[97] Elsewhere, he talks of how Derrida "is trying to get a game going which cuts right across the rational-irrational distinction."[98] And again, "Derrida does not want to comprehend Hegel's books; he wants to play with Hegel."[99] None of this sounds like he thinks Derrida is doing anything serious, which is because he doesn't. He thinks that Derrida is a good joker, someone playing around, "trying to get a game going." Of course, not everyone feels that people in Derrida's position (sold as somewhere between a philosopher and a literary critic but, crucially, not primarily a creative artist) should be so casual about what they say. Rorty feels that there is an imbalance between how Derrida's work is treated and how someone like Yeats is treated: "If you advertise yourself as a novelist or a poet you are let off a lot of bad questions, because of the numinous haze that surrounds the 'creative artist.' But philosophy professors are supposed to be made of sterner stuff."[100] The obvious rejoinder here is that, surely, this inequality is just the payoff for being taken seriously: people listen to philosophers in a way that that they don't listen to Yeats. There may be an aesthetic aspect to philosophy, just as there may be a philosophical aspect to poetry, but you don't have to agree with Yeats's views on spiritualism (which Rorty calls "all that guff"[101]) to enjoy his poetry any more than you have to like Kant's writing style to agree with his philosophy. But these distinctions between the aesthetic and the philosophical (or perhaps form and content; medium and message) are precisely the type of distinctions that Rorty would like to see collapsed. Rorty likes Derrida, in part, because he doesn't have to take him seriously. In Derrida's "game," as Rorty sees it, the aesthetic dimension is as important as the philosophical content, and this is something Rorty himself often cashes in on.

One of the most frequent criticisms of Rorty is that he is only a rhetorician, playing with the language rather than the ideas. Bernard Williams takes issue with this playfulness. Rorty's comment that philosophy happens "when language goes on holiday" is for Williams "a remark which, one might say, is, like some others of his, deeply shallow."[102] This is something literary critics are also sometimes accused of doing—playing with language, finding puns and slippage in the texts they study, and, more controversially, making their own puns and their own ambiguities. (Examples of this are not hard to come by. Here is Irving Malin, one of the more enthusiastic practitioners, looking at the word *occupants*: "'Occupants' seems easy—except for the fanciful idea that 'oc' sounds like *Ach* as in *Achtung* or that 'u' sounds like 'you' or that 'pants' makes me re(member) 'paints'.")[103] Rorty sees this not as a weakness of literary criticism, but as its great strength. Because Derrida is not playing by "any antecedently known rules," Rorty urges we see "his purpose as the same autonomy at which Proust and Yeats aimed," that is, a freedom from disciplinary constraints. Rather than "dissecting his writing along lines laid down by somebody else," we should instead "sit back and enjoy it."[104] Here, as before, we see Rorty happily acknowledging that no one takes literary critics seriously, and seeing this as a benefit. The problem is that some of them do want to be taken seriously.

Rorty conflates literature with criticism, treating them as one type of discourse. He does this, in part, because he doesn't see the point in (or the possibility of) separating the object from talk about it, the analyst and the analyzed. This is reflected in his attitude toward science and how scientists do not simply "find" but make. But it also has come from the way Frye talked about the critic as someone who is just as creative as the author. In part it is from Harold Bloom and the Yale School of critics, whom Rorty calls "textualists," people who want to say that the creativity of the critic is just as important as the creativity of the poet. Here is Rorty on Bloom in relation to more traditional critics: "The kind of textualist who claims to have gotten the secret of the text, to have broken its code, prides himself on not being distracted by anything which the text might previously have been thought to be about or anything its author says about it. The strong misreader, like Foucault or Bloom, prides himself on the same thing, on being able to get more out of the text than its author or its intended audience could possibly have found there."[105] Of course, Bloom is saying just that when he talks about how every strong reading is a misreading. In *The Anxiety of Influence*, Bloom claims: "The issue is reduction and how best to avoid it. Rhetorical, Aristotelian, phenomenological, and structuralist criticisms all reduce, whether to images, ideas, given things, or phonemes. Moral and other blatant philosophical or psychological criticisms all reduce to rival conceptualisations. We reduce—if at all—to another poem. . . . There are no interpretations but only misinterpretations, and so all criticism is prose poetry."[106] Rorty makes a distinction between the traditional humanistic critic and the textualist. An all-out "strong textualist" like Bloom (as Rorty reads him) does not merely treat the text as autonomous, ignoring the intentions of the author (as Frye insisted we do), but goes one step further and ignores the intentions of the text as well. "The critic asks neither the author nor the text about their intentions but simply beats the text into a shape which will serve his own purpose. He makes the text refer to whatever is relevant to that purpose." The weaker textualist critic Rorty dismisses as simply a "decoder," someone who thinks there is a meaning to be found, a stable sense to the text that the right type of analysis will yield up. Such a critic is, Rorty believes, "just doing his best to imitate science—he wants a method of criticism, and he wants everybody to agree that he has cracked the code. He wants all the comforts of consensus. . . . The strong textualist is trying to live without comfort." The central point here, and the reason why the approach so impresses Rorty, is that (like the pragmatist) the textualist critic is concerned with making rather than finding. The textualist is aware that he is constructing the readings he produces, but believes that this is all anyone ever does and so will "treat the scientist as naïve in thinking that he is doing something more than putting ideas together, or constructing new texts." Because the textualist is awake to the real possibilities of engagement and not, like the scientist, deluded by a false realism, Rorty is able to recast the hierarchy and make what he calls "the plausible claim that literature has now displaced religion, science, and philosophy as the presiding discipline of our culture."[107] This is a rather audacious and seemingly baseless compliment to pay. It jars with Rorty's later comments that he doesn't want "to assign science a *lower* position on [the] pecking order"[108] and seems inimical to the more central pragmatist belief in the relativity of descriptions to purposes. To make sense of this (and assuming it is any more than provocative rhetoric—which is not an unrealistic suggestion), we must first agree with Rorty that scientists really are mistaken in believing that they are accurately describing the physical universe; secondly, we must share his preference for the strong misreaders (Harold Bloom, Paul De Man, Geoffrey Hartman) over the "weak decoders" (M. H. Abrams, Frye, Leavis). Given Rorty's conviction on these two points, it becomes easier to see why he thinks literary studies is so impressive. However, the qualities he looks for in criticism are not so highly valued by all critics, nor (in light of the concerns displayed in books like Kernan's *The Death of Literature*, John Ellis's *Literature Lost*, or even Harold Bloom's own doubts for the future of literary studies outlined in *The Western Canon*)[109] is there much evidence that critics themselves would share his optimism. In an essay in which he takes issue with Rorty's "defence" of literary criticism, Michael Fischer sums up the disjunction. "Many professors of literature, disappointed by dwindling enrolments, shrinking job opportunities and stagnant salaries, will be surprised to learn from Rorty that they are conquering heroes, that their depleted classrooms and budgets signal victory over the minds of 'bright youth'."[110]

Fischer concedes that a rationale for literary studies is "sorely needed," but believes that Rorty's account, far from offering such a rationale, "in fact, demeans the study of literature, or fails to remedy what many see as its present aimlessness."[111] Rorty stresses the chaotic nature of literary development. "One can achieve success by introducing a quite new genre of poem or novel or critical essay *without* argument. It succeeds simply by its success, not because there are good reasons why poems or novels or essays should be written in the new way rather than the old."[112] There are a number of issues here. It is surely one thing for a poem to succeed without "argument" and quite another for a critical movement to do the same, but because Rorty conflates them, this difference is concealed. Fischer finds Rorty's account vacuous, remarking on the tautology of literature's "succeeding simply by its success." On a generous reading, we might excuse Rorty by arguing that "succeeding" is meant in the sense of "succession," and gloss the phrase as meaning, "One theory takes the place of another simply by being more popular with the community involved, rather than by being a more rigorous or more convincing argument." This would be consistent with his broad definition of literature as "the areas of culture which, quite self-consciously, forego agreement on an encompassing critical vocabulary, and thus forego argumentation,"[113] and with his fondness for wordplay. But as a defense, this still rings hollow, inasmuch as it still fails to account for why the community was convinced in the first place by the new style of poetry or criticism. That is, without a persuasive reason (which means an argument), it is not clear what it is that propels change. In addition, very often there exists an aesthetic manifesto behind the shifts between literary movements or styles (we need only think, for example, of Romanticism, Modernism, Surrealism, the New Journalism).[114] This is, for Fischer, excessively casual. He complains that Rorty "exaggerates the shapelessness of the literary culture that interests him. Put more bluntly, though not scientists, literary critics speak a more stable vocabulary and heed firmer rules than Rorty supposes. Instead of resembling the shouting match described by Rorty, literary culture, in short, qualifies as a conversation."[115] Fischer's "conversation" is carefully defined. "Contrasted to a certain kind of argument—a debate, for example, or a scientific paper—a conversation seems loose in structure. . . . While a conversation may be less confining than an argument, it is nevertheless highly restrained, bound by conventions." Fischer is happy to assent to Rorty's conflation of literary works and literary criticism, but sees both activities not as "chatter" but as "free-flowing, yet controlled, discussion." Simply because "literary intellectuals break the rules of argument laid down by some philosophers" is no reason to conclude, as Rorty does, that they do so *"without* argument." Fischer agrees with Rorty that philosophy and literature have much in common, but "not, however, in dispensing with rules and a stable vocabulary, but in probing their limits, often in dialogues."[116] So when Rorty claims that literature is "a usurping discipline" that has "put the other disciplines in their places" he doesn't think it is because literature has shown itself to be "cognitive, serious, powerful and responsible" but because philosophy has shown itself to be "like literature: imprecise, capricious and methodologically dishevelled." Fischer emerges disappointed with the defense: "Instead of strengthening literature, Rorty leaves it impotent."[117]

That Rorty's allegiance should be unwanted is not without precedent. Many of the philosophers Rorty calls in for support have expressed reservations about how he has used them. W. V. O. Quine says: "One of the quiet pleasures that a philosophical writer is sometimes vouchsafed is that of reading a colleague's favourable and faithful account of one's views. When, on the other hand, the account is favourable but mistaken, it is with some regret that one undertakes to set the colleague straight; for the colleague might no longer favour one's views if he saw them aright." Quine sounds like a man eager to distance himself from Rorty's views; his response to this praise for him is punctuated with denials. Answering Rorty's account of his philosophy, Quine goes on to say, "Not quite," "No, I favour no such invidious distinctions," "No, it is a naturalistic claim," "I disown. . . ," "I deny that. . . ."[118] There is also Thomas Kuhn, whom Rorty describes as "the most influential philosopher to write in English since the Second World War," but Rorty (a self-professed "Kuhn-disciple") is forced to admit that "Kuhn would have been embarrassed by my defence of him" and that "[i]n interviews Kuhn took pains to distance himself from 'Rorty's relativism'."[119] Rorty also admits that Donald Davidson would have "slim sympathy"[120] for the uses Rorty puts him to, claiming, "Davidson and [William] James are both pragmatists," and "Davidson, however, has explicitly denied that his break with the empiricist tradition makes him a pragmatist."[121] That so many philosophers feel that Rorty has misread them is perhaps a consequence of Rorty's admiration for textualist critics like Harold Bloom, which is to say, the misreadings may not be entirely innocent and accidental. Rorty is a strong misreader of philosophy. He thinks that "literary critics seeking help from philosophy may take philosophy a bit too seriously," and that rather than try to choose philosophers according to "antecedently plausible principles," "[i]t would be better for critics to simply have favorite philosophers (and philosophers to have favorite literary critics)."[122] Because Rorty is willing to treat "both science and philosophy as, at best, literary genres,"[123] they are, like literary works, open to being beaten "into a shape which will serve his own purpose."[124] To reiterate Fischer's criticisms, Rorty's defense of literary study only works if you are willing to see it and the other disciplines as ideally lacking in structure. Rorty has collapsed the hierarchy, but at a cost. It seems to be the case that literary studies can accept Rorty's compliment only if it is first willing to accept its own irrationality.

5
Relativism and the Commonsense Realists

WHILE RORTY MAY THINK OF LITERARY STUDIES AS IRRATIONAL AND inefficacious, is this a model he wants other disciplines to follow, or is the ideal (like the practice) also discipline specific? As discussed above, Rorty is ambivalent on this point; he claims both that literature is the presiding discipline and that there is not a pecking order. Although he does not share Feyerabend's explicitly (and perhaps not altogether serious)[1] anarchistic agenda, Rorty's society of "edifiers"—more interested in reinventing themselves than inventing technologies—seems liable to yield similarly anarchistic results. Pragmatism in the Rortean mode (sometimes "neopragmatism" to distinguish) has the potential to be ironically impractical. Because Rorty's account puts all skills on a level, all "equal comrades with diverse interests," there is no guilt associated with pursuing work that does not contribute to the material welfare of society. Although it was the utility of applied science he admired, Rorty's belief that people "have, and ought to have, many different purposes"[2] means that he doesn't think these are compelling reasons to study science. Consequently, by his own lights Rorty would be under no obligation to answer Snow's demand to acquire scientific knowledge.[3] Scientific knowledge is strictly for the scientists, and Rorty sounds complacent about his inefficacy. Just because the sciences are more useful for manipulating the material world is no reason to accord them a higher status, nor should this (undisputed) material usefulness serve as a rationale to support the idea that it is in any sense our moral or intellectual duty to learn science.

"We admire the people who possess the practical wisdom we want; but we don't quarrel with them. Then why should they quarrel with us? Live, and let live, we say to them. Live upon your practical wisdom, and let us live upon you!" This isn't Rorty, but Harold Skimpole, from Dickens's *Bleak House*.[4] Like Skimpole, Rorty seems to be technologically and materially dependent on a network of people whose work would apparently struggle to proceed without their belief in a tight correspondence between their theories and the world those theories purport to describe. This is the basis of the charge brought against relativism by those scientists and supporters of science who suspect that Rorty's position, and other forms of relativism, are either a purely academic posture or else a luxury afforded by the common-sense realism of the majority. Richard Dawkins uses a similar tack for what he calls his "knock-down argument" against relativism: "Show me a cultural relativist at thirty thousand feet and I'll show you a hypocrite. Airplanes built according to scientific principles work. They stay aloft and they get you to a chosen destination. Airplanes built to tribal or mythological specifications, such as the dummy planes of the cargo cults in jungle clearings or the beeswaxed wings of Icarus, don't."[5] SSK proponent Sarah Franklin takes up the challenge and critiques Dawkins's argument along lines that would be familiar to Rorty. "What," she asks, "is so self evident about the fact that planes could fly? This feat could easily be described as sophisticated tool use instead of an indicator of epistemological certainty."[6] The central objection is that the airplanes are not built according to theory but that theories are constructed after the fact to explain how airplanes work. The force of Dawkins's point is that it becomes harder to call science "merely a social construction" when that same science is holding your plane aloft. Franklin is hoping that, if you can separate the scientific theory from the technological practice, this can be shown to trade on the same sort of circularity that theists employ to argue that, as part of His creation, it is ungrateful (and moreover, blasphemous) to deny God's existence. Dawkins wants you to admit that either the science of aerodynamics is true or else the airplane is not flying or flying by luck alone.[7]

Although unsympathetic with much of the SSK's program,[8] Stephen Jay Kline reminds us that "we can make innovations without any science at all."[9] The relationship between science and technology is considerably more tangled than Dawkins suggests with his airplane argument, and the type of after-the-fact theorizing that Franklin wants us to recognize may well be the primary mode of theory production within the sciences. Many scientists treat technology as the direct application of their primary laboratory work. This enables them to claim as their own any success, prestige, and utility attached to technological progress and innovation. But the success of technologies can, Kline believes, be only partially attributed to scientific progress. He argues that because many of the skills needed to bring technologies into being (he's thinking of the mechanical engineering skills) are not themselves scientific skills; it is thus too simplistic to think of the various technologies "as merely application of the related fields of science." In addition, Kline draws attention to what he calls "technology-induced science," where problems in engineering lead directly to new directions in scientific research so that "the flow of information is backwards from the picture of science setting off innovation; here innovation sets off science." Kline includes fluid dynamics as one such example of this technology-induced science, with Ludwig Prandtl (who is recognized as the founder of the subject in its modern form) prompted to think about how airplane wings create lift only *after* the Wright brothers' first successful flight.[10]

Perhaps recognizing that the relations between technological progress and scientific change are less clear than is needed for arguments that base the utility of science on the utility of technology, scientists notoriously choose to make this bond only selectively. This choice is doubtless made because there is, of course, a flip-side to science being the same as technology. Here is Weinberg reiterating the familiar case for moral immunity of scientific knowledge, conceding that science has "made its own contribution to the world's sorrows." Weinberg wants to say that it has done so only by "giving us the means of killing one another, not the motive."[11] Once again, we see this switch between science as a moral force (curing illness or increasing agricultural yield) to science as an amoral activity, more mathematics than ethics, and the switch occurs over the practical influence of scientific theories: science claiming any benefits as its own doing and any losses as technology's. Hence, he calls the Nazi regime (which, although never a science, claimed scientific support to better effect its atrocities) and "eugenics" "perversions of science."[12] This is thin ice, particularly when only a page before Weinberg has been arguing that the same cannot be said for the application and misapplication of religion. "It is not safe to assume that religious persecution and holy wars are perversions of true religion," he claims, going on to add that: "It should not be surprising that *some* of the people who take these teachings seriously should sincerely regard these divine commands as incomparably more important than any merely secular virtues like tolerance or compassion or reason."[13]

It is unclear where Weinberg thinks the difference between applications and misapplications emerges; that is, why Weinberg thinks that the evil in "evil scientist" floats free of the wider enterprise of science itself, but the evil in "evil religious zealot" attaches to religion as a whole. (This is the same problem Holton had with his Beast.)[14] It might make more sense if Weinberg wanted to argue that religion could constitute a worldview, including a philosophy, whereas science could not. But he does nothing of the sort. Instead, Weinberg classifies his own "working philosophy" as a "rough and ready realism, a belief in the objective reality of the ingredients of our scientific theories," which is, crucially, "learned through the experience of scientific research."[15] Science then seems perfectly able to construct and to constitute a world-view[16] and one that, if Weinberg is representative (and he claims to be, maintaining that that this rough-and-ready realism is held by "most of us," meaning most scientists[17]), leaves little room for (cultural) relativism in the scientific mind.

Sharing Weinberg's commonsense realism and his disdain for philosophical talk, Dawkins believes that relativism is an untenable notion for practical engagement with the world and that it is a purely academic position that nobody seriously believes. As Dawkins sees it "no philosopher has any trouble using the language of truth when falsely accused of a crime, or when suspecting his wife of adultery. 'Is it true?' feels like a fair question, and few who ask it in their private lives would be satisfied with logic-chopping sophistry in response."[18] Perhaps surprisingly, Rorty agrees: "'There is no truth.' What could that mean? Why should anybody say it? Actually, almost nobody (except Wallace Stevens) does say it. But philosophers like me are often said to say it. . . . [S]ince most people think that truth is correspondence to the way reality 'really is,' they think of us as denying the existence of truth."[19] To reiterate, Rorty's position is not that there isn't a real world, just that "[i]t is only the relative about which there is anything to say."[20] The world is there, but we can only talk about our perceptions of it. This is partly a rejection of nomenclature ("We pragmatists shrug off charges that we are 'relativists' or 'irrationalists' by saying that these charges presuppose precisely the distinctions we reject"[21]). More substantially, it represents a misunderstanding on the part of critics like Dawkins of what the "relativist" position is supposed to be. Relativists rarely claim that science and technology don't work, only that they do not necessarily work in the way the scientists think they work. The airplane argument assumes that if you don't think science is accurately describing the world then you don't think its technologies work (and accordingly insist on the tight link between scientific theory and technological practice). Relativists think that technology works with or without a quasitheistic account of Truth making things happen. Relativists are often found trying to assure their audience that dire consequences will not ensue if we all accept their relativism in place of universal Truth. In a passage quoted above, Katherine Hayles pleaded against sensationalism. "If we grant that knowledge is not universal, does the sky fall as a result?"[22] Feyerabend ended *Against Method* with the suggestion that we stop entrusting scientists with the job of deciding what is or is not real and true and, in the interests of democracy, put their pronouncements to the vote instead, promising that "[t]here is no need to fear that such a way of arranging society will lead to undesirable results."[23]

Hayles's implicit appeal to common sense is interesting in light of Dawkins's assessment of relativistic interpretations of truth, because common sense seems to support Dawkins's argument, too. He says, "Yes, there are philosophical difficulties about truth, but we can get a long way before we have to worry about them."[24] He leaves it unclear quite how far we can get before we run into the epistemological difficulties he thinks are out there. The likelihood is that he doesn't want to be too specific about where we will start to encounter stress-points in common sense because he wants to have it both ways. On this occasion, he wants to use commonsense to bolster his case against relativists; at other times, he will ask us to reject our common sense assumptions by accepting his gene-centric view of life.[25] This is where the "rough and ready realism" starts to look more rough than ready. Christopher Norris draws attention to the invalidity of this style of appeal from within the sciences "so much of the current debate among physicists regarding various rival (e.g., 'many-minds' and 'many-worlds') interpretations of Q[uantum] M[echanical] phenomena takes place at a rarefied speculative level that is just as remote from any realist worldview and which leaves no room for pointed comparisons with the kinds of misunderstanding put about by people on the cultural left.'"[26] Working under Dawkins's rationale, a parallel case could be made for the rejection of quantum physics along the lines of, "Yes, there are difficulties with classical mechanics, but we can get a long way before we have to worry about them." The point in both cases is about specialism, and how unnecessary specialist vocabulary appears to be from the outside.

In part, this is because the terms just aren't as simple as either Dawkins or Weinberg would like them to be.[27] Rorty takes issue with Steven Weinberg for just such philosophical naïveté. "If you imagine that you can explicate 'real' by saying 'you know, like rocks'—you had better not think that you understand the epistemico-ontological status of physical laws."[28] For Rorty, who works with them every day, the problems of philosophy are very real. He criticizes Weinberg for "blowing smoke": "He is throwing around terms ('objectively real', 'one-to-one correspondence', etc.) that have been the subject of endless philosophical reflection and controversy as if he and the common reader knew perfectly well what they meant, and could afford to ignore the pseudo-sophistication of the people who have spent their lives trying to figure out what sense, if any, might be given to them."[29] Much as the problems of quantum physics rarely intrude on the lives of non-physicists, so the problems of philosophy rarely appear as problems for non-philosophers. This seems true of most disciplines. If what counts as a description and what counts as a proof are discipline specific, so too is what counts as a problem. Problems are localized, and what the scientists see as rhetorical trickery is to the philosophers a substantial difficulty that cannot be dismissed by an appeal to robust common sense. Due in part, perhaps, to shared historical origins and a continued interest in the same issues (both will claim to be using the most appropriate vocabulary for talking about and understanding reality), scientists, arguing confidently from a materialist-empiricist position, display a particular lack of interest in and even contempt for the problems of philosophy—an attitude seen already in Wilson's comment about philosophy being unfinished science[30] and from Weinberg who claims, "It is just that a knowledge of philosophy does not seem to be of use to physicists—always with the exception that the work of some philosophers helps us to avoid the errors of other philosophers."[31]

Looming behind many of these criticisms from scientists like Dawkins, Weinberg, and Lewis Wolpert, who have little patience for the "logic-chopping sophistry"[32] of philosophers like Rorty, is the belief that a familiarity with scientific method and working practices would render the problems that occupy much of modern philosophy and the antiscience movement within the humanities irrelevant. The assumption here is that the various relativisms (like the social constructivism of the SSK or Rorty's antirealism) do not make sense if you are a scientist. It is, they argue, simply not possible to entertain intellectual doubts about the ontological status of the tools and objects of scientific inquiry when your everyday experience involves the manipulation of these very things. This was what Weinberg was saying when he spoke of how the rough-and-ready realism of working scientists was acquired "through the experience of scientific research and rarely from the teachings of philosophers."[33] It is the force behind Dawkins's airplane argument: here is working technology that proves the science by practical engagement. Many of the errors of the humanities, claim the scientists, can be seen to arise from scientific ignorance (or at least this sort of unfamiliarity with the methods and practices of working scientists) and, consequently could be remedied by learning about science. The problems that occupy antiscientific movements like the SSK would evaporate (along with the pesky SSK, hope the scientists). In addition, the humanities would benefit from the corrective science could provide; the type of commonsense-realist position held by Dawkins and Weinberg (and consistent with a scientific worldview) would act as a methodological constraint that would prevent many of the deep and serious errors that are (they contend) at present incubated by the methodological sloppiness of the humanities.

When the scientists present a case for the dangers of relativism (and the irrelevance of the humanities in general) to the business of modern life, they often trade on assuming, "What would happen if *everyone* did this?" (which translates to "it is dangerous"). This is clearly too strong a condition to impose, as there is no single occupation or discipline that could survive such a test.[34] It is only effective when inverted, so as to ask, "What would we *lose* if *nobody* did this?" (which translates to "it is irrelevant"), and in this form it can be used to argue for elimination. As discussed above, eliminativism is the doctrine that seeks to remove from normal discourse those explanations and theories that can be more fully explained by a causally prior, more fundamental theory (normally understood as one that also accounts for a broader range of phenomena). The usual assumption for the eliminativist, as was seen in the case of the Churchlands, is that the theory to be eliminated is not only a false postulate, but also a misleading one.

How is literary study related to this process? Most scientists who write about eliminative reductionism are quick to reassure nonphysicists that they will retain their disciplinary autonomy. Physics is unlikely to make a hostile bid for chemistry, but they like to imply that it is well within their power to make such moves. For example, Steven Weinberg writes: "I see no reason why chemists should stop speaking of such things [as valence, bond structure, acidity, colour, taste, smell] as long as they find it useful or interesting. But the fact that they continue to do so does not cast doubt on the fact that all the notions of chemistry work the way they do because of the underlying quantum mechanics."[35] This statement can be paraphrased as, "Physicists don't want to envelope chemistry. Yet." John Gribbin goes so far as to claim, "With the new understanding of atoms and molecules that is provided by quantum physics, of course, the old joke of physicists that chemistry is simply a branch of physics has become much more than half true."[36] It is important to realize that these takeovers are not just threatened within the sciences (intrascientific). As was seen above with reference to the interests of evolutionary psychology in literature, the firewall between the subject matter of the humanities and that of the sciences (and the sciences' present lack of interest in literary study) need not be a permanent condition. The issue at the overlap is as much methodological as disciplinary autonomy, which may amount to the same thing. Literary study will almost certainly continue to exist, but in what form? In the ongoing process of explaining culture under a Darwinian description, evolutionary psychology has begun to offer accounts of literature and art. While these are as yet nascent, a matured evolutionary psychology might eclipse the existing mode of literary study as the primary vocabulary for talking about fiction. From the perspective of current literary study, evolutionary psychology—or, for that matter, cognitive or formalist accounts—seem to offer an impoverished and clipped account of the range of issues currently embraced by literary critics. Adopting evolutionary psychology or cognitive science as a research model or program would allow smooth intertheoretic transitions between the sciences and the arts, but constrain the types of things that could legitimately be said. That is, what does and does not count as knowledge would be affected with much of current literary criticism likely to be eliminated on the basis that if it cannot be said scientifically, it cannot be said. So the elimination that is threatened by the sciences is a replacement of one vocabulary for another. The hostile bid is for the way we talk about books. The threat is of methodological monism across the disciplinary spectrum.

What motivates the sciences to make such demands? It could be argued here that in fact, no scientists do make such demands—not explicitly, at least. The radical reductionist is perhaps just a bogeyman for the humanities scholar, or else a straw man to catalyze debate. This is something Stephen Jay Kline rejects. He writes that "[i]n the late twentieth century, some (seemingly quite a few) people in the physical sciences hold this view, but I repeat, I have no reliable statistics on how many people do hold such a view." He does, however, find at least one writer willing to make such claims for a Laplacean "omniscient superphysicist" who could know the future and past, on the basis that "[a]ll the information needed to build the universe at any moment in its history has always existed and will always exist, however mixed up it becomes."[37] Another would be Wilson. So although there are not people calling for the excision of literary studies from the academy, there *are* radical reductionists, and while the excision of literary study is surely not their aim in pursuing such a project, it remains a realistic consequence.

It is hard to discern if this is an extension of the desire to predict and control that characterizes the scientific approach to the natural world, or else a sincere feeling that theirs is a method universally applicable and universally successful at organizing a coherent account of the subject of study, whatever that subject might be. (These two options are not, of course, exclusive or exhaustive.) That the scientist should wish to treat culture as they have nature is to be expected. Behind the enfolding of the human world into the natural world is the realization that if you are a materialist, then nothing can be considered outside of the domain of the sciences (on the basis that a suitable and causally basic way to discuss matter is in terms of physics). This, course, was one of the consequences discussed by Oppenheim and Putnam in their theory of hierarchies: each level is causally dependent on the level immediately below it, and each level contains all the levels above it. The idea, traceable through Laplace, the logical positivists, and recently revivified by Wilson, is that a completed physical theory would suffice for an exhaustive account of the world, from the bottom up.

To argue against the bottom-up determinists, it seems necessary either to depart from the materialist worldview altogether and introduce something non-material into your account (usually a soul or a deity) that remains untouched by the laws of physics, or else to try and argue that the causality that the physicists have assumed to be wholly bottom-up may in part be top-down. Bottom-up and top-down explanations are sometimes called reductionist and synoptic explanations. Consistent with the hierarchies discussed above, "top" is humans thinking about things, and "bottom" is atoms and quarks, from which we are all made. Causal powers are usually assumed to be bottom-up, and that is how the physicists want it. They need it to be this way or their fundamental theories will lose much of their power and cease to comprehensively explain such disciplines as chemistry, and on top of that, biology, and on top of that neurology, and so on, up to explaining the behavior and motivations of individual persons. But there is also a strand of thinking, even within the sciences, that has room for top-down explanation. So instead of saying, "These two chemicals behave in this way because their atoms behave in this way," the top-down explanation allows the macroscopic object—or at least a macroscopic organizing principle—to dictate the behavior of the microscopic components. So we might instead say, "These atoms behave in this way because someone put this reagent in the solution." The thinking behind this inversion was well summarized in the comment by Jerry Fodor, seen earlier, "Causal powers supervene on local microstructure."[38]

How might this work? Theoretical biologist Brian Goodwin gives the example of vortices in fluids, such as water. Vortices are explained by reference to physical laws about how fluids behave, collectively known as hydrodynamics. On the atomic level, there's nothing interesting happening. There is no perceptible difference in organization between water molecules in a vortex and those in a stream or a beaker. But the manifest behavior of the water is quite different at the macroscopic scale, and it does seem that the vortex is dictating "from above," as it were, how the individual molecules should behave "down below."[39]

Kline's case against the exclusivity of either scheme works on insufficiency. While he agrees that the world is made of only atoms and the void, he doesn't think that radical reductionism (the strong version of bottom-up determinism seen in Laplace) can by itself provide a complete account of causality. Kline accepts the existence and even necessity of hierarchies,[40] but he is cautious about how they should be employed and keen to impose limits on their use. He finds neither the reductionist nor the synoptic view[41] wholly adequate and, further, thinks that both the radical reductionist (bottom-up determinism) and radical synoptic (top-down determinism) programs are impossible "even in principle," This last phrase often appears as a prop in arguments about radical reductionism.[42] He believes that bottom-up determinism moves from the true belief that "all material objects are made up of 'particles' of matter" to the "totally false" belief that "one can therefore aggregate the [various representations of the system under study] for particles and thereby find (or derive) all the behaviours for all systems."[43]

Kline thinks that only both views together can approach a sufficient account, and holds with what he calls an "interface of mutual constraint," whereby bottom dictates possibility and top dictates direction. He thinks this because he believes that, "In systems with hierarchical structure and interfaces of mutual constraint, we cannot find adjacent levels merely by aggregation to a higher level or by disaggregation to a lower level, because the adjacent levels only mutually constrain, and do not determine each other." That is, the constituent parts (atoms, molecules, bricks, cells, and so on) limit the possibilities of organization but do not determine what to do within the range of that possibility. The organizing principles exist only at a higher level of the hierarchy, and, crucially, the organization is invisible to the constituent elements. This allows for top-down causation, which, as Kline points out, has the profound consequence that "[i]n hierarchically structured systems, the levels of control (usually upper levels) 'harness' the lower levels and cause them to carry out behaviours that the lower levels, left to themselves, would not do."[44]

This notion of top-down causality is close to what in philosophy is often called supervenience. Supervenience has been enormously profitable as a defense against reductionism, as it offers a way of recognizing the essential materiality of the world without insisting that reference to the material structure is the best or only way to talk about the world. This can be understood by recognizing that another descriptive vocabulary becomes available at a certain level of complexity. The original descriptive vocabulary (perhaps that of physics or chemistry) is not invalidated by the availability of the new vocabulary, but it ceases to be the most efficient way of talking about the phenomenon or subject matter. The higher-level vocabulary is thus said to supervene on the lower-level vocabulary.

Why this is interesting here is that it seemingly offers a means by which to release the higher-level disciplines from the tyranny of fundamentalist physics.[45] A top-down approach would allow for the causal properties of higher-level subject matter to control (that is, supervene on) the behavior of the physical matter of which they were composed. Said like this, it sounds easy and trivial, but the point is that it is the macroscopic organization that does the work. It's how the painting isn't just the paint, and the book not just the words; and it is how Kripke's statue was the same even when cast in different materials. Nothing magical is introduced to accomplish this, just that there is physical matter, so many atoms, and then there are relations. All the interesting work goes on in the relations, in the organization. The top-down approach from supervenience is a functionalist approach, insofar as it says that although the organization is *of* matter (that is, matter is the thing being organized), it was always the organization that the higher-level disciplines have been interested in, never the matter that grounded it.

Setting aside the validity of the argument from top-down causality, why resist the threatened methodological monism? Rorty's answer was that we should value variety over truth. To support his case, he first argues that what the scientists feel they have captured with "truth" is never the whole picture, but only a fragment, a view from a particular perspective. This is also the logic used by opponents of science within the SSK, who argue for the cultural contamination of scientific belief by their strategic corrosion of the boundary between the contexts of discovery and justification within the sciences. Rorty's second move is that he doesn't want to hear everyone speaking in the same voice. Something approaching a definable subgenre of literature speaks to this intuition: books like Zamyatin's *We*, Huxley's *Brave New World*, and Orwell's *Nineteen Eighty-Four*, which propose a future of immaculate (and highly technologized) order, where the right to be wrong has been removed (a theme prefigured by Dostoevsky in books like *Notes from Underground*). In the world of practicing scientists—or at least those who have become sufficiently well known to speak to audiences outside their specialism—are plenty of voices willing to justify the concern. Steven Weinberg, for example, says, "It would be foolish to expect that any discovery of science could in itself purge the human race of all its misconceptions, but the discovery of the final laws of nature will at least leave less room in the imagination for irrational beliefs."[46] We need only recognize the close proximity of "irrational beliefs" to "individual beliefs" to see how near Weinberg's vision is to Orwell's. Because it is seen as a real threat, these cautions continue outside fiction from writers anxious about the influence of science on society in books like Anthony O'Hear's *Beyond Evolution*, the Roses' *Alas, Poor Darwin*, and, making its debt to the fiction explicit, Brian Appleyard's *Brave New Worlds*. These works critique the claims of the biological sciences to provide a sufficient explanatory ground for the richness of human culture and caution against uncritically embracing the newly available genetic technologies that, in the days of Zamyatin, Huxley, and Orwell, were still a distant prospect.

Unfortunately, the drift of these works can make their adherents look like technophobes or, in C. P. Snow's language, luddites. The counterclaim from the sciences is that those resistant to science are in fact resistant to progress and cultural amelioration, which for the scientists is the natural result of their work. Resistance to science is simply an expression of an ignorance of science. So here is another reason why the humanities would profit from a closer familiarity with scientific knowledge and practice: not only would it prevent those mistakes peculiar to thinkers removed from the sciences, but also it would help the resistant overcome their fear of scientific progress (itself a concept neutered for many science sceptics by accounts of scientific change that do not necessarily rely on progressive improvement, like Kuhn's incommensurability thesis). The scientists offer their knowledge as a panacea to the humanities. There are, however, problems. Most immediate is the question of quite how the scientifically ignorant are to be converted and how the science is to be learned and why. A discrepancy exists between the reasons given for learning science and the remedial measures suggested by some of the critics. Popular science is presented as a means for nonscientists to understand science, but the accommodations it makes in the service of comprehensibility necessarily affect the type of understanding available.[47] The effects of these accommodations are seemingly in conflict with the reasons given for the urgency of learning science in the first place.

For the purposes of argumentative clarity, I have been using the term "scientists" to label all those who evangelize the benefits of scientific knowledge, which perhaps conceals the fact that there is a wide range of attitudes toward the humanities from science and mathematics. At the weak end, is something like curiosity, even envy. Dawkins, displaying uncharacteristic humility, reports that Auden's comment about feeling like "a shabby curate who has strayed by mistake into a drawing room full of dukes"[48] "is pretty much how I and many other scientists feel when in the company of poets."[49] Some scientists, however, are happy to play the duke. For example, Raymond Tallis, a professor of geriatric medicine who has published several books attacking the antirealism of French literary theory, along with collections of his own poetry and fiction, is hostile to the point of alienating even fellow scientists. One proscience reviewer of his 1996 book *Newton's Sleep*, who describes the first section as being "written in a kind of lucid rage," remarks that Tallis's "defence of science is so zealous that even his admirers (of whom I am one) may find some of his arguments extreme."[50] Here at the strong end is the incomprehension shading into hostility that Snow spoke of. The following is a sign hung outside the door of mathematician Ron Graham: "ANYONE WHO CANNOT COPE WITH MATHEMATICS IS NOT FULLY HUMAN. AT BEST HE IS A TOLERABLE SUBHUMAN WHO HAS LEARNED TO WEAR SHOES, BATHE, AND NOT MAKE MESSES IN THE HOUSE."[51] Clearly, Graham's intentions here are as much to amuse as convert, but the sign does draw attention to how the mathematically competent regard with a real sense of wonder those who find mathematics difficult. The sign also inverts a popular theme of the two-cultures debate: while there is doubtless mutual ignorance, there is an asymmetry in the shame. The shame of ignorance is assumed to be one-way, with many commentators recording a generalized willingness to admit mathematical or scientific ignorance coupled with an inverse reluctance to appear ignorant of the arts (see Snow, Tallis, and Pinker, below). Literary intellectuals have a reputation for exactly this type of shameless scientific ignorance. A character in one of Ian McEwan's novels complains that "you 'arts' people, you're not only ignorant of these magnificent things, you're rather proud of knowing nothing."[52] This may be a caricature, or may be a situation that no longer exists, but the perceived social acceptability of scientific ignorance in contrast to the perceived unacceptability of literary ignorance has been important as regards the motives behind and direction of the two-cultures debate.

For C. P. Snow, it seems to have been the prompt for his Rede lecture. Snow was concerned that our notion of "culture" was too closely tied to literary knowledge and that a person could be considered "cultured" without knowing any science—a situation exacerbated by the literary intellectuals who, Snow maintains, "still like to pretend that the traditional culture is the whole of 'culture', as though the natural order didn't exist."[53] It was this Eliotic conception of culture as "traditional culture" that Snow wanted to revise. Snow argued that, despite scientists and literary intellectuals being "comparable in intelligence,"[54] the bias toward culture-as-traditional-culture meant that the possession of literary knowledge was both a necessary and sufficient condition for being cultured, whereas scientific knowledge was neither necessary nor sufficient. Those whose knowledge was limited to the sciences were accordingly excluded from discussions of culture and cultured discussions. Snow records the social isolation of the Cambridge scientists. "Oh, those are mathematicians! We never talk to them."[55] Consequently, there was a sense in which "intellectual" came to exclude the scientists. It had, complained Cambridge's own G. H. Hardy, acquired a "new definition which certainly doesn't include Rutherford or Eddington or Dirac."[56] It seems unlikely that this is still the case, and it was only dubiously true for Snow. By 1959, Einstein was already four years dead and his reputation secure. Fellow physicists, such as Heisenberg, Schrödinger, and Oppenheimer, were recognizable names, who had long since achieved sufficient cultural and celebrity status to have their voices heard in books and in interviews on issues that went far beyond the narrow remit of scientific popularization granted them by their achievements within physics. The scientific intellectual was never quite as marginalized as Snow required for his argument. Yet even today, the feeling clearly remains among scientists that while they are allowed some play in cultural debate, their scientific credentials alone will not award them status of "cultured." This is Steven Pinker, writing in 1995: "In a gathering of today's elite, it is perfectly acceptable to laugh that you barely passed Physics for Poets . . . and have remained ignorant of science ever since, despite the obvious importance of scientific literacy to informed choices about public health and public policy . . . But saying that you have never heard of James Joyce . . . is . . . shocking . . . , despite the obvious *un*importance of your tastes in leisure time activity to just about anything."[57] The roots of this asymmetry may lie in what is usually meant by "culture" (that is, the vernacular sense, which Snow was keen to revise, that restricts the term to the arts), or it may lie in a difference between how scientists and literary intellectuals treat those who do not share their interests. Scientists are apparently less scathing of the scientifically ignorant. That, or else they have simply been less effective in their insults than literary critics, who have acquired a formidable reputation for belittling the unread.[58] Certainly, this was apparent in Leavis's reply to Snow—a response so abrasive that it has often overshadowed discussion of the central issues and, for some contributors (notably Raymond Tallis), come to define the terms of engagement. What is shocking about never having heard of James Joyce is the response; it raises a memory of Leavis saying "Snow is, of course, a—no, I can't say that; he isn't; Snow thinks of himself as a novelist. . . . [F]or as a novelist he doesn't exist; he doesn't begin to exist. He can't be said to know what a novel is."[59] To some extent, Snow seemed to have anticipated this, commenting on how the literary intellectuals offer "a pitying chuckle at the scientists who have never read a major work of English literature. They dismiss them as ignorant specialists."[60] And

Pinker, it seems, was not simply suffering a persecution complex when he felt there was no room for literary ignorance; recall that Joseph Carroll was happy to confirm his fears, deriding Pinker's "literary tastes and judgement" as those of an "undergraduate."[61]

Pinker's argument above is similar to that of John Allen Paulos in *Innumeracy: Mathematical Illiteracy and its Consequences*.[62] Both stress how disabling scientific ignorance and mathematical illiteracy are, and how broad and deep the use of scientific knowledge is, in contrast to literary knowledge, which is useful in a much more limited sphere. Scientific knowledge and mathematical literacy are transferable skills; Paulos gives examples of how those whom he calls innumerates find themselves repeatedly duped by statistics and percentages that they cannot comprehend. The consequences here are more damaging than the temporary social discomfort following an admission of literary ignorance, as innumerates find themselves missing bargains or losing their possessions in debts they have signed up for without understanding the conditions, and this on top of the world of wonder they miss out on because they cannot appreciate large numbers, logarithmic scales, squared and cubed numbers, and so on.

Another voice is that of Raymond Tallis, who agrees with Lewis Wolpert that "[s]cience is arguably the defining feature of our age"[63] and is disappointed that Western Civilization can remain so ignorant of this. "It is," writes Tallis in *Newton's Sleep*, "deeply unsatisfactory that most people should be so distant from the major cultural force of our time, being engulfed in science but having no insight into its basis, its methods, its powers and its limitations."[64] This sense of exclusion has not gone unrecognized outside of the sciences; a character in Martin Amis's *The Information* is described as being "[u]ngratefully dependent, like all of us, on technologies he did not understand."[65] What this confession and the criticisms above share is an insistence that learning more about science would be useful in a way that learning more about literature would not. All trade on the utility of science, with Tallis going so far as to subdivide *Newton's Sleep* into "Part I: The Usefulness of Science" and "Part II: The Uselessness of Art." Overwhelmingly, the reasoning for learning science is given in straightforward utilitarian terms,[66] but how appropriate is this register? At first blush, the stance seems to be that "non-scientists should learn science because science accomplishes useful and worthy things," but on examination, it appears to be closer to "non-scientists should learn science because *scientists* do useful and worthy things," and this is not the same thing at all.

When Snow asked a group of literary intellectuals if any of them knew the Second Law of Thermodynamics, he recalled receiving "cold and negative" looks,[67] despite this being, by Snow's estimation, the scientific equivalent of asking if they had read a work of Shakespeare's. It is not clear, however, if Snow would have been satisfied if the literary intellectuals he had asked *had* been able to repeat the Second Law back to him. It seems that behind the complaint common to many advocates of science—"You don't know any science"—is another complaint, far less easy to remedy—"You're not a scientist." This becomes more apparent on examining some of the challenges issued to nonscientists in order to highlight their scientific ignorance.

Snow's "scientific equivalent of *Have you read a work of Shakespeare's?*"[68] is rephrased by Tallis but emerges essentially the same when he charges that "though most [literary intellectuals] will have caught up with Copernicus' daring heliocentric conjecture, it is a safe bet that few will be able to give any evidence for it."[69] The reason, he goes on to suggest, has something to do with the fact that "[e]ven an elementary equation, such as the one representing the universal law of *gravitation* . . . is more opaque to non scientists than the most intractably obscure modern verse."[70] Wolpert makes much the same point. "I doubt that of those who do believe the earth moves round the sun, even one person in 100,000 could give sound reasons for their conviction."[71] (Although Wolpert does concede that "the evidence and the arguments for supporting such a belief are in fact quite complex."[72]) Alan Sokal frames his question in very similar terms in an appendix to *Intellectual Impostures.* "Ask an average undergraduate: Is matter composed of atoms? Yes. Why do you think so? The reader can fill in the response."[73]

On the one hand, these observations are intended to draw attention to gaps in the nonscientist's worldview and thereby to show it wanting. But equally, the second condition of each question—can you give any evidence?—demonstrates that rote learning alone will not satisfy. Claims for the importance of science run parallel to tales of its difficulty. Tallis picks up on this theme, contrasting the accessibility of the novel with the exclusivity of science, that, he claims, "is difficult for many people because they find it hard to concentrate on and this in turn because it is as remote as possible from gossip." He goes on to argue "The humanities are closer to this ordinary gossipy interest than science is. The kind of effort routinely demanded of professional scientists is rarely required of humanist intellectuals. Reading a novel appeals to something closer to our everyday curiosity than reading a scientific treatise."[74] Snow was making much the same point when he said "[the scientific] culture contains a great deal of argument, usually much more rigorous and almost always at a higher conceptual level, than a literary person's arguments."[75] The thrust is that science is hard work, and moreover is *harder* work than literary studies. In his introduction to *The Faber Book of Science*, John Carey makes this subtext explicit, "Though most academics are wary of saying it straight out, the general consensus seems to be that arts courses are popular because they are easier, and that most arts students would simply not be up to the intellectual demands of a science course."[76] It is difficult to say if this was Snow's implication when he asked the literary people if they knew the Second Law, but it certainly seems to be the thinking behind the challenges from Tallis, Wolpert, and Sokal. Of course, the obvious reply is that if science really is so much harder, why are the literary intellectuals not excused from answering questions on it? This opens up problems for science advocates from the Snow/Tallis school. They seem to be saying both that you should learn science (Tallis going so far as to charge that "those whose experience of disciplined thought has been confined to the humanities . . . cannot be considered adequately educated"[77]) and also that science is very difficult to learn. The scientists cannot have it both ways on this issue: either science is difficult, and it is therefore unfair to expect nonscientists to comprehend its machinations, or else it is simple, and the claims for conceptual superiority are unwarranted. The confusion seems to arise from there being two senses of scientific knowledge at play here. It isn't just the names of scientists and scientific principles that the literary intellectual is supposed to have remembered; they must also have understood those principles with their context and applications. Tallis and Sokal, in particular, are hard to please. Both demand a more thorough awareness of science from nonspecialists, but differ significantly on how the requisite knowledge should best be acquired.

Tallis suggests that as "there is no shortage of reliable popularisations," scientific ignorance is inexcusable; "all that is required is some effort."[78] But the type of knowledge Tallis apparently demands is simply not attainable through these means. Would any popularization really explain the Schrödinger Wave equation (as Tallis suggests in *Newton's Sleep*[79])? Stephen Hawking's *Brief History of Time* doesn't, nor even does John Gribbin's *In Search of Schrödinger's Cat*, a text more or less devoted to this issue. Both go some way to explaining the issues that surround the equation and offer some of its uses and implications, but an intimate knowledge of the algebra is simply unnecessary at this level. Unnecessary because readers of popular science are (usually) not scientists and are not expected to be inserting variables into equations and to be calculating values. Unnecessary and, it seems, unwanted. In the preface to *Brief History*, Hawking reports, "Someone told me that each equation I included in the book would halve the sales. I therefore resolved not to have any equations at all. In the end, however, I *did* put in one equation, Einstein's famous equation, $E = mc^2$. I hope that this will not scare off half of my potential readers."[80] Contrary to what we might hope in reading them, what can be learned from popularizations of science doesn't include the ability to practice it. If such complex science *was* accessible through popularizations, then higher education in the sciences would swiftly become redundant. Familiarity with *The Selfish Gene* doesn't make you a geneticist, or *Brief History* a cosmologist, anymore than the *Reader's Digest Medical Guide* makes you a doctor. Aldous Huxley was aware of these limitations and of the compromise brokered between information and attention: "However elegant and memorable, brevity can never . . . do justice to all the facts of a complex situation . . . But life is short and information endless: nobody has time for everything. In practice we are generally forced to choose between an unduly brief exposition and no exposition at all. Abbreviation is a necessary evil . . ."[81] Popularizations inevitably offer restricted descriptions, and popular science is successful at the price of scientific explanation. Physicist Richard Feynman, fielding questions from journalists looking to condense copy, is said to have replied, "Listen, buddy, if I could tell you in a minute what I did, it wouldn't be worth the Nobel Prize."[82]

Alan Sokal and Jean Bricmont, both theoretical physicists, seem more aware than Tallis of the shortcomings of popular science. Anxious about what they consider to be the abuse of science at the hands of postmodern philosophers and critics,[83] Sokal and Bricmont want to place limits on the spread of pseudoscientific discourse. As they say, "It's a good idea to know what you're talking about. Obviously, it is legitimate to think philosophically about the content of the natural sciences. . . . But, in order to address these subjects meaningfully, one has to understand the relevant scientific theories at a rather deep and inevitably technical level; a vague understanding, at the level of popularizations, won't suffice."[84] Arguably, Sokal and Bricmont are not so much addressing the problem of scientific ignorance so much as the quite different problem of scientific pretension. As such, it is difficult to gauge how useful they believe popularizations are. While they admit that "it is usually possible to explain [difficult scientific concepts] in simple terms, at some rudimentary level,"[85] they are quick to illustrate the limitations of such knowledge. Concerning conflicting findings by different researchers working on solar neutrino emission levels (a study not quite inside Sokal or Bricmont's field), they claim "we could get a rough idea by examining the scientific literature on the subject; or failing that, we could get an even rougher idea by examining the sociological aspects of the problem, for example, the scientific respectability of the researchers involved in the controversy. . . .

But the degree of certainty provided by this kind of investigation is very weak."[86] This last issue of "scientific respectability" highlights another problem for the keen amateur, which Tallis fails to recognize. As Norris points out "one need only glance at a typical number of upmarket popularizing journals like *New Scientist* or *Scientific American* to see how narrow is the line that separates 'advanced' theoretical physics from the crankier versions of New Age thinking or sheer science-fiction fantasy.... [O]ne just can't be sure ... which are (supposed to be) the purveyors of mere fashionable nonsense and which are reputable scientific sources."[87] The reason why it is hard to tell the sense from the nonsense is in part due to the ever-widening gulf (discussed above) between theoretical physics and commonsense beliefs about the world, and in part rooted in the type of understanding available to thinkers whose lack of scientific training limits their reading matter/input to popularizations (rather than technical journals). Unlike medical ethics or even evolutionary psychology, no intuitions are available against which to measure the feasibility of ideas like "superstrings" and "wormholes."[88] Be that as it may, many nonscientists exhibit an almost religious faith[89] in the pronouncements of theoretical physics. In an interesting inversion of the two-part questions that Snow, Wolpert, Tallis, and Sokal were asking, Wayne C. Booth reports, "I have known science majors who would go to the stake ... for $E = mc^2$ ... though I have never found one yet who professed to be able to reconstruct Einstein's reasoning in support of this interesting proposition."[90] The type of uncritical acceptance Booth is interested in is itself a special sort of scientific ignorance. It is interesting to note the similarities between the credulity being criticized by Booth and the type of scientific pretension being criticized by Sokal. Both Booth and Sokal are interested in people who employ a scientific vocabulary without necessarily understanding the science behind the terminology. For Sokal, this manifests in conspicuous misuses of the vocabulary by poseurs and manipulators, and these misuses occur as a result of (and their success depends on) the same uncritical acceptance of science being critiqued by Booth. The same point is being made by both Sokal and Booth—that is, that scientific authority does not consist in simply saying the words, and that saying the words and knowing what they mean are not the same thing.

The type of knowledge available to the nonspecialist may be able to answer Snow or Tallis's pop quizzes, but it comes preassembled, a conclusion for which the premises—the evidence and the mechanisms—must be taken on trust. Wolpert is well aware that "many people accept the ideas of science because they have been told these ideas are true rather than because they understand them."[91] Sokal makes a similar point. "The teaching of mathematics and science *is* often authoritarian; and this is antithetical not only to the principles of radical/pedagogic democracy but to the principles of science itself."[92] Yet it seems undeniable that, without access to the relevant equipment and without the years of study necessary to make sense of that equipment (and the results it offers), the only scientific "facts" available to the non-scientist (and nonspecialist) come as received wisdom—unchecked and for the main part uncheckable.[93] A minimum amount of training and preparation is necessary and a certain worldview. As Ian Hacking notes, "[this is] surely inescapable. Science without background beliefs makes no sense."[94] In addition to scientific training and familiarization with the tools and equipment is the idea that science proceeds from mathematics and that an understanding of mathematics is the crucial attribute dividing the scientists from the laymen. Richard Feynman is unequivocal on this point. "It is impossible to explain honestly the beauties of the laws of nature in a way that people can feel, without their having some deep understanding of mathematics."[95]

Feynman draws attention to one of the apparently unavoidable blocks on non-mathematical explanations. "Physicists cannot make a conversion to any other language. If you want to learn about nature, to understand nature, it is necessary to understand the language that she speaks in."[96] The contention here is that only so much science can be explained without recourse to mathematics, and there seems to be no place for such mathematics in popularizations. Richard Dawkins thinks there may be a way out. "It is possible to enjoy the Mozart concerto without being able to play the clarinet.... Couldn't we learn to think of science in the same way?"[97] Can we separate learning to "play" science from learning how to listen to it? Snow described the scientifically ignorant as "tone-deaf." "Except this tone-deafness doesn't come by nature, but by training, or rather the absence of training."[98] Feynman was more pessimistic. He thought that science without mathematics wasn't just a case of learning to listen rather than learning to play, it was like teaching music to the deaf.[99] Perhaps Dawkins is implicitly conceding the redundancy of popularizations by utilitarian standards. The correlation Tallis finds between "useful" and "worthy" simply doesn't obtain in popular science. As former *Times* editor Simon Jenkins says, "I can think of very few science books I've read that I've called useful. What they have been is wonderful ... I think that science has a wonderful story to tell. But it isn't useful."[100]

How should this discrepancy between Jenkins and Tallis be understood? Dawkins considers the notion that science is wonderful but useless "so idiosyncratic that I shall pass over it." He adds, "Usually, even its sternest critics concede that science is useful, perhaps all too useful."[101] But Jenkins's point need not be a criticism. One way to explain the discrepancy is to recognize the ends to which that scientific knowledge can be put. For the nonspecialist such as Jenkins, science books can be interesting, informative and, as he says, wonderful, but the type of information they offer is not "useful" insofar as it cannot be put to any use. What Booth was questioning is not whether $E = mc^2$ is true or false, but whether or not as nonscientists we are qualified to say. Booth holds that "as believed by most of us . . . it is nether true nor false but simply meaningless." It is, of course, legitimate as a free citizen to have an opinion on whether or not $E = mc^2$ is true (although this would only be "an opinion about an opinion"), but he maintains that such an opinion is not the same thing as an idea. Booth is trying here to set up a sharp distinction between ideas and opinions. On this account, ideas are those opinions for which we can "reconstruct the reasons for believing them." So, unless we know "in a nonhistorical sense, where they came from," our beliefs are only opinions. Ideas must be "earned," they must be understood from the ground up. Consequently, opinions are "almost always proved to be false," and ideas are "seldom shown to be false though they may prove to have been inadequate."[102] Booth is advocating a more ready admission of ignorance during arguments where the subject matter under debate (say, $E = mc^2$) is one that is poorly understood by the parties involved. One result of this is that two people could say the same sentence and it could have a different epistemological status in each utterance, Coming from Booth, "$E = mc^2$ is true" is an opinion about an opinion; for Einstein (and presumably most physics professors), it is an idea. Booth's claim then, is that while what we say might be true for someone who understood the processes, it can never be anything but meaningless for someone who did not. (Its truth value isn't false, but it certainly isn't true.) The upshot is that truth is (in this respect) domain relative; that is, the statements we make are applicable only within "the world of discourse we have chosen to operate in, and within that world, whatever it is, there are always rigorous standards which dictate decisions as to truth or falsehood."[103] So by Booth's rationale, a nonscientist giving an answer to Snow's questions is simply making a meaningless utterance.[104]

This use of "ideas" and "opinions" is a little idiosyncratic, and it is easy to predict the difficulties of preserving a word like *idea* as a specialized concept. But it is not important to agree with Booth's choice of terms to recognize the distinction he is making. Booth's point is that science is only science in the hands of scientists, which is to say, what makes science good is what makes it useful, and what makes it useful can't be (even partially) conveyed by rote learning, and it certainly cannot be learned from popularizations. An alternative terminology is found with Gilbert Ryle's demarcation between "knowing how" and "knowing that."[105] "Know how" is the type of hands-on, functional knowledge that allows practical engagement; to "know that" is to possess abstract knowledge such as a list of names or an index of equipment and parts. The type of knowledge Jenkins, as a nonspecialist, can glean from reading science books (by which he presumably means popular science books as opposed to textbooks) is only ever knowing that; which is to say, facts un-supplemented by the type of know-how Dawkins and Tallis (as trained scientists) can bring to their readings. In Booth's language, it is only ever opinions and never ideas. And because it is usually only popular science books and not science textbooks that are accessible to nonspecialists, the only science the nonspecialist can acquire is almost certain to be "useless." That is, it is of no scientific function or value, isolated as the findings are from the evidence and the nonspecialist reader from the proofs.

So there are two types of scientific knowledge here: that which functions as science (and may incidentally be astonishing) and that which cannot function as science but does retain much of its power to astonish (perhaps all the more so because the mechanisms are opaque and mysterious). A functionalist thinker might want to say that the second type of knowledge is not science at all, but something like "trivia," a separate domain with its own vocabulary and unique applications (answering questions, for example). Given the limits placed on the nonscientist's comprehension of scientific information, it is normally only this inert type of scientific knowledge that we can expect to find in the possession of the nonspecialist. That this distinction seems hard for a scientist such as Dawkins to appreciate is perhaps not surprising given that, for the scientist, proofs exist and are recognized and understood at every level up to the "wonder" of a conclusion. But it is surprising (and disappointing) to find many scientific commentators consistently failing to recognize that if science is ever going to feed into literature, the most likely way for it to do so is through popularizations; and not only that it may do so, but that it has. Saddened by what he sees as the neglect of science by serious writers, Dawkins writes, "It is my thesis that poets could better use the inspiration provided by science."[106] This echoes Snow's regret that "[t]here seems then to be no place where the two cultures meet" and that "the clashing point of two subjects . . . ought to produce creative chances."[107] It seems that these "creative chances" can (and do) occur, but in terms of popularizations and in terms of knowing *that* rather than knowing *how*. Novelist Richard Powers appears acutely aware of this distinction. Reading through scientific literature, he writes, "I took the math on faith, having long ago sacrificed my math to the study of fiction." He adds, "I could follow the *story* of the math, if not the substance."[108] For Powers, this separation of "story" from "substance" is essential. The know-how has long ago been forsaken for specialization elsewhere, but the story is still within reach.

Science's use and practical function come only with the know-how, and while whole shelves of popularizations can explain the structure of DNA and its process of translation and transcription, not one will offer step-by-step instructions for gene therapy or cloning. Popular science can only ever teach the story, a fact that Sokal and Bricmont are uniquely placed to appreciate. The type of overreaching pseudoscience they are criticizing is the *story* of science mistaking itself for the *substance*. For worthwhile, practical engagement, "a vague understanding, at the level of popularizations, won't suffice."[109] For a man credited with bringing about a renaissance of science and employed to promote the public's understanding of science, Dawkins seems curiously unsure as to what the public's understanding is for. That it will not achieve practical engagement (as Sokal and Bricmont have shown) is not to say that it will not enable engagement at all. What popular science offers is the story without the substance, a mathematics taken on faith that for all its uselessness can still inspire wonder. Perhaps to argue in this fashion is to commit a simple category mistake—to have access to all the parts and still fail to recognize the whole. Perhaps knowing enough about science is the same thing as knowing science, and this seems true for what Oppenheim and Putnam called higher level sciences, such as zoology or botany. But at a more fundamental level it seems scientific awareness is just not the same as scientific knowledge, just as listening to music is not the same as playing it. What popular science offers is scientific awareness; it offers a route out of appearing scientifically ignorant, but it doesn't offer full-blooded scientific knowledge. It is through popularizations that science seems most likely to feed into the minds of humanities scholars if only because specialization elsewhere has rendered "real" science inaccessible.

Across these accounts is a pessimism about the possibilities of interdisciplinarity. Booth and Sokal and, in their own ways, Dawkins, Tallis, and even Leavis insist on the importance of disciplinary boundaries. It is not a matter of etiquette and territorialism; it is a firm and frank belief that contributions to professional discourse at anything less than a professional level of specialization will be useless. What's being blocked here is not the possibility of creative borrowings and inspirations, it is the hope that literary critics and scientists could sit at the same table and talk in nontrivial terms about each other's discipline. But this seems impossible, and the reason for this is that they are all using highly specialized vocabularies. They cannot make themselves understood. There are two responses to this. Stephen Jay Kline believes that we ought to try to create a "multidisciplinary" vocabulary in addition to and not in place of the existing specialist disciplines; a point of interface between the cultures, a place where specialists could exchange ideas. Stanley Fish is more pessimistic, and because he thinks that a discipline is constituted by its vocabulary, he cannot see a way for two disciplines to both make exchanges *and* retain autonomy.[110] In Fish's view, as soon as you start trying to do historical literary criticism, you have started doing history and stopped doing literary criticism, and as soon as the scientist starts popularizing, his science becomes redundant, stops being science, and starts to be story Fish's line is similar to that taken by Feynman, rather than Dawkins regarding the importance of mathematics to understanding science Both used musical analogies, but recall that where Dawkins felt there was a legitimate space to teach people to listen to science rather than play it,[111] Feynman believed that trying to teach science without mathematics was like teaching music to the deaf. The Dawkins line here basically assumes that communication is possible (although given where his reputation rests, this is unsurprising),[112] whereas Feynman is more skeptical, or attaches more importance to what is lost in abbreviation.

The issue for Feynman and Fish is the impossibility of exporting specialized concepts in anything like their useful sense (which is to say embedded within their disciplinary context) outside of the boundaries of the specialism.[113] The reason the concepts are no longer useful is discussed above in relation to the neutering of science at its own borders, but it is easy to see that if we follow Stanley Fish and assume that the vocabulary of a professional discourse exhausts the discipline, then it is clear that he can only argue in one direction here. There's nothing magical about this claim. All it is saying is that within a specialism words and concepts are used as part of a larger set of interrelations. is from these other interrelated words and concepts that the words and concepts acquire their meaning and their importance, and the specialism its identity. Take them out of that web, and they no longer have their connotations, and may, in fact, acquire new connotations.

In stressing the untranslatability of discipline-specific concept Feynman and Fish take an almost Whorfian position, and the idea that scientific theories in particular have profound effects on our observations has been much discussed within the philosophy of science. I the prefatory material to *The Structure of Scientific Revolutions*, Thom Kuhn acknowledges a debt to Benjamin Lee Whorf.[114] The most co troversial sections of that book have always been and continue to be the parts where he claims that there is a nontrivial sense in which "after a revolution scientists work in a different world."[115] This is the strong end of the Kuhnian thesis, and it continues to be a contentious issue. Whorf's is an explicit version of the idea that our language makes our world, and this is close to what Kuhn is claiming when he talks of theory limiting perception. A good deal of the confusion arises from Kuhn's inclusion of sentences like this: "Though the world does not change with a change of paradigm, the scientist afterwards works in a different world."[116] *World* is being used in two quite distinct senses: in the first instance, to refer to something like "the material universe as physical matter, independent of observers"; and in the second, to refer to the mental image of a situated and language-using observer exposed to that material universe. To sharpen this contrast, we might call these differences *physical universe* and *worldview*. If you substitute these senses, the sentence loses its gleam. "Though the *universe* does not change with a change of paradigm, the scientist afterwards works [with]in a different *worldview*." So language makes *our* world but not *the* world—an interpretation Rorty might be expected to be in sympathy with (albeit on the condition that *the* world was something we could never get to; so as far as we are concerned, *our* world is *the* world).

Benjamin Lee Whorf is often criticized for the Hopi translations that serve as evidence in his argument for linguistic relativism, which claims that "the structure of a human being's language influences the manner in which he understands reality and behaves with respect to it."[117] The strong version of the Whorfian thesis is linguistic determinism, which claims that the language a person speaks determines which phenomena he or she is able to observe. That is, two observers who speak different languages may find that one can see or understand something that the other categorically cannot, because it is excluded by his or her language. It implies that language can generate perceptual and conceptual blindspots. The weaker version is linguistic relativity, which makes the far less troubling claim that the language an observer speaks may affect which phenomena he or she is prepared to count as significant. This doesn't claim that the phenomena not labeled by the language won't be seen, only that they might be more easily overlooked. In *Language, Thought and Reality* where he talks of Hopi containing "abstractions for which our language lacks adequate terms,"[118] Whorf writes, "In order to describe the structure of the universe according to the Hopi, it is necessary to attempt—insofar as it is possible—to make explicit this metaphysics, properly describable only in the Hopi language."[119] Whorf then includes a translation in English, a point that has been picked up on by Donald Davidson, among others. As Norris explains, "Whorf is here attempting to have it both ways, on the one hand declaring that Hopi cannot be 'calibrated' with English, while on the other presuming to describe *in English* those various lexical and grammatical features of Hopi that supposedly render such description impossible."[120] But being generous, the issue isn't so much that the basic idea is untranslatable, it's that the bit that does the work is untranslatable, and Whorf continues the passage above by explaining that this translation will work "by means of an approximation expressed in our own language, somewhat inadequately it is true, yet by availing ourselves of such concepts as we have worked up into relative consonance with the system underlying the Hopi view of the universe."[121] The salient part here is the hope of achieving "relative consonance." You can convey the ideas of Einstein to an audience of nonscientists, but the audience can't do science with them, they come over as inert. Rorty (who favors the stronger interpretation of Kuhn's claim that scientists working within different paradigms work in different worlds) makes a similar point about "the intuition behind the false romantic claim that great poems are untranslatable. They are, of course, translatable; the problem is that the translations are not themselves great poems."[122] That is closer to what is at stake: the bit you are actually interested in (the nuance, the special significance of how something is said) gets lost in the move, and the most that can be achieved is relative consonance.

The claim by Feynman that certain concepts within mathematics cannot be translated into English is a quite different type of claim than Whorf's belief about the impossibility of calibrating certain natural languages (such as Hopi and English). A plausible case can be made for the content of mathematical theories being untranslatable into natural language, but this is not support for Whorf's argument, rather a matter of numbers and words being different types of things. Mathematics is hermetic, internally consistent and world-independent, and not a language in the usual sense at all. It is only syntactic, a system of rules specifying relations between numbers. As mentioned earlier (with reference to Frye's desire to see literary criticism achieve a similar hermeticism), the philosophical difficulty for mathematicians is not internal consistency, but external application; that is, explaining why their models appear to fit the world at all. So it is coherent for Feynman to make the claim that nature cannot be understood by nonscientists only insofar as the mathematical concepts that prohibit nonscientists' comprehension accurately describe nature. If nature does work on mathematical rules, then it may be the case that only those suitably trained in mathematics could ever really appreciate those relations, with the corollary that they could never talk or even think about them in nonmathematical terms.

Fish's case is different inasmuch as he wants to make the claim that concepts are sensible only within the disciplines that generated them (and of which they are constitutive), that is to say, only within their interrelations. But all this amounts to is the claim that without knowledge of the context, a term loses its sense. That sense isn't untranslatable, it just requires a good deal of background knowledge to be properly understood. Of course, untranslatability is only one part of the Whorf-Kuhn thesis, the corollary being the claim that the untranslatable vocabulary or theory either produces or is the product of a distinct and incommensurable conceptual scheme. It is unclear if either Fish or Feynman would want to say that possession of specialized vocabulary affects our perception of the world in this more profound sense, although given Feynman's commonsense realism, it seems very unlikely that he would want to say that he lived in a different world to nonscientists, or to previous scientists. Feynman did not think only scientists could experience the wonder of nature, but rather, that this was felt by everyone already, and that the purpose of teaching scientific knowledge "is to appreciate wonders even more. And that the knowledge is just to put into [the] correct framework the wonder that nature is."[123]

Given that these arguments about the importance of professionalism trade on a version of linguistic relativism, it is unfortunate that Whorf is often dismissed within linguistics for not being a professional (he was a fire inspector for an insurance company who never held an academic position, although he was apparently offered them). But the argument here is not about being a nominal professional; it is about knowing the professional vocabulary and being able to work with it. Here's Kline on multidisciplinarity: "It is not much of an exaggeration to say that in our late-twentieth-century universities we have acted as though there were a 'First Commandment of Academe' which reads, 'Thou shalt not transgress thy disciplinary boundary'."[124] Kline makes it sound as if the problem were simply territorial, but the issue is as much about possibility. It's not that people object to others working within their specialism (although with competition for jobs and funding being tight, this is obviously a factor), just that when people who haven't devoted years of study to it start to pronounce on a given specialism, they are likely to say silly things. This is what we saw between Rorty and Weinberg. Weinberg *does* sound naïve to philosophically trained ears when he starts to talk about "epistemico-ontological" issues that have taxed philosophers for centuries as if they really could be dismissed as easily as saying "you know, *real*; like rocks." One of the problems here is that Rorty seems to be in a situation where he wants to use his own specialism to close down the types of things that the scientists can talk about, but is unwilling to have the scientists close down the types of things he can say. The question in this case is: who knows most about reality? And it is unclear who should take priority. The physicists say, "We work all day with the very ground of matter, with the particles from which everything else is composed. I think we're in a good position to say what is and isn't real." And the philosophers reply, "You physicists don't even know what questions to ask. You start with assumptions about objectivity and reality that are tailored to the types of things you are willing to call real, and so, unsurprisingly, you find what you expect."

We see this same conflict replayed between Sokal and the literary theorists and in criticisms by biologist H. Allen Orr of Dennett's foray into evolutionary theory. Orr is quite scathing at times, particularly of Dennett's failure to consider the "neutral theory" of Kimura: "What can account for this astonishing omission?" he writes. "One possibility is that Dennett may not know about the neutral theory. Kimura *is*, after all, a tad harder to read than the pop biology Dennett appears to devour."[125] Orr is repeating Sokal's complaint that popularizations offer insufficient detail to permit meaningful contributions. The substance of the complaints is the same: and it isn't territorial; it is that the outsider says silly things because he or she simply doesn't speak the same (professional) language. Like the two interlocutors trading misunderstood concepts in Booth's example, nonspecialists or specialists from separate domains simply argue past each other. Their exchanges will be meaningless. The possibilities of assent are constrained by this condition.

In summary, this chapter has attempted to braid three related arguments. The first is an argument for the separation of science and technology. This says that the putative usefulness of science is actually the usefulness of technology. Here is another way to understand Jenkins's comment about the science he has read being of no use, and that is to recognize a difference between science (which is an academic discipline and source of theories about natural phenomena) and technology (which is equipment that solves a problem in the material world). While technology may be informed by many of the findings of science, it is possible to see science's relation to technology as similar to the relation between mathematics and science. Even though a particular technology has been made possible by scientific knowledge, insofar as the final product continues to work whether or not we understand the theory, we can say that science is only a handmaiden to technology, just as mathematics is a handmaiden to science. Mathematics by

5: RELATIVISM AND THE COMMONSENSE REALISTS

itself (that is, independent of science) makes nothing happen. Science by itself (that is, independent of technology) is similarly inefficacious. In material terms, only technology is useful.

Scientists are well aware of this division and use it strategically. The link between science and technology is embraced by scientists when they want to make claims about their practical worth and virtue (in contrast to the inefficacy of literary study), but denied when the products of technology threaten to question the moral responsibility of science. At this point scientists usually retreat to a claim that insists on the separation of science (as something like the love of knowledge and discovery for its own sake) and technology (as the use of certain scientific principles by nonscientists, such as engineers, craftsmen, and farmers, for purposes beyond the scope of scientific control). What happens here is that the scientists claim to dictate technological limits but not technological direction: they supply the tools but have nothing to say about how to employ them. (A stronger version of this argument would claim that science does not even dictate technological limits; very often, working technology awaits an explanation from the sciences. For example, analgesics like paracetamol/acetaminophen were manifestly effective long before they received a comprehensive explanation from neurochemistry, so the job of science is very often to reverse engineer a technology to explain how it works.)

This feeds into the second argument, which is about top-down control or at least the nonexclusivity of bottom-up determinism as a causal power. This argument is about what level of scale is doing the work. The scientists' arguments for the primacy of their vocabulary comes from an assumption that causal forces move only upward from fundamental particles to macrostructures, but a good case can be made for the relationship being more complex than this. Kline offered a system of "mutual constraints" whereby the macrostructure is limited in its possibilities by the microstructure, but that the microstructure is controlled or directed by the macrostructure. So the macroscopic supervenes on the microscopic. Scientists from higher-level sciences (for example, evolutionary biology) often use this same line of reasoning to argue against the threat of genetic determinism.[126] They will say genes offer limits on possibility, a cap on potential, but they do not tell you what to do with the potential you do have. It is easy to see how the same thinking maps over determinism in physics. Top-down causality is also the most efficient explanation for many phenomena. It makes more sense to say that it is the emergent properties of the higher-level objects that dictate and coordinate the behavior of the lower-level objects, and that a degree of causal autonomy exists with respect to these emergent boundaries.

The third part argues for the usefulness of science only within the sciences, that is, the uselessness of science to nonscientists. This argument is about the unavailability of a suitable vocabulary for the translation of much scientific knowledge into nonscientific terms and aims to show that the type of questions Snow, Tallis, Wolpert, Sokal, and Dawkins are asking humanities scholars to know the answers to are not questions about scientific knowledge, but are in fact trivia questions whose subject happens to be science. Because the questions are about scientific theories ("What is the Second Law of Thermodynamics?" "Who proposed the Universal Law of Gravitation?") they seem to be testing scientific knowledge. However, being able to answer questions such as these does not demand a knowledge of how the concepts involved are important for the scientific fields from which they emerge. Such facts are meaningful only when part of a wider understanding of how they fit together with other scientific beliefs. Isolated in this fashion, they are inert. Consequently, scientific ignorance is more difficult to remedy than thinkers like Snow imply.

To a large extent, the argument for the superiority of science trades upon an argument for the utility of science, and this in turn on maintaining a tight connection between science and technology. But pure science, when considered apart from technology, starts to looks as inefficacious as literature and literary criticism. Literature being chastized for its uselessness by Tallis and company seems a far less threatening criticism if we separate science from technology. All too often the wonder of science is conflated with its use. If science is useful, it is only while it is being done by scientists; and if its use is its virtue, then it is virtuous only in the hands of scientists. The facts and figures nonspecialists possess will never function as the scientific know-how of Tallis or Dawkins can function; they can never be of *use*. But a synthesis of literature and science surely never could. In the realization of Snow's "creative chances," science's use and function are lost, and only the awe and the wonder survive.

6
Centralities of Language and Matter

MUCH OF THE CONFLICT BETWEEN THE RELATIVISTS AND THE commonsense realists is centered on an understandable reluctance to relinquish a characteristic way of speaking about the world. Neither vocabulary suffices to describe successfully the things the other is interested in. The problem with replacing one vocabulary with another is that we may find that there are things that we used to be able to say using the old vocabulary that we cannot say with the new vocabulary. To some extent, this became apparent when Wilson was trying to argue for an account of the world ultimately reducible to the language of physics, but to do so, he found himself employing a series of different levels of explanation. Oppenheim and Putnam suggested this approach in their theory of the hierarchy, and Putnam went on to explore the idea with his notion of appropriate levels of description. It is tied to what Rorty called the relativity of descriptions to purposes.

From here, it is then a comparatively short step to the stronger case for disciplinary autonomy that claims that the particular vocabulary a discipline employs to do its work is constitutive of that discipline. This is Fish's position, which he expounds at length in his 1995 book *Professional Correctness*. Fish holds that a discipline is not a natural kind—he is keen to stress that he does not take an essentialist line on disciplinary identity—but instead describes literary studies as a "conventional activity, one shaped by the vocabulary, distinctions, and questions it employs," and because of this, "it behoves us to be wary of discarding its machinery." In Fish's account, to discard the machinery, to adopt a new vocabulary, is to lose the discipline. This is because he holds that any conventional activity "lives and dies by the zeal with which we ask its questions and care about the answers." The language of literary study is thus "a specialized and artificial vocabulary which is generative of the phenomena it picks out." Consequently, "If that vocabulary falls into disuse, the facts it calls into being will no longer be produced or experienced." If no one any longer asks What is the structure of this poem? or What is the intention of the author and has it been realized? or In what tradition does the poet enrol himself and with what consequences for that tradition?, something will have passed from the earth and we shall read the words of what was once literary criticism as if they were the remnants of a lost language spoken by alien beings."[1] The intuition that Fish is appealing to here is the idea that literary studies was not always a part of the university and may cease to be so in the future. He is not calling for a lockdown on interdisciplinary work (actually, he says the very idea is a nonsense, that apparent interdisciplinarity is really only ever one of the supposedly cooperating subjects, and never both), but the implication is clear: you can alter the way we do this only so much, and then it becomes something else. At a sufficient distance from the original type, speciation occurs. The discipline vanishes with the way of talking, because the way of talking was all the discipline was. The flip side to the impossibility of meaningful exchanges is the necessity of professional discourses and the professionals to speak them. Fish becomes a Scheherazade-figure; as soon as he stops talking like a literary critic, the discipline vanishes behind him. If serious about his claims, then he's talking to save his job, to keep it in existence.

There are some parallels here between Fish's (entirely serious?) claim about the unintelligibility of literary studies in a future where its remaining productions were now long-unread journals and books, lost in the storerooms of libraries, and Rorty's concession to the physicists that it might just be possible to predict the future, but not to know what it means.[2] It is not clear if the productions of literary critics really would be "alien," although this would presumably be a question for archaeologists to sort out. The productions of literary study would surely be no more alien than they currently are to nonspecialists: in a future where literary study had ceased to exist, people would view the orphaned books and journals in much the same way as scientists and mathematicians view them today. (Perhaps this is alien enough.)

Fish calls for a recognition of the necessity of professionalization. His closing comment is, "When there's a job to be done, and you want it done correctly, call in a professional."[3] Professionals have expert knowledge in a limited field. That's why Fish uses the word: it puts specialism in a good light. This works by reminding us of professionals like plumbers and doctors, individuals trained in particular specialist skills. Analogously, we think that a plumber is to a leaking pipe as a doctor is to an illness (and then) as a literary critic is to a text in need of interpretation. But this is where the argument falls down. Leaking pipes and illnesses are things we want sorting out; they are problems for which an expedient solution allows us to get on with the things we want to do. But an uninterpreted text is not an obstacle in this sense.

The question of why anyone should bother examining and interpreting literary texts is less clear and, at the end of Fish's defense, remains unanswered. It has been suavely avoided in all the talk of generative vocabularies and disciplinary professionalization, but it is the question that criticisms of literary study inevitably want to address. Complaints about the lack of rigor within literary studies or the dissolution of the canon are usually only technical ways of getting to the thing that puzzles those unsympathetic to literary study: what's the point of studying books in this manner? In the first place, what does it do (apart from keep people like Fish in employment)? An answer to "why study literary texts?" is the hollow at the middle of Fish's argument. (Rorty had an answer with his notion of edification: it makes us aware of new ways of thinking about ourselves, and perhaps Fish would agree.) This is nothing new. Frye had encountered a similar problem regarding the "use or value" of studying literary texts. Doubtful about the possibilities of persuading those external to the discipline of its worth, he saw a circularity involved with the familiar appeals to aesthetic experience as an end in itself. "Most 'defences of poetry' are intelligible only to those well within the defences." Anxious about answering directly questions about the *use* of studying literature, Frye diverts the issue to the question of "What follows from the fact that it is possible?"[4]

What is being asked for when literary study is being criticized is usually a definition of the subject so that its merits might be evaluated. Fish, however, claims that a definition in this sense cannot be given; that such discursive definitions do not exist outside of performative demonstrations. To this end, he devotes nine pages to a reading of the opening words of Milton's *Lycidas*. The reading he offers is designed to both satisfy those expectant of a definition and also to underline his belief that a discipline is no more than its unique approach, what he calls its "distinctiveness." Consequently, if we significantly alter this approach, then the distinctiveness of the discipline vanishes, and because a discipline is no more than its distinctive approach, the discipline vanishes, too.

This account of "distinctiveness" means that literary study is defined as whatever literary studies departments do. That this all sounds a little circular is half the point; the act of approaching a text as a poem is generative of the discipline of literary study and generative of the poem itself. Fish believes that the act of interpretation "makes" the poem, that our willingness to treat a text as a poem is (something like) the special quality that formalists like the early Jakobson had searched for in terms of locating and defining the property of "literariness." If there is something different about literary and nonliterary texts, it does not exist—or is at least only latent—until a reader has decided to look for it. "Linguistic and semantic density is not something poems announce, but something that readers actualize by paying to texts labelled poetic a kind of attention they would not pay to texts not so labelled."[5]

Preserving the distinctive approach of a discipline is therefore the same project as preserving the discipline itself. For this reason, Fish wants us to share his concerns about the possibility of literary critics making waves in the world outside the narrow field of fellow scholars. His condition of professionalization means that the opinions of literary critics on subjects outside of literary criticism, such as racism or terrorism or feminism, will have a limited impact. "It is not so much that literary critics have nothing to say about these issues, but that so long as they say it *as* literary critics no one but a few of their close friends will be listening, and, conversely, if they say it in ways unrelated to the practices of literary criticism, and thereby manage to give it a political effectiveness, they will no longer be literary critics."[6]

Of course, this apparent block on the field of legitimate contributions for literary critics ultimately cuts in favor of literary criticism: the corollary is that the wall that keeps the literary critics in keeps the scientists out. It is not unrealistic to see Fish's whole argument here as serving a primarily defensive role. For all the talk of the limited scope of professional contributions, there was never any real danger that literary critics were going to drift *en masse* out of literature and into politics. What Fish has done, however, is to outline an account of disciplinary identity that seems to offer a means of legitimizing an overlap of subject matter between disciplines without demanding either relinquish the way it usually deals with its subjects of study (like travelling abroad without learning the language).

Under this account, it is possible to review the interest of evolutionary psychology in fiction, and the interest of literary criticism in evolutionary psychology, and to recognize that the interaction is both less promising than some had hoped and less threatening than some had feared. It seems that the hope and fear arises from a misapprehension of what evolutionary psychology is trying to do with literature. It does not and cannot provide empirical support for value judgments, nor can it serve as a heuristic device for unveiling new meanings; rather, evolutionary psychology wants to explain the urge for and object of criticism and is not itself a type of criticism.

While Carroll's position as laid out in *Evolution and Literary Theory* was bound to meet with resistance from those involved with or sympathetic to the poststructuralist positions he attacks, a wider rejection of the use of evolutionary psychology as a critical tool has come from critics whose objections tend to center on two claims: first, that as an heuristic tool, evolutionary psychology seems to offer no original insights; and second, that evolutionary psychology offers a crude account of literary fiction. These claims are related and have a common explanation.

In an article called "Questioning Interdisciplinarity,"[7] literary critic Tony Jackson surveys attempts to employ evolutionary psychology and cognitive science in the service of literary study. He levels the familiar charge that these scientific approaches have nothing to add that literary critics didn't already know. Reading Carroll's *Evolution and Literary Theory*, he complains that "[h]is interpretations are worth reading in a general sense, but as with his claims about literature per se, he does not really offer us anything new. And it is not clear that Darwin or biology have made any interesting difference in getting at the interpretations he does provide." And again with Robert Storey's *Mimesis and the Human Animal*: "Though he has good, useful things to say, he does not really offer much that sounds revolutionary." And again, of Steven Pinker's account from *How the Mind Works*: "Pinker is very smart and a very good writer, and everything he says is true, but he tells us nothing that is not already widely known."[8]

These criticisms stem from a mistaken idea about what it is that evolutionary psychology is meant to be doing with literature. Evolutionary psychology is looking for confirmation that its assertions and expectations are correct, and literature—broadly conceived as traditional narrative fiction—is the type of place where any panhuman cognitive traits might emerge as recognizable continuities. If such continuities can be found, then the evolutionary psychologist is in a stronger position to repeat his claim that man has a human nature and it is always and everywhere the same. Proving this claim is the extent of evolutionary psychology's interest in literature. It does not aim (and may be unable) to function as a heuristic device for producing new meanings. It is still the job of literary criticism to produce new readings and not the job of evolutionary psychology. If evolutionary psychology *did* start to turn up readings radically divergent from the standard positions of literary criticism, then there would be questions asked about how correct it all was.

The reason that Jackson finds so much to criticize is that he assumes that "if the interweaving of evolutionary psychology and literary interpretation are to matter, presumably we will have to hear *new* interpretations."[9] But this is not the case. It is not necessary that Carroll introduce new interpretations, just that he offer a rationale for the set of interpretations he does provide. For although Carroll and critics like him do indeed seem to be using evolutionary psychology as a framework for saying things that have been said without this framework, this need not be a failure, even though it is possible that removing all references to evolutionary psychology would yield the same (literary critical, if not scientific) account. To say that all the talk of evolutionary psychology is not essential to preserve the content of Carroll's account, but is instead wholly and cleanly detachable, is not to say that evolutionary psychology has no relevance to Carroll's account. On the contrary, it is the decision procedure for what types of comments are permissible, that is, which types of things are (by Carroll's rationale) sensible things to say and which are not. The issue here is filtering.

Using an analogy with physics, Frye wrote of how the perspectives of "externally derived critical attitudes" (of which evolutionary psychology is one)[10] acted as "color-filters."[11] It is instructive to pursue this analogy so far as color filters do not add anything to the light they filter. A red filter will not "turn" all the white light red; there is transformation only insofar as there is blockage. All a red filter does is block those sections of the spectrum that are not red light (this was the novel part of Newton's theory of optics). So in an important sense, the filter is taking nothing away but variety: filters homogenize.

Carroll's filter allows anything consonant with evolutionary psychology to pass through, and nothing that isn't. This means that the reading that emerges is not a more various view but a less various one—which may or may not be more illuminating. The reading from evolutionary psychology fits this. This is the reason why an account such as Carroll's seems like it could have been produced without all the talk about Pleistocene man and the hunter-gatherers of the African savannah. Existing literary criticism could have constructed such an account, and for the main part, already had. All the evolutionary talk did was decide which elements of the existing literary criticism were admissible.

This all becomes much clearer when Jackson writes, "For Carroll, evolutionary theory is going to save literature and criticism from poststructuralism."[12] Jackson is perhaps being hyperbolic here, but this is nonetheless exactly what Carroll wants. In fact, it is hard to tell whether Carroll's motives for adopting and endorsing the evolutionary psychology view are motivated by a genuine belief in the program or, more shrewdly, because he doesn't value poststructuralism and believes that by encouraging the adoption of evolutionary psychology he might veto the poststructuralists by proxy: render their vocabulary invalid and moot everything they say before it's said.

So Carroll demands of and expects from evolutionary psychology the type of account he can already get from literary criticism, but one blessed by science. He wants this because he is taking sides. As explained above, the way he cuts the pack is poststructuralism on one side and science on the other. Anything allied to poststructuralism must go, and anything that can be allied with science should be preserved and examined more closely, as the new focus allows. He likes books and literary criticism, but seems to feel ashamed and disheartened that he cannot talk about these books with the authority with which practitioners of other disciplines—particle physicists and molecular biologists—are able to talk about their interests in atoms and molecules. He seems to feel that this authority was once possessed by literary critics (presumably, judging by the weight given to Pater and Arnold, around the late nineteenth and early twentieth century), but has since been lost in the subsequent ascendancy of both science and poststructuralism (subjects he construes as inherently antagonistic). By producing an account of literary study that will not offend at least this one branch of science, Carroll perhaps hopes to receive wider acclaim from the scientific community as a whole.[13] So it is not invalid for Carroll to invoke evolutionary theory in his account, although it may be that he is doing so disingenuously; that is, because he thinks it is useful only *instrumentally*, only insofar as it blocks poststructuralist readings.

Another common response to evolutionary psychology is the accusation that it is a too crude and clumsy method of interpretation that fails to account for much of what literary studies is interested in. This usually takes the form of a falsification argument. One of the universals E. O. Wilson talks about is a preference for a 20 percent level of detail redundancy in visual art, something found in Chinese ideograms and Mondrians.[14] Here is architecture critic Charles Jencks having fun with the idea that it might be possible to write an algorithm for artistic productions: "What about the Modern Masters? Did they have the right degree of redundancy? Of Simplicity divided by Complexity? [. . .] There must be some limit on the degree of labyrinthine complication; Wilson must be right. Too bad James Joyce, too bad T. S. Eliot, your *Waste Land* is just too . . . complex, not enough redundancy."[15] Jencks's sarcasm here is misplaced, attacking a claim that Wilson does not make. Wilson, and the researchers from whom he takes his data, are not claiming 20 percent redundancy is a necessary condition for artistic productions, and certainly not that it is sufficient, only that there is a marked tendency toward this level of redundancy in many instances of visual design from different geographical and historical periods. In addition, the claim is made only for visual art, so invoking either Joyce or *The Waste Land* as counterexamples seems puzzling or just plain obtuse.[16] What Jencks's criticisms underline, however, is the common and persistent misunderstanding of the aims and extent of explanations from evolutionary psychology.

Evolutionary psychology is interested in explaining the existence and origins of art and literature and in sketching out the types of things art and literature will generally tend to concern themselves with describing. It is interested in broad trends, not specific works. Those who object to the use of evolutionary psychology in the service of explaining the existence of art and literature tend to do so by appeal to an anomalous counterexample, as if taking evolutionary psychological theories to be falsifiable by a single anomaly. That is not the case. Evolutionary psychology proposes statistical results—trends, not axioms—and an anomalous datum does not refute a trend. To object then, as some critics do, that such accounts fail to touch the literary greats is to have mistaken what it was that evolutionary psychology was trying to do with literature in the first place.

It is unfortunate, given the many things wrong with Wilson's program, that the types of objections heard are more commonly these. What this should not do is make us reject evolutionary psychology on the grounds that it is dull and overdetermines criticism. What it should make us realize is the superfluous character of extraliterary interpretations. (For example, Carroll's bizarre defense of *Wuthering Heights* on the grounds that it doesn't violate the Westermarck effect works on an implicit assumption that *Wuthering Heights* would be somehow less compelling if it *did*.) In other words, we should not expect evolutionary psychology to do what literary criticism does.

This goes some way to answering the criticism that evolutionary psychology offers only crude and simplistic readings and offers no separate account of literary fiction. If these types of criticisms recall some of the complaints heard before regarding linguistic analyses (such as Jakobson's), it is because they have the same explanation. Linguistic readings of literary texts were interested only in the linguistic features of the text and lacked an apparatus for providing an account beyond this of the text's excellence or literary merit. Likewise, evolutionary psychology is interested in culture generally and narrative fictions only incidentally (as instances of this broader field). And as with linguistics, evolutionary psychology is not interested in qualitative judgments but only in popular trends. Seeking to explain the anomalous popularity of works like *The Waste Land* or *Ulysses*, which may not fit their expectations, evolutionary psychologists would likely be more interested in the social status and authority of literary critics in shaping public opinion than they would in analyzing the texts themselves for appealing content.

Looking again at the argument between Carroll and Pinker,[17] it becomes possible to better understand where they diverge. Carroll is first a literary critic and second an adherent of evolutionary psychology. Pinker, on the other hand, approaches literature from inside evolutionary psychology as one of its foremost public advocates. These separate agendas mean there are differences in how each utilize their materials. If Carroll was using evolutionary psychology only instrumentally, then Pinker is using literature only instrumentally. Pinker is saying the same things as Aristotle *deliberately;* or at least, it does not touch him to complain that his account is consistent with traditional accounts because his argument only works if the mind has always been this way. The project here is not about novelty but consistency, and Pinker's job is to reach the same conclusions using novel methods, that is, according to the expectations of evolutionary psychology.[18] He is not a literary critic, and it is wrong to treat him as one. For the same reason, he's not interested in giving an account that recognizes literature outside fiction. Pinker's is a theory of aesthetics only in the nonevaluative sense. Like linguistics, evolutionary psychology isn't interested in giving a value account and would have no grounds on which to construct such an account outside its own account of the types of things it would expect people to find valuable.

As regards evolutionary psychology's obligation to explain the existence of literary texts outside fiction generally, there is the option of leaning on an argument from sexual selection—something Geoffrey Miller might want to take up. Miller claims that a preference for "costly and wasteful display" distinguishes the "elite" individual from "the common run of humanity."[19] This works well for exclusive items such as expensive jewelry and clothes, but less well for reading habits, except insofar as they display education. The sexual worth of literary fiction might then lie in showing off intelligence. Reading difficult books is one way of vicariously being clever or signaling intelligence. Of course, this reasoning alone hardly serves as an explanation for why Joyce is held in such esteem: those features that separate Joyce from popular fiction are better explained with reference to values intrinsic to literature, and their connection to sexual attractiveness (and biological fitness) is almost uselessly distant. The most such an account can offer (and the most evolutionary psychologists could be expected to provide) is an explanation for why there is a division at all between high and low art, and it appears Miller is aware of this limitation. "The human tendency to regard works of art as a fitness indicators is being used here as a clue to art's evolutionary origins—not as a prescription for how art should be made or viewed."[20]

Centrally, evolutionary psychology is, or is at least *trying to be*, a science looking to explain the origins of culture and the reasons for the popularity of some forms of cultural production over others. If we stop interpreting the interests of evolutionary psychology (or cognitive science) in literature as replacements for the current vocabulary and begin instead to interpret them not as instances of criticism but as instances of science, then many of the problems evaporate. The sciences are interested in what it is that makes people interested in literature. Insofar as evolutionary psychology is a scientist's look at literature, it is also a disinterested look—with neither the intention nor the capacity to make evaluative judgments. It is not trying to answer the types of questions literary study tries to answer, and nor will it provide a foundation for what Northrop Frye called the "donkey's carrot of literary criticism,"[21] the demonstrable value judgment.[22] To use the terms Fish employed, whatever personal interest an evolutionary psychologist (or linguist, or cognitive scientist) has invested in literature, their professional interest (and accordingly what they can say in a professional capacity) will be limited to the types of things their profession is concerned with.

Armed with this account of the divergence of professional purposes, literary critics needn't fear that an account of literature from evolutionary psychology will invalidate the way they currently talk about books. Both literary criticism and now evolutionary psychology find themselves trying to describe creativity. The role of literary study is to make those descriptions in the intentional language appropriate for answering questions about intentional projects.[23] The role of evolutionary psychology is to make those descriptions in terms of trying to answer their quite separate questions about the origins of creativity and to try and understand the enduring popularity of certain narratives and visual images. So an overlap of subject matter does not imply a conflict of purposes, and it is purposes that ensure disciplinary autonomy and not subject matter.

This is not intended as an argument either for or against evolutionary psychology's interest in literature any more than one might sensibly argue against the interests of biochemists in zoology. All that is being said is that their interest is neither threatening nor misplaced; it is disinterested scientific inquiry, running on separate tracks and with separate goals from those of literary criticism. The scientists see the enormous and enduring cultural significance of literature and wonder how they can best fit that into their worldview (which aims to comprehensively explain phenomena), and evolutionary psychology is one of the best tools they have for attempting to do that. It is science's way of explaining what's going on; that is, science's way into literature and not (as Carroll had hoped) literature's way into science.

Does this then imply that literary study gains none of science's prestige from the type of empirically grounded organization that evolutionary psychology seems to offer? While evolutionary psycholog

6: CENTRALITIES OF LANGUAGE AND MATTER 167

cannot provide any support for evaluative claims about literary and subliterary fiction, it might still function as a hub on which to center an account of literature, such as Frye's, that seeks to organize literature in conceptual (rather than historical) space. In short, Frye needs an account like that offered by evolutionary psychology to anchor his conceptual schema to. Without it, his taxa (like Polti's thirty-six dramatic situations) risk appearing arbitrary.

As covered in Chapter 2, Frye described his intention to organize literature thematically. Rather than see literature as involved in a linear, historical progression, he wanted to see if it would be possible to see it as a complication in conceptual space. It is a fundamental assumption of any such scheme that forces are at work greater than the efforts of individual writers. This needn't sound so mysterious. Another way to say it is that such schemes must assume levels of organization exist above the individual, and that these higher-level organizations supervene on individual efforts to grant the type of coherence that Frye and so many others have seen in literature as a whole. The alternatives are to say either that any large patterns are coincidental (something rejected by evolutionary psychology or cognitive science, which takes regularity to be evidence for the existence of a universal human nature), or to say that large patterns are forced impositions. This is the case if the patterns are made by the critics and are not themselves an emergent property of the data. Scientific interpretation proceeds from the belief that the scientist is working with a ready-made world that is in need of explanation. The claim from Frye is that the taxa (whether that is the same scheme he suggests or some other doesn't matter) are *real*; that they are found and not made. He is claiming they are the product of an "inductive survey" of literature. Frye's is not the first such attempt, and he expects that his taxa will be revised and/or augmented, stressing that his is a preliminary effort. When Frye wonders if it would be possible to organize a "science of criticism," he is asking whether hard rules exist for literary organization.

When scientists find patterns, they are usually working with unconscious subject matter. Nature fits a coherent scheme because (this is the reductionist's justification) it is constructed according to very simple, iterative rules. As a result, patterns and trends can be explained in terms of the complication of simple rules. Literature, too, could fit patterns if there were similar rules governing the behavior of mankind. This is, of course, the thesis of evolutionary psychology, and it is hard to see how Frye could support his scheme without some similar sort of account of a commonality in humans. Where it meets problems is in the difference between finding patterns in the behavior of ant colonies and sand dunes (or whatever) and that of sentient humans. Could such simple rules be at work behind artists, shaping their work into fitting a pattern?

A scheme like Frye's needs top-down causality in something like the sense suggested by Kline's claim that "[i]n hierarchically structured systems, the levels of control (usually upper levels) 'harness' the lower levels and cause them to carry out behaviours that the lower levels, left to themselves, would not do," or Fodor's claim that "[c]ausal powers supervene on local microstructure."[24]

The higher levels of control here would be commonalities of human minds (on the assumption that physically similar human minds would share functional similarity) such that all human minds would tend to be internally similar and consequently exhibit similar responses to similar stimuli. These similarities would engender what Patrick Colm Hogan called "default tendencies," meaning that all human minds (or at least, the mean average human mind) would tend to find similar stimuli similarly interesting or dull. Consequently, they would tend to tell the same types of stories. (Although it has been stressed above, it is worth repeating that this does not imply a limit on the number of *possible* stories, only that there may be a limit on the number of *entertaining* stories. The set of possible stories could still be infinite, of which the set of entertaining stories is a finite subset. Again, "entertaining" is a nonevaluative label understood in terms of what is popular.)

It doesn't make sense to talk of a pattern in the whole without the parts being organized and shaped by the pattern. It doesn't make sense to think there are themes in literature that are not also themes for individual writers. Unless they have similar minds, it doesn't make sense that they collectively produce similar works. Frye's account is bound up with a view of creativity that is entirely consistent with the account offered by evolutionary psychology. To talk about there being a possibility of conceptual organization is to shave a little autonomy from the individual writer. The threat from evolutionary psychology is determinism: the author cedes a little creativity when he admits that his work is part of a panhuman expression, and the same is true for any account that seeks to impose a conceptual net wider than the actions of one individual acting autonomously.

This also goes some way to explaining why it is a commonplace within literary criticism that the poet[25] is not necessarily an authority on his own work. Recall that Frye believed actually being Dante does not in itself make you a good critic of Dante: "what he says has special interest but not special authority." As discussed above, he points out that people accept that a poet may not be able to fairly judge the *value* of his own work (for obvious reasons), but think that the poet should be consulted for learning about the *meaning* of the work, and that the author's account of the text's meaning would be definitive. For Frye, the assessment of both the value *and* the meaning of a text were to be tasks for the critic, not the poet. He dismissed as "the absurd quantum formula" the idea that it is the critic's task to get out of the text the meaning that the author put in. [26] But if these meanings are to be any more than critical imposition, we must assume that there is unconscious behavior by the creative writer; that the writer was including meanings of which he was not aware. This effects an abduction of authorial control from the poet into the hands of the critic. It is a strategic move, enabling the critic to wriggle free of accusations of parasitism and to consequently ensure a level of interpretive autonomy unachievable if the decisive reading and final say on interpretation stays with the poet.

This does not in itself open the way for wild misreadings and free interpretation of texts, but it does importantly allow the critic to better claim that the poets are acting in obedience to larger patterns—something we might expect individual writers to deny: being told that we are behaving in a typical fashion is an insult to our sense of personal autonomy. It is a sort of weak determinism, and it is the same thing that grates against us when evolutionary psychologists claim we are behaving in species-typical ways. It implies that our behavior, if not quite tropistic, is at least close to it. But if a taxonomic scheme in anything like the sense envisaged by Frye exists, then either artists are consciously designing their work to slot into one of its categories (perhaps true of some commercially motivated genre works), in which case some conscious awareness of the scheme must exist, or else there is no conscious awareness of the scheme and the scheme therefore precedes the authorial decision-making process. This second take is the one that shaves authority off the author. This suggests that artists are acting to some extent in blind obedience to a system of which they are a part. For Frye's scheme to work, he has to treat the poet as a herd animal. Only then does it make sense to think that literature could ever be organized around anything larger or more coherent than thousands of individual conceptual schema.

Once you have artists in a position of bovine obedience to unconscious forces, it becomes possible to talk of their productions with a similar authority with which scientists talk of the natural world. This is because it enables interpretations unfettered by worries about the creator's intentions and designs. It doesn't matter what the artist wanted; this is what we have. What is being imitated here, consciously or otherwise, is a version of what in science is known as the two contexts of discovery and justification.

Literary criticism employs the distinction whenever there is talk of the irrelevance of a writer's biography to a writer's art (following the New Critics or following the Proust of *Contra Sainte-Beuve*). What goes into the life is supposed to have no bearing on our opinions about what comes out in the art. Although counter-intuitive, this allows critics to avoid charges of parasitism. If the art is immune to the opinion of its creator, then the critic could be as creative and as important as the artist.

This is a clever trick, but one that physicists have been doing much longer. Take out the Creator, and all you have is an object and your interpretation; there is no need to worry about design and intention. The difference, however, is that physicists seek a stability of interpretation, whereas critics seek idiosyncrasies of interpretation. Frye builds this into his account of what a science of criticism might look like, and it is crucial, because it keeps criticism from ever completing its work. Unlike science, which seeks to exhaust nature in its description and would welcome this event as a triumph, criticism takes its subject to be inexhaustible, and seeks to proliferate readings. As Frye famously has it, the inexhaustibility of literature holds even if new works cease to be produced.[27]

In the same way scientists talk of "raw data" in the context of discovery, the text before interpretation is "bare." Here is a context of discovery, the text itself, and a context of justification, the reading a critic makes of that text: In modern literary criticism it does not seem too strong to claim that this reading really does float free of the text as much as the scientist's proofs and conclusions float free of the conditions of their discovery.[28]

From here, it is not overreaching to see the efforts of the critics to strip the author of post-publication authority (as regards interpretation of meaning) as a conscious or subconscious imitation of the relationship that scientists hold between the world and their work; that is, one of found subjects (the devising of a series of taxonomic systems for the interpretation of nature), rather than created subjects (the author whose finite capacity to create will limit the interpretive act). With intention out of the way, it becomes possible to talk about "art" outside "artists." So finding patterns in the whole implies less control in at least this one respect.

We needn't, of course, immediately collapse into a fatalistic determinism, but it is worth questioning the claim that for every way in which we are like other people we are that much less free. This cuts both ways: it could be used to support the liberal-egalitarian idea that all men are created equal, but it could also support the idea that our flaws are ineradicable. On the strong view of this sort of determinism are the tropisms. A tropism is a reflex that affects the movement of the whole organism; so blinking is a reflex, but not a tropism. A flower's turning to the sun is called a phototropistic response. There are also animal tropisms, and the account is familiar enough, as James Rachels explains. "We may mistakenly believe that an animal is behaving rationally, but in reality the animal's movement is only a machinelike, unreasoning response to a stimulus." To give the flavor of how these might work, he offers some examples of tropistic behavior in animals: "When the male nocturnal moth mates with the female, we may be tempted to see in his evident zest something analogous to the lusty desire of a man—yet it turns out that the male moth's behaviour is triggered entirely by the odour produced by two scent organs near the female's abdomen. When these are removed the male will attempt to mate with the organs, ignoring the nearby female. Again, upon analysis, we seem to find nothing but a fixed, unreasoning response to a stimulus."[29] Rachels goes on to ask, "One key question is whether all animal behaviour is to be regarded as tropistic, or only some of it." He asks this partly because he is concerned with animal welfare, but to this end, he is also interested in establishing a continuum between man and animal, which he sees as a logical consequence of accepting Darwin's ideas about evolution and speciation. It is quite uncontroversial to claim that the behavior of moths or the sphex wasp (Darwin's example, and now a stock case) is tropistic in this sense, but quite a different thing to consider the behavior of rats, dogs, chimps, and ultimately humans in the same way. Exploring the possibilities, Rachels asks, "But what if *all* behaviour is tropistic, including the most impressive performances of the higher animals?"[30] The tropistic behavior of higher animals would have to be more complex, but it is conceivable that any tropistic behavior could be made more sophisticated by the addition of a subroutine and still be a tropism. In theory, there is no limit to the number of subroutines the tropism may have and still be a tropism.

As should be clear from the talk of subroutines, the argument for tropisms in higher animals works from an analogy with computer programs. Consistent with his project of describing the human mind in computational terms, Daniel Dennett wonders what number of subroutines you'd have to add to make the sphex wasp look intelligent: "There will always be room for yet one more set of conditions in which the rigidly mechanical working out of response will be unmasked, however long we spend improving the system. Long after the wasp's behaviour has become so perspicacious that we would not think of calling it tropistic, the fundamental nature of the systems controlling it will not have changed; it will just be more complex. In this sense any behaviour controlled by a finite system must be tropistic."[31]

Rachels concludes that "Since all animal behaviour is controlled by finite systems, we might by this reasoning come to regard even the most "intelligent" behaviour of the higher animals as in principle similar to the behaviour of the bee, the moth, and the wasp. . . . Human behaviour, too, is under the control of a finite system—the human brain—and this means that the human repertory, no matter how vast, also has some limits."[32] Being told that our behavior is analogous (however distantly) with the behavior of moths and flowers is a blow to our sense of personal control, but consistent with the decentering science effects.

The Kuhnian view of scientific change rejects the idea of cumulative knowledge, alleging that what the scientists often call progress is better understood as a series of new beginnings. Be that as it may, the history of paradigm shifts does have a core theme constituting a progression of sorts, and this becomes apparent when listing the major revolutionaries: Copernicus, Newton, Darwin, and Einstein. As well as being attached to scientific revolutions, these names are among the most famous science has produced. What unites them and explains their cultural value is that each pushed mankind a little further from the traditional, theistic view, that had humanity at the center of the physical universe and the closest to God. Each successive and culturally significant scientific development has involved a reconception that has moved man further and further from the central figure he was. The trend in the history of science has been the decentering of the human subject.

The cultural significance of scientists is usually related to the extent to which their work contributes to this decentering. What is *scientifically* significant about Newton is that he proposed a universal law of gravitation, invented the calculus, or pioneered the almost autistic attitude to data collection standardized as the modern scientific method. What is *culturally* significant is that he offered us an account of the universe that didn't need intentionality. You can do a lot of work in science and not change our position in the universe. Darwin and Copernicus force re-thinkings in a way that Mendeleyev's elegant periodic table or even Watson and Crick's double helix do not. The scientific community already believed in an atomic universe, Mendeleyev simply organized that system. Similarly, so far as the work of Darwin and Mendel had already persuaded the scientific community that some or other mechanism existed for the transmission of genetic material, all Watson and Crick's discovery did was provide a model for how this could be realized. (The profound point at the center of Darwin's work was that mankind is just another animal.) This is not to try to undermine the importance for the scientific community of what Mendeleyev or Watson and Crick achieved, but their work does not shift humanity any further from the center of the universe than where the atomists and evolutionists had already put us; it only secures that position.

It is part of the materialist credo that our lives are insignificant to a mechanistic universe whose continued operation does not need us or our native obsessions about purpose and meaning and intention. Explanations from science are almost defiantly anti-intentional. (What makes science rational is the absence of what Dennett called "skyhooks," an appeal to anything outside of a mechanistic causal explanation.) Given this prohibition, it comes as no surprise to hear that Steven Weinberg finds "a chilling impersonality in the laws of nature": or that Richard Dawkins believes in "an orderly universe, one indifferent to human preoccupations," where "nature is not cruel, only pitilessly indifferent. . . . neither good nor evil, neither cruel nor kind, but simply callous—indifferent to all suffering, lacking all purpose"; or to hear Stephen Jay Gould saying, "Nature does not exist for us, had no idea we were coming, and doesn't give a damn about us."[33]

To say that decentering has been a constant theme in the history of science is not to say that decentering is a deliberate aim of science. The removal from center stage of the human is surely a secondary effect of trying to account for phenomena without recourse to teleological or intentional explanations. When scientists talk of aiming for objectivity, what they are trying to capture is the idea of a third person account; to see things as they are, rather than as we see them. (That this is something that thinkers like Rorty have rejected as a nonsense helps locate much of the argument between the commonsense realists and the relativists, as discussed above.) Recognizing that our own senses are fallible (that they can be misled by illusions, for example), the scientist becomes skeptical of appearance and of intuitive accounts and may attempt to construct apparatus to measure the world for him (relocating the problem of measurement to the movement of dials). The effect, as Anthony O'Hear puts it, is "to present the human being and his modes of perceiving the world as incidental parts of the picture" and, consequently, "of no more significance than any other incident in the development of the cosmos."[34]

On account of its apparent independence of human perceptions, the scientific view is also credited with being an epistemologically more secure and, therefore, satisfying view. Recall that Steven Pinker described science as a "uniquely satisfying kind of understanding."[35] The rationale for this is easy to follow: the truth is how things are, and not necessarily how they appear to be, so a view unclouded by human perception is a more truthful one, and the truthful view is ultimately more satisfying than a fabricated view. Accordingly, the extent to which a view is independent of human perceptions is proportional to its accuracy and truthfulness. This is why Dawkins believes that the universe "indifferent to human preoccupations" he speaks about "is a more beautiful, more wonderful place than a universe tricked out with capricious, *ad hoc* magic."[36] It is no accident that Dawkins splits the options this way: anything that seems remotely interested in the merely human must be nonsense.

The consistency with which anthropocentric accounts have been shown to be erroneous has led to a situation where the presence of anthropocentrism in a theory becomes sufficient grounds for its outright rejection. In much the same way as the patent office will not consider applications for perpetual motion machines because they entail a violation of the inviolable second law of thermodynamics, the presence of anthropocentrism flags an account as ultimately unsound, as wrong from the start. Accordingly, it is the mark of a respectable account of the cosmos that it does not require human beings. Most long-range sciences, such as cosmology, geology, or evolutionary theory, work from the principle and accept as a truism that there was a world long before there were people living in it, and that there will still be a world if people disappeared.[37] They accordingly hold that the world was neither created for humans nor that humans are an endpoint for evolutionary change (the very idea of an endpoint, barring extinction, being inimical to and a nonsense in terms of evolution).[38]

All this flies in the face of the traditional teleological and theistic conception of the universe and (on the smaller scale of life on earth) of the relative importance of different forms of life. Accordingly, appeals to the *prima facie* special sanctity of human life are invalidated, and the value of nonhuman life reassessed. In *Created from Animals*, Rachels embraces this position to argue for the development of a "better ethic concerning the treatment of both human and non-human animals. Human life will no longer be regarded with the kind of superstitious awe which it is accorded in traditional thought, and the lives of non-humans will no longer be a matter of indifference. This means that human life will, in a sense, be devalued, while the value granted to non-human life will be increased. A revised view of such matters as suicide and euthanasia, as well as a revised view of how we should treat animals, will result."[39] Rachels wants to use Darwinian thinking as a supplementary argument in support of vegetarianism and environmental protection. He is an ethicist, and his is an ethical argument, interested in the question of how ought we to act, given this revised account of the importance of human beings.[40] As when ethicists ask questions like "what is wrong with killing?" or "what is wrong with rape?",[41] Rachels is not looking to overturn our sense of right and wrong, but to question our assumptions so as to better ground our beliefs. "Abandoning the idea that human life has special importance does not leave us morally adrift; it only suggests the need for a different and better anchor."[42]

What Rachels wants is for the implications of the decentering to have some positive impact outside of science—here, on our behaviour toward animals. His argument is in line with Peter Singer's account of animal welfare. Both claim that a proper consideration of the relative importance of humans and other animals should make us recognize that an appeal to the special concerns of humans constitutes a prejudice, analogous to sexism and racism, which Richard Ryder called "speciesism." Rachels uses Darwin to support his belief that speciesism is to be resisted as another type of anthropocentrism.

Because of the shared concern with avoiding anthropocentrism, we might expect scientists to be sympathetic to an account like Rachels's. Here is Richard Dawkins apparently doing just that: "The attitude that living things are placed here for our benefit still dominates our culture, even where its underpinnings have disappeared. We now need, for purposes of scientific understanding, to find a less human-centred view of the natural world. . . . We must learn to see the world through non-human eyes."[43] It should, however, be stressed here that when Dawkins talks about looking at the world through nonhuman eyes, he is not trying to talk about the moral benefits of a more objective worldview. "Non-human" is not meant as "free-floating" or "disembodied" or in any such Nagelian view-from-nowhere sense. When Dawkins says "non-human" he means only that. He is thinking that we should do the other Nagelian thing: that is, to imagine what it would be like to be a bat, or a bee, or any other creature with significantly different perceptual apparatus to ourselves. That is why he places the emphasis on the available gains for *scientific understanding*. Although it is dressed up as an ethical point, analogous to Rachels's, Dawkins's is an argument for environmental protection only insofar as there can be gains for human life and human understanding. In a sense, his is another version of the idea that the world exists for our pleasure, but here the pleasure is calibrated by scientific discovery: the better we are to the environment, the more Dawkins (as a zoologist) has to investigate. (It is a bit like thinking of a wealthy literary critic patronizing creative writers so that he might have more books and poems to interpret.) Dawkins sees anthropocentrism as an epistemological problem; Rachels saw it as an ethical one.

That Rachels seems to accept that human behavior may be tropistic and that Dawkins looks forward to an age where the human viewpoint is marginalized is not to say that all scientists are happy with the decenterings and accordingly fatalistic about agency. Although obviously an advocate of the sciences, Tallis finds fault with the trend toward decentering insofar as it creates "a climate of intellectual opinion in which individual human consciousness and the part it might play in bringing about change for the better is marginalised." Tallis thinks that the success of mechanical explanations within the sciences has led to a generalized eagerness to employ mechanistic explanations where once intentional explanations had been employed, with the result that the sphere of human agency is reduced. He points out that since "[i]t is the mark of a science that it does not consult its object in order to find out the truth about it," there is a tendency for thinkers wishing to scientize their subject to insist on "the autonomy of the object of study (language, society, etc.)." Accordingly, various determinisms—physical, biological, psychological—replace what had been thought to be free choice and rational action. As indicated by the title of his book *Enemies of Hope,* Tallis fears that a desire among the humanities (he says "human sciences") to become more scientific has led some thinkers into too readily ceding control to forces outside of human influence, and hence becoming unduly pessimistic about the possibility of escaping biological (or psychological, or social, and so on) constraint. Among these thinkers, Tallis targets Marx's historical determinism and Freud's emphasis on the subconscious as examples of what he calls "marginalising consciousness."[44]

Rather happily, Freud explicitly claims to do just this: situating his own work as another stage in the successive decenterings of science. He claims that "in the course of two centuries the *naïve* self-love of men has had to submit to two major blows at the hands of science. The first was when they learnt that our earth was not the centre of the universe but only a tiny fragment of a cosmic system of scarcely imaginable vastness.... The second blow fell when biological research destroyed man's supposedly privileged place in creation and proved his descent from the animal kingdom and his ineradicable animal nature."[45] Then, in what Stephen Jay Gould has called "possibly the least modest statement of intellectual history,"[46] Freud claims that it is from his own work that "human megalomania will have suffered its third and most wounding blow." First Copernicus removes humans from the center of the universe (the cosmological blow), then Darwin removes them from the center of the animal kingdom (the biological blow), and now Freud "seeks to prove to the ego that it is not even master in its own house, but must content itself with scanty information of what is going on unconsciously in its mind."[47] This last, Freud's psychological blow, is a wresting away of control from the patient into the hands of the psychoanalyst; it carries the subtext that, although access to the unconscious mind is denied to the individual, it may yet be accessible to the Freudian analyst.

This is the same model Frye and the New Critics had employed to think about the poet's reading of his or her own work, seen again in the output-based Skinnerean behaviorism, and seen again today in how neuropsychologists will favor brain scans over direct reports of mental experience. It opens the way for claiming that an individual may be deluded about his or her motivations. While not amounting to a claim that behavior is tropistic, it is an important first step toward doing so. In this respect, it is also a different type of blow to the decenterings effected by the Copernican and Darwinian revolutions. Writing on the same subject in a later lecture, Freud would stress this difference: "Although thus humbled in his external relations, man feels himself to be supreme within his own mind." Freud becomes quite emphatic: "You feel sure that you are informed of all that goes on in your mind if it is of any importance at all, because in that case, you believe, your consciousness gives you news of it. . . . Indeed, you go so far as to regard what is 'mental' as identical with what is 'conscious'. . . . Come, let yourself be taught something on this point! What is in your mind does not coincide with what you are conscious of. . . ."[48] This intuition that the conscious is not coextensive with the mental has endured and found support from modern psychology in spite of the widespread rejection of Freudian psychoanalysis. The claim being made is that the conscious mind is less efficacious than we are led by the conscious mind to believe. Because the conscious is, by definition, that part of the mind (and the *only* part of the mind) to which the individual has access, this becomes an essentially irrefutable argument in support of the existence of the unconscious. Recognizing this strength, Freud uses our resistance to any reduction in the influence of consciousness as evidence of his being correct on this point: "No wonder, then, that the ego does not look favourably upon psychoanalysis and obstinately refuses to believe in it."[49]

It is an argumentative technique that would later be employed again through the efforts of evolutionary theorists to convince us that our conscious reasons for action are, if not supplementary to, at least not independent of the dictates of our genes. Matt Ridley, following an argument made by Robert Trivers, uses a similar fail-safe to counter our gut resistance to genetic determinism. "If man has evolved the ability to override his evolutionary imperatives, then there must have been an advantage to his genes in doing so. Therefore, even the emancipation from evolution that we so fondly imagine we have achieved must have evolved because it suited the replication of genes."[50] The tightness of this sort of appeal[51] has meant that some evolutionary psychologists are accordingly fond of talking about the "real" reason for liking literature or falling in love as being the biological reason, and calling any other account delusional.

Richard Dawkins is often cited as being one such thinker. Although he explicitly denies this toward the start of *The Selfish Gene* ("I am not going to argue about whether people who behave altruistically are 'really' doing it for secret or subconscious selfish motives. Maybe they are and maybe they aren't, and maybe we can never know . . ."[52]), it is something implicit in his work in that it is the basis of his metaphorical inversion (it is the *gene* that is selfish, not the person), and the reason his books have attracted so much attention. It is this aspect of the evolutionary perspective, the threat of determinism, that meets with the fiercest resistance from critics of the project. Whether or not this is something evolutionary psychologists are actually saying, it is something that they are thought to say and something consistent with their accounts.

As Freud recognized,[53] advocates of the delusion thesis find an ally in Schopenhauer, who relegated romantic love to the role of a trick used to dupe the species into reproducing.[54] In Schopenhauer's view, "all love, however ethereally it may bear itself, is rooted in the sexual impulse alone." Consonant with modern biology, this impulse—reproduction—is no less than "the ultimate goal of almost all human effort." Schopenhauer's account has some striking parallels with the biologistic theories of behavior offered by evolutionary theorists, but with none of Dawkins's reservations about whether the biologistic reasons are the "real" reasons for our actions. So love is a way to "deceive our consciousness; for nature requires this stratagem to achieve its ends." Deception is necessary because the job of reproducing the species is, like respiration or the regulation of the heartbeat, simply too important to be trusted to absent-minded consciousness, and so nature, like capitalist marketing, makes an appeal to our reliable self-interest: "nature can only achieve its ends by implanting a certain illusion in the individual, on account of which that which is only a good for the species appears to him as a good for himself, so that when he serves the species he imagines he is serving himself."[55] Although he calls love an "illusion," it is not clear that this is justified. It is important to recognize that Schopenhauer's identification of romantic love with a pragmatic end doesn't demand the elimination of love, any more than the identification of the cause of a pain (the doctor says it is a sprained ankle) would have any effect on the felt intensity of that pain. Equally, learning that a pain is a certain type of neural activity in the brain doesn't, unfortunately, make that pain illusory.[56] The explanation from a different level isn't "actually," but rather "also" the reason, and the apparent interference doesn't seem to occur.

Lacking both Freud's unconscious and the Modern Synthesis vocabulary, Schopenhauer spoke not of "genes," but of "the genius of the species," a hazily defined subconscious force that pushed human behavior in directions that would benefit the species rather than the individual. Although the emphasis on species-level selection has since been rejected by orthodox evolutionary theory, Schopenhauer's delusion argument sits surprisingly easy alongside the rhetoric of the neo-Darwinists. Here is Ridley again, laying out the bones of his thesis in the opening pages of *The Red Queen:* "reproduction is the sole goal for which human beings are designed; everything else is a means to that end."[57] It is possible, of course, that Ridley, as a popularizer, is only trying to attract browsers with such a line. It is unlikely that many evolutionary theorists would assent to this statement without careful qualification—the kind of qualification to which Ridley will devote the rest of his book.[58] But the current here is toward downplaying the potency of conscious intention. If we are not conscious of being controlled by our genes or by our unconscious mind, it must be because it is in the "interests of" the genes or the unconscious mind to conceal their influence from our conscious experience. Repeatedly, one reads references to being "worked through" and "manipulated by" and "tricked into." It is as if we are no longer in control.

Yet there is something almost seductive about this sort of fatalistic determinism, too. Rather than see it as a loss of control, it can be switched around and seen as a release from responsibility. Martin Amis seems to be doing just this when, in his autobiography, he claims, "My respect for the unconscious continues to grow.... Really, the conscious mind can afford to give itself a rest. The big jobs are done by the unconscious. The unconscious does it all."[59] This sort of resignation is precisely what Tallis was worried about: determinism becomes an excuse, another way in which things are not our fault, a dereliction of social and ethical duties.

Equating a reduction in agency with a release from the existential pressure to choose and decide our own fate is an only dubiously praiseworthy consequence of decentering, and while Amis is probably quite serious when making claims for the power of the unconscious, it seems unlikely that in so doing he is advocating a collapse into the type of impotent fatalism experienced by the homuncular narrator of his

Time's Arrow: condemned to simply watch events unfold and absolutely powerless over the body in which he finds himself. Freud, too, overstates his case when he claims that consciousness is no longer "master in its own house."[60] The conscious mind is not as enfeebled as Freud would have us believe. (At the very most, following Freud's metaphor, the staff are occasionally disobedient.) There are, however, ways in which the reduction in the potency of consciousness and a more humble conception of our place in the universe can be seen as positive moves. The way Freud tells it, the decentering revolutions constitute attacks, wounding what he calls our "naïve self-love" and effectively driving wedges between humanity and God. But it is equally possible to see them as historian Bruce Mazlish (following Jerome Bruner)[61] suggests: namely, as continuities between man and nature. The further from God's favor we slide, the closer we come to a natural harmony:

> In this version of the three historic smashings of the ego, humans are placed on a continuous spectrum in relation to the universe, to the rest of the animal kingdom, and to themselves. They are no longer discontinuous with the world around them. In an important sense, once humans are able to accept this situation, they are in harmony with the rest of existence. Indeed, the longings for a sense of "connection" seen in the early nineteenth-century romantics and all "alienated" beings are, unexpectedly, partially fulfilled.[62]

Note that Mazlish sees this sort of materialism as sympathetic to Romanticism, a sharp contrast with Dennett, who sees scientific materialism as destructive of Romanticism, opening *Consciousness Explained* with a denial of the possibility of "'true love'—as if this were some sort of distinct substance (emotional gold as opposed to emotional brass or copper)."[63] Mazlish's agenda is to remove what he calls "the fourth discontinuity," the break between man and machine.[64] Mazlish, like Boden, believes that silicon technology is soon to provide a demonstration that our mental powers are not unique: that the materialist claim that the mind is just another machine will receive the same near-universal assent as the Copernican claim that the earth is just another planet, and the Darwinian claim that man is just another animal. Reviewing Robert Jastrow's *The Enchanted Loom*, Stephen Jay Gould embraces Mazlish's idea to add his voice to those calling for a recognition of our more humble place in nature "by forging a true discontinuity in the physical history of intelligence on earth, we may force ourselves to appreciate our own deep embeddedness in nature. Of course, any paleontologist knows that too deep an embedding can lead to oblivion

This, indeed, is the paradox we may soon face."[65] The "oblivion" in question is a conceptual alteration: a gestalt shift in how we think of ourselves in relation to the universe—from figure to ground. This, Gould believes, is the consequence of accepting the decenterings. (It is passivity in the face of this oblivion that some commentators—like Tallis, above—have found pernicious inasmuch as it seems to encourage fatalism about our potential for change.) It is an idea that Gould would return to in an essay from 1990, "The Golden Rule: A Proper Scale for Our Environmental Crisis."[66] Once again, Gould draws on his experience as a paleontologist to resituate humanity in a more minor role.

Here, Gould is analyzing the claims made by environmental ethicists to the effect that the ecosystem is fragile and at dire risk from humanity's unchecked and destructive spread, and that, consequently, it falls to humanity to protect the environment and (as the slogan says) "save the planet." Perhaps surprisingly for someone professionally concerned with the environment (but consistent with the drive to reduce the importance of humans), Gould attacks the claim that we are in a position to "save the planet" on the grounds that we could not destroy the world in the first place, dismissing the rationale behind these arguments as a monstrous arrogance. "Such views, however well intentioned, are rooted in the old sin of pride and exaggerated self-importance. We are one among millions of species, *stewards of nothing*." Gould's take on the problem of environmental damage is based on his understanding of geological "deep time," which talks in terms of millions of years rather than hours and seconds. Consequently, the existence of human beings becomes a far smaller fraction of the whole, and the importance of an individual life is slivered to insignificance.[67]

Gould is well aware that deep time is not a useful way to think about environmental preservation, and this is why he talks instead of choosing the "proper scale": that we couldn't destroy all the bacterial life is not to say that we couldn't make the planet inhospitable to mammalian life. It is not supposed to be an argument for abandoning green policies and indulging again in reckless pollution.[68] What it is supposed to be is a demonstration of how our interpretation of the scale and nature of a situation is dependent on the scale we choose to view it from.

Another trick with time—this one fictional, but no more comforting—is the perspective offered by the Tralfamadorians in Kurt Vonnegut's *Slaughterhouse-Five*. Billy Pilgrim is a chaplain's assistant in the Second World War who, as Vonnegut has it, "came unstuck in time."[69] The Tralfamadorians see time omnisciently, making no distinction between tenses: "All moments, past, present, and future, always have existed, always will exist. The Tralfamadorians can look at all the different moments just the way we can look at a stretch of the Rocky Mountains, for instance. They can see how permanent all the moments are, and they can look at any moment that interests them. It is just an illusion we have here on Earth that one moment follows another one, like beads on a string, and that once a moment has gone it is gone forever."[70] So time here is nonsequential, composed instead of a presumably infinite number of discrete moments. There are plus sides to this: dead bodies, for example, are only in a poor condition at this particular time, but at other moments are healthy and happy.[71] What the Tralfamadorian perspective inadvertently dissolves, however, is the possibility of change. For the Tralfamadorians, events are fixed like events in a novel. Readers avoid turning to the last pages to preserve the suspense, to discover how events unfold. In narrative fiction, sequence is a convention we willingly play along with. For the Tralfamadorians, sequential time is just such a construct. So the relationship the Tralfamadorians have with time is much like the relationship we have with past events: everything has already happened, is known, and cannot be altered. As far as the Tralfamadorians are concerned, our future is always already someone else's past. Of course, the problem at the foot of this is determinism. (This has always been a vexing problem for theologians seeking to reconcile moral agency with God's omniscience. Either God knows what actions we are going to perform next and, therefore, we have no choice but to perform them and, consequently, no responsibility for them, or else he doesn't know what is going to happen next and is therefore not truly omniscient.) In conversation with one of the Tralfamadorians, Billy notice this apparent incompatibility. "You sound to me as if you don't believe in free will":

> "If I hadn't spent so much time studying Earthlings," said the Tralfamadorian, "I wouldn't have any idea what was meant by 'free will.' I've visited thirty-one inhabited planets in the universe, and I have studied reports of one hundred more. Only on Earth is there any talk of free will."[72]

Vonnegut presents free will as something humans choose to believe in, as something at odds with how the physical universe actually is. The behavior of characters in Billy's world is fixed in the same way that the behavior of people in the past and characters in novels is fixed: everything is already on the page.

As Vonnegut tells it, free will is a condition of there being a present tense toward which events approach and behind which they recede.

6: CENTRALITIES OF LANGUAGE AND MATTER

This sounds as if free will might be just a linguistic construct. In *After Babel*, George Steiner wonders if this could be the case:

> The past-present-future axis is a feature of grammar which runs through our experience of self and being like a palpable backbone. The modulations of inference, of provisionality of conjecture, of hope through which consciousness "maps ahead" of itself, are facts of grammar. Does the past have any existence outside of grammar? . . . No raw data from the past have absolute intrinsic authority. Their meaning is relational to the present, and that meaning is realized linguistically. Memory is articulated as a function of the past tense of the verb.

He goes on to point out that a phrase violating tense structure like "it happened tomorrow" causes a discomforting "nausea of the illogical' which is not the same as the imitation caused by a syntactic impossibility such as 'one men.' "[73] Steiner seems to be implying here (a little too grandly, perhaps) that it is as if we intuitively recognize the plausibility of the Tralfamadorian account of time, but are prevented from experiencing it by the structure of our language that, in turn, is a manifestation of some cognitive limit peculiar to human minds.

Vonnegut's Billy came "unstuck" partly as a coping mechanism, as a way of understanding or coming to terms with the horrors of war. In a fully determined universe, all is as it should be or rather, since, in the absence of alternatives, the normative force of "should" falls redundant, all is as it always has been. At one point, Billy asks how the universe will end, and the Tralfamadorians calmly inform him that they blow it up, accidentally:

> "If you know this," said Billy, "isn't there some way you can prevent it? Can't you keep the pilot from pressing the button?"
> "He has *always* pressed it, and he always *will*. We *always* let him, and always *will* let him. The moment is *structured* that way."[74]

In *Slaughterhouse-Five*'s autobiographical prelude, Vonnegut recalls telling a filmmaker of his intention to write an antiwar novel, to which the filmmaker had replied that he might as well write an antiglacier novel.[75] His point was that wars are inevitable, and the Tralfamadorian perspective is a way of flatly accepting the Dresden fire bombing (which so shocked Vonnegut in reality and Billy in the novel) as something that was always going to happen or, rather, had always happened. Once more, there is a collapse into fatalistic determinism, and it is this same collapse, this abdication of responsibility, that Martin Amis—partly inspired by Vonnegut—explores in *Time's Arrow*.

The novel tells a life story backwards, opening with a man's death and closing with his birth. The central conceit is that Amis writes this in first person. The narrator has never known time to run anything but backwards, and so accepts this as the normal course of things. Much of the narrative is then given over to the confusions this reversal creates. By interfering with the tense structure in this manner, by making the known past someone's future, Amis effectively strips his narrator of control. The narrator is entirely powerless. He becomes a spectator of his own life, a sort of homunculus, passively riding around inside the head of his host, an American doctor called Tod Friendly.[76] The past to which the narrator is inexorably led finds him leaving America (as Tod arrives) and eventually arriving in Auschwitz, where he is (or rather, Tod has been) a Nazi doctor. As with Vonnegut's Tralfamadorian time, Amis's backwards world is perhaps a coping mechanism: a way of understanding what the subtitle of the book describes as "The Nature of the Offence"—as if the scale of the atrocity violates known convention such that it cannot be approached or comprehended directly.

The subtitle is also a reference to "The Memory of the Offence," a chapter of Primo Levi's *The Drowned and the Saved*.[77] (Levi is credited in Amis's author's note.) Tod Friendly's memory of the offense, like the memories Levi examines, is distorted, buried, and inaccessible to the narrator except in guilt dreams, which seem to him prophecies. The emergence of the narrator's consciousness at Tod's death can be seen as a forced reexamination: as if Tod's conscience was so shocked that it traveled the path back again, struggling to understand how everything happened.

Time's Arrow is an exercise in the narrative potential of determinism, inasmuch as it is all about not having any choice. Expanding on the fatalism embedded in the cliché that all roads lead to Rome, for the narrator, working backwards against a causal web of choices, every route leads to the same conclusion. The phrase works on the rationale that the Romans built all the roads, and the logical corollary is simply that following any one road back to its origin will find you in Rome. The Holocaust becomes an analogue of that for the narrator and in the wider sense in which Amis is setting up the Holocaust as an attractor toward which memory is drawn. It is possible to think of historical events as having a metaphorical gravity, and the gravity of the Holocaust is such that all history sufficiently close behind and everything sufficiently far ahead gets drawn in. Just as Levi finds complicity in the deliberate silence of those living near the camps, it is as if the surrounding time becomes complicit, too, implicated in the offense. It is a massive body, a black hole in memory, distorting our interpretation of the past, informing our view of the present. The narrator is drawn back into it, compacted into a child, and eventually reduced to a singularity.

Amis isn't the first to tell a life backwards. There have been short stories by science fiction writers such as Phillip K. Dick and J. G. Ballard where time is run backwards. It threatens to be a silly thing to do, and Salman Rushdie cautions his fellow writers against it in *Shame*: "no, ends must not be permitted to precede beginnings and middles, even if recent scientific experiments have shown us that within certain types of closed system, under intense pressure, time can be persuaded to run backwards, so that effects precede their causes. This is precisely the sort of unhelpful advance of which storytellers must take absolutely no notice whatsoever; that way madness lies!"[78] But of course, for the narrator, effects don't precede causes in *Time's Arrow:* there is still suspense, and the only certainty is the narrator's eventual death (albeit in birth), but that's a given for characters in conventional narrative, too. What Amis does is offer us a grand piece of dramatic irony with the joke on the narrator, who is the only one who doesn't realize what's happening. In terms of sense perception, of course, everything has a certain internal logic: unsupported bodies fall upwards, food is delivered in dustbins. Most things can be made to fit, but the glitch is control—the causal power to influence events, to alter the environment, and of that, the narrator has and can have none. The determinisms here are manifold. There is the determinism of physics, the inversion of what Arthur Eddington had called "time's arrow"; and the set term of our natural lives, that archaic sentence meted out to the condemned. But even here the term of a natural life has the peculiar property of being fixed because, as the narrator realizes, in a life whose end is birth there is no possibility of suicide.

The germ of *Time's Arrow* seems to have been a short story from Amis's 1987 collection *Einstein's Monsters*, "Bujak and the Strong Force: Or God's Dice."[79] Polish Bujak is an ex-strongman, now East End suburbanite with an interest in physics:

> Einsteinian to the end, Bujak was an Oscillationist, claiming that the Big Bang will forever alternate with the Big Crunch, that the universe would expand only until unanimous gravity called it back to start again. At that moment, with the cosmos turning on its hinges, light would begin to travel backward, received by the stars and pouring from our human eyes. If, and I can't believe it, time would also be reversed, as Bujak maintained (will we move backward too? will we have any say in things?), then this moment as I shake hands will be the start of my story, his story, our story, and we will slip downtime of each other's lives, to meet four years from now.[80]

Four years later, Amis publishes *Time's Arrow*. Some of the important features of the later work are being asked about already. The parenthetic asides "(will we move backwards too? will we have any say in things?)" are questions *Time's Arrow* answers at length. It is as if Amis, at the end of this story, is warming to his theme. We can almost sense him running with it, catching on to the import of this idea.

There are also early signs here of Amis experimenting with the wordplay he will refine in *Time's Arrow*; with the ways in which some phrases can be turned over to make sense in both directions. He creates a sort of logical palindrome, as when he realizes "we will have our conversations, too, backing away from the same conclusion."[81] We can see here the emergence of a construction that will become familiar in *Time's Arrow*. Amis is playing with the available figurative sense to be made of "backing away," as in retreating from the conclusion because it is horrifying (in "Bujak," nuclear war; in *Time's Arrow*, the Holocaust) and also logically; backing away from the conclusion through the premises, reverse engineering the initial axiom or postulate from the solution.

To switch the register into chemistry, the idea of the elements of a solution spontaneously separating back into their component parts is a violation of the second law of thermodynamics—a classic demonstration, in fact, and one that the Victorian physicist James Clerk Maxwell used as a thought experiment. In a letter of 1870, Maxwell had said that the second law of thermodynamics "[h]as the same degree of truth as the statement that if you throw a tumblerful of water into the sea you cannot get the same tumblerful out again."[82] Which is to say, it is a statistical law. There is a chance that random motion would reassemble the tumbler of water, but the odds are infinitesimally small. It is not possible to unmix things; like the Tralfamadorian's resignation at the world's end, things done cannot be undone.

Locked into his host, the narrator of *Time's Arrow* says, "It just seems to me that the film is running backwards."[83] The second law of thermodynamics is the law that prohibits the film from running backwards. Interestingly, it's also the law that Snow in his "Two Cultures" lecture suggested was so fundamental to the sciences as to be the equivalent of having read a work of Shakespeare's. There's a sense in which Amis can be seen to be demonstrating his scientific literacy on this point. But the second law is an appealing law for fiction writers, too, inasmuch as it is all about entropy, about the shift from order to chaos, and about how you can't put things back together again. *Time's Arrow* can be seen as meditation on the irreversibility of actions, what Richard Menke calls "the thermodynamics of history."[84] In this respect, Amis's trapped and impotent homuncular narrator is also a metaphor for a sort of historical determinism or, at least, the feeling that we can do nothing to alter the course of events, that we are too insignificant to make a difference. The narrator resigns himself early, "Still, I'm powerless, and can do nothing about anything. I can't make myself an exception."[85] It sounds like the guilty excuses people tell themselves for having not resisted. It sounds like a prompt for the title of another one of Levi's books: *If Not Now, When?* The narrator's fatalism on this point is indicative of a greater determinism: that our own fates might be fixed.

It is important not to miss the point behind the central conceit of *Time's Arrow:* time runs backwards here, but away from what? Frye spoke of how literary study is sometimes criticized for being a backward-looking discipline, but that this is a hollow complaint because, of course, we never do face the future, we face the past, moving backwards into the future.[86] Amis takes this line in *Time's Arrow*, "When we drive, we don't look where we're going. We look where we came from."[87] If the narrator is facing the past, then (on his inverted timeline) it is important to think about what it is in the future that he is backing away from. There is a clue to this in the early stages of the book. The narrator, riding around inside Tod in New York, is suddenly struck by the intricacy and the might of the city and what he calls the "notched pillars of the skyscrapers": "Jesus, how do cities get here? One can just about imagine the monstrous labours of the eventual demolition (centuries away, long after my time), and the eventual creation of the pleasant land—the green, the promised. But I'm awfully glad I wasn't around for the city's arrival. It must have just lurched into life. It must have just lurched into life out of a great trodden stillness of dust and damp."[88] This passage assumes a new prominence in light of "Bujak" and Amis's dominant preoccupations at this time. Here is a description of what Amis sees as the inevitable apocalypse for our world (where time moves forward): nuclear annihilation, the other holocaust of the book, just out of sight of the narrator. As terrible as the slow and careful Holocaust, which Amis is born just after in 1949, is the sudden and catastrophic holocaust that his narrator arrives just before and recedes away from. How sudden destruction seems, or as the narrator in his backwards world sees it, "Destruction—is difficult. Destruction is slow. Creation, as I said, is no trouble at all;" "Creation . . . is easy, is quick."[89] Flipping the narrative back: the holocaust is where we have come from, where we're going to is apocalypse. Amis, oscillationist, shuttles between holocausts. What *Time's Arrow* offers is a way of seeing the history of the second half of the twentieth century as bracketed by holocausts: one actual, documented, and one just out of sight, but (for Amis) as inevitable as the Holocaust *Time's Arrow* moves toward.

Just as *Time's Arrow* ends with Odilo's birth, at the close of "Bujak and the Strong Force," Amis briefly imagines the hulking Bujak turned back into a child, weak again, and without his family, as he is at his life's end. "We cry at both ends of life while the doctor watches"[90] and, "then big Bujak shrinks, becoming the weakest thing there is, helpless, indefensible, naked, weeping." The symmetry of this infirmity prompts Amis to ask, "Will that be easier to bear than the other way around?"[91] Amis seems to see our place in history, like the narrator's place in *Time's Arrow*, as trapped and determined. The fate that awaits us is nuclear holocaust, but if we back away from this conclusion (as he puts it), we end up in the other holocaust. It's Big Bang or Big Crunch. Either way, we are at the mercy of events outside our control, and it is this sense of powerlessness in the face of history that Amis is so despairing about in the introduction to *Einstein's Monsters* when he says that nuclear weapons "distort all life and subvert all freedoms. Somehow, they give us no choice."[92] It is this same sense of powerlessness that he dramatizes so effectively through the inversion of time's arrow.

What Eddington was trying to convey when he talked of time's arrow was that, as regards the operations of the laws of physics, the orientation of time's arrow was irrelevant. That is, the equations of physics are reversible in principle, and the second law is why they are not reversible in practice. Both "Bujak" and *Time's Arrow* ask the same question: if time went the other way, what difference would it make? Because for all the confusion our narrator's inversion engenders, there is a disturbing moral equivalency to the reversal of time's arrow. Tod is first bad, then good,[93] whichever way you play the tape, things even out, and that's another sort of determinism.

In this light, *Time's Arrow* can be seen as an almost cynical interpretation of the radical Laplacean claim that all physical events, including the behavior of persons, are subject to deterministic physical laws, that the future was set at the moment of the universe's conception. "God's Dice," the subtitle of the Bujak story, refers to the absence of chance in the account of the universe promised from a matured science. Against such a universe, free will looks like another anthropocentrism, as it did to Vonnegut's Tralfamadorians. As a complication of the principle that "ought implies can," there is blamelessness in inevitability: the manipulation of time by both Vonnegut and Amis translates this inevitability to effect a voiding of moral responsibility (this being the collapse that Tallis was worried about). If things were always going to happen, then (in the important sense in which there was ever a difference between tenses) they have happened already. Guilt and morality are surplus to a deterministic universe. That this doesn't square with experience is precisely the tension that Vonnegut and Amis are exploiting: a tension between the mechanical, physical universe described by science and the existential, lived-world of guilt and blame.

The scientific perspective—or rather, those different perspectives inspired by or realized by or made possible by science—have the uncanny property of taking the individual perspective (and, as importantly, intentionality) out of the picture. By seeing the threat humanity poses to the environment in geological time scales, Gould was able to minimize it. By seeing the Dresden fire bombings as events that had already happened and would always have happened, Vonnegut (or, at least, Billy Pilgrim) was able to void himself of dread and regret, and by reversing time's arrow, Amis was able to better explore what he described as "the nature of the offence." All three views—Gould's deep time, Vonnegut's flat time, and Amis's backwards time—accept a diminished capacity for action. The question is: Does science offer these perspectives to choose from, or force them upon us? Does it become more "proper" to think in these scales and contexts rather than the scale of individuals and the context of our own lives?

The problem here is choosing the appropriate scale. This is very similar to the central problem of Thomas Nagel's *The View from Nowhere*. "How to combine the perspective of a particular person inside the world with an objective view of that same world, the person and his viewpoint included."[94] Nagel is concerned with reconciling the internal and the external, the subjective and the objective, acknowledging the validity of both and without eliminating or giving epistemological priority to either. To this end, he sets the dilemma against terms similar to those used by the scientists when they talk of the indifference of nature. "From far enough outside my birth seems accidental, my life pointless, and my death insignificant, but from inside my never having been born seems nearly unimaginable, my life monstrously important, and my death catastrophic."[95] It's a relatively straightforward point being made, but one surprisingly easy to miss. There is a disjunction between what the scientists claim in their professional capacity (to maintain Fish's terminology) and how they behave in their everyday lives. It's a safe bet that Dawkins and Weinberg do not think themselves so insignificant that they would not attach considerable value to their own lives or (one would hope) to the lives of fellow humans. This is not meant facetiously, but just to underline how often the point is overlooked that the universal scale is not necessarily the correct scale for thinking about all situations.

When scientists say things like this, they are likely just talking tough, displaying through this sort of bravado their commitment to the mechanistic end of the materialist worldview. (It's what Richard Rorty pointedly calls "all this masochistic talk about hardness and directness"⁹⁶). But it is important not to make the mistake of assuming that because they are correct when they say that the universe is indifferent to us that our interest in the "merely human" is somehow less worthy.

More sensitive to this than some of the brasher voices, Richard Feynman confronted the same issue when talking about hierarchies. Given the variety of vocabularies available, and aware that each stratum captures a different kind of subject matter, Feynman climbs gradually from the physical up to the metaphysical:

> And going on, we come to things like evil, and beauty, and hope . . . Which end is nearer to God; if I may use a religious metaphor. Beauty and hope, or the fundamental laws? I think [. . .] that what we have to look at is the whole structural interconnection of the thing; and that all the sciences, and not just the sciences but all the efforts of intellectual kinds, are an endeavour to see the connections of the hierarchies, [. . .]. And today we cannot, and it is no use making believe that we can, draw carefully a line all the way from one end of this thing to the other, because we have only just begun to see that there is this relative hierarchy.
>
> And I do not think either end is nearer to God.⁹⁷

So Feynman shares Wilson's desire to see consilience, but without Wilson's eliminativism. Feynman is adamant on this, maintaining that "to stand with evil and beauty and hope, or to stand with the fundamental laws, hoping that way to get a deep understanding of the whole world, with that aspect alone, is a mistake."⁹⁸ The view from one level doesn't invalidate other levels so long as it continues to capture something unique; that is, something invisible to the other levels as atoms are invisible to humans and aesthetics are invisible to (or rather, simply do not exist for) chemicals. Feynman's ambivalence on which end is closer to God reflects a more sophisticated conception of the problem of scale, one closer to Nagel's worries. The question being asked is where our (intellectual) commitments should really lie—with the personal (the internal, the subjective, the anthropocentric, the indulgent) or with the universal (the external, the objective, the humble), and how best to think of ourselves in light of the information science offers about our place in the universe.

In *The Information* (1995), Amis takes on the same problem, but as it intersects with and impacts upon the place of the novel against science's ever-widening backdrop. The question of how important we really are assumes a new relevance in these terms. The novel, if you take Ian Watt's line, is primarily concerned with an almost absolute anthropocentrism, that is, the indulgent immersion in the consciousness of not just mankind, but one man. Scientifically literate, Amis exploits the available scales to recast apparently important events as inconsequential and apparently trivial events as having massive consequences: "And just by dropping his head like that Richard was changing his temporal relationship with the quasars by thousands and thousands of years. He really did. Because the quasars are so far away and getting further away so fast. This is to put Richard's difficulties in context. The context of the universe."[99] While an available scale, this is obviously not the appropriate scale: it is a clumsy language for trying to understand human action. Amis is well aware of this, and it becomes a way of mocking his protagonist, Richard Tull.

Tull is an eminently unlikable character. A writer of serious and difficult fiction, he is intensely bitter about the commercial and critical success of fellow writer and old friend, Gywn Barry, whose utopian fable *Amelior* enjoys a level of praise inexplicable to Tull. Much of the novel follows Tull's jealousy through various revenge plots and attempts to come to terms with Gwyn's success by undercutting the critical standards of the establishment. These latter segments involve minimizing Gwyn's success by recasting it in progressively wider contexts. Tull's jealousy centers on what he sees as the parochialism of Gwyn's writing. By seeing Gwyn in the context of his importance to the universe, Tull finds he is able to make him and his novel appear petty and useless.

Recast in the context of the universe, the joke is on Tull: his criticism is too strong. The universal scale is simply too big; it makes *everything* seem unimportant. This was what Gould was trying to poke at when he talked about our inability to wipe out life on earth: deep time is the wrong perspective for assessing our impact on the environment. At the other end of the scale, it is the same point Putnam was making when he argued that the atomic account was a an unworkable and effectively useless way of explaining why square pegs won't pass through round holes. Tull's work, as much as Barry's, ends up appearing parochial and irrelevant. It becomes clear that against the universal scale, it is difficult to find anything that isn't parochial. Amis wonders throughout the book about what all "the information" is leading up to, what conclusions we should draw from recognizing our diminished potency in an indifferent universe, finally deciding, "the information is nothing. Nothing: the answer to so many of our questions. What will happen to me when I die? What *is* death anyway? Is there anything I can do about that? Of what does the universe primarily consist? What is the measure of our influence within it? What is our span, in cosmic time? What will our world eventually become? What mark will we leave—to remember us by?"[100] But then we are forced to recognize that nothing—not love, not tragedy, not war—matters at the cosmological scale. In what has been a recurrent theme throughout this study, we find Amis confronting the problem of how best to situate ourselves. Clearly the universal is the wrong language for trying to capture human behavior. It's too massive, too imprecise.

Imprecision is not always accidental. Dawkins recalls how a fellow zoologist would make the claims that "to a first approximation all species are insects." A little more counterintuitively, Gould recalls a colleague who would open lectures with the line, "To a first approximation, all species are extinct." Steven Pinker makes a similar claim for language, citing Chomsky's argument that "aside from their mutually unintelligible vocabularies," a visiting Martian would to a first approximation conclude that "Earthlings speak a single language."[101] First approximation is sufficient to demonstrate group similarity, but it is often too broad a category to offer useful information. The generalization clips too much detail, as if we were to claim, "To a first approximation, everything is brown" or "To a first approximation, I never go to sleep." Similarly, the universal offers a hopeless binary, becomes either the universe or the everyman (against a solipsistic "me"). As Gould warned, the perspective of the universal results in an oblivion. Man has become ground, and the figure is the whole universe on which he was previously set and against which he is now indistinguishable. Or, to adopt Mazlish's continuity thesis, figure and ground are no longer instructive (or valid) ways to separate man from environment.

With the parochial being something unavoidable, it falls to Amis to select from the available scales one able to offer some sort of comfort from the strange and modern isolation that comes from being absorbed and camouflaged in this manner. The horrible realization for Tull is that this type of comfort is precisely what the homely parochialism of Gwyn Barry's novels offer. "So that's what you'd have to do. That's what you have to do, to make it all new again. You'd have to make the universe *feel smaller*." And this Gwyn achieves by an inversion of Tull's decentering perspective: "Of course, in Gywn's novels, there wasn't much talk of astronomy. There was talk of astrology. And what was astrology? Astrology was the *consecration* of the homocentric universe. Astrology went further than saying that the stars were all about *us*. Astrology said the stars were all about *me*."[102] The return to astrology (and by extension all things New Age) constitutes a flight from the indifference of scientific rationalism. In addition, it allows people to reconcile the universal with the individual: astrology accepts the cosmologist's account of an inconceivably vast universe, but perverts the data to its own ends, these being the elevation of the human. It lifts the individual out of the background, repairing and reinflating the ego after the successive woundings Freud spoke of. It also promises a means of reintroducing the hero to literature (a hero being something quite absent from *The Information*), and Amis/Tull makes reference to Frye's theory that the history of Western literature sees an ever-decreasing heroism in its protagonists.

Frye's theory of modes—one of the conceptual organizing principles he saw behind the history of literature, and the first essay of the *Anatomy*—says that fictions "may be classified, not morally, but by the hero's power of action, which may be greater than ours, less, or roughly the same."[103] He explains that, using this standard, we can sort fictions into a matrix comprising:

1. *Myth*, where the protagonist is "superior in *kind* both to other men and to the environment of other men" (for example, divine beings and gods)
2. *Romance*, where the protagonist is "superior in degree to other men and his environment" (for example, human but heroic folk heroes)
3. *High mimetic*, where the protagonist is "superior in degree to other men but not to his natural environment" (for example, human leaders such as kings)
4. *Low mimetic*, where the protagonist is "superior neither to other men nor to his environment" (one of us)
5. *Ironic*, where the protagonist is "inferior in power or intelligence to ourselves" (for example, a villain or peasant)

Frye notes that it is possible to "see that European fiction, during the last fifteen centuries, has steadily moved its centre of gravity down the list."[104]

What Amis does is to map Frye's theory of modes over the history of scientific decenterings described above, pairing writers with their contemporaries in the sciences, seeing the shift Frye recorded in the history of the decreasing power of protagonists as running parallel to the history of the decreasing power of man in the face of an (epistemologically and, as Hubble would show, literally) expanding universe. Amis's Richard Tull explains his plan for "a big bold book he never wrote called *The History of Increasing Humiliation*": "literature, Richard said, describes a descent. First, gods. Then demigods. Then epic became tragedy: failed kings, failed heroes. Then the gentry. Then the middle class and its mercantile dreams. Then it was about *you* . . . : social realism. Then it was about *them:* lowlife. Villians. The ironic age. And he was saying, Richard was saying: now what? Literature, for a while, can be about us . . . : about writers. But that won't last long. How do we burst clear of all this? And he asked them: whither the novel?"[105] Tull's fear—and, it seems fair to infer, Amis's—is that the importance of the novel seems to find itself bound up with and contingent on the importance of the individual.

After Ian Watt's *The Rise of the Novel*, Amis seems to be speculatively charting its decline. Watt saw that ascent as bound up with a shift in the early eighteenth century toward individualist thinking: "The novel's serious concern with the daily lives of ordinary people seems to depend upon two important general conditions: the society must value every individual highly enough to consider him the proper subject of its serious literature; and there must be enough variety of belief and action among ordinary people for a detailed account of them to be of interest to other ordinary people, the readers of novels."[106] But if the novel is a form tied to documenting the lives of the *ordinary* people, then it starts already low on the list of modes and can only slide down. This is something Amis accepts as inevitable, writing elsewhere (and a year before the publication of *The Information*), "If art has an arrow, then that is the way it points: straight downward, from demigod to demirep."[107] As the universe and what we know of it gets bigger, the importance of the individual (and more generally, mankind's role) diminishes. Amis/Tull even speculates that scientific understanding is not riding benignly behind the ever-decreasing potency of literary protagonists, but actively displacing them. "Supposing that the progress of literature (downwards) was forced in that direction by the progress of cosmology (upwards—up, up). For human beings, the history of cosmology is the history of increasing humiliation."[108] Those same blows to humanity's importance that Freud saw himself capping off are seen now as causal in the simultaneous demotion of the importance of the humanities. It is as if Amis is suggesting that modern science, far from endorsing Frye's tentative system for a science of criticism, has invalidated it. It is as if science has so changed our world as to make redundant the patterns traditionally used to organize literature. In this scientific age, it is as if Frye's "conceptual centre" cannot hold.

Early in the book, Amis interrupts his narrative to directly address us in one of the many short lectures on literary theory (often voiced through Tull, but there are lectures on other subjects, too) offered throughout the novel. "Consider. The four seasons are meant to correspond to the four principal literary genres. [. . .] Close this book for a minute and see if you can work it out: which season corresponds to which genre. It's obvious really. Once you've got comedy and tragedy right, the others follow."[109] Amis again follows Frye's *Anatomy*[110] here, in according summer to romance, autumn to tragedy, winter to satire, and spring to comedy. But then Amis returns these correlations back to the real seasons, as opposed to how the seasons are meant to be, and finds that the mapping doesn't work. "Something had gone wrong with summer"[111] he writes, and this becomes a way of saying: something had gone wrong with romance.

From here, he maps back again, as if these relations were concrete—fixed and interdependent. "We keep waiting for something to go wrong with seasons. But something has already gone wrong with the genres. They have all bled into one another. Decorum is no longer observed."[112] In the gradual dissolution of clear seasonal breaks, Amis sees a corresponding dissolution of the literary genres. It is unclear whether he thinks that the breakdown of literary genres is affecting the seasons, or if the absence of clear seasonal boundaries is affecting our ability to keep separate the genres.

It may be that Amis feels that the system Frye saw as a means of organizing Western literature simply no longer holds and that the seasonal tropes have lost much of their relevance in an increasingly technologized society insulated from the natural rhythms on which it was previously dependent. The industrial revolution, the ease of international trade, the efficiency of agriculture, and climate-controlled interior environments have all contributed to a diminution in our awareness of seasonal change. It might be snowing outside, but the food we eat is the same, and the temperature inside (where we spend most of our time) remains a constant 20°C. It is as if our scientific and technological age demands a new model for organizing our genres; it is as if the seasonal tropes are too geocentric and, like Gywn Barry's novels, too parochial.

Toward the end of the book, Amis reintroduces the seasonal analogy ("It was spring, season of comedy"[113]), then self-consciously wonders if *this* novel will manage to fit the scheme. "But we haven't had much luck with our seasons. Not yet, anyway. We did satire in summer, and comedy in autumn, and romance in winter."[114] It is as if Amis is questioning his own ability as a narrator to remain obedient to the conventions. In doing so, he is alerting us to how artificial those conventions have become.[115] If he thinks the seasonal analogy doesn't work, he can refute it by deliberately not using it or by revising it. To this end, he can be found tentatively suggesting a new model: one drawn not from direct experience, but from the findings of cosmology.

As part of his effort to shift our perspective from the parochial to the universal, or rather, to recognize the implications of effecting such a shift, Amis says it might help if we knew where we are, where we are going, and what we are made of. He then answers these questions in astronomical terms. "Where we are" becomes an address of increasing generality ("This or that street, . . . This or that country, The Earth, The Superior Planets," and so on up to "The Universe"). "Where we are going" is given in terms of orbits and galactic movements ("Astronomically, everything is always getting further away from everything else."). And "what we are made of" is stars "that explode when they die.") Maintaining this dislocation from more familiar ways of thinking of our situation, he goes on to talk of how "we are warmed and hatched and raised by a steady-state H-bomb, our yellow dwarf: a second-generation star on the main sequence."[116] The main sequence is a diagonal cluster on the Hertzsprung-Russell (HR)-diagram, which is a scatter-graph used by astronomers as a method of indexing stars by luminosity and surface temperature. By talking of our sun as if it were just another star (as astronomers do), Amis is again inviting us to acknowledge our normality and the typicality of our part of space. He returns to the subject of yellow dwarves later in the novel, punning fairly crudely on the double-referent. "Where I live there's a yellow dwarf I keep seeing . . . . She is young and yellow and less than four feet tall." His description here is literal, but (bluntly) alerts us to where the lateral move into metaphor will be coming from.[117] So we have the "half-Asian, half-Carribean, pale-eyebrowed, white lashed" dwarf, but Amis wants us to encourage his readers to think of her not as an individual, but as a type. To this end, he shifts from the specific to the general. "The yellow dwarf is not exotic. Yellow dwarves are not exotic."[118] Of course, "yellow dwarves" understood as four-foot-tall Asian-Caribbean people are surely hard to come by, and by this standard, exotic; so it's clear that referent has shifted now. Amis proceeds to shuttle back and forth between star and human, threading analogies between them.[119]

The main point of this seems to be in pursuing the possibilities for grading types of people into types of stars. It is as if Amis is suggesting the HR-diagram of the (Copernican) universe as a substitute for the worn-out (largely Ptolemaic) tropes that Frye had chosen to work with. But such a revision here was perhaps anticipated by Frye, who was well aware that those patterns in literature that mapped so well onto the idealized seasons and heavens of the medieval age fit the real world less closely. Frye's fondness for the neatness of that correspondence is such that he is unwilling to abandon the old system altogether and thinks he may have a means of preserving it. Recognizing that cosmology probably has more in common with poetry than it does with descriptive science, "the thought suggests itself that symmetrical cosmology may be a branch of myth."[120] He explains that "[i]t has long been noticed that the Ptolemaic universe provides a better framework of symbolism, with all the identities, associations, and correspondences that symbolism demands, than the Copernican one does."[121] He even suggests that the ancient version of cosmology was never more than a literary device. "Perhaps it not only provides a better framework of poetic symbols but *is* one, or at any rate becomes one after it loses its validity as science, just as Classical mythology became purely poetic after its oracles had ceased."[122] Inapplicable within the sciences, Frye sees no reason why the Ptolemaic system shouldn't still function as an organizing principle for literature: it is, after all, the intuitively correct account of heavenly motion. He seems almost nostalgic for a time when the Ptolemaic universe held: and why shouldn't he? After all, if he is right, its existence is testament to a society that values the literary over the scientific. That's not the world he finds himself in now (and here we see one of the reasons behind his desire to scientize literature).

Amis's position seems to be that we perhaps can update it, that there may yet be a way to reconcile the anthropocentrism necessary to sustain the humanities with the apparent indifference of a scientific universe. So is Amis trying to rope the Copernican universe into the service of the poets? With the old systems of organization used by Frye rendered invalid, Amis's reworking suggests that it may still be possible to employ the new cosmology as model and metaphor. Exploring these, he contrasts the banality of yellow dwarves with the possibilities:[123] "She is ordinary, in the big picture. Who will ever tell her? She is ordinary. Not like the other stars of the street. Not like the red giant flailing and falling under the overpass, not like the black hole behind the basement window, not like the pulsar on the roundabout in the deserted playground."[124] In thinking of people as stars, Amis is surely also referring back to the literal truth of this, based on his previously having informed us that all matter was produced in stellar explosions, in "stars that explode when they die."[125] So some of the yellow dwarf (person) used to be a yellow dwarf (star): he is drawing attention to the continuities that Mazlish spoke of, of the inseparability of mankind from the universe.

What we have arrived at is the central premise of scientific materialism: all things—animals, planets, stars, brains, and their minds—are made of the same building blocks, the same elementary particles, and can ultimately, in principle, be understood through an understanding of those elementary particles. In tracing a path from the secure anthropocentrism of the ancient world to the vertiginous sense of irrelevance we first feel in the face of Einstein's universe, Amis finds not a dislocation, but an almost complete continuity: materialism unifies all matter.

If Frye wanted to stop with the anthropocentric myth-science of Ptolemaic cosmology, then Amis wants to push all the way forward to Einstein's relativity, because in the Einsteinian universe, the individual again assumes a curious centrality. Einstein's relativity theory says there is no absolute frame of reference, and in this sense, it is the ultimate decentering, but the flip side of there being no center is that everywhere is the center: Einstein's contribution to the decenterings is to dissolve the sense behind the very idea of a center. Relativity puts us back in the middle of the universe, but on the condition that being in the center means nothing, becomes particular to each observer. So the shift Amis is registering in his calibrating the collapse of the hero with the ascent of science ultimately returns to a centrality of the individual, albeit on the egalitarian condition that everyone shares it equally, and the centrality that science returns to us is a curiously washed-out version: we can be just as important as the stars, but only because we are as irrelevant.

Conclusion: Tessellation Patterns

That amis's attempt to understand the information should arrive at this continuity between man and the material world is in some ways expected. The lesson from science—because the information is always scientific information—is that if we are going to take seriously the materialist thesis, then we must be prepared to accept that if it explains stars and atoms (and what they do) then it also explains humanity (and what humans do). Given this, and working with an account that sees the identity of a discipline decided by the subject matter it studies, then at first sight it doesn't make sense to maintain a distinction between what is covered by the humanities and what is covered by the sciences: the former was always a subset of the latter, and any apparent separation was an illusion caused by science's previously lacking a vocabulary for talking about the subject matter of the humanities. Properly considered, everything could be covered by the sciences, and the humanities would be superfluous, vestigial disciplines.

That, of course, was the rationale behind Wilson's drive for unity. It comes as something of a surprise that *Consilience* ends not with a design for how the academy might be restructured so as to facilitate his plan for unified study, but with a polemic on the importance of environmental protection, making dire predictions for the future of humanity if we fail to recognize the fragility of the ecosystem. Reviewing the book, Tzvetan Todorov complained that this final section was tacked on and had nothing to do with the rest of the project.[1] But in one sense, if Wilson is even halfway right in all that has come before, then it has everything to do with the project. *Consilience* is Wilson's account of what he thinks would happen if everyone adopted scientific materialism. That is, the unification of the disciplines is not so much Wilson's aim but what he sees as an inevitable consequence of recognizing the situation (or perhaps, "situatedness") of humans in the natural world. From *Sociobiology* onward, Wilson's argument has always been that man is within nature, not external to it, and certainly not above it. Behind the physics imperialism, his call, finally, is for humility.

This is much the same conclusion that Lévi-Strauss drew from his work with the indigenous civilizations of the South American forests, and what he perceived as their symbiotic relationship[2] to nature, in contrast to Western civilization's destructive parasitism. Lévi-Strauss's particular take on the continuity between man and nature picks up on how the etiquette of table manners in Western civilization reveals a conception of humanity as clean and the natural world as dirty. In marked contrast, the South American Indians, as José Merquior explains, "behave on the assumption that man smears the world: whilst we use cutlery and canned food to protect our meals from infection, they think it is the world that needs protection against our activity."[3] Lévi-Strauss explicitly links this to an increased ecological awareness, concluding that "correct behaviour, is to be found . . . in deference towards the world—good manners consisting precisely in respecting its obligations."[4] He offers us "a lesson in humility which, it is to be hoped, we may still be capable of understanding." "In the present century, when man is actively destroying countless living forms, . . . it has probably never been more necessary to proclaim, as do the myths, that sound humanism does not begin with oneself, but puts the world before self interest: and that no species, not even our own, can take the fact of having been on this earth for one or two million years . . . as an excuse for appropriating the world as if it were a thing and behaving on it with neither decency nor discretion."[5] But although Merquior is clearly sympathetic to the general direction of such an argument—describing Lévi-Strauss's position as "a wise and useful warning against mindless, ruthless forms of economic and technological drives, well in tune with the growing consciousness of our duties toward mother nature"[6]—he suspects that this endorsement of the Indians has as much to do with tacitly condemning the attitudes of the West. Susan Sontag describes Lévi-Strauss's position in *Tristes Tropiques* as a "heroic, diligent, and complex modern pessimism."[7] Merquior says that Lévi-Strauss's position is pessimistic, but not heroic: "I fail to see where lies the heroism of such an outlook. By that I do not mean, of course, that Professor Claude Lévi-Strauss . . . is defective in any moral dimension. All I am saying is that his worldview speaks of detachment and despondency, not of resistance and defiance. Like Schopenhauer, he is not a heroic thinker, but a subtle master of renunciation."[8] The pessimism in question is Lévi-Strauss's attitude toward man's place in nature; the renunciation is of control (hence the comparison with Schopenhauer). The heroism that Sontag detects here is just that willingness to relinquish privilege. Insofar as this secession sees mankind reduced to the level of animals, then it is also pessimistic because—in line with Schopenhauer, Freud, and the evolutionary psychologists—it leaves our sphere of agency (and so our capacity for right action) reduced. What Merquior sees as "the spectacle of a first-rate writer indulging in one of the favourite games of contemporary intellectuals: kick the West, bash modernity, down with progress,"[9] we ought instead to see as an attack on our acceptance of the biological imperative to indefinitely better our conditions, at any price. This is an attack on progress only insofar as progress entails environmental destruction.

Wilson and Lévi-Strauss both argue from a recognition of material continuity between man and nature to a position that advocates a more humble relationship between man and nature. James Rachels made exactly the same move when he demanded a revision of our view of the natural world as a proper response to Darwinism. For Rachels (picking up Richard Ryder's concept of "speciesism"), anthropocentrism is not simply awkward ideological baggage; it is another type of prejudice, analogous to (and as insidious as) sexism and racism. The prohibition on anthropomorphism from the sciences collapses the figure and ground relationship of man superimposed on and qualitatively superior to his environment into a new model that has man inside and part of his environment: a product of natural processes and subject to natural constraints.

What apparently happens, if this line of thought is pursued long enough, is that humans start to seem increasingly awkward. Humans become an aberration; they don't fit in anywhere. Both within and above nature, we are outsiders. The broader sphere of the Darwinian world reintegrates with our person-centred world in such a way as to demand a shake-up of our value system. Out of this come two strands of environmental concern, sometimes called the Shallow and the Deep Ecological movements. The Shallow movement advocates the preservation of environment and the conservation of natural resources with a view to the well-being of present and future generations. In other words, it is a way of saying that the earth and its contents are here for our consumption, but now recognizing that those resources are finite and so, in the interests of human welfare, ought to be used considerately. The concern here is not for the environment, but for the persons for whom the environment is important. To the extent that environmental preservation is an instrumental rather than intrinsic good, it is an anthropocentric view.[10]

The Deep Ecology movement, initiated by Norwegian philosopher Arne Naess in the 1970s,[11] seeks to replace the image of "man-in-environment" with a relational image. Naess calls this "biospherical egalitarianism," a dissolution of the master-slave relationship implied by the Shallow view.[12] Typically, the Deep Ecology movement sees natural diversity as an intrinsic good, rather than an instrumental good for humanity. The Deep movement rejects the idea that "'resource' means resource for humans" in favor of the idea that "'resource' means resource for living beings."[13] The value of the environment is accordingly "independent of the usefulness of the nonhuman world for human purposes."[14]

What is crucial is that these distinctions turn on how important humans are. What this reflects is the decentering project of science being turned on environmental ethics. The disdain displayed by the scientists for anthropocentric accounts (as a move consistent with the historical trajectory of science) is embraced by the environmentalists who find themselves with a convenient rationale to support their long-held intuition that the environment must not be willfully destroyed. They speak of "biocentrism" to draw attention to precisely this contrast. So the block on anthropocentrism is no longer just an efficient means of displaying affinity with the sciences, it is also—as Wilson, Lévi-Strauss, Rachels, and the Deep Ecologists have it—an ethical statement of humility. After scientific materialism, there seems to be a general convergence on this conclusion.

Yet beside the ecologists' talk of being at one with nature comes an awareness of the artificiality of such claims: our self-knowledge makes "blending in" a forced condition. That same, unique level of consciousness, which fed in the first place what Freud called the megalomania of self-love, also made us rational enough to accept the decenterings. Similarly, there is something disingenuous about pretending to be entirely subject to unconscious forces or genetic constraints. It is the same sort of specious argument that sees defendants claiming their crimes were committed because of their genes; which is to say, consciousness of any such underlying determinism also cancels out much of its power to control us.

Doubtless an opportunity has arisen to see literature as a site for exploring this disjunction between the twin legacies of culture and biology, of rationalism and genetics. If science's progressive decenterings seem to be invalidating the traditional appeal to the centrality and importance of human life, this is only as a more general consequence of accepting the materialist view. That such a perspective increases our awareness of the importance of environmental conservation while simultaneously decreasing the importance of literary study points to a new and deeper tension between the two cultures. It is what Amis meant when he wrote of how the progress of cosmology entailed the decline of literature. The importance of human individuality has been seen as a condition of possibility for the novel. By undermining human individuality, the sciences threaten to unbalance the conceptual foundations of literature. From this view, if literary study risks becoming irrelevant in the face of an increasingly omniscient scientific community, it is not directly because of any uncivil, territorial hostility of the type recorded by Snow, but only as an indirect corollary of the decenterings science effects. That is, if literature becomes irrelevant, it is because human life itself doesn't seem so important from the scientific perspective (or rather, the sciences have no rationale to support a claim for the *special* importance of human life). The humanities are, by definition, anthropocentric at a time when this is shorthand for wrong, epistemologically and ethically.[15] Against the spread of physics imperialism, there seems little hope for such defiantly anthropocentric disciplines as literary study. If acceptance into the academy of the future depends on successful tessellation with the sciences, then it seems an obvious candidate for ejection.

By dividing the disciplines according to their respective adherence to forms of anthropocentrism, it is clear that here is that sharp break between the humanities and the sciences. The substance of the two-cultures arguments can be understood in this manner: at the most basic and fundamental level, the arts and (natural) sciences divide over the importance of human beings to the validity of their conclusions. The (natural) sciences do not require the existence of humans for their conclusions to hold; without humanity, the humanities are *prima facie* inconceivable. This apparent independence from humanity is what the scientists mean by objective, and it is precisely what relativists like Rorty want to undercut when they redefine objective to mean consensus-based (what the scientists would probably call inter-subjective).[16] Seen like this, the conflict between science and literary study is a branch of this much wider conflict between those disciplines that revere conscious human achievement and those that revere unconscious natural processes or those disciplines that make a distinction between willed human action and spontaneous or natural processes. So there is room for the sciences to revere human achievement, but as a type of natural process, rather than as the autonomous achievement of a person to whom admiration could be sensibly directed.[17] This broader understanding perhaps explains why the subject of Snow's "Two Cultures" lecture has ballooned to involve so many disciplines in the debate.

Thinking about the two-cultures arguments in terms of anthropocentrism does not, of course, answer all the questions at once, but it does suggest that the rift between the humanities and the sciences is deeper than a simple shift of methodology could repair, and it also helps us to understand what it was that was so unsatisfying about the accounts of fiction that the evolutionary psychologists and cognitive scientists had to offer. In contrast to these universally anti-intentional, mechanistic accounts, literary study offers us the type of explanation that acknowledges the individual author's intention and purpose, and it is in this ability that literary study can hope to maintain its place within the academy.

Literary study without a certain reverence for the conscious achievements of human minds doesn't make sense—something that became problematic for Jakobson's linguistic readings and any similar account that seeks to relegate apparent acts of conscious will to unconscious, mechanical processes. This is also the substance of many of the grievances held against evolutionary psychology: if the behavior can be explained in mechanistic, biological terms, then the intentional account of creativity becomes an adjunct and can be eliminated. Scientific understanding threatens to demystify and mechanize creativity. The objection to the interest of the sciences in artistic production is founded on a fear that creativity will cede to just such a destructive mechanistic understanding. At the very least, assigning a function to art risks making art appear purely functional (a stimulus simulator, or whatever, tricking responses from our nervous system).

Marginalizing the conscious will of the author in favor of a behaviorist-style insistence on the autonomy of the text and (which is really the same thing) emphasizing the importance of the unconscious mind to the creation of literature were critical strategies aimed at escaping charges of parasitism and the most effective way of making the study of literature look more like a scientific business. Emulation here trades on the idea that science is characterized by not asking questions of its object of study directly. This is the difference seen in how a psychiatrist might talk to someone who is thought to be insane and how he might talk to his colleagues: the doctor does not engage with the patient, disinterest means treating the subject as an object (or rather, it means treating everything as an object). Accordingly, the critic who wishes to be more scientific will seek to interpret the text (as object), and ignore the author (as subject). As was seen above, a criticism that doesn't care for what the author is trying to say ends up by missing out on many of the answers. Jakobson's meticulous poetry analyses never did decide if the texts were also good poems, and deliberately never sought to ascertain what they meant. By retaining an approach that recognizes intentionality, literary critics retain a niche in the academy. The problem for tessellation is that the same anthropocentrism that is anathema to the dominant sciences is both desirable and useful to criticism.

This also goes some way to explaining the appeal of relativism to besieged scholars within literary study. Relativism (in the sense that is opposed to objective scientific knowledge) is deeply anthropocentric: everything is centered on the observer, everything filtered through his or her concerns, his or her ideology and observations. In this sense, relativism is a way to get back into the middle of things: it puts the observer, the individual, back in the middle of the universe and legitimizes again the focus on the individual.

Frye's nostalgia for the geocentric universe of medieval times arises precisely because the Ptolemaic universe is so anthropocentric: it provides a cosmology that supports the importance of man, something literary study demands in order to escape from seeming irrelevant. What has replaced that universe is a place where free will is a plurality of determinisms, where man is another animal, a universe indifferent for the main part and positively hostile beyond earth's atmosphere. The "new" Copernican model invalidates not just those archaic structures Frye had hoped might organize literature, but also the very importance of writing stories in the first place. It seems difficult for a writer like Amis to square his belief in a universe obedient to scientific principles with the elevation of man necessary to sustain or justify the writing of a novel. (One wonders if this revised perspective had any bearing on Amis's subsequent book *Koba the Dread* [2002], a factual and sobering account of the horrors of the Stalinist government.) Amis's concerns about the possibility of literary study after the decentrings are echoed here by Alan Sinfield:

> The collapse of Man has made the traditional project of Englit absurd; it has become an edifice built over a void. So the students drift away, for if professional attainment is the only reason for studying literature, why not choose a more useful major—law, for instance? [Today's critics] are sustaining many of the old routines while knowing, really, that their validity has evaporated. That is why, very often, work is admired, not because it is right or useful (it may well be barely comprehensible), but because it is *smart*.[18]

Of course, this is exactly what Rorty thinks literary study should be: his admiration for the "textualists" and his enthusiasm for reading philosophy as if it were fiction is one way to deal with the displacement. Rorty's willingness to elide the boundary between substance and style is a tempting prospect; the linguistic turn is an about-face from scientific materialism and the requirement to do materially useful things.

If science does pose a threat to literary study, it is unlikely to be a methodological threat—nothing so direct as the hostile takeover that the radical reductionist wants to achieve—and it won't be a gradual takeover of the subject matter by disciplines such as evolutionary psychology and cognitive science. But it might conceivably occur as a secondary consequence of the growing acceptance of scientific materialism. It seems possible that the gradual absorption of the consequences of the decenterings might lead to scholars and writers questioning the ethical value of pursuing work in the humanities. But this is not a new worry, and concerns about the disutility of literary study have been active since its inception in the late nineteenth century (see, for example, the first chapter of Alvin Kernan's *The Death of Literature*). Simply put, literary study can retain disciplinary autonomy so long as it does work that the sciences cannot.

The advantages of such an account are clear. It shows interdisciplinary hostilities to be misguided, and it removes the need to either scientize literature or to construct or borrow arguments that attempt to deny the effectiveness of scientific knowledge. The threat of excision from the academy is made more real when literary critics respond by siding with the constructivists and relativists. The denial of scientific knowledge is neither necessary nor is it sensible. As stressed repeatedly, the threat to literary studies from science's interest in literature—be that by evolutionary psychology, cognitive science, or even linguistics—can be neutralized by recognizing that the shared subject matter does not entail a destructive interference so long as the purposes for which that subject matter is employed remain distinct. The threat posed by science is contingent on disciplinary identity being decided by subject matter. It has been a recurrent claim of this study that disciplinary autonomy is ensured not by exclusive access to a unique subject matter, but by the particular approach that discipline takes toward its subject of study.

A second level of threat here was first encountered with reference to Wilson's *Consilience* and is implicit in the claim from the radical reductionists that, as physics is the discipline that studies the fundamental particles, it is therefore the fundamental discipline, and that (ultimately) physics is sufficient to do the work currently done by the various other disciplines, both scientific and nonscientific. It is useful to make an analogy with the limits of linguistics here. To reiterate what was said with reference to the global claims of the linguists: while it is true that linguistics is the subject that studies written material, it is an invalid inference to conclude from this that linguistics is the only tool necessary for the interpretation of all written material (or else linguistic readings of scientific texts would be sufficient). Likewise, it is invalid for the physicists to conclude that theirs is a comprehensive and satisfying account of the behavior of all physical things. Physicists do physics when they look at atoms anywhere, but they do not by extension do all those disciplines whose business also happens to rely on the existence of atoms.

It is not necessary to undermine science in order to champion literary study. The two cultures need not interfere destructively. Thinkers within the humanities can accept what science has to say and still maintain disciplinary autonomy. On some level, that has been the central claim of this work. It is about the impossibility of challenging science without first being a scientist, the futility of trying to do this, and how literary study needn't either become a science or revert to relativism. It is possible to hold with scientific materialism and still believe in the validity of literary study as long as literary study continues to offer answers to questions that the sciences have no access to. Objectifying literary study in emulation of the sciences is intended to insure the discipline against obsolescence. The hoped-for effect is to make literary study appear epistemically defensible. The actual effect is to disable the discipline's ability to answer its own questions. So it is a peculiar injustice that the result of the efforts to scientize the discipline has been to make literary study seem not more relevant, but less.

Notes

Introduction

1. Bas C. van Fraassen, "Empiricism in the Philosophy of Science," *Images of Science: Essays on Realism and Empiricism, with a Reply from Bas C. Van Fraassen*, ed. Paul M. Churchland and Clifford A. Hooker (Chicago: University of Chicago Press, 1985), 245–308; ibid., 258.

2. W. H. Auden, *The Dyer's Hand and Other Essays* (London: Faber, 1963), 81.

3. Richard Dawkins, *River Out of Eden: A Darwinian View of Life* (London: Wiedenfeld, 1995), 31–32.

4. The inception of psycholinguistics, as a subdiscipline straddling psychology and linguistics, is evidence of how the sciences enjoy mutual compatibility and, consequently, is something that attaches scientific validity to *both* parent disciplines. This mutual reinforcement occurs because compatibility is a distinguishing feature of the sciences. The smooth intertheoretic transitions and reductions allowed between chemistry and molecular physics or between biochemistry and biology attest to a shared set of criteria of proof that is usually absent from nonscientific subjects.

5. It is worth noting at this stage that James and Chomsky are the intellectual fathers of many of the ideas discussed in this work: both the evolutionary psychologists John Tooby and Leda Cosmides and their opposite part, the philosopher Richard Rorty, acknowledge a filial debt to James; and Chomsky is the figure who brings linguistics into the domain of the sciences. In his argument for the modularity of mind, it is not an overstatement to say that Chomsky makes possible evolutionary psychology, and he creates the conceptual link that allows the linguist Steven Pinker to legitimately write books about evolutionary psychology and, as he puts it, *How the Mind Works*.

6. Hilary Putnam, "Why Reason Can't Be Naturalized," in *After Philosophy: End or Transformation?*, ed. Kenneth Baynes, James Bohman, and Thomas McCarthy (Cambridge, MA: MIT Press, 1987), 222–44; ibid., 226.

7. Richard P. Feynman, *The Character of Physical Law* (1959; Cambridge, MA: MIT Press, 1990), 13.

8. See, for example, Steven Pinker, *How the Mind Works* (Harmondsworth, UK: Penguin Books, 1998), 522–23.

9. There is no "Popular Lit-crit." There is, of course, popular fiction, but it is criticism and not fiction that is usually taught in the universities. That is to say, popular science is a less scholarly version of science as it is taught in the universities, but there is no popularized equivalent of literary studies as it taught in the universities.

10. For example, N. Katherine Hayle, *The Cosmic Web: Scientific Field Models and Literary Strategies in the Twentieth Century* (Ithaca, NY: Cornell University Press, 1984); Daniel Cordle, *Postmodern Postures: Literature, Science and the Two Cultures Debate* (Aldershot: Ashgate, 1999); and Gillian Beer, *Open Fields: Science in Cultural En-*

counter (Oxford: Clarendon, 1996). All are excellent guides to the field, and though less well known, Cordle's book is especially clear.

11. Don DeLillo, interview by Tom LeClair, in LeClair and Larry McCaffery, eds., *Anything Can Happen: Interviews with Contemporary American Novelists* (Urbana, IL: University of Illinois Press, 1983), 84.

12. We need only think of how emotions are described; of how adjectives for emotion are usually drawn from some physical process or event. An angry man is simmering (or even seething, a word almost entirely used for emotional states now, but originally used to describe a state of boiling, which is another emotion word). It is difficult to think of emotions being used to name something physical, except, of course, the poetic device of pathetic fallacy, which is usually a projection of emotion onto the environment and therefore designed to draw attention to the poet or character's emotion, not serve as a description of his or her environment.

13. Beer, *Open Fields*, 194.

14. What Beer is tacitly doing is assuming that proponents of the sociology of scientific knowledge have been successful in their strategic erosion of the barrier between discovery and justification. These are to some extent internal standards of proof, but that is no reason to see them as invalid.

15. John Limon, *The Place of Fiction in the Time of Science: A Disciplinary History of American Writing* (Cambridge: Cambridge University Press, 1990), 11.

16. e. e. cummings, "Picasso," *Complete Poems*, vol. 1 (n.p.: MacGibbon and Kee, 1968), 195.

17. Michael Frayn, having employed uncertainty as the controlling metaphor for his play about Heisenberg and Bohr, *Copenhagen*, includes an interesting discussion of this confusion in an essay published as the postscript to the revised edition (*Copenhagen*, rev. ed. [London: Meuthen, 2000], 95–132).

18. Cognitive science has inspired, for example, Joseph Tabbi's *Cognitive Fictions* (Minneapolis: University of Minnesota Press, 2002), and Mark Turner's *Reading Minds: The Study of English in the Age of Cognitive Science* (Princeton: Princeton University Press, 1991). It's interesting to note that cognitive science, emerging in the late twentieth century, attracts more critics interested in contemporary fiction; whereas those critics interested in evolutionary theory, which emerged in the nineteenth century, tend to concentrate on nineteenth-century fiction. This correlation occurs because such critics are often involved with trying to demonstrate an awareness of contemporary science in authors and to suggest an active dialogue between science and literature.

19. Aldous Huxley, foreword to *Brave New World Revisited* (London: Chatto and Windus, 1959).

20. Mary Midgely, "Rival Fatalisms: The Hollowness of the Sociobiology Debate," in *Sociobiology Examined*, ed. Ashley Montague (Oxford: Oxford University Press, 1980), 15–38; ibid., 20.

21. David Foster Wallace, "Rhetoric and the Math Melodrama," review of *The Wild Numbers* by Philbert Schogt and *Uncle Petros and Goldbach's Conjecture* by Apostolos Doxiadis, *Science* (22 December 2000): 2263–67; both quotations at page 2266.

1. Scientism

1. C. P. Snow, *The Two Cultures and a Second Look: An Expanded Version of The Two Cultures and the Scientific Revolution* (Cambridge: Cambridge University Press, 1964), 4.

2. Ibid., 11.
3. Ibid., 17.
4. Ibid., 16.
5. Edward O. Wilson, *Consilience: The Unity of Knowledge* (London: Little, Brown, 1998), 297.
6. Ibid.
7. Ibid.
8. Kathleen Lennon, "Reduction, Causality, and Normativity," in Lennon and David Charles, eds., *Reduction, Explanation, and Realism* (Oxford: Clarendon, 1992), 225.
9. Wilson, *Consilience*, 105.
10. Paul Oppenheim and Hilary Putnam, "Unity of Science as a Working Hypothesis," in *Minnesota Studies in the Philosophy of Science*, ed. Herbert Fiegl, Michael Scriven, and Grover Maxwell, vol. 2, *Concepts, Theories, and the Mind-Body Problem* (Minneapolis: University of Minnesota Press, 1958), 3–36; ibid., 3.
11. Erwin Chargaff, "Building the Tower of Babble," *Nature* 248 (1974): 776–79; ibid., 777.
12. Joshua Lederberg, foreword to *Haldane's* Daedalus *Revisited*, ed. and intro. Krishna R. Dronamraju (Oxford: Oxford University Press, 1995), vii–ix; ibid., vii.
13. Oppenheim and Putnam, 9.
14. The bottom end of this list possibly blurs into energy, granting the physicists' their concerns about all matter being interaction, and going by the consequences of $E = mc^2$ (which is to say, you can talk of matter in terms of energy, and that mass is a form of energy). This is apparently discounted by Oppenheim and Putnam, unless they intend to use "elementary particles" to refer to whatever is the elemental base, be that quarks and muons or something even more ephemeral. On a similar theme, it might be argued that talk of "elementary particles" and "fundamental laws" is somewhat question begging (in the philosophers' sense of the term) although, again, this is not applicable if "elementary particles" is being used to refer to whatever turns out to ground matter. At the top end of the scale, we might want to insert "perception" above "social groups," although this is perhaps a metacategory, a category-creating category.
15. Quoted in O. Hanfling, ed., *Essential Readings in Logical Positivism* (Oxford: Blackwell, 1981), 128.
16. Oppenheim and Putnam, 7.
17. Ibid.
18. Wilson, *Consilience*, 7.
19. Ibid., 6.
20. Ibid., 10.
21. Ibid., 9.
22. Lennon and Charles, 2.
23. Identity theory says that for every mental act there exists an identical physical state in the brain, and that identical thoughts will be physically identical, as much as it makes sense to the unexperienced ear to talk of thoughts as having a physical location.
24. Paul M.Churchland, *Matter and Consciousness: A Contemporary Introduction to the Philosophy of Mind*, rev. ed. (Cambridge, MA: MIT Press, 1988), 43
25. For example, in the production of oxides, as seen in rusting iron, green copper, and respiration in living bodies. See Hazel Rossotti, *Fire* (Oxford: Oxford University Press, 1993), 261–65 for the origins and history of the phlogiston hypothesis.
26. The apparent paradox of believing there are no beliefs is remedied by realizing

that the eliminativist doesn't claim to have the replacement framework provided by neuroscience just yet, but that when it arrives, there will be something similar to our notion of "to believe that . . ." (what David Braddon-Mitchell and Frank Jackson term "belief*" in Braddon-Mitchell and Jackson, *Philosophy of Mind and Cognition* [Oxford: Blackwell, 1996], 242) with which he will express his lack of sympathy with folk psychology. Eliminativism is a speculative position in this regard, and some might argue it was premature, a case of killing chickens before they were hatched. A stronger version of eliminativism would want to do away with talk of folk psychology even if accurate, as a case of overdetermination. This would argue that if every mental event was also a physical event then talk of physical events alone would be sufficient and anything surplus to this (namely, talk of propositional attitudes) would be otiose and misleading (insofar as it sustains and encourages a dualism of mind and body). For why this might not be sensible, see the section on smooth reductions and appropriate levels, below.

27. Paul Churchland, *Matter and Consciousness*, 43.

28. Peter Smith, "Modest Reductions and the Unity of Science," in Lennon and Charles, 19–43; ibid., 20.

29. The one-to-one match-up between genes and chromosomal sites is less precise than is commonly assumed. Whilst this does complicate the reduction, it is not a block to its success, because even if the physical locations of a given gene are not adjacent or as coherent as might be hoped, they are still present, just a little more complex than was once thought.

30. Jennifer Hornsby, "Physics, Biology, and Common-sense Psychology," in Lennon and Charles, 155–77; ibid., 155.

31. Richard Rorty, *Philosophy and the Mirror of Nature* (Oxford: Blackwell, 1979): 217.

32. And because they explain inheritance in more comprehensible terms than talk of amino acids and protein synthesis (see section below on interest-relative explanations).

33. This is not to say that the materialist ontology is unproblematic, nor does it claim that merely announcing that all real objects are made of atoms amounts to anything approaching a complete description of the world. The physicist's ontology also includes such nonphysical things as spatial relations, the electromagnetic spectrum (cf. C. L. Hardin, *Color for Philosophers: Unweaving the Rainbow* [Indianpolis, IN: Hackett, 1988], 60), and other factors that affect particle interactions and yet do not obtain at the atomic or subatomic level. As Richard Dawkins has complained, there is more to giving an explanation in terms of physics (or any of the other lower levels of the hierarchy) than simply stating that the world is made of atoms: "'In terms of' covers a multitude of highly sophisticated causal interactions, and mathematical relations of which summation is only the simplest. Reductionism, in the 'sum of the parts' sense is obviously daft, and is nowhere to be found in the writings of real biologists" (R. C. Lewontin, S. Rose, and L. Kamin, "Sociobiology: The Debate Continues," rev. of *Not in our Genes*, *New Scientist* (January 24, 1985): 59–60). The physicist, then, will admit into his ontology something like "pattern" or "organization" where this refers to a mathematically definable/analyzable subject matter whose shape and interrelations are causally efficacious in a specified manner (for example; digital code, such as binary switches in a computer, the three-dimensional structure of a protein or chemical receptor, the outer shell of electrons in a covalent bond, and so on). Problems arise when the physicist tries to reconcile the simple picture of the world being only a heap of atoms in a certain order with a picture that includes causal relations as real properties. Putnam argues that such an account cannot help but be interest-rela-

tive because the account we give of a given event and cause will rarely involve the *total* cause of that event, only one or two factors, and what these factors are will be determined by the types of questions we ask (for example, what causes the car to speed up is the wheels turning faster, more gas in the engine, depression of the accelerator pedal, the driver realizing he is ten minutes late, and so on, each true and each only a part of the total cause). (See Putnam's "Why There Isn't A Ready-Made World," in *Realism and Reason* [Cambridge: Cambridge University Press, 1983], 205–28; ibid., 221–22.)

34. Wilson, *Consilience*, 10.

35. In *Against Method*, Paul Feyerabend uses the Latin phrase *"extra scientiam nullas salus"*—there is no knowledge outside science—as exemplary of the attitude here. See Feyerabend, *Against Method: Outline of an Anarchistic Theory of Knowledge* (London: New Left Books, 1975), 306.

36. Barkow, Tooby, and Cosmides argue that the relation is not one of reduction but of consistency, what they call "conceptual integration." "A conceptually integrated theory is one framed so that it is compatible with data and theory from other relevant fields. Chemists do not propose theories that violate the elementary physics principle of the conservation of energy: Instead, they use the principle to make sound inferences about chemical processes," in Jerome H. Barkow, Leda Cosmides, and John Tooby, eds., *The Adapted Mind: Evolutionary Psychology and the Generation of Culture* (New York: Oxford University Press, 1992), 4.

37. Oppenheim and Putnam, 10.

38. Wilson, *Consilience*, 297.

39. Oppenheim and Putnam, 10.

40. Steven Weinberg, "Can Science Explain Everything? Anything?" *New York Review of Books* (31 May 2001): 47–50; ibid., 48.

41. It feeds into functionalism because these arguments are used to ground his belief that what is important to philosophy of mind should not be the matter of the mind (and the physical location of certain mental processes), but rather, the *functions* those minds perform: because the functions of the mind can theoretically be realized in multiple substrates (e.g., silicon-based) it is misleading (and unnecessary) to focus on the realization that they do have (i.e., carbon-based).

42. Putnam, *Mind, Language and Reality* (Cambridge: Cambridge University Press 1975), 296.

43. Ibid., 296.

44. Putnam, *Realism and Reason*, 213.

45. Ibid., 214.

46. Putnam concedes that you can call such a deduction an explanation, but "it is just a terrible explanation, and why look for terrible explanations when good ones are available?" *Mind, Language and Reality*, 296.

47. Ibid., 297.

48. Outlined in "Why There Isn't A Ready-made World," in Putnam, *Realism and Reason*, 205–28.

49. Ibid., 219.

50. Elliott Sober, *Philosophy of Biology* (Boulder, CO: Westview, 2000), 8. It might also be the case that our understanding of A was flawed, but this need not affect the relations between B and C; so there is an extent to which the proximal accounts are autonomous with respect to more distal causes.

51. Ibid., 8.

52. Midgely, "Rival Fatalisms," 15–38; ibid., 25; ibid.

53. Wilson, *Consilience*, 297.

54. Ibid., 73–77; 82–84; 247–64.
55. Rorty, "Against Unity," *Wilson Quarterly* 22:1 (1998): 28–38. *The Wilson Quarterly*, it should be noted, is named after the street on which its offices are located, and his in turn after President Woodrow Wilson, and not Edward O. Wilson.
56. Ibid., 30.
57. In John Brockman, *The Third Culture* (New York: Simon and Schuster, 1995), 32.
58. Niles Eldredge and Ian Tattersall, *The Myths of Human Evolution* (New York: Columbia University Press, 1982), 13.
59. Rorty, "Kuhn," in *A Companion to the Philosophy of Science*, ed. W. H. Newton-Smith (Oxford: Blackwell, 2000), 203–6; ibid., 204.
60. Dennett speaks of how the different "stances" we take toward objects we encounter affect the type of explanation we give. An intentional explanation is one that tries to "explain a bit of behaviour, an action, or a stretch of inaction, by making it reasonable in light of certain beliefs, intentions, desires ascribed to the agent" (Daniel C. Dennett, *Brainstorms: Philosophical Essays on Mind and Psychology* [Hassocks, Sussex: Harvester, 1979], 236). While this sort of explanation will chiefly be used for explaining the behavior of other people, there are times when the behavior of a complex system other than a human can be most effectively predicted by adopting the intentional stance, that is, by acting as if the system has intentions, beliefs, and desires. Taking the intentional stance does not entail that you really think the system (for example, a chess-playing computer) has intentions, just that its behavior can be most successfully predicted by acting as if it did. (In the case of the chess-playing computer, it should be fairly obvious that taking the intentional stance is far easier than trying to figure out the computer's next move by thinking about the electrical activity in the circuit boards, or even the programming code in which the game is written.)
61. Rorty, "Against Unity," 28.
62. As discussed above, saying that there are different ways to talk about the same thing that do not cover each other's ground—the irreducibility of vocabularies—can seem to be leaning toward property dualism. It makes no sense to talk about the "truth value" of a particular neuronal arrangement, but this does not mean that we need deny that the proposition whose truth value is in question is constituted by anything more than that particular neuronal arrangement. Like Kripke's statue/ball of clay, what is different about the two things are the statements that are true of them. And it is not just that nonscientific accounts are shorthand accounts of the fuller scientific explanation, the issues discussed at higher levels simply have no common ancestor in physical accounts. The reason why a quantum physical explanation of the-square-peg-will-not-pass-through-the-round-hole fails is not just that it is a cumbersome and confusing account, but because that exact atomic arrangement will never recur, whereas it will always be true in rigid bodies that a square one inch will not pass through a circular aperture of diameter one inch, whether the rigid material is wood, plastic, metal, or whatever.
63. Rorty, "Against Unity," 31.
64. Ibid., 38.
65. This has been a long-standing interest of Rorty's; compare the following, from 1979. "The gap between explaining ourselves and justifying ourselves is just as great whether a programming language or a hardware language is used in the explanation" (*Philosophy and the Mirror of Nature*, 249).
66. Rorty, "Against Unity," 34.
67. Ibid.

2. A Science of Criticism

1. Steven Pinker, *The Language Instinct: How the Mind Creates Language* (Harmondsworth, UK: Penguin Books, 1995), ix.
2. This is not to say that Chomsky would necessarily be sympathetic to Wilson' program. He has, to the dissatisfaction of advocates such as Pinker, expressed reserva tions about the explanatory power of exclusively Darwinian evolutionary mechanism (see Pinker, *The Language Instinct*, 11).
3. Noam Chomsky, *Reflections on Language* (New York: Pantheon, 1975), 10.
4. Ibid., 29.
5. Ibid., 11.
6. Ibid.
7. See Raymond Tallis, "Evidence-Based and Evidence-Free Generalizations: Tale of Two Cultures," in David Fuller and Patricia Waugh, *The Arts and Sciences Criticism* (Oxford: Oxford University Press, 1999), 71–93.
8. John M. Ellis, *Literature Lost: Social Agendas and the Corruption of the Humaniti* (New Haven, CT: Yale University Press, 1997), 193.
9. Northrop Frye, *Anatomy of Criticism: Four Essays* (1957; Harmondsworth, UI Penguin Books, 1990).
10. Ibid., 7.
11. Ibid., 8.
12. Frye, "The Archetypes of Literature" (1951), in *Myth and Literature: Contemp rary Theory and Practice*, ed. John B. Vickery (Lincoln, NE: University of Nebras Press, 1966), 87–97; ibid., 88.
13. Frye, *Anatomy of Criticism*, 364. It is perhaps significant that this quotatic forms the very last words of the book.
14. The troubling problem is not establishing that mathematics is internally cohe ent, but trying to understand how it is that numbers seem to also work in descriptio of the physical world. See, for example, Thomas Tymoczko, ed., *New Directions in t Philosophy of Mathematics: An Anthology*, revised and expanded edition (Princeton, N Princeton University Press, 1998); especially Reuben Hersh's essay, "Some Propos for Revising the Philosophy of Mathematics," 9–28.
15. Frye, *Anatomy of Criticism*, 118.
16. Murray H. Abrams, *Doing Things with Texts: Essays in Criticism and Critical Tr ory*, ed. Michael Fischer (New York: Norton, 1989), 230–31.
17. The popular version is a condensation of Einstein's words. The original te reads, "The eternal mystery of the world is its comprehensibility . . . The fact tha is comprehensible is a miracle." From a paper called "*Physik und Realität* [Physics a Reality]," *Journal of the Franklin Institute* 221 (1936): 313–47. See *The Oxford Dictic ary of Quotations*, ed. Elizabeth Knowles (Oxford: Oxford University Press, 1998), qt. 1.
18. Wayne C. Booth, *Now Don't Try to Reason with Me: Essays and Ironies for a Cr ulous Age* (Chicago: University of Chicago Press, 1970), 106.
19. Borges, "Kafka and His Precursors," trans. James E. Irby, in *Labyrinths: Selec Stories and Other Writings*, ed. Donald A. Yates and James E. Irby (Harmondswor UK: Penguin Books, 1970), 234–36.
20. Making explicit the connections, he continues by recognizing that '[a] belief the order of nature, however, is an inference from the intelligibility of the natu sciences" (Frye, *Anatomy of Criticism*, 17).
21. See "The Archetypes of Literature," in Vickery, 87–97.
22. Ibid., 97.

23. Which is to say, we expect to find order. On some level we must believe in the unity or at least the similarity of the minds that individually produce and consume the literature. Without this assumption, it doesn't make sense to expect a pattern to emerge. This is discussed in the closing sections, tying Frye to evolutionary psychology.

24. Frye, *Anatomy of Criticism*, 17; ibid., 118; ibid.
25. Frye, "The Archetypes of Literature," 89.
26. Frye., *Anatomy of Criticism*, 134–35, 140.
27. Ibid., 135.
28. Chomsky's *Syntactic Structures* was published in 1957, the same year as Frye's *Anatomy*.
29. Frye, *Anatomy of Criticism*, 133.
30. Ibid., 133.
31. Ibid., 17.
32. Ibid., 7.
33. Ibid., 6–7.
34. Wayne C. Booth, *The Rhetoric of Fiction*, 2nd ed. (1961; Chicago, IL: University of Chicago Press, 1983), 37; n. 27.
35. Frye, "The Archetypes of Literature," 91; ibid., 90.
36. Georges Polti, *The Thirty-Six Dramatic Situations*, trans. Lucille Ray (1921; Boston, MA: Writer, 1977).
37. Frye, *Anatomy of Criticism*, 71.
38. Polti, 8.
39. Frye, *Anatomy of Criticism*, 7.
40. Polti, 9.
41. Ibid., 119.
42. Ibid., 120.
43. Ibid.
44. Ibid., 121.
45. That said, he does add that the number thirty-six is not to be considered an immutable figure, "There is, I hasten to say, nothing mystic or cabalistic about this particular number; it might perhaps be possible to choose one a trifle higher or lower, but this one I consider the most accurate" (ibid., 9). This confession is somewhat at odds with the general sense of necessity surrounding his other proclamations, particularly as regards the one-to-one correlation he detects between the dramatic situations and the human emotions.
46. Ibid., 9.
47. In terms of universal facial expressions (see Paul Ekman and R. J. Davidson, eds. *The Nature of Emotion* [New York: Oxford University Press, 1994]), universal decorative patterns (see Ellen Dissanyake, *Homo Aestheticus: Where Art Comes From and Why* [Seattle, WA: University of Washington Press, 1995]; Irenäus Eibl-Eibesfeldt, *Human Ethology* [New York: Gruyter, 1989]), even universal responses to certain landscapes (see "Environmental Aesthetics" in Barkow et al., *The Adapted Mind*, 552ff.).
48. Polti, 129.
49. Ibid., 130.
50. Ibid., 126.
51. Ibid., 8.
52. Joseph Carroll, "Wilson's *Consilience* and Literary Study," *Philosophy and Literature* 23.2 (1999): 393–413; ibid., 397.
53. Frye, *Anatomy of Criticism*, 29.
54. Joseph Campbell, "Bios and Mythos: Prolegomena to a Science of Mythology," in Vickery, 15–23; ibid., 15.

55. James George Frazer, *The Golden Bough: A Study in Magic and Religion* (abridged edition), edited and introduction by Robert Fraser (Oxford: Oxford University Press, 1994), 507. Frazer also reports that transubstantiation was "familiar to the Aryans of ancient India long before the spread and even the rise of Christianity" (ibid., 507). In *Unweaving the Rainbow*, Richard Dawkins attempts to explain the recurrence of transubstantiation rites with reference to "an obsession with things representing other things that they slightly resemble" ([Harmondsworth, UK: Penguin Books, 1998], 181), and attributes this to the tendency to draw connections by metaphor. "Skill in wielding metaphors"—as the bestselling author of *The Selfish Gene* and *The Blind Watchmaker* is only too happy to point out—"is one of the hallmarks of scientific genius" (ibid., 185). But, cautions Dawkins, such associations are normally "superficial and meaningless," their authors are too often "drunk on metaphor . . . , which misleads [them] into seeing connections which do not illuminate the truth in any way" (ibid., 186). The innate tendency to connect ideas by metaphor has been explored by Mark Turner in *Reading Minds*.

56. Bastian calls them *Elementargedanke* and *Volkergedanke*; the translation is Campbell's. Bastian's work was published as *Das Beständige in den Menschenrassen und die Spielweite ihrer Veränderlichkeit* (Berlin: Dietrich Reimer, 1868).

57. Campbell, "Bios and Mythos," 15–16.

58. Robert Fraser, introduction to Frazer, *Golden Bough*, xx; ibid., xx; ibid., xl.

59. Sometimes they are called "the Cambridge Anthropologists" or just "the Cambridge Group," despite Murray's being an Oxford scholar.

60. Wendell V. Harris, *Dictionary of Concepts in Literary Criticism and Theory* (New York: Greenwood, 1992), 247.

61. Quoted in Maud Bodkin, *Archetypal Patterns in Poetry: Psychological Studies of Imagination* (1934; Oxford: Oxford University Press, 1974), 1.

62. John Keats, letter to Reynolds (19 February 1818), in *The Complete Poems*, edited by John Barnard, 3rd ed. (Harmondsworth, UK: Penguin Books, 1988), 541; Bodkin, 29.

63. Bodkin, 2.

64. Ibid., 24.

65. In his *Philosophie Zoologique* of 1809, Lamarck claimed that "numerous repetitions of . . . organized activities strengthen, stretch, develop and even create the organs necessary to them. . . . every change that is wrought in an organ through a habit of frequently using it, is subsequently preserved by reproduction. . . . Such a change is thus handed on to all succeeding individuals in the same environment." In William C. Dampier and Margaret Dampier, eds. *Readings in the Literature of Science* (New York: Harper, 1959), 205.

66. The only possible escape route here would seem to be mitochondrial DNA, which are passed exclusively from mother to child, but micochondrial DNA have no effect on phenotypic development.

67. Joseph Carroll, *Evolution and Literary Theory* (Columbia, MI: University of Missouri Press, 1995), 27.

68. Bodkin, 24.

69. Ellis, *Literature Lost*, 193.

70. Ibid., 193–94.

71. Polti, 124.

72. First, nature and science are opposed, and second, analysis and experience or thought and feeling. See e. e. cummings, "since feeling is first," in *Complete Poems*, 290, and for science's "naughty thumb," see "O sweet spontaneous earth" (ibid., 46). The thumb here is likely a reference to Whitman's "Spontaneous Me," where he de-

scribes the penis as the "thumb of love" (line 13) (Whitman, *Complete Poems*, ed. Francis Murphy [Harmondsworth, UK: Penguin Books, 1986], 138). This equation of knowledge with violation, nature's innocence being corrupted by humanity's hunger for rational explanation, stretches back to Genesis and remains a familiar theme, particularly for poets, which Richard Dawkins moves against in *Unweaving the Rainbow*.

73. Dennett, *Consciousness Explained* (Boston, MA: Little, Brown, 1991), 22–23.

74. Stanley Fish, "What Is Stylistics and Why Are They Saying Such Terrible Things About It?" in Seymour Chatman, ed., *Approaches to Poetics* (New York: Columbia University Press, 1973), 109–52; ibid., 109.

75. A. L. Binns, "'Linguistic' Reading: Two Suggestions of the Quality of Literature," in Roger Fowler, ed., *Essays on Style and Language* (London: Routledge, 1966), 118–34; ibid., 118.

76. Ibid., 119. Of course, to a materialist—and especially an eliminativist—finding no soul in dissection would actually be quite compelling evidence that no soul existed to be found. In this respect, his point is perhaps a little misleading. However, substituting "soul" for something less ontologically problematic like "personality" or "capacity to suffer" retains his general point and is less open to argument on these grounds. Unfortunately, this only opens up another problem; namely, is literary quality more like a soul or a capacity to suffer? That is, might it be like pain, both felt and explicable in physical terms (in this case, perhaps nerve fibers, or particular neural structures), or might it be like a soul and open to elimination as an illusory epiphenomenon of causally prior and physically describable structures.

77. In lectures given between 1907 and 1911, Saussure had proposed a shift in linguistic thought from the then-prevalent historical study of language origin and change, to an analytic study, where the focus would be on how language functioned as a system.

78. Tzvetan Todorov, "Structural Analysis of Narrative," *Novel* 3 (Fall 1969): 70–76; ibid., 71.

79. "Linguistics and Poetics," 62–94; "Poetry of Grammar and Grammar of Poetry," in Roman Jakobson, *Language in Literature*, ed. Krystyna Pomorska and Stephen Rudy (Cambridge, MA: Belknap-Harvard University Press, 1987), 121–44.

80. Ibid., 63.

81. Ibid., 198–215, especially "Shakespeare's Verbal Art in 'Th' Expense of Spirit,'"; and, in collaboration with Lévi-Strauss, an analysis of Baudelaire's "Les Chats," ibid., 180–97.

82. Jakobson, *Language in Literature*, 190. "The remarkable rhyme which links the two tercets ["un rêve sans fin" (line 11) and "un sable fin" (line 13)] is the only homonymous rhyme in the whole sonnet and the only one among its masculine rhymes which juxtaposes different parts of speech. There is also a certain syntactic symmetry between the two rhyme words, since both end subordinate clauses, one of which is complete, the other elliptical" (ibid., 192).

83. Ibid., 213.

84. Ibid., 214 (substitution Jakobson's).

85. Ibid., 215.

86. Frye, *Anatomy of Criticism*, 5.

87. Jakobson, *Language in Literature*, 250.

88. There are exceptions here, like the "automatic writing" of the surrealists and beats.

89. Jakobson, *Language in Literature*, 250.

90. Sometimes "Khlebnikov," I have retained the spelling used by Pomorska and Rudy in Language and Literature.

91. Quoted in ibid., 251 and 263.
92. Ibid., 251.
93. Ibid., 250–51.
94. Ibid., 251.
95. Ibid., 253. Jakobson seems almost dismayed by Xlebnikov's inattentiveness, complaining about "the substantial gaps in his observations concerning the quintuple pattern of the discussed tristich," and "even more when in the next sentence of the same essay he deplores the lack of such arrangement in his militant quatrain . . . and thus surprisingly loses sight of its six quintets" (ibid, 253).
96. Frye, *Anatomy of Criticism*, 4.
97. Ibid., 5.
98. Ibid., 6.
99. Ibid., 17.
100. Ibid., 11.
101. Ibid., 12.
102. Ibid., 4.
103. E. D. Hirsch, Jr., *Validity in Interpretation* (New Haven, CT: Yale University Press, 1967), 20
104. Ibid., 21; ibid., 20.
105. Ibid., 22.
106. Dawkins, *Unweaving the Rainbow*, 301.
107. William H. Calvin, "A Stone's Throw and its Launch Window: Timing Precision and its Implications for Language and Hominid Brains," *Journal of Theoretical Biology* 104 (1983): 121–35, especially 124–25. For a summary, Calvin, *How Brains Think: Evolving Intelligence, Then and Now* (London: Weidenfield, 1997), 97.
108. Calvin, "A Stone's Throw and Its Launch Window," 125; and see Dawkins, *Unweaving the Rainbow*, 301.
109. Hirsch, 1.
110. As Hirsch was aware, it also becomes a problem for the critic to maintain that he is fully in control of the meanings of his own language.
111. Jakobson, *Language Literature*, 250.
112. See "Supraconscious Turgenev," in ibid., 262–66. The comment apparently translates as "Radish! Pumpkin! Mare! Turnip! Peasant Woman! Kasha! Kasha!" Jakobson deals with the Russian. It is interesting to note that both in this title, "Supraconscious Turgenev," and others, for example, "Subliminal Verbal Patterning in Poetry" (ibid., 250–61), Jakobson deliberately emphasises the nonconscious dimension to the aspects of writing that he is looking at.
113. Jakobson writes, "Both cola of the trisyllabic formula 'I like/Ike' rhyme with each other, and the second of the two rhyming words is fully included in the first one (echo rhyme), /layk/—/ayk/, a paranomastic image of a feeling which totally envelops its object. Both cola alliterate with each other, and the first of the two alliterating words is included in the second: /ay/—/ayk/, a paranomastic image of the loving subject enveloped by the beloved object. The secondary, poetic function of this campaign slogan reinforces its impressiveness and efficacy" (ibid., 70).
114. Ibid., 250.
115. Jakobson, "Modern Russian Poetry: Velimir Khlebnikov" [excerpts] in *Major Soviet Writers: Essays in Criticism*, trans. and ed. Edward J. Brown (London: Oxford University Press, 1973), 58–82, at 62.
116. Binns, 120–21.
117. This, in effect, is another version of Frye's claim that literature "is, so far as we know, an inexhaustible source of new critical discoveries, and would be even if new

works of literature ceased to be written" (*Anatomy of Criticism*, 17). For this to be the case, the intention of the author (which was limited at the time of writing) must take a backseat to the interpretive faculties of the critic (which have no limits and can be endlessly renewed). This enormously profitable strategy for the continuation of literary criticism is apparently still fashionable. Here is Paul H. Fry (writing in 1999), who concludes that literature is just "that form of discourse which is not exhausted by interpretation" ("Beneath Interpretation: Intention and the Experience of Literature," in Fuller and Waugh, 164–79; ibid., 179).

118. Fish, "What Is Stylistics . . . ," 112.

119. Frye reached the same conclusion. "Shakespeare, we say, was one of a group of English dramatists working around 1600, and also one of the great poets of the world. The first part of this is a statement of fact, the second a value-judgement so generally accepted as to pass for a statement of fact. But it is not a statement of fact. It remains a value-judgement, and not a shred of systematic evidence can ever be attached to it" (*Anatomy of Criticism*, 20).

120. Tzvetan Todorov, *The Poetics of Prose*, trans. Richard Howard (Oxford: Blackwell, 1977), 19.

121. Jakobson, *Language in Literature*, 63.

122. Jonathan Culler, introduction to Todorov, *The Poetics of Prose*, 9–10.

123. James R. Bennett, "Todorov and the Structuralist Science of Poetics," *Phenomenology, Structuralism, Semiology. Bucknell Review*, ed. Harry R. Garvin (Lewisburg, PA: Bucknell University Press, 1976), 127–39; ibid., 134.

124. Todorov, "Structuralism and Literature" in Chatman, 153–68; ibid., 154–55; also quoted in Bennett, 134.

125. Bennett, 135.

126. Ibid., 139.

127. "Modern Russian Poetry" in Jakobson, *Language in Literature*, 59–60.

128. Alvin Kernan, *The Death of Literature* (New Haven: Yale University Press, 1990); Harold Bloom, *The Western Canon: The Books and Schools of the Ages* (London: Papermac-Macmillan, 1995); Ellis, *Literature Lost*.

129. Kernan, 19.

130. This is an appeal to what Stephen Jay Kline calls Kelvin's dictum. "If I can make a mechanical model, then I can understand it; if I cannot make one, I do not understand it," in *Conceptual Foundations for Multidisciplinary Thinking* (Stanford, CA: Stanford University Press, 1996), 313.

131. An example of such work can be found in Edmund Bertschinger, "Simulations of Structure in the Formation of the Universe," *Annual Review of Astrophysics* 36 (1998): 599–654. I am grateful to the cosmologist Claudio Dalla Vecchia for this article.

132. Margaret Boden, *The Creative Mind: Myths and Mechanisms* (London: Cardinal, 1992).

133. Ibid., 170.

134. Ibid., 170.

135. See John Searle, "Is the Brain's Mind a Computer Program?" *Scientific American* 262 (1990): 20–25; and "Minds, Brains, and Programs" in David Rosenthal, ed., *The Nature of Mind* (Oxford: Oxford University Press, 1991), 509–19.

136. Boden, 163.

137. Ibid., 179.

138. Pinker, *The Language Instinct*, ix.

139. This is the difference Dennett underlined between the ways beavers build dams and the way humans do. See *Darwin's Dangerous Idea* (New York: Simon and Schuster, 1995), 372–73.

140. Dennett, *Brainstorms*, 234.

141. Of course, there is probably room to argue here that all the computer would be simulating is the construction of a plot, and appeal to the idea—discussed above with reference to Polti—that plot was always formulaic. This line of argument would work only so long as the computers didn't use innovative poetic language.

142. That said, the popularity of Disney cartoons suggests we also have no trouble imagining talking animals. In *The Illusion of Conscious Will* (Cambridge, MA: Bradford-MIT Press, 2002), neuropsychologist Daniel Wegner cites a classic study by the psychologists Heider and Simmel (conducted in 1944) that suggests we are more than willing to ascribe intentionality to (appropriately) moving images. Using images far more basic than the heavily anthropized mice and ducks of Disney, Heider and Simmel showed volunteers a film of geometric shapes (two triangles, T and t, and circle, c) revolving around a box with an opening, "in such a way that people almost always described T as chasing t and c around a house" (16).

143. Boden, 179.

144. Carroll, *Evolution and Literary Theory*, 31.

145. Pomorska, introduction to Jakobson, *Language in Literature*, 1.

146. David Robey, ed. *Structuralism: An Introduction*. (Oxford: Clarendon, 1973), 2.

147. Ibid., 2.

148. Norris, *Deconstruction and the "Unfinished Project of Modernity"* (London: Athlone, 2000), 162.

149. See, for example, Leonard Jackson, *The Poverty of Structuralism: Literature and Structuralist Theory* (London: Longman, 1991).

150. Wilson, *Consilience*, 169.

3. Evolutionary Psychology

1. Barkow, Cosmides, and Tooby, *The Adapted Mind*, 4.

2. This particular integration, which the authors call the Standard Social Science Model, or SSSM, is the target of their critique. The mutual, reciprocal consistency of sociology and anthropology, according to Barkow, Tooby, and Cosmides, counts for nothing unless there is also consistency with the natural sciences (the internal consistency of which, in turn, counts for nothing unless there is a consistency with physics).

3. Barkow, Tooby, and Cosmides, 4.

4. Ibid., 4.

5. Clifford Geertz, *The Interpretation of Cultures: Selected Essays* (New York: Basic Books, 1973), 37.

6. Wilson, *Consilience*, 139.

7. See Martin E. P. Seligman and Joanne L. Hagar, eds. *Biological Boundaries of Learning* (New York: Appleton-Century-Crofts, 1972).

8. Wilson, *Consilience*, 165.

9. Barkow, Tooby, and Cosmides, 19–136.

10. Ibid., 38.

11. Pinker, *The Language Instinct*, 356.

12. Matt Ridley, *The Red Queen: Sex and the Evolution of Human Nature* (London: Viking, 1993), 3.

13. The official difference between the two approaches is that evolutionary psychology posits a Pleistocene environment as the source of any and all adaptations, and so demands that to understand human behavior in the present, we must first recognize the peculiar concerns of Pleistocene hominids. Evolutionary psychology is specific to

humanity. Sociobiology, on the other hand, is a more general thesis about the social behavior of fauna, and human sociobiology is therefore only a fragment of this larger project. That said, most one-time sociobiologists are now writing as evolutionary psychologists, and so for practical purposes evolutionary psychology represents little more than a rebranding of sociobiology so as to shed the taint of Social Darwinism. For a comprehensive history of this shift, see Ullica Segerstråle's *Defenders of the Truth: The Battle for Science in the Sociobiology Debate and Beyond* (Oxford: Oxford University Press, 2000).

14. Barkow, Tooby, and Cosmides, 5.

15. The other main reason is that such adaptations run into developmental constraints. The existing architecture of the body would get in the way; an adaptation doesn't start form scratch but always has to build on the existing bodyform, and this is linked to the insistence that an adaptation (like a wing) be useful at every stage of its development (the common objection being: "what use is half a wing?").

16. Denis Dutton, "Art and Sexual Selection," *Philosophy and Literature* 24 (2000): 512–21; ibid., 514.

17. Barkow, Tooby, and Cosmides, 5.

18. Notwithstanding the distinction made between sociobiology and evolutionary psychology, "evolutionary psychology" and "evolutionary biology" are being used here interchangeably because the point extends beyond psychology and into physiology. Evolutionary psychologists talk of anatomical monomorphism as a parallel to psychological unity with such regularity that it seems they want to see the brain as another organ to be studied by biology and not by the separate discipline of psychology, which, if "conceptually integrated" properly, would surely be indistinguishable from biology anyway. This underlines how little there is between conceptual integration and elimination.

19. See Margie Profet in Barkow, Tooby, and Cosmides, 327–66.

20. See "Environmental Aesthetics" section of Barkow, Tooby, and Cosmides, 552ff.

21. Underlining the untestability of these postulates, an alternative theory of human evolution has our ancestors beginning to adapt to an aquatic or semiaquatic lifestyle. Presented by Alistair Hardy and popularized by Elaine Morgan, the so-called aquatic ape theory offers highly plausible accounts of bipedalism, vocal ability, subcutaneous fat, the salinity of sweat and tears, and the direction and amount of body hair. The theory has met with much derision from the scientific establishment, although it is unclear if the objections are on ideological or scientific grounds. See Roede, et al., eds, *The Aquatic Ape: Fact or Fiction?* (London: Souvenir, 1991).

22. John Searle is one of the dissenters from this view. He argues that function is a property of intention, that there is no function without there being a designer. That is to say, you can only call something functional if it was designed to do that particular thing. See John Searle, *The Rediscovery of Mind* (Cambridge, MA: MIT Press, 1992).

23. Dennett, *Darwin's Dangerous Idea*, 245.

24. Pinker, *How the Mind Works*, 37.

25. Geertz, *The Interpretation of Cultures*, 18.

26. Daniel Dennett cheerfully corrects Gould and Lewontin on this, pointing out that what they refer to are actually not spandrels at all, but pendentives (*Darwin's Dangerous Idea*, 272). But since "spandrel" is as good as a neologism to non-architects, what it has come to mean in biology is probably much clearer than what it points out in construction.

27. S. J. Gould and R. C. Lewontin, "The Spandrels of San Marco and the Panglossian Paradigm," *Proceedings of the Royal Society of London* B 205 (1979): 581–98; ibid., 581.

28. It is tempting to talk here in terms of effects and side effects. The problem with such talk is that invites us to posit the existence of a designer who intended certain effects, rather than others. This is because, as Katherine Hayles has pointed out ("Consolidating the Canon" in *Science Wars*, ed. Andrew Ross [Durham, NC: Duke University Press, 1996], 226–37), there are no side effects, only effects, and what decides which of those effects are relegated to the status of side effects is the intended purpose of the operation at hand.

29. This is the "panglossian" element to their critique where Dr. Pangloss, Voltaire's Leibniz parody from *Candide*, comes in. The idea is that, like Dr. Pangloss (and, sometimes, Leibniz), the adaptationists tend to think that things are as they are because they were meant to be that way, ruling out accident and failure as happenings contrary to God's grand and mysterious design. Serving as an exemplar of optimization—the idea that everything is as good as it could be—Dr Pangloss remarks that "Things cannot be other than they are . . . Everything is made for the best purpose. Our noses were made to carry spectacles, so we have spectacles" (quoted in Gould and Lewontin, 149).

30. Dennett, *Darwin's Dangerous Idea*, 371.

31. Ibid., 144.

32. Barkow, Tooby, and Cosmides, 29. Social constructivists on these strong terms may well be mythical, as Tooby and Cosmides seem themselves to admit when they claim "all coherent behavioural scientists accept the reality of evolved mechanisms" (ibid., 39).

33. Quoted in ibid., 29.

34. Ibid., 39

35. Eibl-Eibesfeldt, 19.

36. Dennett, *Darwin's Dangerous Idea*, 372–73.

37. Chomsky, 10. Here, again, the analogy is with bodily organs, eliding the difference between psychology and biology.

38. Following Darwin's *The Expression of the Emotions in Man and Animals* (1872; Chicago: Chicago University Press, 1965), Paul Ekman's work on the six basic facial expressions was decisive here (see Ekman and Davidson, *The Nature of Emotion*.

39. Dennett, *Darwin's Dangerous Idea*, 373.

40. Chomsky, 11.

41. It is, of course, possible to invent novel grammatical structures, but they are significantly more difficult to learn and will not be adopted easily. In contrast, it is easy to replace words; but as with the development between generations from pidgin to Creole, infants using a new vocabulary will invariably insert them into familiar structures.

42. Pinker, *The Language Instinct*, 20. He goes on to point out that eating with hands rather than feet is also universal, but "we need not invoke a special hand-to-mouth instinct to explain why."

43. Recall that Chomsky formulated the grammatical principles as "highly restrictive," and Tooby and Cosmides regretfully list M. Konner's *The Tangled Wing: Biological Constraints on the Human Spirit* (New York: Holt, Rinehart, and Wilson, 1982); Seligman's own *Biological Boundaries of Learning;* and R. Gelman's "Structuralist Constraints on Cognitive Development," (*Cognitive Science* 14 (1990): 3–9. See Barkow, Tooby, and Cosmides, 36.

44. Barkow, Tooby, and Cosmides, 32.

45. Paul R. Gross, "The Icarian Impulse," *Wilson Quarterly* 22, no. 1 (1998): 39–49; ibid., 49.

46. See, for example, Raymond Tallis's *Newton's Sleep* (London: MacMillan, 1995).

47. Dennett, *Darwin's Dangerous Idea*, 357.
48. Dissanayake, *What is Art For?* (Seattle, WA: University of Washington Press, 1988), 6
49. That is, not "wise man" but "artistic man." See Dissanayake, *Homo Aestheticus*.
50. Graham Richards, *Human Evolution: An Introduction for the Behavioural Sciences* (London: Routledge, 1987), 309.
51. Alexander Marshack, "Upper Paleolithic Symbol Systems of the Russian Plain: Cognitive and Comparative Analysis," *Current Anthropology* 20, no. 2 (1979): 271–311; ibid., 293–94. See also Marshack, "Explaining the Mind of Ice Age Man," *National Geographic* 147, no. 1 (1975): 62–89. Both articles discussed in Richards, *Human Evolution*, 309.
52. Richard Dawkins, *The Selfish Gene*, 2nd ed. (1976; Oxford: Oxford University Press, 1989), 192.
53. Dawkins, *Unweaving the Rainbow*, 302.
54. Dawkins, *The Selfish Gene*, viii–ix.
55. Dennett, *Darwin's Dangerous Idea*, 347.
56. Ibid., 346.
57. Dawkins, *The Selfish Gene*, 189–201.
58. Ibid., 194.
59. See Dawkins, "Viruses of the Mind" in Bo Dahlbom's *Dennett and His Critics: Demystifying Mind* (Oxford: Blackwell, 1993), 13–27.
60. "Unbelievers": that is, those unwilling to carry the God meme in its active form. Dawkins himself obviously carries a version of the God meme, but it is inert. Dawkins's knowledge of religion is not for evangelical purposes, but fulfills a negative role; his is a knowledge of religion intended to cut against religion. That is, not love your enemy but know your enemy.
61. Dawkins, *The Selfish Gene*, 194–98.
62. Ibid., 192.
63. Dennett, *Darwin's Dangerous Idea*, 344.
64. Dawkins, *The Selfish Gene*, 197.
65. Ibid., 194.
66. Dennett, *Darwin's Dangerous Idea*, 348.
67. Quoted in Manfred Eigen (with Ruthild Winkler-Oswatitsch), *Steps Toward Life: A Perspective on Evolution* (1987; Oxford: Oxford University Press, 1992), 124.
68. Wilson, *Consilience*, 149.
69. David Hull, "Identity and Selection," *Annual Review of Ecology and Systematics* 11 (1990): 311–32; ibid., 300.
70. Dennett, *Darwin's Dangerous Idea*, 356.
71. For example, Patrick Colm Hogan, not a biologist, but writing on evolutionary psychology, talks of "default tendencies" ("Literary Universals," *Poetics Today* 18, no. 2 (1997): 223–46; ibid., 229) in poetry, a phrase that captures well the sense in which an innate behaviour is not dictatorial, but can be unlearned or overridden. Similarly, in *The Language Instinct*, Steven Pinker stresses the difference between constraint and determinism (473–75).
72. Wilson, *Consilience*, 241.
73. The stress on chance is important, given the intended analogy with Darwinian selection.
74. "Real" is in scare-quotes here to stress that although the stimulus is faked, the response is real in the sense that it is chemically identical to the response that would have been produced had the stimulus been real.
75. Susan Sontag, "The Pornographic Imagination," *A Susan Sontag Reader* (Harmondsworth, UK: Penguin Books, 1983), 205–33; ibid., 206.

76. Denis Dutton, "Sociobiology and Art," *Philosophy and Literature* 23 (1999): 451–57; ibid., 452.

77. Carl Gustav Jung, *The Spirit in Man, Art, and Literature*, vol. 15, *Complete Works*, trans. R. F. C. Hull, 2nd ed. (Princeton, NJ: Princeton University Press, 1966), 87–88.

78. Sigmund Freud, "Creative Writers and Day-Dreaming," in *Art and Literature: Jensen's Gravida, Leonardo da Vinci and Other Works* [The Penguin Freud Library, vol. 14.] trans. James Strachey, ed. Albert Dickson (Harmondsworth, UK: Penguin Books, 1990), 131–41; ibid., 137.

79. Freud, "Creative Writers," 138.

80. Ibid., 138.

81. Chomsky, 10.

82. See Denis Dutton, "Sociobiology and Art," in *Philosophy and Literature* 23, no. 2 (1999): 451–57; ibid., 451.

83. Pinker, *The Language Instinct*, 21.

84. Ellis, 193.

85. Dissanayake, *Homo Aestheticus*, 33.

86. Wilson, *Consilience*, 233–64.

87. Like Freud, but owing the idea more directly to Boden, Wilson believes creativity to be a universal human ability, "common to everyone in varying degrees" (ibid., 237) but possessed in incrementally different quantities. "Behind Shakespeare, Leonardo, Mozart, and others in the foremost rank are a vast legion whose realized powers form a descending continuum to those who are merely competent" (ibid., 236).

88. Ibid., 237.

89. Rorty, "Against Unity," 34.

90. Joseph Carroll, "Wilson's *Consilience* and Literary Study," *Philosophy and Literature* 23.2 (1999): 393–413; ibid., 406.

91. Pinker, *How the Mind Works*, 525.

92. Ibid., 524.

93. Ibid., 542.

94. Ibid., 543.

95. Pinker's *How the Mind Works* references: Woody Allen, 542; *Animal House*, 548; Bob Dylan and Lou Reed, 535; Shakespeare, 528; Dryden, 539; Joyce, 541; and Kafka, 541.

96. Joseph Carroll, "Steven Pinker's Cheesecake for the Mind," *Philosophy and Literature* 22, no. 2 (1998): 478–85; ibid., 479.

97. Sontag, "The Pornographic Imagination," 206.

98. Any account, that is, that resists the reduction of literature to scientifically digestible terms.

99. George Levine, *Darwin Among the Novelists: Patterns of Science in Victorian Fiction* (Cambridge, MA: Harvard University Press, 1988), 5.

100. Rorty, "Against Unity," 38.

101. We can assume that by "other disciplines" Carroll means mainly the scientific ones.

102. Carroll, *Evolution and Literary Theory*, 26–27.

103. Ibid., 126.

104. Ibid.

105. Ibid., 468.

106. Ibid., 170.

107. Ibid.

108. E. O. Wilson, *On Human Nature* (Cambridge, MA: Harvard University Press, 1978).
109. Carroll, *Evolution and Literary Theory*, 170.
110. Ibid.

4. THE UNITY OF CULTURE

1. Don DeLillo, interview with Tom LeClair, in LeClair and McCaffery, *Anything Can Happen*, 84.
2. "New Age" itself is an astrological concept, this being the Age of Aquarius.
3. Thomas Kuhn held this to be the key difference between art and science, arguing that, for all their similarities, they display "sharply divergent responses to their discipline's past. . . . Unlike art, science destroys its past." *The Essential Tension* (Chicago: University of Chicago Press, 1977), 345.
4. Andrew Ross, ed. and intro., *Science Wars* (Durham, NC: Duke University Press, 1996), 9.
5. Ibid., 9.
6. Gerald Holton, *Science and Anti-science* (Cambridge, MA: Harvard University Press, 1993), 181.
7. Ross, 9.
8. Holton, 184.
9. Quoted in Ullica Segerstråle,. *Defenders of the Truth: The Battle for Science in the Sociobiology Debate and Beyond* (Oxford: Oxford University Press, 2000), 223.
10. Richard J.Herrnstein and Charles Murray, *The Bell Curve: Intelligence and Class Structure in American Life* (New York: Free Press-Simon, 1994).
11. Steiner is referenced in an anonymous editorial regarding the scope of scientific research and the moral responsibility of scientists, "Truth At Any Price?", *Nature* 271 (2 February 1978): 391: "Some of the truths that turn up or might be capable of turning up could be in conflict with the ideals of social justice or even survival."
12. Bernard B. Davis, "The Moralistic Fallacy," *Nature* 272 (1978): 390.
13. Ibid., 390.
14. Ibid., 390.
15. N. Katherine Hayles, "Consolidating the Canon," in Ross, ed., *Science Wars*, 226–37; ibid., 228.
16. Donna Haraway, *Primate Visions* (New York: Routledge, 1989).
17. Carpenter could, of course, reply that realistic budgetary constraints only permit the exploration of a finite number of experimental approaches, and it seems unlikely that he would protest if other researchers were to carry out similar experiments, now removing only females, now only infants, and so forth. Rather, we might expect Carpenter to welcome such research as only building upon his findings—an augmentation, not a contradiction. Indeed, he appears to do just this, admitting that while, "In almost all natural groupings which have been carefully studied, the male or males play the most prominent role in controlling the group. . . . This does not preclude the fact that, among the females, as among males, there is also a dominance gradient" and that "some of the most dominant females are more dominant than some of the least dominant males" (Carpenter, 361). He concludes by arguing that the dominance gradients of both sexes "affect social controls in the group" (ibid., 361). See C. R. Carpenter, ed., *Naturalistic Behaviour of Nonhuman Primates* (University Park, PA: Pennsylvania University Press, 1964).
18. It seems Carpenter wants to link the behavior of the rhesus macaques to hu-

mans explicitly. "The kinship of non-human primates to man makes it reasonable to assume that the study of these types may yield data which can be readily employed in understanding basic kinds of human motivations" (Carpenter, 358). Note that the linkage moves from physiological similarity to behavioral similarity.

19. For example, Jean-Marie Vidal, Michel Vancassel, and René Quris in "Introducing Anthropomorphism, Discontinuities and Anecdotes to Question Them," *Behavioural Processes* 35 (1995): 299–309) claim the block "follows from the [adoption of] overly limited Popperian scientific standards" that are unrealistically severe, imposing "a restriction that most scientists transgress at some time or other in their research" (ibid., 307). The approach may in fact be beneficial. "The effort required to repress our anthropomorphic thoughts is probably futile. It is undoubtedly more interesting to exploit their heuristic value by elaborating tools to sort between alternative hypotheses" (ibid., 307). The position here is the same as that described by Daniel Dennett when he talks of taking the "intentional stance" toward subject matter whose behavior can be fruitfully understood in terms of intentions, beliefs, and desires. The adoption of the intentional stance does not demand that we believe that the subject matter actually has conscious intentions, but simply involves a recognition that the subject matter is best understood and its behavior best predicted by acting as if it did.

20. Anthony O'Hear, *Beyond Evolution: Human Nature and the Limits of Evolutionary Explanation* (Oxford: Clarendon, 1997), 90; ibid., 91.

21. Hayles, "Consolidating the Canon," 288.

22. Werner Heisenberg, *Physics and Beyond* (New York: Allen, 1971), 63.

23. Patricia Smith Churchland, *Neurophilosophy: Toward a Unified Science of the Mind Brain* (Cambridge, MA: Bradford-MIT Press, 1986), 405.

24. It would be pointless asking a nonscientist (and even a nonspecialist) to look down a microscope and either affirm or deny that any mitochondria present are abnormal. Not only would the untrained eye fail to identify in the mess which patches of darkness were the mitochondria, but recognition of abnormality requires a familiarity with normality that could only be acquired through considerable experience. You normally have to know what you are looking for. This ability to sort through data, to decode and classify the enormous deluge of information our senses present to us is largely taken for granted, but not qualitatively different from what practicing scientists do.

25. Kekulé in Laura Otis, ed., *Literature and Science in the Nineteenth Century: An Anthology* (Oxford: Oxford University Press, 2002), 431–33.

26. Hayles, "Consolidating the Canon," 229.

27. Ibid., 231.

28. Ibid., 233.

29. "All things are made of atoms" was the one piece of information Richard Feynman said he would preserve if the rest of scientific knowledge was to be cataclysmically lost. He believed it was possible to extrapolate an enormous amount of science from this insight. James Gleick, *Genius: Richard Feynman and Modern Physics* (London: Abacus, 1995), 358. "Water boils at 100°C" is probably a bad example, because the centigrade scale is calibrated by the boiling point of water, thus making the statement "Water boils at 100°C" necessarily true. It is not easy to see how these statements might be differentiated from more complex science, apart from in their familiarity. The differences, then, are only incremental, of complexity but not of type, and as science slides away from common sense, skepticism sets in.

30. Feyerabend, *Against Method*.

31. Ibid, 309.

32. Ibid., 301–2.

33. That "everyone concerned" would probably vote Copernicanism back in, so to speak, isn't really a threat for Feyerabend. He once quipped "argument is not confession" and is no doubt Copernican himself, and the point of the ballot is not so much to usurp scientific norms, but to give a broader range of people decision-making powers, to let them feel that the truth is their own, and to take the secrecy out of science. That said, the "secrecy" is really not a result of deliberate obscurantism, but one of science's incidental complexity—a complexity that would doubtless have to mastered for the vote to be legitimate. So perhaps the ballot is a backhanded way of spreading the scientific gospel after all.

34. Feyerabend, *Against Method*, 78.

35. Ibid., 302.

36. Ibid., 300.

37. Feyerabend writes "Scientists have *ideas*. And they have special *methods* for improving ideas. The theories of science have passed the test of method. They give a better account of the world than the ideas which have not passed the test. The fairy-tale explains why modern society treats science in a special way, and why it grants it privileges not enjoyed by other institutions" (ibid., 300).

38. Ibid., 302.

39. Ibid., 28.

40. Ibid., 75.

41. If he is correct in his belief that there is a fallacy of method, then the proposal of "anything goes" is really not that radical because this would be the non-method already in use. That is, he argues only for an acceptance of "anything goes" and not its implementation. Anything *already* goes, and always has.

42. Feyerabend, *Against Method*, 296.

43. These examples throw up further issues; although the discovery itself was perhaps just "lucky," the presence of the background knowledge to recognize or develop that discovery was not. As a disgruntled Louis Pasteur supposedly remarked, "Where observation is concerned, chance favours the prepared mind."

44. There is a work that attempts to recreate this book, entitled *For and Against Method: including Lakatos's lectures on scientific method and the Lakatos-Feyerabend correspondence*, ed. and intro Matteo Motterlini (Chicago: University of Chicago Press, 1999).

45. Feyerabend, *Against Method*, 7.

46. Ibid.,147–49, 166–68.

47. Ibid., 167.

48. Ibid., 308. He doesn't perhaps hold a belief in myths, nor does he hold such beliefs against those who do, and his comment about the particular superstition of science is no insult because he likes superstitions. He is very tolerant of everything but dogma.

49. Ibid., 305.

50. Ibid., 301, 300.

51. George Levine, "What Is Science Studies For, and Who Cares?" in Ross, ed., *Science Wars*, 123–38; ibid., 136.

52. One of the features that characterizes science is the high degree of consensus between practitioners, and the purported objectivity of science is not incidental to this. Objectivity is tied up with consensus in something like a causal role, usually understood as being something like "the higher the degree of objectivity, the more likely consensus will be achieved." Pragmatism in the tradition of John Dewey and William James, however, inverts this relation, and makes the claim that what we call objectivity only ever consists in a recognition of a higher level of consensus. Richard Rorty sees

objectivity as not the cause of consensus, but an accolade we tag onto any disciplines where this sort of consensus is achieved. The obvious objection here is that if it isn't objective and checkable correspondence with something like how the world really is, then what else impels consensus in the sciences?

53. Stanley Fish, *Professional Correctness: Literary Studies and Political Change* (Oxford: Clarendon, 1995), 83.

54. Rorty is often described as either a "relativist" or a "postmodernist," or both terms in combination. But like many relativists and postmodernists, Rorty denies that he is either. "I think that 'relativism' and 'postmodernism' are words which never had any clear sense, and that both should be dropped from our philosophical vocabulary." *Philosophy and Social Hope* (Harmondsworth, UK: Penguin Books, 1999), xiv. He is, he insists, a pragmatist, in the tradition of William James and John Dewey, who was also called a relativist, but "of course, we pragmatists," he claims, "never call *ourselves* relativists" (ibid., xvii). Rorty says he would rather define himself negatively, in opposition to the things he doesn't agree with, so he is an "anti-Platonist," an "anti-foundationalist," an "anti-metaphysician" (and elsewhere, "anti-representational"). To allow himself to be called a relativist is, he says, to accede to a vocabulary that already implicitly acknowledges the existence of the type of found-made or absolute-relative distinctions he is trying to remove, and to accept this to have no place to argue from. "We cannot allow ourselves to be called 'relativists', since that description begs the central question. That central question is about the utility of the vocabulary which we inherited from Plato and Aristotle" (ibid., xviii). And again, "We pragmatists shrug off charges that we are 'relativists' or 'irrationalists' by saying that these charges presuppose precisely the distinctions we reject" (ibid., xix). If he accepts he is a relativist, then there is no room left to argue that the apparently objective discoveries of science are not found but made, because then the way is open for his opponents to ask what he calls the "awkward question, viz., Have we *discovered* the surprising fact that what was thought to be objective is actually subjective, or have we *invented* it?" (ibid., xviii). So for Rorty's project to even get off the ground, it is imperative that he denies from the start the validity of such labels and the distinctions they imply. However, for the purposes of explaining his views, and those of his critics, the "relativist" label is here retained, because it describes clearly what he is to those who are not.

55. Rorty, "Against Unity," 38.

56. Rorty, *Philosophy and Social Hope*, 188.

57. Ibid., 188.

58. Rorty, *Consequences of Pragmatism: Essays: 1972–1980* (Brighton: Harvester, 1982), 142.

59. Rorty, *Philosophy and Social Hope*, 186.

60. Fish, *Professional Correctness*, 72.

61. Obviously, zoology is reducible to physics if you trace backwards through biology to biochemistry to chemistry to physics and is in this respect mathematically formalizable. However, talk of zoology in terms of biochemistry or physics obscures the salient features that zoology studies; in other words, talking about zoology in terms of biochemistry is not talking about zoology qua zoology because, at the biochemical level, the animals don't exist anymore than colors exist at the atomic level.

62. Physicist Steven Weinberg is keen to point out that although "quantum mechanics can seem rather eerie if described in ordinary language," this is no reason to draw the invalid conclusion (as Andrew Ross does) that science "can no longer account for matter at the quantum level" (quoted in Weinberg, "Sokal's Hoax," 12; from Ross, *Strange Weather: Culture, Science, and Technology in the Age of Limits* [New York: Verso, 1991], 42). Physicists can, Weinberg assures us, "obtain a complete

quantitative description of atoms using what is called the 'wave function' of the atom" ("Sokal's Hoax," 12). That said, Rorty's point holds here inasmuch as what is at issue is not whether the physicists can understand quantum mechanics, but whether there is any simple way to explain it to a nonprofessional audience. Apparently there is not.

63. Van Fraassen, "Empiricism in the Philosophy of Science," 245–308; ibid., 258.
64. Rorty, *Philosophy and the Mirror of Nature*, 217.
65. Rorty, *Philosophy and Social Hope*, 186.
66. Richard Rorty, *Objectivity, Relativism, and Truth* (Cambridge: Cambridge University Press, 1991), 38.
67. Rorty, *Philosophy and the Mirror of Nature*, 335.
68. His thinking here is informed by William James, who said "*ideas (which are themselves but parts of our experience) become true just in so far as they help us to get into satisfactory relation with other parts of our experience.*" James, *Pragmatism: A New Name for Some Old Ways of Thinking* (1907; London: Longmans, 1910), 58. Also see John Dewey, who said "[r]ationality . . . is the attainment of working harmony among diverse desires." Dewey, *Human Nature and Conduct: an Introduction to Social Psychology* (London: Allen, 1922), 196. Both quotes appear in Rorty, *Consequences of Pragmatism*, 205. Although Rorty describes himself as a pragmatist to align himself with both James and Dewey, his position is informed as much by the post-Wittgenstein "linguistic turn" in philosophy, and to stress this difference, he is often referred to as a "neopragmatist."
69. Rorty, *Philosophy and Social Hope*, xxvi.
70. When we say "given" in this sense, what we mean is that "this is how a phenomena will appear before we have begun layering theory onto it," as opposed to "made," which is usually used to describe constructed interpretations (such as, "parking in that zone was wrong" or "the Germany-France border"). This is, of course, what Rorty says, too, but he wants to stress that the given is as much a human perspective as the made. In the sense that we don't choose the given but do choose the made (or, at least, our culture chooses the made), there does seem to be a difference: they are both necessarily human perspectives, but one is a universal human perspective, true for all humans (perhaps "the sky is blue"), and one is culturally limited.
71. Rorty sensibly adds that you'd need to be a language-using amoeba for his point to hold.
72. Rorty, *Philosophy and Social Hope*, xxvi.
73. What Eddington called "Table No. 1" and "Table No. 2" (in Arthur S. Eddington, *The Nature of the Physical World* [1928; Cambridge: Cambridge University Press, 1944], xi–xix). When Eddington says "there are duplicates of every object about me—two tables, two chairs, two pens" (ibid., xi) it should be clear that he doesn't mean there are *actually* two tables, just that there are two ways of describing the one table; geometrically and atomically, a macro- and a microstructure. Eddington also goes on to add, "The external world of physics has thus become a world of shadows. In removing our illusions we have removed the substance, for indeed we have seen that substance is one of the greatest of our illusions. . . . Perhaps, indeed, reality is a child which cannot survive without its nurse illusion. But if so, that is of little concern to the scientist, who has good and sufficient reasons for pursuing his investigations in the world of shadows and is content to leave to the philosopher the determination of its exact status in regard to reality" (ibid., xvi). Rorty is only too happy to play the philosopher, but it seems probable that Eddington would not have approved of his conclusions about where this all leaves "reality."
74. Putnam himself is not so clear on this. The upshot of his famous "Twin Earth" thought experiment supports an essentialist position that argues for the denotation of

a word being guaranteed by causally basic (usually atomic) structures. Twater (Twin-Earth's water analogue) is not water because twater is XYZ and not H_2O. These functional analogues are nonetheless different things; when a Twin Earthian says "water is wet" it does not mean the same thing as this same utterance on Earth by virtue of a nonidentity at the chemical (and so, causal) level. See "Meaning and Reference" in A. P. Martinich, ed., *The Philosophy of Language*, 3rd ed. (New York: Oxford University Press, 1996), 284–91, and "The Meaning of 'Meaning'" in Putnam, *Mind, Language and Reality*, 215–71; especially 223–27.

75. Rorty, *Philosophy and Social Hope*, xxvi.

76. Jerry A. Fodor, *Psychosemantics: The Problem of Meaning in the Philosophy of Mind* (Cambridge, MA: Bradford-MIT Press, 1987), 44. This is not to imply that Fodor would wholly agree with Rorty. Fodor maintains a link between these layers of scale. The way Rorty tells it, as far as we can ever know, the different vocabularies do describe different worlds. The way Fodor tells it, these are different ways of describing the same world, and we use a different language to talk about micro- and macrostructure because the relationships at the macro level simply do not obtain at a micro level but supervene on the micro level.

77. This point, if it isn't clear, applies at every level, right down to atoms themselves. The lessons of quantum physics and subatomic physics seem to be teaching us that even atoms are not quite as basic (which is to say, not quite as atomic) as Democritus had hoped, but also subject to change, and that on some level, it is all just matter and energy in flux. Physicist Richard Feynman mimics the haiku to claim that you cannot reduce one to the other, "You can't say A is made of B/or vice versa. / All mass is interaction" (in Gleick, *Genius*, 5).

78. Rorty, "Against Unity," 31.

79. Ayer's letter comes in response to an article Rorty had published in the *London Review of Books* entitled "The Contingency of Language," *LRB*, 17 April 1986, 3–6 ibid., 4, revised and reprinted in *Contingency, Irony, and Solidarity* (Cambridge: Cambridge University Press, 1989), 3–22.

80. Rorty, *Philosophy and Social Hope*, 151. This is, of course, really quite evasive. All that's really being said is, "It works doesn't it? What more do you want?" What we want to know (as scientists), is "What are the mechanisms under the surface that make this theory able to successfully predict phenomena?" The assumption is, that these mechanisms will be universally applicable.

81. Atomic or geometric, these are both valid descriptions, none more true than the other, but, are *all* descriptions valid? Presumably not, insofar as some will be useless and misleading. The intuition here is to mentally add "some accounts will be closer to how it really is." When we ask, "do all descriptions (that is, *any* description) work?" what we are thinking is something like "do all these accounts describe how *really* is?" Because, to go back to the square peg/round hole, you can say "it's the atoms, here, now" (atomic) or you can say, "it's that the area of the aperture in the board is smaller than the area of the face of the peg" (geometric), and both are true but only one is useful. What if, however, you tried to say, "it's because the peg is blue and the board is red" or "it's because squares and circles are enemies." Would these descriptions be valid? How would you tell? What if you said something like "that typical of triangles and hexagons," would this be an inaccurate description? How, indeed, can objects (any objects) be picked out? Once again, we seem to be close saying, "well, one would be true to (something like) how it really was and one wouldn't." Because it seems for each purpose, there is only one description that works properly. If the purpose is explaining to me why the peg won't go through the hole the geometric argument, and maybe something about the solidity of the materials i

volved, is going to work best. The other explanations—color, speculation about antagonism between different shapes, false descriptions of the shapes (assuming we can talk of false descriptions when we can't talk of true ones), and so on—are irrelevant and even misleading. One assumes Rorty would probably agree that only one description really works, but he would stress that it worked only in light of the certain purpose I had in mind (explaining "why doesn't the peg pass through the hole?").

82. Rorty, *Philosophy and Social Hope*, xxv.
83. Feyerabend, *Against Method*, 100; ibid., 298–309.
84. Rorty, *Objectivity, Relativism, and Truth*, 89.
85. Ibid., 81.
86. See, for example, "tools in a toolbox" (Rorty, *Philosophy and Social Hope*, 186); see "the plumber-carpenter or the carpenter-electrician distinction" (Rorty, "Against Unity," 30); see "Is the carpenter's or the particle physicist's account of tables the true one?" (Rorty, *Philosophy and Social Hope*, 153). This is doubtless also a vestige of the original rhetoric of pragmatism, where thinkers like John Dewey used similar juxtapositions to stress the importance of practical familiarity for all sorts of knowing. "The scientific man and the philosopher like the carpenter, the physician and politician know with their habits not with their 'consciousness.' The latter is eventual, not a source" (Dewey, *Human Nature*, 182–83).
87. "Texts and Lumps" in Rorty, *Objectivity, Relativism, and Truth*, 83.
88. Dawkins, *Unweaving the Rainbow*, 125–26.
89. Rorty, *Philosophy and Social Hope*, xxiv.
90. Ibid., 268.
91. Ibid., 146.
92. Davis, "The Moralistic Fallacy," 390.
93. Ibid., 390.
94. Rorty, *Philosophy and Social Hope*, 149.
95. Fish, *Professional Correctness*, 85.
96. Rorty, *Philosophy and the Mirror of Nature*, 61, 373, 377, 372.
97. Rorty, *Philosophy and Social Hope*, xx–xxi.
98. Rorty, *Contingency, Irony, and Solidarity*, 133.
99. Rorty, *Consequences of Pragmatism*, 96. Rorty does think that Derrida also has a "very serious" side. "He is serious about the need to change ourselves, serious about what he calls 'deconstruction.'" (ibid., 98), and Rorty likes this "shadowy, deconstructive, good side," which he opposes to the "luminous, constructive, bad side" (ibid., 99). It is also worth noting that what Rorty means when he talks about Derrida's lack of seriousness is "simply this refusal to take the standard rules seriously, conjoined with the refusal to give a clear answer to the question, 'Is it the old game played differently, or rather a new game?'" (ibid., 98). When Rorty speaks of games, it is usually in the Wittgensteinian sense of language games, of participating in social procedures with certain rules, or even John Von Neumann's sense of "game theory," the logic of competition, but there is also a sense in which he is capitalizing on the ambiguity here and probably intends to also suggest the levity of a game. If he believes his own claims, then Rorty is intent on rejecting the terms and conditions of the rationale of his opponents, so it follows that he probably does not take their criticisms very seriously.
100. Ayer, *Contingency, Irony, and Solidarity*, 133.
101. Ibid.
102. Bernard Williams, "Auto-da-Fé: Consequences of Pragmatism," in Alan Malachowski, ed., *Reading Rorty: Critical Responses to Philosophy and the Mirror of Nature (and Beyond)* (Oxford: Blackwell, 1990), 26–37; ibid., 32.

103. In Steven G. Kellman and Irving Malin, eds., *Into "The Tunnel": Readings of Gass's Novel* (Newark: University of Delaware Press, 1998), 132. It's unclear how seriously Malin wants to be taken. It is tempting to interpret his style as parodic, but if so, the joke is on the language, Malin's point presumably being that there is a greater layer of linguistic slippage and depth than we commonly realize.

104. Rorty, *Contingency, Irony, and Solidarity*, 133.

105. Ibid., *Consequences of Pragmatism*, 151–52. It follows, of course, that if the author could not have "found" these meanings in his or her text, he or she certainly could not have consciously intended them to be read in this way.

106. Harold Bloom, *The Anxiety of Influence: A Theory of Poetry* (Oxford: Oxford University Press, 1973), 94—95.

107. Rorty, *Consequences of Pragmatism*, 151, 152, 140, 155.

108. Ibid., *Philosophy and Social Hope*, 186.

109. Bloom writes, "I have very little confidence that literary education will survive its current malaise." See *The Western Canon: The Books and Schools of the Ages* (1994; London: Papermac-Macmillan, 1995), 517; ibid., 517–28.

110. Michael Fischer, "Redefining Philosophy as Literature: Richard Rorty's 'Defence' of Literary Culture," in Malachowski, *Reading Rorty*, 233–43; ibid., 236.

111. Fischer, 233.

112. Rorty, *Consequences of Pragmatism*, 142.

113. Ibid., 142.

114. Rorty's thinking here is informed by a Kuhnian notion of theory change whereby the revised vocabulary is incommensurable with the old one. The idea is there is no intermediate vocabulary to argue for the change, although this sits uncomfortably with the response to artistic change. Modern art does not invalidate the art of the renaissance. As Kuhn himself points out, "Picasso's success has not relegated Rembrant's paintings to the storage vaults of art museums." "Comment on the Relations of Science and Art," *The Essential Tension*, 340–51; ibid., 345.

115. Fischer, 237.

116. Ibid., 238–39.

117. Ibid., 241; ibid.; ibid., 117.

118. W. V. O. Quine, "Let Me Accentuate the Positive," Malachowski, 117–19.

119. Rorty, *Philosophy and Social Hope*, 175, 182, 187, 188.

120. Rorty, *Consequences of Pragmatism*, 17.

121. Rorty, "Pragmatism, Davidson and Truth," *Truth and Interpretation: Perspectives on the Philosophy of Donald Davidson*, ed. Ernest LePore (Oxford: Blackwell, 1986), 333–55; ibid., 335; ibid., 333.

122. "Texts and Lumps," in *Objectivity, Relativism, and Truth*, 78; ibid., 79; ibid., 78.

123. Party, *Consequences of Pragmatism*, 141.

124. Ibid., 151.

5. COMMONSENSE REALISTS

1. In his autobiography, *Killing Time*, Feyerabend stresses that *Against Method* was only ever a collage, without an overall coherence, and expresses reservations about his commitment to philosophical argument. "Didn't I care about what I had written? Yes and no. I certainly didn't feel the religious fervor some writers apply to their products; as far as I was concerned, *Against Method* was just a book, not holy writ. Moreover, I could be easily convinced of the merits of almost any view. Written texts, my own

text included, often seemed ambiguous to me." *Killing Time: The Autobiography of Paul Feyerabend* (Chicago: University of Chicago Press, 1995), 145.

2. Rorty, "Against Unity," 31.

3. That said, Rorty (who was trained in formal logic) almost certainly could acquit himself before Snow's questioning. In one aside, Rorty recalls being "forced to learn the proofs to some of Goedel's results in order to pass my Ph.D examinations." *Philosophy and Social Hope*, 178.

4. Charles Dickens, *Bleak House* (1852–53; Oxford: Oxford World Classics, 1996), 624–25; chapter 43.

5. Dawkins, *River Out of Eden*, 32n., 31–32.

6. Sarah Franklin, "Making Transparencies: Seeing Through the Science Wars," in Ross, ed., *Science Wars*, 151–67; ibid., 153.

7. Franklin doesn't make this explicit, but note that Dawkins here inverts the way scientific principles get to be useful. The way Dawkins tells it, Frank and Orville Wright might simply have used a recognized list of equations to design their airplane, knowing it would work because they had built it in obedience to those equations. But in fact, the relationship between the physics of airplanes and the actual engineering is more complex, and the science behind aeronautics emerged hand in hand with the messier and more confusing task of experimentally testing hundreds of different designs and composing and editing the theories of aerodynamics according to the results of these attempts. Aviation authorities and manufacturers do not simply greenlight the launch of a new passenger plane because it is obedient to the equations used for designing airplanes, but instead insist that numerous tests are run. (One might reply to Dawkins, "Show me a physicist on a test flight.") Which is to say, it is practical function rather than fidelity to theory that satisfies. Franklin's argument is that explicit knowledge about the principles of aeronautics is not essential for building airplanes and will (and in fact did) emerge only after practical success. Rorty and company do not doubt that there may be laws that decide how airplanes fly, only that, to build and fly airplanes, the manufacturers do not need to know them explicitly. (This reasoning follows the analogy that you needn't know the science of combustion to start a fire; it's enough to know through trial and error that wet materials are less likely to catch than dry ones.)

8. He stresses that "I have no wish to deny the power and the utility of the methods of science *within their proper domain*"—although note the limit placed on applications within a specific and bounded domain. Stephen Jay Kline, *Conceptual Foundations for Multidisciplinary Thinking* (Stanford, CA: Stanford University Press, 1996), 113; my emphasis.

9. Ibid., 210.

10. Ibid., 210–11.

11. Steven Weinberg, *Dreams of a Final Theory* (New York: Pantheon, 1992), 259.

12. Ibid., 259. The quote marks around eugenics are Weinberg's; presumably included so as to distance the pernicious science of eugenics from the beneficent science of nuclear physics he is himself a practitioner of.

13. Ibid., 258.

14. Tom Sorrell talks of the linkage here between the noun and the modifier as hinging on hyphenation. The "evil-scientist" is evil because of something about the way scientists look at the world, but the "evil scientist" is simply a scientist who happens to be evil. The issue is whether the nature of the belief system impacts on the worldview and ethics of the individual, and Weinberg is answering a no for science and a yes for religion.

15. Weinberg, *Dreams of a Final Theory*, 167.

16. Weinberg finds science's "moral core" in its "agnosticism" (in Thomas H. Huxley's sense of the word). "It is not the certainty of science that fits this role"—that is, to "preserve a sane world"—"but its *uncertainty*" (Ibid., 259).

17. Ibid., 167.

18. Dawkins, *Unweaving the Rainbow*, 21.

19. Rorty, *Truth and Progress* (Cambridge: Cambridge University Press, 1998), 1.

20. Ibid., 3.

21. Rorty, *Philosophy and Social Hope*, xix.

22. Hayles, "Consolidating the Canon," in Ross, ed. *Science Wars*, 233.

23. Feyerabend, *Against Method*, 309.

24. Dawkins, *Unweaving the Rainbow*, 21.

25. For this reason, Dawkins's appeal to simple robust common sense is surprising. Common sense is something that scientists would do well to leave out of their reasoning, as appeals to common sense can be made from either side here, something Dawkins's colleague Lewis Wolpert is well aware of. Rather than being intuitively obvious, science is often highly counterintuitive, and Wolpert's 1992 book *The Unnatural Nature of Science* makes just this point. Wolpert believes that science is reliable, but that more often than we realize, "both the ideas that science generates and the way in which it is carried out are entirely counterintuitive and against common sense. . . . Science does not fit with our natural expectations." Lewis Wolpert, *The Unnatural Nature of Science* (London: Faber, 1992), 1. As the evolutionary psychologists would say, common sense is not necessarily the best tool for sorting out truth, but evolved as a rough-and-ready strategy of "best-fit" in a world which to all approximations obeyed Newtonian mechanics. Common sense, of a sort, says heavy objects fall faster, and common sense alone would probably suggest dualism as a theory of mind. (Needless to say, common sense rejects quantum mechanics.) On the other hand, common sense favors the correspondence theory of truth and rejects Rortean pragmatism and the social constructivism of the SSK.

26. Christopher Norris, *Deconstruction and the "Unfinished Project of Modernity"* (London: Athlone, 2000), 195.

27. Weinberg, for example, in wanting to be a realist about quantum physics, finds himself at an initially surprising variance with the positivists. In opposition to Wilson (who was sympathetic to the positivists), Weinberg is a realist *as opposed to* a positivist. Weinberg, surrounded by elementary particles that are categorically unobservable, cautions against "taking too seriously the doctrine of positivism, that science should concern itself only with things that can be observed. Other physicists including myself prefer another, realist, way of looking at quantum mechanics." *Dreams of a Final Theory*, 251. At the scale Weinberg is concerned with, what will count as an observation is less clear than it is for Dawkins the zoologist or for Wilson the synthesist.

28. Rorty, *Philosophy and Social Hope*, 185–86.

29. Ibid., 183.

30. Wilson, *Consilience*, 10.

31. Weinberg, *Dreams of a Final Theory*, 168.

32. Dawkins *Unweaving the Rainbow* , 21.

33. Weinberg, *Dreams of a Final Theory*, 167.

34. One need only think about how a world of skilled doctors would make the pharmaceuticals they require.

35. Weinberg, *Dreams of a Final Theory*, 43–44.

36. John Gribbin, *In Search of Schrödinger's Cat* (London: Black Swan, 1996), 30.

37. Kline, 112, 216; ibid., 216.

38. Fodor, *Psychosemantics*, 44.

39. This looks complicated because the discipline that studies vortices is hydrodynamics, which is part of physics, and the water molecules are the domain of chemistry; so to some extent, it's physics dictating chemistry all over again. The point here is that there is an organizing principle that does not exist at the atomic level that seems to be controlling the behavior of objects at the atomic level. See again Fodor's comment, which sums it up neatly. Goodwin's vortex example is intended to ease the passage of his more controversial thesis about structural biology, whose proponents want to argue that form (or "morphology") in biology is dictated by structural as much as functional rules. See Rudolf A. Raff, *The Shape of Life: Genes, Development, and the Evolution of Animal Form* (Chicago: University of Chicago Press, 1996).

40. He writes, "Hierarchy is nearly ubiquitous as a structural form in our world. If we deny the existence of hierarchy in structure, we will end up confusing ourselves about how things are put together, how they work, and also about how we think, communicate, and use concepts" (Kline, 105).

41. He actually has more complex categories than this, five types in all. "Synoptic; reductionist; a belief in the synoptic and reductionist views, held as an existential paradox; explicit attempts to reconcile the two conflicting views; and abandonment of these attempts to form an overview (and thus live without any coherent view of our world)" (ibid., 111). For these purposes, the split between the two is sufficient.

42. For example, the proreductionist Rudolf Carnap writes, "No scientific reason is known for the assumption that such a derivation should be *in principle* and forever impossible" (quoted in O. Hanfling, *Essential Readings in Logical Positivism*, 128; my emphasis). The ambivalent Oppenheim and Putnam write, "If this is achieved, then psychological laws will have, *in principle*, been reduced to the laws of atomic physics" ("Unity of Science as a Working Hypothesis," 7; my emphasis). And the antireductionist Eldredge and Tattersall write, "Theoretically, *in principle*, a reductionist could explain human evolution in terms of the laws of physics" (*The Myths of Human Evolution*, 14; emphasis preserved).

43. Kline, 111, 128, 113.

44. Ibid., 121, 119.

45. Also, it seems like a way to reintroduce free will to an otherwise bleakly determinist universe. This is pleasant side effect. If higher levels command the behavior of lower levels, then the picture suggests that will is supervening on the atomic laws, that is, will is (literally) moving matter.

46. Weinberg, *Dreams of a Final Theory*, 240.

47. For a more detailed analysis of the changes made to scientific data between peer-review journals and popular repackaging, see Jeanne Fahnestock, "Accommodating Science: The Rhetorical Life of Scientific Facts" in Murdo William McRae, ed., *The Literature of Science: Perspectives on Popular Science Writing* (Athens: University of Georgia Press, 1993), 17–36.

48. The quotation comes from Auden's essay "The Poet and the City" in Auden, *The Dyer's Hand and Other Essays*, 72–89; ibid., 81.

49. Dawkins, *Unweaving the Rainbow*, 15.

50. Richard Webster, "The Great Enterprise," rev. of *Newton's Sleep*, by Raymond Tallis, *TLS*, 16 February 1996, 30.

51. Paul Hoffman, *The Man Who Loved Only Numbers* (London: Fourth Estate, 1998), 16.

52. Ian McEwan, *The Child in Time* (London: Vintage, 1997), 45.

53. Snow, *The Two Cultures and a Second Look*, 14. This is putting the case too strongly; for the literary people are not, of course, denying the *existence* of the natural order, they are simply saying that it seems an unsuitable candidate for what we might call "culture."

54. Snow, 2.
55. Ibid., 3.
56. Quoted in Snow, 4. That is, Ernest Rutherford, Arthur Eddington, and P[aul]. A. M. Dirac, all physicists. Rutherford and Dirac were both Nobel laureates (1908 and 1933, respectively).
57. Pinker, *How the Mind Works*, 522–23.
58. There is even a word for artistic ignorance, "philistinism." If there were a scientific equivalent, it would probably be "Luddite." Neither quite captures the deficiency being criticized, but can and often are used in these senses. For "philistine," *The Shorter OED* offers (rather unhelpfully given the concepts under discussion), "An uneducated or unenlightened person; a person indifferent to culture, or whose interests are commonplace and material." But does specify that the philistine is usually "aesthetically unsophisticated," which clearly chimes with Carroll's criticism of Pinker. For "Luddite" the dictionary suggests, "A person opposed to increased industrialization, or the introduction of new technology." Snow's use of the term is probably meant to appeal to the fact that the dictionary describes the original Mr Ludd as "insane."
59. F. R. Leavis, *Nor Shall My Sword* (London: Chatto and Windus, 1972), 44–45.
60. Snow, 14.
61. Joseph Carroll, "Steven Pinker's Cheesecake for the Mind," *Philosophy and Literature* 22 (1998): 478–85; ibid., 479.
62. John Allen Paulos, *Innumeracy: Mathematical Illiteracy and its Consequences* (London: Viking, 1989).
63. Wolpert, *The Unnatural Nature of Science*, ix.
64. Raymond Tallis, *Newton's Sleep: Two Cultures and Two Kingdoms* (London: MacMillan, 1995), 3.
65. Martin Amis, *The Information* (London: Flamingo, 1995), 232.
66. Note that this utility extends beyond proficiency in the sciences: the skills acquired in the study of science (basic numeracy, familiarity with statistics, techniques for accurate measurement, etc.) are offered as useful for business affairs and home management.
67. Snow, 15.
68. Ibid., 15.
69. Tallis, *Newton's Sleep*, 5.
70. Ibid., 6.
71. Wolpert, ix–x.
72. Ibid., x.
73. Alan Sokal and Jean Bricmont, *Intellectual Impostures* (London: Profile, 1998), 256.
74. Tallis, *Newton's Sleep*, 8.
75. Snow, 12.
76. John Carey, ed., *The Faber Book of Science* (London: Faber, 1995), xxvi.
77. Tallis, *Newton's Sleep*, 40.
78. Ibid., 7.
79. Ibid., 6.
80. Stephen Hawking, *A Brief History of Time* (Toronto: Bantam, 1995), vi–vii.
81. Aldous Huxley, *Brave New World Revisited*.
82. Feynman quoted in Gleick, *Genius*, 378.
83. Mainly French academics, including Jacques Lacan, Julia Kristeva, Luce Iriguay, Jean Baudrillard, Gilles Deleuze, and Felix Guattari. To underline the distinction between use and wonder, it is important to note that their criticisms do not extend to science in fiction.

84. Sokal and Bricmont, 176.
85. Ibid., 176. They add, "For example, although neither of us has any training in biology, we are able to follow, at some basic level, developments in that field by reading good popular or semi-popular books" (ibid., 176–77). Regarding the difficulty of comprehension outside of specialization, see Chargaff, "Building the Tower of Babble," 776–79. As mentioned above, Chargaff feared that acute scientific specialization would eventually bring communication between scientists to a halt, and a situation would arise where nobody could ever "know more than an ever smaller portion of what they must know in order to function properly" (ibid., 777).
86. Sokal and Bricmont, 87.
87. Norris, *Deconstruction and the "Unfinished Project of Modernity,"* 197.
88. It is also surely no coincidence that these ideas—some of the most abstract and difficult to explain even to scientists—are those most appealing to popular readers. It seems reasonable to assume that it is this difficulty that licenses popular writers to not even attempt to explain the mechanisms.
89. "Religious" is not intended here in any pejorative sense. The scientific beliefs of nonscientists are religious insofar as they seem to ask believers to accept the word as true and do not demand proof beyond this authority.
90. Booth, *Now Don't Try to Reason with Me*, 85. It's perhaps worth asking if the case was not that they could not provide an explanation at all, but that they could not offer anything that Booth, as a nonscientist, would have recognized as a proof or explanation.
91. Wolpert, *The Unnatural Nature of Science*, x.
92. Sokal and Bricmont, 256.
93. It is interesting that Sokal and Bricmont argue that the "main reason for believing scientific theories (at least the best verified ones) is that they explain the coherency of our experience" (ibid., 55), as this goes strongly against Wolpert who, as mentioned above, believes that science is reliable, but that more often than we realize, "does not fit with our natural expectations" (*The Unnatural Nature of Science*, 1).
94. In Andrew Pickering, ed., *Science As Practice and Culture* (Chicago: University of Chicago Press, 1992), 45.
95. Feynman, *The Character of Physical Law*, 39–40.
96. Ibid., 58.
97. Dawkins, *Unweaving the Rainbow*, 36.
98. Snow, 14.
99. Feynman, *The Character of Physical Law*, 58. See also John Carey's introduction to *The Faber Book of Science*, xvii.
100. Quoted in Dawkins, *Unweaving the Rainbow*, 37.
101. Ibid., 37.
102. Booth, *Now Don't Try to Reason with Me*, 85, 85, 83, 83, 83. It should be clear that because the students Booth has met who would go to the stake for $E=mc^2$ were unable to explain or reconstruct Einstein's reasoning, they would be going to the stake for a mere opinion. This is Booth's criticism: it may or may not be foolish to go to the stake for an idea, but it is certainly foolish to go there for an opinion.
103. Ibid., 90.
104. It isn't really meaningless, of course, because it will (hopefully) mean something to the interrogator. Nor is it meaningless if we recognize the role it plays socially, as an almost symbolic and ritualized exchange between the scientifically trained and those without such training. The point is that *as science* it doesn't work anymore, and so it is meaningless in this capacity.
105. Gilbert Ryle, *The Concept of Mind* (Oxford: Oxford University Press, 1949), 25–61; especially 27–32.

106. Dawkins, *Unweaving the Rainbow*, 17. It's interesting to compare this with Steven Weinberg, who writes, "The problem seems to be that we are trying to be logical about a question that is not really susceptible to logical argument: the question of what should or should not engage our sense of wonder" (*Dreams of a Final Theory*, 238).
107. Snow, 16.
108. Richard Powers, *Galatea 2.2* (New York: Farrar, Straus, Giroux, 1995), 74.
109. Sokal and Bricmont, 176.
110. That is, both disciplinary and methodological autonomy; for Fish, the method is the discipline.
111. There is a case for Dawkins's point here in that it is necessary to learn a good deal about music to genuinely appreciate the depth of a Bach fugue, for example. This type of knowledge, musicology, doesn't include the ability to play the instruments, but it does require a good deal of specialist language and careful attention to the music. The difference is sometimes explained in terms of the difference between *hearing* and actually *listening*. Poetry appreciation is another example; simply reading the words or hearing them said is insufficient, and we talk of "trained ears" to distinguish the type of sensitivity skilled readers or listeners have acquired. But what is learned to appreciate poetry or music in this deeper sense is probably as hard to teach as the mathematics itself. It's another professional and specialist skill and equally prone to any criticisms about the impossibility of exporting specialist terms outside the specialism.
112. Dawkins is the first holder of the Charles Simonyi Chair for the Public Understanding of Science at Oxford University. In *The Selfish Gene*'s 1989 preface, Dawkins says: "I prefer not to make a clear separation between science and its 'popularization'" (xi).
113. Put like this—that specialist language only works within a specialist context—it seems impossible to achieve meaningful interdisciplinary exchanges, and that is Fish's point. Once you have accepted his thesis that the vocabulary exhausts the discipline, you are logically bound to accept the consequential impossibility of transporting it outside the boundaries and retaining disciplinary identity.
114. Thomas S. Kuhn, *The Structure of Scientific Revolutions*, 2nd ed. (Chicago: University of Chicago Press, 1970), vi.
115. Ibid., 135.
116. Ibid., 121.
117. John B. Carroll, introduction to Benjamin Lee Whorf, *Language, Thought, and Reality: Selected Writings of Benjamin Lee Whorf* (Cambridge, MA: MIT Press, 1956), 23.
118. Whorf, 58.
119. Ibid., 58.
120. Donald Davidson, "On the Very Idea of a Conceptual Scheme," *Inquiries into Truth and Interpretation*, 2nd ed. (Oxford: Clarendon, 2001), 183–198; ibid., 184. Christopher Norris, *New Idols of the Cave* (Manchester: Manchester University Press, 1997), 145.
121. Whorf, 58.
122. Rorty, *Philosophy and the Mirror of Nature*, 355.
123. Richard P. Feynman, *The Pleasure of Finding Things Out: The Best Short Works of Richard P. Feynman*, ed. Jeffrey Robbins (London: Allen Lane-Penguin, 2000), 102.
124. Kline, 5.
125. H. Allen Orr, "Dennett's Dangerous Idea," rev. of *Darwin's Dangerous Idea* by Daniel C. Dennett, *Evolution* 50, no. 1 (1996): 467–72; 468.
126. See, for example, Pinker, *The Language Instinct*, 473–78.

6. Centralities of Language

1. Fish, *Professional Correctness*, 70.
2. In *Philosophy and the Mirror of Nature* (206), Rorty discusses the claims of Laplacean physics determinists that an adequate knowledge of the current position and velocity of atomic particles would be sufficient to exactly predict future events, including the behavior of future humans. Even if this were possible (and there are many reasons why it is not, even in principle), Rorty maintains that the knowledge-productions of future humans would be meaningless to us without our understanding of their context within the future society from whence they came—an understanding that could only be achieved by immersion within the culture. This is a strongly historicist view. Meaning is assumed to be almost emergent, a property of interaction.
3. Fish, *Professional Correctness*, 126.
4. Frye, *Anatomy of Criticism*, 10.
5. Fish, *Professional Correctness*, 13.
6. Ibid., 1.
7. Tony Jackson, "Questioning Interdisciplinarity: Cognitive Science, Evolutionary Psychology, and Literary Criticism," in *Poetics Today* 21.2 (2000): 319–47.
8. Ibid., 328, 334, 336. Similar criticisms come from Frederick Adams, writing in the *Stanford Humanities Review* 4, no. 1 (*http://www.stanford.edu/group/SHR/4–1/text/adams.commentary.html*) dedicated to responses to psychologist Herbert Simon's take on cognitive science's promise for literary study. "Some of his offerings do not seem to add things that are new or more precise than any literary critic would have known" (quoted in Tony Jackson, 336). The "precision" claim is important in this case because Simon had explicitly advertised precision as a virtue of his approach.
9. Tony Jackson, 335.
10. Of course, the critical approach will only be considered "externally derived" by those unsympathetic to or skeptical of its effectiveness. An avowed Marxist would presumably maintain that the literature is a product of the socioeconomic environment from which it emerged. Likewise, an adherent of evolutionary psychology can be expected to believe that their approach is not external to literature, but constitutive of it: that in evolutionary psychology they have identified the source of literature's character and condition of its possibility.
11. Frye, *Anatomy of Criticism*, 7.
12. Carroll, *Evolution and Literary Theory*, 327.
13. Of course, the problem with this is that evolutionary psychology has *not* received the universal acclaim of the scientific community that Carroll needs. One of the better essays denouncing the scope of evolutionary psychology comes from Stephen Jay Gould, "More Things in Heaven and Earth" in Steven Rose and Hilary Rose, eds. *Alas, Poor Darwin: Arguments Against Evolutionary Psychology* (London: Jonathan Cape, 2000), 85–105. Gould doesn't attack the more conservative claims of the evolutionary psychologists: he agrees that the mind is an evolved organ, but is hesitant about assenting to the ability of evolutionary psychology to explain every feature of human behavior by natural selection alone. He seizes on the Lamarckian nature of cultural evolution, and argues that this effectively eclipses any Mendelian effect that Dawkins and Dennett want to reintroduce through talk of memetics. The meme is intended to facilitate and encourage an analogy between Mendelian genetic evolution and the "evolution" of thoughts and ideas. Gould and others, including Mary Midgely ("Why Memes?" in Rose and Rose, 67–84) and biologist H. Allen Orr (from whom Gould borrows the bulk of his argument in "Dennett's Dangerous Idea," 467–72), however, hold that the analogy is fundamentally skewed because cultural evolution is

Lamarckian (not Mendelian) in character. They argue that the desire of the ultra-Darwinists to account for every aspect of humanity—physiological and psychological—in terms of evolved adaptations has forced them to invent the meme. In an irony probably designed to rankle Dennett (who had written "an excoriating caricature of [Gould's] ideas" where it was hard to find an argument "amid the slurs and sneers" [Gould in Rose and Rose, 94]), Gould effectively dismisses the meme as a skyhook. Cutting against the memetic theory, Mary Midgely makes the further claim that belief is not granular (like the genes in DNA), in the sense that Dawkins and Dennett need for the memetic theory to hold. The correct register for talking about memes, these critics argue, is not that of genetics, but of epidemiology. (Oddly, Dawkins himself seems to recognize this, writing a typically hostile account of religious belief entitled "Viruses of the Mind" in Bo Dahlbom, ed., *Dennett and His Critics* [Oxford: Blackwell, 1993], 13–27.) It is unclear whether or not memes are essential to evolutionary psychology: some proponents talk about them but most do not. Carroll himself never draws on the memetic theory explicitly, so a criticism of memes perhaps misses him.

14. See Wilson, *Consilience*, 245–46.

15. In Rose and Rose, 39. Ellipses Jencks's unless in brackets.

16. Jencks does also list Jackson Pollock as an anomaly, but this is met by Dutton's point that Pollock's art, like that of Duchamp, was controversial: that is, it shocked and offended and is still largely an *avant garde* concern. Any wider popularity Pollock now enjoys is not based on the immediate appeal of his work, but rather, its critical success and consequent dissemination in the form of book-covers and poster prints. Unlike a pastoral Constable or the work of the Hudson River School, Jackson Pollock is not universally popular with audiences. The same is true of *The Waste Land* or *Ulysses*, a view Frye explicitly endorsed when he made the claim that "Whatever popularity Shakespeare and Keats have now is . . . the result of the publicity of criticism" (*Anatomy of Criticism*, 4). Jencks writes complacently for an audience already persuaded that the biological approach is wrong. This leads to carelessness and easy, often facile sniping. The volume's editors, Hilary and Steven Rose, describe Jencks's essay as "stylishly ironic" (Rose and Rose, 9). Jencks apes Danny Kaye's *Court Jester* patter ("The pellet with the poison's in the flagon with the dragon; the vessel with the pestle has the brew that is true" [*Court Jester*, director Melvin Frank and Norman Panama, 1956]). "The issue of the tissue is the sound which is found in the nose, I suppose. What?" (in Rose and Rose, 31–32).

17. See Carroll's essay, "Steven Pinker's Cheesecake for the Mind," 478–85.

18. A Kuhnian would call this an example of normal science. See *The Structure of Scientific Revolutions:* the translation of "*mere* facts" (35) into science comes with their absorption into the paradigm. In a discussion about the reception of Coulomb's experimental data, Kuhn explains that this "is why that result surprised no one and why several of Coulomb's contemporaries had been able to predict it in advance. Even the project whose goal is paradigm articulation does not aim at the *unexpected* novelty" (35). What is being sought by experimenters working within a paradigm is corroboration: "the aim of normal science is not major substantive novelties" (35).

19. See Geoffrey Miller, *The Mating Mind: How Sexual Choice Shaped the Evolution of Human Nature.* (London: Heinemann, 2000), especially 258–291; ibid., 284.

20. Ibid., 285.

21. Frye, *Anatomy of Criticism*, 20.

22. "The demonstrable value-judgement is the donkey's carrot of literary criticism, and every new critical fashion, such as the current fashion for elaborate rhetorical analysis, has been accompanied by a belief that criticism has finally devised a definitive technique for separating the excellent from the less excellent. But this always turns out to be an illusion of the history of taste" (ibid., 20).

23. Of course, this all becomes complicated by the tendency of many critics to use a behaviorist approach to literary production. See section on Frye below.

24. Kline, 119; Fodor, 44.

25. For argumentative clarity (and consistent with Frye's usage), the term "poet" is used here to denote the creative writer or artist as distinct from the critic or interpreter.

26. Frye, *Anatomy of Criticism*, 5, 4–6, 17.

27. Ibid., 17, 133.

28. The two contexts mark the same division that is used to argue within political circles that a man's personal life has no impact on his ability to make professional decisions. In fact, the two contexts idea is something that runs throughout intellectual thought. The idea that a contribution should be judged by its merit within the debate rather than on the identity of the speaker is something that is central to standards of academic integrity. If Hitler says, "Genocide is wrong," the statement is not rendered untrue. It becomes perhaps a little senseless in Hitler's mouth, but the moral worth of such a prohibition survives because it rests not on the identity of the speaker but on the validity of the contribution.

29. James Rachels, *Created from Animals* (Oxford: Oxford University Press, 1991), 144. Daft as the moth's behavior might seem, that a similar principle applies to human males is apparent from the popularity of pornography, where the olfactory stimulus is replaced by a visual stimulus.

30. Ibid., 145.

31. Daniel C. Dennett, *Brainstorms*, 245.

32. Rachels, 146.

33. Weinberg, *Dreams of a Final Theory*, 245; Dawkins, *Unweaving the Rainbow*, xiii; *River Out of Eden*, 96; Gould, "The Golden Rule: A Proper Scale for Our Environmental Crisis" in Louis P. Pojman, ed., *Environmental Ethics: Readings in Theory and Application* (Boston, MA: Jones and Bartlett, 1994), 164–68; 168. Dawkins makes similar comments later in *River Out of Eden*. "In a universe of blind physical forces and genetic replication, some people are going to get hurt, other people are going to get lucky, and you won't find any rhyme or reason in it, nor any justice. The universe we observe has precisely the properties we should expect if there is, at bottom, no design, no purpose, no evil and no good, nothing but bland, pitiless indifference" (133).

34. Anthony O'Hear, *The Element of Fire* (London: Routledge, 1988), 14–15.

35. Pinker, *The Language Instinct*, ix.

36. Dawkins, *Unweaving the Rainbow*, xiii.

37. This is what is meant by the independence of scientific ideas from humans, as opposed to the humanities, which are so called because they are entirely dependent on the existence of humans. It may be possible to push this further and to claim that they must be biological *homo sapiens*, too, and not just intelligent persons. It might be that the humanities would make no sense to intelligent aliens, but the scientists are fairly sure that their work would.

38. James Rachels stresses that this has been a tenet of Darwinian thinking right from the start, "For Darwin there was nothing in the constitution of any organism that propels its development in any particular direction. Nor were there any 'higher' or 'lower' forms of life; nor any 'progress': there were only organisms adapted in different ways to different environments, by a process ignorant of design or intention" (*Created from Animals*, 116). There is a pleasant symmetry between Rachels's paraphrasing of Darwin and the way that that Rorty talks about the relativity of descriptions to purposes and the corresponding absurdity of ranking disciplines in the academy. See also Stephen Jay Gould's *Wonderful Life* (1990; London: Vintage, 2000)

and *Life's Grandeur* (London: Cape, 1996) for a lengthy account of how evolutionary theory is non-teleological.

39. Rachels, 5.

40. In making such a case, Rachels is well aware that he is skirting a violation of the naturalistic fallacy, and so is careful to stress the relations between the naturalistic reasons found in the acceptance of a Darwinian account of life and the normative conclusions about how we should behave with regard to the environment. "In providing reasons, one need not be claiming that the facts logically entail the moral judgement. One need only claim that they provide good reasons for accepting the judgement" (96–97).

41. See, for example, R. M. Hare's essay "What Is Wrong with Slavery?" in Peter Singer, ed., *Applied Ethics* (Oxford: Oxford University Press, 1986), 165–83.

42. Rachels, 4.

43. Dawkins, *Climbing Mount Improbable*, 238.

44. Raymond Tallis, *Enemies of Hope* (London: MacMillan, 1997), 221, 226, 225, 220.

45. "Fixation to Traumas—the Unconscious," *Complete Works*, vol. 16, 284–85. (See "A Difficulty in the Path of Psychoanalysis," *Complete Works*, vol. 17, 137–44.) See Sigmund Freud, *The Standard Edition of the Complete Psychological Works of Sigmund Freud*, trans. and gen. ed. James Strachey (London: Hogarth, 1955). Note how Freud equates anthropocentrism with narcissism. In a slightly later lecture, he is more forgiving and allows that unaided sense perception is consistent with geocentrism.

46. Stephen Jay Gould, *An Urchin in the Storm* (New York: Norton, 1987), 214.

47. Freud, *Complete Works*, 16:285.

48. "A Difficulty in the Path of Psychoanalysis," ibid., 17:141, 142–43.

49. Ibid., 17:143.

50. Ridley, *The Red Queen*, 9.

51. There is a contradiction here, too. The first premise allows that man can override his evolutionary imperatives, but then Ridley seems to switch back to claim that this emancipation is only fondly imagined. But it is either emancipation or it isn't. To use Ridley's intentional language, if the genes "let us free," then their motives for doing so are rendered irrelevant, because they don't have the power anymore.

52. Dawkins, *The Selfish Gene*, 4.

53. Freud was aware that he was not the first to suggest that we might not be the best reporters of our own mental lives and credited Schopenhauer with being a significant forerunner, claiming that his "unconscious 'Will' is equivalent to the mental instincts of psycho-analysis" (*Complete Works*, 17:143–44).

54. Arthur Schopenhauer, "The Metaphysics of the Love of the Sexes," in *The World As Will And Idea* (1883; London: Routledge, 1948), 3:336–75.

55. Ibid., 3:339, 339, 341, 345–46.

56. There is a chance that the situation is analogous with the identification of microorganisms as the cause of disease: it is not in itself a cure, but may point the way for a cure.

57. Ridley, *The Red Queen*, 4.

58. He immediately admits this to be "an astonishingly hubristic claim" but then says "[y]et I know of no other way that human nature can have developed" (ibid., 4).

59. Martin Amis, *Experience* (London: Cape, 2000), 80.

60. Freud, *Complete Works*, 16:285.

61. Bruce Mazlish, *The Fourth Discontinuity* (New Haven: Yale University Press, 1993), 3–4; Jerome Bruner, "Freud and the Image of Man," *Partisan Review* 23, no. 3 (Summer 1956): 340–47.

62. Mazlish, 4.
63. Dennett, *Consciousness Explained*, 23.
64. When you think on it, Mazlish's fourth discontinuity is much more in the spirit of Darwin and Copernicus than Freud. Mazlish's is really just a special case of materialism: recognizing a continuum between the organic and the inorganic and between the mind and the brain. Freud's is an epistemological concern about the security of our self-knowledge, whereas Darwin and Copernicus's claims were more ontological: Where are we? What are we like?
65. See "The Perils of Hope," in Gould, *An Urchin in the Storm*, 208–15; ibid., 215.
66. In Louis P. Pojman, ed., *Environmental Ethics* (Boston, MA: Jones and Bartlett, 1994), 164–68.
67. Gould, "The Golden Rule," 167. He goes on to add, "We are virtually powerless over the earth at our planet's own geological time scale. All the megatonage of our nuclear arsenals yield but one ten-thousandth the power of the asteroid that might have triggered the Cretaceous mass extinction. Yet the earth survived that larger shock and, in wiping out the dinosaurs, paved the road for the evolution of large mammals, including humans" (168).
68. Gould is trying to puncture the overblown rhetoric of the environmentalist movement in the name of intellectual honesty, but it's not at all clear that this is a particularly responsible move.
69. Kurt Vonnegut, Jr., *Slaughterhouse-Five, Or The Children's Crusade: A Duty Dance with Death* (1968; New York: Dell, 1976), 30.
70. Ibid., 27.
71. Ibid., 27.
72. Ibid., 86.
73. George Steiner, *After Babel*, 2nd ed. (1975; Oxford: Oxford University Press, 1992), 137–38; ibid., 138.
74. Vonnegut, 117.
75. Ibid., 3.
76. As the book moves back through time, "Tod Friendly" emerges to be a pseudonym, one of several, culminating in his being called Odilo Unverdorben. Although there may be a sense in which Amis wants us to think of these as discrete selves and question the identity of self over time, for clarity, I will usually refer to the host as Tod.
77. Primo Levi, *The Drowned and the Saved* (1986. London: Abacus, 1989), 11–21.
78. Salman Rushdie, *Shame* (London: Cape, 1983), 22.
79. Martin Amis, *Einstein's Monsters* (Harmondsworth, UK: Penguin Books, 1988), 27–48.
80. Ibid., 47.
81. Ibid., 47.
82. Keith J. Laidler and John H. Meiser, *Physical Chemistry*, 2nd ed. (Boston, MA: Houghton, 1995), 693–94.
83. Martin Amis, *Time's Arrow: Or, The Nature of the Offence* (Harmondsworth, UK: Penguin Books, 1991), 16.
84. Richard Menke, "Narrative Reversals and the Thermodynamics of History in Martin Amis's *Time's Arrow*," *Modern Fiction Studies* 44.4 (1998): 959–80; ibid., 959.
85. Amis, *Time's Arrow*, 16.
86. "The preoccupation of the humanities with the past is sometimes made a reproach against them by those who forget that we face the past: it may be shadowy, but it is all that is there" (Frye, *Anatomy of Criticism*, 345).

87. Amis, *Time's Arrow*, 30.
88. Ibid., 26; 31.
89. Ibid., 26, 23 (ellipsis preserved).
90. Ibid., 129.
91. Amis, *Einstein's Monsters*, 48; ibid., 48.
92. Ibid., 2.
93. To clarify this, the narrator feels that the work Tod does in his old age as a charitable doctor is bad (because charity = stealing from the needy, and doctoring = unpicking stitches and inflicting wounds), and that the work he does in the concentration camps is good (making a race of people out of ashes and populating Europe with them). In forward time, the work Tod does in his youth is bad, and the work he does in his old age is good. If you reverse the arrow, morality is also reversed, so the effect is the same.
94. Thomas Nagel, *The View from Nowhere* (New York: Oxford University Press, 1986), 3.
95. Nagel, *The View from Nowhere*, 209.
96. Rorty, "Texts and Lumps," in *ORT*, 81.
97. Feynman, *The Character of Physical Law*, 125 (ellipses preserved, unless in brackets).
98. Ibid., 125–26.
99. Martin Amis, *The Information* (London: Flamingo, 1995), 163–64.
100. Ibid., 452.
101. Dawkins, *Climbing Mount Improbable*, 97; Gould, "The Golden Rule," 166; Pinker, *The Language Instinct*, 248.
102. Amis, *The Information*, 437; ibid., 437.
103. Frye, *Anatomy of Criticism*, 33.
104. Ibid., 33–34.
105. Amis, *The Information*, 435; ibid., 435–36. It seems safe to assume that Amis has not come to the same conclusion independently: there is evidence that Amis is familiar with Frye. in the introduction to his selected essays and reviews, *The War Against Cliché* (London: Vintage, 2002), Amis recalls having discussions about literary criticism in the early 1970s, citing Frye's work as one of the topics (xi). There is even a chance that Amis heard these ideas firsthand. in a letter to Kingsley reprinted in his autobiography, *Experience* (231–32, dated, vaguely, as "July? 1971?"), Martin mentions that he is attending a series of seminars given by Frye at Oxford. Although the "History of Increasing Humiliation" is presented as Richard Tull's (and the debt to Frye unacknowledged), it seems probable that Amis also subscribes. In an essay from 1994 (a year before *The Information* is published), Amis can be found offering the theory in his own name. Responding to a writer who has recorded a downward trajectory of heroism in cinema over the second half of the twentieth century, Amis points out that the trend is much wider than just cinema: "literature . . . has been following exactly the same graph line for two thousand years" (note that Amis has five hundred on Frye). He goes on to say, "If art has an arrow, then that is the way it points: straight downward, from demigod to demirep" (Amis, *The War Against Cliché*, 15).
106. Ian Watt, *The Rise of the Novel* (1957; London: Hogarth, 1987), 60. As a typical example, Watt says, "The novel is surely distinguished from other genres and from previous forms of fiction by the amount of attention it habitually accords both to the individualisation of its characters and to the detailed presentation of their environment" (17–18).
107. Amis, *The War Against Cliché*, 15.
108. Amis, *The Information*, 436.

109. Ibid., 52.

110. In Frye's "theory of mythos," comprising the third essay of his *Anatomy*, genres are allotted to seasons. Amis uses the pattern of the *Anatomy* rather than simply Frye's pattern, because, as discussed earlier, Frye is inconsistent with his allocation. In 1951, Frye linked the genre of romance with Spring and comedy with Summer. By the publication of the *Anatomy* six years later, these had been inverted. So it isn't *that* obvious, even to Frye.

111. Amis, *The Information*, 52.

112. Ibid., 53.

113. Ibid., 479.

114. Ibid., 479.

115. One of the conditions for Frye's schema was that they were being acted on unconsciously. The anatomy was never intended to be prescriptive; it was diagnosis, not direction. In the hands of authors familiar with the theory, there is a risk of manipulation, although the risk is all to the validity of the theory. Perhaps this is just another way in which criticism cannot be a predictive science. Frye might want to treat the author like an object, by the author will always react like a subject.

116. Ibid., 64–65.

117. Ibid., 124. There is, of course, a yellow dwarf visible from where he lives, and all the talk of astronomy leads the reader into assuming he is talking technically of the sun. The passage resolves itself only when he gives her physical description, and he then switches between registers.

118. Ibid., 124–25.

119. For example, the prohibitions on staring at the sun or staring at the congenitally deformed. "I will never be able to meet the eye of the yellow dwarf. Its stare will never soften; its defiance will be always be absolute" (Amis, *The Information*, 125).

120. Frye, *Anatomy of Criticism*, 161.

121. Ibid., 161.

122. Ibid., 161.

123. Of course, it's worth realizing that if you push the analogy, it collapses. Stars do not remain stationary on the HR-diagram, but travel along the main sequence over time; yellow dwarves can become red giants.

124. Amis, *The Information*, 125.

125. Ibid., 65.

Conclusion

1. "Wilson's last chapter is a convincing cry of alarm about the dangers of genetic technology, overpopulation, and the destruction of the ecosystem, but it bears no visible relation to the rest of the work." Todorov, "The Surrender to Nature," translated by Claire Messud, review of *Consilience* by Edward O. Wilson, in *The New Republic*, 27 April 1998, 29–33; ibid., 29.

2. By symbiosis, I mean the vernacular sense of mutually beneficial cooperation, what is sometimes called "social mutualism" or "parabiosis," to distinguish it from parasitism, which is also a form of symbiosis, but not the sense intended.

3. J. G. Merquior, *From Prague To Paris* (London: Verso, 1986), 106.

4. Claude Lévi-Strauss, "The 'Moral of Myths,'" in *The Origin of Table Manners*, trans. John Weightman and Doreen Weightman (London: Cape, 1978), 496–508; ibid., 507.

5. Ibid., 508 (closing words).

6. Merquior, 105.
7. Susan Sontag, *Against Interpretation* (New York: Farrar, Straus, Giroux, 1966), 81; and quoted in Merquior, 104.
8. Merquior, 104.
9. Ibid., 106.
10. It is also the view usually endorsed by those mainstream politicians who take an interest in the environment. Al Gore, for example, rejects Deep Ecology precisely on the grounds that it is "anti-humanistic." See Gore's *The Earth in Balance* (Boston: Houghton Mifflin, 1992) and the essay "Dysfunctional Civilisation" in Louis P. Pojman, ed., *Environmental Ethics: Readings in Theory and Application* (Boston, MA: Jones and Bartlett, 1994), 473–82.
11. Arne Naess, "The Shallow and the Deep, Long-Range Ecological Movement," in Pojman, *Environmental Ethics*, 102–4.
12. Ibid., 103.
13. Bill Devall and George Sessions, "Deep Ecology," in Pojman, *Environmental Ethics*, 106.
14. Ibid., 115.
15. It is clear that this is precisely the association those disciplines currently fashioning themselves as the "Social Sciences" are trying to escape: a Social Science can produce claims potentially true for all social groups, humans being only an incidence of this field, and not its extension.
16. It is also the central claim of most relativist positions that the sciences are equally dependent on human perspectives, and any apparent independence from such perspectives is an illusion of there being no alternative viewpoint. Obviously, this objection appears to flounder on the mathematical sciences, where internally consistent logic holds regardless of the symbols used or the language spoken. This difference between a mathematical axiom (which is true in virtue of the meaning of the terms used, or "analytic") and a scientific theory (which is true in virtue of an agreement with empirical data, or "synthetic") was probably the reason why Orwell chose "$2 + 2 = 5$" (and not, say, "the speed of light is a constant") as the unthinkable proposition forced on Winston Smith in *Nineteen Eighty-Four* (Orwell, *Nineteen Eighty-Four* [1949; Harmondsworth, UK: Penguin Books, 1989], 270, 290, 303).
17. That is, they admire the mechanism behind the action. So, while the art lover might make a comment such as, "What a wonderful artist Michelangelo was," the scientist may reply, "You are right, the human mind is indeed an amazing thing." It looks like consensus, but they are actually talking about quite different things. The scientist is interested in the mechanism and subsumes intention into that as a mere epiphenomenon of the mechanism, which is for him the really interesting thing, and was all along.
18. Alan Sinfield, *Faultlines: Cultural Materialism and the Politics of Dissident Reading* (Oxford: Clarendon, 1992), 287.

Works Cited

Abrams, Meyer H. *Doing Things with Texts: Essays in Criticism and Critical Theory*, edited by Michael Fischer. New York: Norton, 1989.
Amis, Martin. *Einstein's Monsters*. 1987. Harmondsworth, UK: Penguin Books, 1988.
———. *Experience*. London: Cape, 2000.
———. *The Information*. London: Flamingo, 1995.
———. *Time's Arrow: Or, The Nature of the Offence*. Harmondsworth, UK: Penguin Books, 1991.
———. *The War Against Cliché: Essays and Reviews 1971–2000*. London: Vintage, 2002.
Auden, W. H. *The Dyer's Hand and Other Essays*. London: Faber and Faber, 1963.
Ayer, A. J. Letter. *London Review of Books*, May 8, 1986.
Barkow, Jerome H., Leda Cosmides, and John Tooby, eds. *The Adapted Mind: Evolutionary Psychology and the Generation of Culture*. New York: Oxford University Press, 1992.
Beer, Gillian. *Open Fields: Science in Cultural Encounter*. Oxford: Clarendon, 1996.
Bennett, James R. "Todorov and the Structuralist Science of Poetics." In *Phenomenology, Structuralism, Semiology*. Bucknell Review, edited by Harry R. Garvin. Lewisburg, PA: Bucknell University Press, 1976.
Binns, A. L. "'Linguistic' Reading: Two Suggestions of the Quality of Literature." In *Essays on Style and Language: Linguistic and Critical Approaches to Literary Style*, edited by Roger Fowler. London: Routledge, 1966.
Bloom, Harold. *The Anxiety of Influence: A Theory of Poetry*. Oxford: Oxford University Press, 1973.
———. *The Western Canon: The Books and Schools of the Ages*. 1994. London: Papermac-Macmillan, 1995.
Boden, Margaret. *The Creative Mind: Myths and Mechanisms*. London: Cardinal, 1992.
Bodkin, Maud. *Archetypal Patterns in Poetry: Psychological Studies of Imagination*. 1934. Oxford: Oxford University Press, 1974.
Booth, Wayne C. *Now Don't Try to Reason with Me: Essays and Ironies for a Credulous Age*. Chicago, IL: University of Chicago Press, 1970.
———. *The Rhetoric of Fiction*. 1961. 2nd ed. Chicago, IL: University of Chicago Press, 1983.
Borges, Jorge Luis. *Labyrinths: Selected Stories and Other Writings*, edited by Donald A. Yates and James E. Irby. Harmondsworth, UK: Penguin Books, 1970.
Braddon-Mitchell, David, and Frank Jackson. *Philosophy of Mind and Cognition*. Oxford: Blackwell, 1996.
Brockman, John. *The Third Culture*. New York: Simon and Schuster, 1995.

Buss, David M. *The Evolution of Desire: Strategies of Human Mating*. New York: Basic, 1994.
Calvin, William H. *How Brains Think: Evolving Intelligence, Then and Now*. Science Masters. London: Weidenfield and Nicolson, 1997.
———. "A Stone's Throw and Its Launch Window: Timing Precision and Its Implications for Language and Hominid Brains." *Journal of Theoretical Biology* 104 (1983): 121–35.
Campbell, Joseph. "Bios and Mythos: Prolegomena to a Science of Mythology." 1951. In Vickery, *Myth and Literature*.
Carey, John, ed. *The Faber Book of Science*. London: Faber and Faber, 1995.
Carpenter, C. R., ed. *Naturalistic Behaviour of Nonhuman Primates*. University Park, PA: Pennsylvania University Press, 1964.
Carroll, Joseph. *Evolution and Literary Theory*. Columbia, MI: University of Missouri Press, 1995.
———. "Steven Pinker's Cheesecake for the Mind." *Philosophy and Literature* 22, no. 2 (1998): 478–85.
———. "Wilson's *Consilience* and Literary Study." *Philosophy and Literature* 23, no. 2 (1999): 393–413.
Chargaff, Erwin. "Building the Tower of Babble." *Nature* 248, no. 5451 (26 April 1974): 776–79.
———. "On the Dangers of Genetic Meddling." Letter. *Science* 192, no. 4243 (4 June 1976): 938–40.
Chatman, Seymour, ed. *Approaches to Poetics*. New York: Columbia University Press, 1973.
Chomsky, Noam. *Reflections on Language*. New York: Pantheon, 1975.
Churchland, Patricia Smith. *Neurophilosophy: Toward a Unified Science of the Mind-Brain*. Computational Models of Cognition and Perception. Cambridge, MA: Bradford-MIT Press, 1986.
Churchland, Paul M. *Matter and Consciousness: A Contemporary Introduction to the Philosophy of Mind*. Rev. ed., Cambridge, MA: MIT Press, 1988.
Cordle, Daniel. *Postmodern Postures: Literature, Science and the Two Cultures Debate*. Aldershot: Ashgate, 1999.
cummings, e. e. *Complete Poems*. 2 Vols. N.p.: MacGibbon and Kee, 1968.
Dahlbom, Bo, ed. *Dennett and His Critics: Demystifying Mind*. Oxford: Blackwell, 1993.
Dampier, William C., and Margaret Dampier, eds. *Readings in the Literature of Science: Being Extracts from the Writings of Men of Science to Illustrate the Development of Scientific Thought*. New York: Harper, 1959.
Davidson, Donald. *Inquiries into Truth and Interpretation*. 2nd ed. Oxford: Clarendon, 2001.
Davis, Bernard B. "The Moralistic Fallacy." *Nature* 272, no. 5652 (30 March 1978): 390.
Dawkins, Richard. *Climbing Mount Improbable*. Harmondsworth, UK: Viking-Penguin Books, 1996.
———. *The Selfish Gene*. 1976, 2nd ed. Oxford: Oxford University Press, 1989.
———. "Sociobiology: The Debate Continues." Rev. of *Not in our Genes* by R. C. Lewontin, S. Rose, and L. Kamin. *New Scientist*, 24 January 1985: 59–60.

———. *River Out of Eden: A Darwinian View of Life.* Science Masters. London: Weidenfeld and Nicolson, 1995.
———. *Unweaving the Rainbow: Science, Delusion and the Appetite for Wonder.* Harmondsworth, UK: Penguin Books, 1998.
Dennett, Daniel C. *Brainstorms: Philosophical Essays on Mind and Psychology.* Hassocks, Sussex: Harvester, 1979.
———. *Consciousness Explained.* Boston, MA: Little, Brown, 1991.
———. *Darwin's Dangerous Idea: Evolution and the Meanings of Life.* New York: Simon and Schuster, 1995.
———. *The Extended Phenotype: The Long Reach of the Gene.* Afterword by Daniel C. Dennett. Oxford: Oxford University Press, 1999.
Dewey, John. *Human Nature and Conduct: an Introduction to Social Psychology.* London: Allen, 1922.
Dickens, Charles. *Bleak House.* 1852–53, edited and introduction by Stephen Gill. Oxford: Oxford World Classics, 1996.
Dissanayake, Ellen. *Homo Aestheticus: Where Art Comes From and Why.* Seattle, WA: University of Washington Press, 1995.
———. *What Is Art For?* Seattle, WA: University of Washington Press, 1988.
Dronamrafu, Krishna R., ed. *Haldane's Daedulus Revisited.* Foreword by Joshua Lederberg. Oxford: Oxford University Press: 1995.
Dutton, Denis. "Art and Sexual Selection." *Philosophy and Literature* 24, no. 2 (2000): 512–21.
———. "Sociobiology and Art." *Philosophy and Literature* 23, no. 2 (1999): 451–57.
Eddington, A[rthur]. S. *The Nature of the Physical World.* 1928. Cambridge: Cambridge University Press, 1944.
Eibl-Eibesfeldt, Irenäus. *Human Ethology.* New York: Walter de Gruyter, 1989.
Eigen, Manfred, with Ruthild Winkler-Oswatitsch. *Steps Toward Life: A Perspective on Evolution.* 1987, translated by Paul Woolley. Oxford: Oxford University Press, 1992.
Ekman, P., and R. J. Davidson, eds. *The Nature of Emotion.* New York: Oxford University Press, 1994.
Eldredge, Niles, and Ian Tattersall. *The Myths of Human Evolution.* New York: Columbia University Press, 1982.
Ellis, John M. *Literature Lost: Social Agendas and the Corruption of the Humanities.* New Haven, CT: Yale University Press, 1997.
Feyerabend, Paul K. *Against Method: Outline of an Anarchistic Theory of Knowledge.* London: New Left Books, 1975.
———. *Killing Time: The Autobiography of Paul Feyerabend.* Chigaco, IL: University of Chicago Press, 1995.
Feynman, Richard P. *The Character of Physical Law.* 1959. Cambridge, MA: MIT Press, 1990.
———. *The Pleasure of Finding Things Out: The Best Short Works of Richard P. Feynman,* edited by Jeffrey Robbins. London: Allen Lane-Penguin, 2000.
Fischer, Michael. "Redefining Philosophy as Literature: Richard Rorty's 'Defence' of Literary Culture." In Malachowski, *Reading Rorty,* 233–43.
Fish, Stanley. *Professional Correctness: Literary Studies and Political Change.* Oxford: Clarendon, 1995.

———. "What Is Stylistics and Why Are They Saying Such Terrible Things About It?" In Chatman, *Approaches to Poetics*, 109–52.

Fodor, Jerry A. *Psychosemantics: The Problem of Meaning in the Philosophy of Mind.* Cambridge, MA: Bradford-MIT Press, 1987.

Franklin, Sarah. "Making Transparencies: Seeing Through the Science Wars." In Ross, *Science Wars*, 151–67.

Frayn, Michael. *Copenhagen*. Rev. ed. London: Meuthen, 2000.

Frazer, James George. *The Golden Bough: A Study in Magic and Religion*, abr. ed., edited and introduction by Robert Fraser. Oxford: Oxford University Press, 1994.

Freud, Sigmund. "Creative Writers and Day-Dreaming." *Art and Literature: Jensen's Gravida, Leonardo da Vinci and Other Works*. The Penguin Freud Library. Vol. 14, edited by Albert Dickson and translated by James Strachey. Harmondsworth, UK: Penguin Books, 1990.

———. *The Standard Edition of the Complete Psychological Works of Sigmund Freud*, translated and edited by James Strachey. London: Hogarth, 1955.

Frye, Northrop. *Anatomy of Criticism: Four Essays*. 1957. Harmondsworth, UK: Penguin Books, 1990.

———. "The Archetypes of Literature." 1951. In Vickery, *Myth and Literature*.

Fuller, David, and Patricia Waugh. *The Arts and Sciences of Criticism*. Oxford: Oxford University Press, 1999.

Geertz, Clifford. *The Interpretation of Cultures: Selected Essays*. New York: Basic Books, 1973.

Gleick, James. *Genius: Richard Feynman and Modern Physics*. London: Abacus, 1995.

Gould, S[tephen]. J[ay]., and R. C. Lewontin. "The Spandrels of San Marco and The Panglossian Paradigm." *Proceedings of the Royal Society of London* B 205 (1979): 581–98.

Gould, Stephen Jay. "The Golden Rule: A Proper Scale for Our Environmental Crisis." In Pojman, *Environmental Ethics*.

———. *Life's Grandeur: The Spread of Excellence from Plato to Darwin*. London: Cape, 1996.

———. *An Urchin in the Storm: Essays about Books and Ideas*. New York: Norton, 1987.

———. *Wonderful Life: The Burgess Shale and the Nature of History*. 1990. London: Vintage, 2000.

Gribbin, John. *In Search of Schrödinger's Cat*. London: Black Swan, 1996.

Gross, Paul R. "The Icarian Impulse." *Wilson Quarterly* 22, no. 1 (1998): 39–49.

Hanfling, O. ed. *Essential Readings in Logical Positivism*. Oxford: Blackwell, 1981.

Haraway, Donna. *Primate Visions: Gender, Race, and Nature in the World of Modern Science*. New York: Routledge, 1989.

Hardin, C. L. *Color for Philosophers: Unweaving the Rainbow*. Indianapolis, IN: Hackett, 1988.

Harris, Wendell V. *Dictionary of Concepts in Literary Criticism and Theory*. New York: Greenwood, 1992.

Hawking, Stephen. *A Brief History of Time: From the Big Bang to Black Holes*. Toronto: Bantam, 1995.

Hayles, N. Katherine. "Consolidating the Canon." In Ross, *Science Wars*, 226–37.

———. *The Cosmic Web: Scientific Field Models and Literary Strategies in the Twentieth Century*. Ithaca, NY: Cornell University Press, 1984.

Heisenberg, Werner. *Physics and Beyond: Encounters and Conversations*, translated by Arnold J. Pomerans. New York: Allen and Unwin, 1971.

Herrnstein, Richard J., and Charles Murray. *The Bell Curve: Intelligence and Class Structure in American Life*. New York: Free Press/Simon and Schuster, 1994.

Hirsch, E. D., Jr. *Validity in Interpretation*. New Haven, CT: Yale University Press, 1967.

Hoffman, Paul. *The Man Who Loved Only Numbers: The Story of Paul Erdos and the Search for Mathematical Truth*. London: Fourth Estate, 1998.

Hogan, Patrick Colm. "Literary Universals." *Poetics Today* 18, no. 2 (1997): 223–46.

Holton, Gerald. *Science and Anti-science*. Cambridge, MA: Harvard University Press, 1993.

Hornsby, Jennifer. "Physics, Biology, and Common-sense Psychology." In Lennon and Charles, *Reduction, Explanation, and Realism*.

Huxley, Aldous. *Brave New World Revisited*. London: Chatto, 1959.

Jackson, Leonard. *The Poverty of Structuralism: Literature and Structuralist Theory*. London: Longman, 1991.

Jackson, Tony. "Questioning Interdisciplinarity: Cognitive Science, Evolutionary Psychology, and Literary Criticism." *Poetics Today* 21, no. 2 (2000): 319–47.

Jakobson, Roman. *Language in Literature*, edited by Krystyna Pomorska and Stephen Rudy. Cambridge, MA: Belknap-Harvard University Press, 1987.

———. "Modern Russian Poetry: Velimir Khlebnikov [Excerpts]." In *Major Soviet Writers: Essays in Criticism*. Edited and translated by Edward J. Brown. London: Oxford University Press, 1973.

James, William. *Pragmatism: A New Name for Some Old Ways of Thinking*. 1907. London: Longmans, 1910.

Jung, Carl Gustav. *The Spirit in Man, Art, and Literature*, translated by R. F. C. Hull. 2nd ed. Princeton, NJ: Princeton University Press, 1966. Vol.15 of *The Collected Works of C. G. Jung*. 18 vols., edited by Herbert Read, Michael Fordham, Gerhard Adler, and William McGuire.

Keats, John. *The Complete Poems*, edited by John Barnard. 3rd ed. Harmondsworth, UK: Penguin Books, 1988.

Kellman, Steven G., and Irving Malin, eds. *Into "The Tunnel": Readings of Gass's Novel*. Newark, DE: University of Delaware Press, 1998.

Kernan, Alvin. *The Death of Literature*. New Haven, CT: Yale University Press, 1990.

Kline, Stephen Jay. *Conceptual Foundations for Multidisciplinary Thinking*. Stanford, CA: Stanford University Press, 1996.

Kuhn, Thomas S. *The Essential Tension: Selected Studies in Scientific Tradition and Change*. Chicago, IL: University of Chicago Press, 1977.

———. *The Structure of Scientific Revolutions*. 1962. 2nd ed., enlarged. *International Encyclopedia of Unified Science*. Vol. 2, no. 2. Chicago, IL: University of Chicago Press, 1970.

Kurzweil, Edith. *The Age of Structuralism: Lévi-Strauss to Foucault*. New York: Columbia University Press, 1980.

Laidler, Keith J., and John H. Meiser. *Physical Chemistry*. 2nd ed. Boston, MA: Houghton Mifflin, 1995.

Leavis, F. R. *Nor Shall My Sword: Discourses on Pluralism, Compassion and Social Hope*. London: Chatto and Windus, 1972.

LeClair, Tom, and Larry McCaffery, eds. *Anything Can Happen: Interviews with Contemporary American Novelists*. Urbana, IL: University of Illinois Press, 1983.

Lennon, Kathleen, and David Charles, eds. *Reduction, Explanation, and Realism*. Oxford: Clarendon, 1992.

Levi, Primo. *The Drowned and the Saved*. 1986. Translated by Raymond Rosenthal. Introduction by Paul Bailey. London: Abacus, 1989.

Lévi-Strauss, Claude. *The Origin of Table Manners*, translated by John Weightman and Doreen Weightman. London: Jonathan Cape, 1978. Vol. 3 of *Introduction to a Science of Mythology*. 4 vols. Originally published as *Mythologiques: 3*, 1968.

———. *Structural Anthropology*, translated by Claire Jacobson and Brooke Grundfest Shoepf. New York: Basic Books, 1963.

Levine, George. *Darwin Among the Novelists: Patterns of Science in Victorian Fiction*. Cambridge, MA: Harvard University Press, 1988.

———. "What Is Science Studies For, and Who Cares?" In Ross, *Science Wars*.

Limon, John. *The Place of Fiction in the Time of Science: A Disciplinary History of American Writing*. Cambridge Studies in American Literature and Culture. Cambridge: Cambridge University Press, 1990.

Malachowski, Alan, ed. *Reading Rorty: Critical Responses to "Philosophy and the Mirror of Nature" (and Beyond)*. Oxford: Blackwell, 1990.

Martinich, A. P. ed. *The Philosophy of Language*. 3rd ed. New York: Oxford University Press, 1996.

Marshack, Alexander. "Upper Paleolithic Symbol Systems of the Russian Plain: Cognitive and Comparative Analysis." *Current Anthropology* 20, no. 2 (1979): 271–311.

Maynard Smith, John. "Constraints on Human Behaviour." Rev. of *On Human Nature*, by E. O. Wilson. *Nature* 276, no. 5684 (November 9, 1978): 120–21.

Mazlish, Bruce. *The Fourth Discontinuity: The Co-Evolution of Humans and Machines*. New Haven, CT: Yale University Press, 1993.

McEwan, Ian. *The Child in Time*. London: Vintage, 1997.

McRae, Murdo William, ed. *The Literature of Science: Perspectives on Popular Science Writing*. Athens, GA: University of Georgia Press, 1993.

Menke, Richard. "Narrative Reversals and the Thermodynamics of History in Martin Amis's *Time's Arrow*." *Modern Fiction Studies* 44, no. 4 (1998): 959–80.

Merquior, J. G. *From Prague to Paris: A Critique of Structuralist and Post-Structuralist Thought*. London: Verso, 1986.

Midgely, Mary. "Rival Fatalisms: The Hollowness of the Sociobiology Debate," In *Sociobiology Examined*, edited by Ashley Montague. Oxford: Oxford University Press, 1980.

Miller, Geoffrey. *The Mating Mind: How Sexual Choice Shaped the Evolution of Human Nature*. London: Heinemann, 2000.

Naess, Arne. "The Shallow and the Deep, Long-Range Ecological Movement." In Pojman, *Environmental Ethics*.

Nagel, Thomas. *The View from Nowhere*. New York: Oxford University Press, 1986.

Newton-Smith, W. H., ed. *A Companion to the Philosophy of Science*. Oxford: Blackwell, 2000.

Norris, Christopher. *Deconstruction and the "Unfinished Project of Modernity."* London: Athlone, 2000.

———. *New Idols of the Cave: On the Limits of Anti-realism*. Manchester: Manchester University Press, 1997.

O'Hear, Anthony. *Beyond Evolution: Human Nature and the Limits of Evolutionary Explanation*. Oxford: Clarendon, 1997.

———. *The Element of Fire: Science, Art and the Human World*. London: Routledge, 1988.

Oppenheim, Paul, and Hilary Putnam. "Unity of Science as a Working Hypothesis." In *Minnesota Studies in the Philosophy of Science*, Vol. 2, *Concepts, Theories, and the Mind-Body Problem*, edited by Herbert Fiegl, Michael Scriven, and Grover Maxwell. Minnesota: University of Minnesota Press, 1958.

Orr, H. Allen. "Dennett's Dangerous Idea." Rev. of *Darwin's Dangerous Idea* by Daniel C. Dennett. *Evolution* 50, no. 1 (1996): 467–72.

Orwell, George. *Nineteen Eighty-Four*. 1949. Harmondsworth, UK: Penguin Books, 1989.

Otis, Laura, ed. *Literature and Science in the Nineteenth Century: An Anthology*. Oxford: Oxford University Press, 2002.

Paulos, John Allen. *Innumeracy: Mathematical Illiteracy and its Consequences*. London: Viking, 1989.

Pickering, Andrew, ed., *Science As Practice and Culture*. Chicago, IL: University of Chicago Press, 1992.

Pinker, Steven. *How the Mind Works*. Harmondsworth, UK: Penguin Books, 1998.

———. *The Language Instinct: How the Mind Creates Language*. Harmondsworth, UK: Penguin Books, 1995.

Pojman, Louis P., ed. *Environmental Ethics: Readings in Theory and Application*. Boston, MA: Jones and Bartlett, 1994.

Polti, Georges. *The Thirty-Six Dramatic Situations*. 1895. Translated by Lucille Ray, 1921. Boston, MA: The Writer Inc., 1977.

Powers, Richard. *Galatea 2.2*. New York: Farrar, Straus and Giroux, 1995.

———. *The Gold Bug Variations*. 1991. New York: Harper Collins, 1992.

Putnam, Hilary. *Mathematics, Matter and Method*. Vol. 1 of *Philosophical Papers*. 3 vols. to date. Cambridge: Cambridge University Press, 1975.

———. *Mind, Language and Reality*. Vol. 2 of *Philosophical Papers*. 3 vols. to date. Cambridge: Cambridge University Press, 1975.

———. *Realism and Reason*. Vol. 3 of *Philosophical Papers*. 3 vols. to date. Cambridge: Cambridge University Press, 1983.

———. "Why Reason Can't be Naturalized." In *After Philosophy: End or Transformation?* edited by Kenneth Baynes, James Bohman, and Thomas McCarthy. Cambridge, MA: MIT Press, 1987.

Pynchon, Thomas. *Gravity's Rainbow*. London: Jonathan Cape, 1973.

Quine, W. V. O. "Let Me Accentuate the Positive." In Malachowski, *Reading Rorty*.

Raff, Rudolf A. *The Shape of Life: Genes, Development, and the Evolution of Animal Form*. Chicago, IL: University of Chicago Press, 1996.

Rachels, James. *Created from Animals: The Moral Implications of Darwinism*. Oxford: Oxford University Press, 1991.

Richards, Graham. *Human Evolution: An Introduction for the Behavioural Sciences*. London: Routledge, 1987.

Ridley, Matt. *The Red Queen: Sex and the Evolution of Human Nature.* London: Viking, 1993.

Robey, David, ed. *Structuralism: An Introduction.* Wolfson College Lectures, Oxford University, 1972. Oxford: Clarendon, 1973.

Roede, Machteld, Jan Wind, John M. Patrick, and Vernon Reynolds, eds. *The Aquatic Ape: Fact or Fiction? The First Scientific Evaluation of a Controversial Theory of Human Evolution.* London: Souvenir, 1991.

Rorty, Richard. "Against Unity." *Wilson Quarterly* 22:1 (1998): 28–38.

———. *Consequences of Pragmatism: Essays: 1972–1980.* Brighton: Harvester, 1982.

———. *Contingency, Irony, and Solidarity.* Cambridge: Cambridge University Press, 1989.

———. *Essays on Heidegger and Others.* Vol. 2 of *Philosophical Papers.* 3 vols. to date. Cambridge: Cambridge University Press, 1991.

———. "Kuhn." In Newton-Smith, *A Companion to the Philosophy of Science.*

———. *Objectivity, Relativism, and Truth.* Vol. 1 of *Philosophical Papers.* 3 vols. to date. Cambridge: Cambridge University Press, 1991.

———. *Philosophy and Social Hope.* Harmondsworth, UK: Penguin Books, 1999.

———. *Philosophy and the Mirror of Nature.* 1979. Oxford: Blackwell, 1980.

———. "Pragmatism, Davidson and Truth." In *Truth and Interpretation: Perspectives on the Philosophy of Donald Davidson,* edited by Ernest LePore. Oxford: Blackwell, 1986.

———. *Truth and Progress.* Vol. 3 of *Philosophical Papers.* 3 vols. to date. Cambridge: Cambridge University Press, 1998.

Rose, Steven, and Hilary Rose, eds. *Alas, Poor Darwin: Arguments Against Evolutionary Psychology.* London: Cape, 2000.

Rosenthal, David, ed. *The Nature of Mind.* Oxford: Oxford University Press, 1991.

Ross, Andrew, edited and introduction. *Science Wars.* Durham, NC: Duke University Press, 1996.

Rossotti, Hazel. *Fire.* Oxford: Oxford University Press, 1993.

Rushdie, Salman. *Shame.* London: Jonathan Cape, 1983.

Ryle, Gilbert. *The Concept of Mind.* Oxford: Oxford University Press, 1949.

———. *Dilemmas: The Tanner Lectures 1953.* Cambridge: Cambridge University Press, 1954.

Scholes, Robert. *Structural Fabulation: An Essay on the Fiction of the Future.* Notre Dame, IN: University of Notre Dame Press, 1975.

Schopenhauer, Arthur. *The World As Will and Idea.* 1883. Translated by R. B. Haldane and J. Kemp. 3 vols. London: Routledge, 1948.

Searle, John. "Is the Brain's Mind a Computer Program?" *Scientific American* 262 (January 1990): 20–25.

———. *The Rediscovery of Mind.* Cambridge, MA: MIT Press, 1992.

Segerstråle, Ullica. *Defenders of the Truth: The Battle for Science in the Sociobiology Debate and Beyond.* Oxford: Oxford University Press, 2000.

Seligman, Martin E. P., and Joanne L. Hagar, eds. *Biological Boundaries of Learning.* New York: Appleton-Century-Crofts, 1972.

Sinfield, Alan. *Faultlines: Cultural Materialism and the Politics of Dissident Reading.* Oxford: Clarendon, 1992.

Singer, Peter, ed. *Applied Ethics.* Oxford Readings in Philosophy. Oxford: Oxford University Press, 1986.

Slade, Joseph W., and Judith Yaross Lee, eds. *Beyond the Two Cultures.* Ames, IA: Iowa State University Press, 1990.

Smith, Peter. "Modest Reductions and the Unity of Science." In Lennon and Charles, *Reduction, Explanation, and Realism.*

Snow, C. P. *The Two Cultures and a Second Look: An Expanded Version of the Two Cultures and the Scientific Revolution.* Introduction by Stefan Collini. Cambridge: Cambridge University Press, 1964.

Sober, Elliott. *Philosophy of Biology.* 2nd ed. Dimensions of Philosophy Series. Boulder, CO: Westview, 2000.

Sokal, Alan, and Jean Bricmont. *Intellectual Impostures: Postmodern Philosophers' Abuse of Science,* translated by Sokal and Bricmont. London: Profile Books, 1998.

Sontag, Susan. *Against Interpretation and Other Essays.* New York: Farrar, Straus and Giroux, 1966.

———. "The Pornographic Imagination." In *A Susan Sontag Reader.* Harmondsworth, UK: Penguin Books, 1983.

Steiner, George. *After Babel: Aspects of Language and Translation.* 1975. 2nd ed. Oxford: Oxford University Press, 1992.

Symes, Colin. "Writing by Numbers: OuLiPo and the Creativity of Constraints." *Mosaic* 32, no. 3 (1999): 87–107.

Tallis, Raymond. *Enemies of Hope: A Critique of Contemporary Pessimism: Irrationalism, Anti-Humanism and Counter Enlightenment.* London: MacMillan, 1997.

———. *Newton's Sleep: Two Cultures and Two Kingdoms.* London: MacMillan, 1995.

Todorov, Tzvetan. *The Poetics of Prose,* translated by Richard Howard. Oxford: Blackwell, 1977.

———. "Structural Analysis of Narrative." *Novel* 3 (Fall 1969): 70–76.

———. "Structuralism and Literature." In Chatman, *Approaches to Poetics.*

———. "The Surrender to Nature," translated by Claire Messud. Review of *Consilience: The Unity of Knowledge* by Edward O. Wilson. *The New Republic* (April 27, 1998): 29–33.

Turner, Mark. *Reading Minds: The Study of English in the Age of Cognitive Science.* Princeton, NJ: Princeton University Press, 1991.

Tymoczko, Thomas, ed. *New Directions in the Philosophy of Mathematics: An Anthology.* Rev. ed. Princeton, NJ: Princeton University Press, 1998.

van Fraassen, Bas C. "Empiricism in the Philosophy of Science." In *Images of Science: Essays on Realism and Empiricism, with a Reply from Bas C. Van Fraassen,* edited by Paul M. Churchland and Clifford A. Hooker. Chicago, IL: University of Chicago Press, 1985.

Vonnegut, Kurt, Jr. *Slaughterhouse-Five, Or The Children's Crusade: A Duty Dance With Death.* 1968. New York: Dell, 1976.

Vickery, John B., ed. *Myth and Literature: Contemporary Theory and Practice.* Lincoln, NE: University of Nebraska Press, 1966.

Vidal, Jean-Marie, Michel Vancassel, and René Quris. "Introducing Anthropomorphism, Discontinuities and Anecdotes to Question Them." *Behavioural Processes* 35 (1995): 299–309.

Wallace, David Foster. "Rhetoric and the Math Melodrama." Review of *The Wild*

Numbers by Philbert Schogt and *Uncle Petros and Goldbach's Conjecture* by Apostolos Doxiadis. *Science* 290, no. 5500 (15 December 2000): 2263–2267.

Watt, Ian. *The Rise of the Novel: Studies in Defoe, Richardson and Fielding.* 1957. London: Hogarth, 1987.

Webster, Richard. "The Great Enterprise." Review of *Newton's Sleep* by Raymond Tallis. *TLS* (16 February 1996): 30.

Wegner, Daniel M. *The Illusion of Conscious Will.* Cambridge, MA: Bradford/MIT Press, 2002.

Weinberg, Steven. "Can Science Explain Everything? Anything?" *New York Review of Books* (31 May 2001): 47–50.

———. *Dreams of a Final Theory.* New York: Pantheon, 1992.

———. "Sokal's Hoax," *New York Review of Books* (8 August 1996): 11–15.

Whitman, Walt. *The Complete Poems*, edited by Francis Murphy. Harmondsworth, UK: Penguin Books, 1986.

Whorf, Benjamin Lee. *Language, Thought, and Reality: Selected Writings of Benjamin Lee Whorf*, edited and introduction by John B. Carroll. Cambridge, MA: MIT Press, 1956.

Williams, Bernard. "*Auto-da-Fé:* Consequences of Pragmatism." In Malachowski, *Reading Rorty.*

Wilson, Edward O. *Consilience: The Unity of Knowledge.* London: Little, Brown, 1998.

———. *Sociobiology: The New Synthesis.* Cambridge, MA: Belknap-Harvard University Press, 1975.

Wolpert, Lewis. *The Unnatural Nature of Science.* London: Faber and Faber, 1992.

———. "Which Side Are You On?" *Observer* (March 10, 2002): Review section, 6.

Index

Abrams, Meyer H., 41, 124
academic, as pejorative, 14–15
acquired characteristics, 54–55. *See also* Jung; Lamarckism
Adapted Mind, The (Barkow, Cosmides, Tooby), 77, 97
adaptive function: of art 85, 86, 95; of narrative 90; in organisms 81. *See also* spandrels
advertising slogans: as subject for linguistic analysis 68, 218 n. 113; use of scientists in, 100
aesthetic(s): manifestos, 125; of philosophy 122; of scientific knowledge, 114
After Babel (Steiner), 183
Against Method (Feyerabend), 109–12, 232 n. 1
"Against Unity" (Rorty), 35
airplane argument (against relativism), 12, 128, 130, 132, 233 n. 7
airport fiction, 90. *See also* genre fiction; literary, distinct from subliterary
Alas, Poor Darwin (Rose and Rose), 138
alchemy, 41
algorithm: for creativity, 72, 99; for literature, 66
Allen, Woody, 95
altruism, 178
Amis, Martin: *The Information*, 16, 190–95; as literary critic, 197–99, 205, 244 n. 105; on technology, 141, *Time's Arrow*, 16, 179, 183–88
analgesics, mechanics of, 155
analytic truths, 246 n. 16
anarchistic theory of knowledge (Feyerabend), 109, 110, 111
Anatomy of Criticism (Frye), 40–41, 43–47, 51, 193–94
Animal House, 95
anthropocentrism: and narcissism, 242 n. 40; and the novel, 202–3; prohibition of, 174, 188–90

anthropology: of art, 85; and entomology, 105; as discipline, 24, 76–77; and literary study, 46, 52
anthropomorphism: permissibility of, 226 n. 19; in primatology, 105
anti-intentionality, 204. *See also* intentionality
anti-realism, 132, 139
anti-science, 102
ants, 23
Anxiety of Influence (Bloom), 123
Appleyard, Brian, 138
appropriate scales, 191. *See also* explanation, levels of; reductionism
aquatic ape hypothesis, 221 n. 21
archetypes: Jungian, 44, 46, 54; in poetry, 53; theory of literature, 94
architecture: as art, 41
Aristotle, 165
Arnold, Matthew, 36, 96, 98
art: arrow of, 194; for art's sake, 50; circle of, 41; elite tastes, 165; history of, 225 n. 3; as luxury, 85; and modern science, 232 n. 114; outwith artists, 170; outwith entertainment, 96; universality of art, 86
artificial intelligence (AI), 70–72
astronomy: as science, 112, 118; versus astrology, 192; as trope, 245 n. 117
Auden, W. H., 12, 138
Auschwitz, 184
autonomy: of literature, 68; of object of study, 176. *See also* determinism; disciplinary
Ayer, A. J., 117

background: beliefs, 146, 153; conditions, 32
Ballard, J. G., 185
Barkow, Jerome, 77, 80–81, 97
Barthes, Roland, 56

Bastian, Adolf, 52–53
Baudelaire, Charles, 59, 60–61, 65
Beardsley, Monroe C., 60
beaver dams, 83, 84, 219n. 139
Beer, Gillian, 17
behavioral genetics, 103
behaviorism, 177, 204. *See also* psychology
Bell Curve, The (Murray and Herrnstein), 103–4
Bennett, James, 67, 68
benzene ring, 107
Beyond Evolution (O'Hear), 138
Bible, 52–53, 88
big bang, 185, 188; as distal cause, 34
big crunch, 185, 188
Binns, A. L., 57–58, 66
biochemists, 166
Birketts, Sven, 69
black holes, 145
blank slate, 83
Bleak House (Dickens), 127
blind watchmaker, 70
Bloom, Harold, 69, 123–24, 126
Boden, Margaret, 70–74, 92, 99, 180
Bodkin, Maud, 53–55
Bohr, Niels, 18
Booth, Wayne C., 42, 46, 145, 147, 149, 154
Borges, Jorge Luis, 42, 71
botany, as higher level science, 149
brain (as bodily organ), 79, 80
Brave New World (Huxley), 137
Brave New Worlds (Appleyard), 138
Bricmont, Jean, 109–10, 112, 144, 149
Brief History of Time, A (Hawking), 143–44
Bruner, Jerome, 180

cabalism, 50
Cage, John, 91
Calvin, William, 64, 73
Cambridge Ritualists, 52–53, 93
Campbell, Joseph, 52, 93
Cantos, The (Pound), 42
Carey, John, 143
cargo-cult science, 128
Carnap, Rudolf, 26
Carpenter, Clarence Ray, 104–6, 108, 225n. 17
Carroll, Joseph, 14, 51, 55–56, 74, 94–99, 141, 160–66; quarrel with Pinker 94–95
cartography, 43
categorization, 40
cause: bottom up and top down, 135–37, 155, distal and proximal, 33, 34; laws of, 71; levels of, 211–12n. 33; total, 32
Cézanne, Paul, 44
chaos theory, 17, 19
Chargaff, Erwin, 25, 237n. 85
Charles, David, 28
"Chats, Les" (Baudelaire), 59
chemistry: as discipline, 119, 135, 136, 186; vocabulary of, 133
Chinese Metaphysics (Midgely), 20, 21
Chinese Room (Searle), 71
Chomsky, Noam, 13, 39–40, 43, 45, 83–84, 192, 208n. 5, 214n. 2
Chomskyan linguistics, 93
Christian belief (versus scientific), 118
Churchland, Patricia, 106, 133
Churchland, Paul, 28–29, 133
Classical mythology, 44, 52, 53, 197
cloud formations, 106
cognitive limits of human minds, 183
cognitive science, 20, 39, 76, 165–67, 203–4, 209n. 18
coherence of literature, 42
coherence theory of truth, 115–17, 120, 203
collective unconscious, 53, 93
commonsense: appeals to, 145, 234n. 25; correspondence theory, 234n. 25; psychology, 28; realists, 157; and science, 131. *See also* folk theories
computer simulations of creativity, 57, 73
conceptual center of literature, 44, 167
conceptual integration, 77, 78, 97, 212n. 36. *See also* reductionism
conscious awareness, 177
Consciousness Explained (Dennett), 57, 180
consensus theory of truth, 113, 227–28n. 52. *See* coherence theory
Consilience (Wilson), 23–24, 34, 74, 82, 94, 113, 199, 206
consilience, 23–24, 27, 36, 39, 73, 85
constructive interference, 15
constructivism (social), 104, 108, 128, 132, 206, 222n. 32
context of discovery / justification, 107, 108, 111, 112, 137, 170, 209n. 14

continuity with nature, 180
Contra Sainte-Beuve (Proust), 17
convergent evolution, 90
Copenhagen Interpretation, 18
Copernican(ism): as belief system, 109, 205; contrasted with Ptolemaic universe, 196–97; revolution, 176–77; vote for, 227 n. 33
Copernicus, Nikolas, 142, 172, 176
Cornford, F. M., 52. *See also* Cambridge Ritualists
correspondence theory of truth, 115–17, 127, 234 n. 25. *See also* coherence theory
Cosmides, Leda, 77–78, 80–81, 83–84, 97–98
cosmology, 70, 174, 194, 196. *See also* astronomy
Created From Animals (Rachels), 174
creationism, 101, 120
Creative Mind, The (Boden), 70, 74
creativity: algorithm, 72, 99; continuum, 224 n. 87; innateness of, 86; simulation, 92; traditional notions of, 56; transcendental account, 96
Creole, 93, 222 n. 41. *See also* pidgin
Crick, Francis, 42, 172, 173
Crime and Punishment (Dostoevsky), 51
cubists, 50
Culler, Jonathan, 67
cultural: evolution, 90; norms, 86; senses of, 140; significance of science, 172
cummings, e. e., 19, 57, 60

Dante, 62, 65, 72, 168
Darwin, Charles, 55, 86–87, 96–97, 161, 171–73, 176
Darwin Among the Novelists (Levine), 97
Darwinian: accounts of art, 133; as belief system, 201; contrasted with Lamarckian, 54; explanation of, 33; revolution, 176, 177; theory, 13, 19, 44, 70, 81
Davidson, Donald, 126, 152
Davis, Bernard, 103, 120
Dawkins: against relativism, 12, 128, 130–32; altruism, 178; anthropocentrism, 173–75, 176, 189; attitude to arts, 138; blind watchmaker program, 70; faith healers, 119, 120; memes, 87–89; utility of popular science, 146, 148–50, 156; as zoologist, 192

daydreams (Freud), 91, 92
De Man, Paul, 124
"death of the author" (Barthes), 56
Death of Literature, The (Kernan), 69, 124, 206
decentering, 172–73, 176, 181, 206. *See also* anthropocentism
deconstruction, 94
Deep Blue (IBM computer), 72
deep ecology, 201–2
deep time, 181, 189, 243 n. 67
defences: of literary criticism, 124; of poetry, 159
DeLillo, Don, 16, 101
delusion, 178–79
democracy (and science), 109, 110, 227 n. 33
Demoiselles d'Avignon (Picasso), 18
"demonstrable value judgements" (Frye), 166
Dennett, Daniel C.: appropriate stances, 36, 213 n. 60; computational theory of mind, 171, 173; criticism of, 154; demystification, 57, 180; evolution, 81–82, 84–85; evolutionary psychology, 37; mechanistic explanations 73; memes, 87–89
Derrida, Jacques, 17, 121–22
Derridian epistemology, 17, 19
Descartes, René, 24–25, 121
descriptions: levels of, 136, 229 n. 73; pluralism, 36; relative to purposes, 116
destructive interference, 15
determinism, 170–71, 179, 183; historical, 176, 186; genetic, 155, 177–78; in literature, 168, 169; physics (Laplacean), 155, 185
Dewey, John, 230 n. 68, 231 n. 86
Dick, Philip K., 185
Dickens, Charles, 127
Dirac, Paul A. M., 140
disciplinary: autonomy, 15, 150, 157, 206; boundaries, 149, 153; identity, 77; obsolescence, 27; vocabulary, 120, 158
Dissanayake, Ellen, 86, 92, 94–95
DNA, 30, 42, 88, 149; mitochondrial, 216 n. 66
Dostoevsky, Fyodor, 137
dreams (and theories), 107. *See also* Kekulé
Dresden, 183, 189

Drowned and the Saved, The (Levi), 184
Dryden, John, 95
dualism: Cartesian, 24, 55; of property, 33, 213 n. 62
Duchamp's urinal ("Fountain"), 91
Dutton, Denis, 80, 91
Dylan, Bob, 95

$E = mc^2$, 144–45, 147, 210 n. 14, 237 n. 102
ecology: shallow versus deep, 201
economics, 37
Eddington, Arthur, 140, 185, 229 n. 73
edification / edifiers, 121, 127, 159
education: humanities, 143; specialization in, 25
Eibl-Eibesfeldt, Irenäus, 49, 83–84
Einstein, Albert, 18–19, 42, 106, 140, 144, 147, 152, 172, 197, 198
Einstein's Monsters (Amis), 185, 188
Eisenhower, Dwight, 65
Ekman, Paul, 49
Eldredge, Niles, 35, 40
"Elementary Ideas" (Bastian), 52, 53
eliminativism, 28–29, 133–34, 190, 210–11 n. 26, 217 n. 76
Eliot, T. S., 163
Ellis, John, 40, 45, 56, 93, 124
emergent properties, 167
empirical facts, 17
Enchanted Loom, The (Jastrow), 180
end of science (idea), 45
Enemies of Hope (Tallis), 176
engineers (contra scientists), 155
entomology, 23, 105
entropy, 186
environmentalism, 175, 181, 199, 201–2
epigenetic rules, 78
equations, 142
escapism (as function of art), 90
essentialism, 78
ethology, 24
eugenics, 129
euphemism, 101
evidence-free generalisations, 40
evil scientists, 129, 233 n. 14
Evolution and Literary Theory (Carroll), 94, 96, 160–61
evolutionary biology, 34
evolutionary epistemology, 14, 86
evolutionary explanation, 33
evolutionary psychology: Chomsky, 208 n. 5, cognitive science, 20; criticisms of, 81, 163; defined, 77, 79–81; determinism, 178–79, 201; divergent attitudes to, 37; explanatory poverty of, 14, 162–63, 203; intuitive appeal of, 145; literary criticism, 38, 94–96, 160–62, 164–69; memes, 87–90; novelty in, 161; post-structuralism, 96–97; scientific status of, 239 n. 13; structuralism, 75–76; taxonomical schema, 49, 91–92, 167–68; threat from, 13, 133–34, 206
evolutionary theory: account of art, 93–94; and cognitive science, 20; growth of, 13, 14; levels of selection, 179; and literature, 97. *See also* Carroll, Joseph; evolutionary psychology
exaptions, 82. *See also* spandrels
explanation: classes of, 24; definitions of, 14; discipline specificity of, 24; evolutionary (criticized), 212 n. 46; geometric (*see* geometric); interest relative explanations, 31–34, 116; levels of, 26, 31, 33–36, 73, 230 n. 76; software/hardware, 36, 37; structural, 30; top-down and bottom-up, 26, 136–37
external attitudes to literature, 45–46, 49, 56, 68, 123, 162

Faber Book of Science, The (Carey), 143
faith: as mind virus, 88. *See also* memes
faith healers, 119
fatalism, 179 183. *See also* determinism
feminism, 45, 46, 56, 160. *See also* external attitudes
Fermat Theorem of Literature, 66, 70
Feyerabend, 109–13, 118, 127, 130
Feynman, Richard Phillips, 14, 144, 146, 150, 152–53, 190
filters, 162
Finnegans Wake (Joyce), 42
first approximations, 192
Fischer, Michael, 124–26
Fish, Stanley, 14, 57, 67, 113–15, 120, 150, 153, 157–58, 160, 166, 189
Flaubert, Gustave, 91
Fleming, Alexander, 110
Fodor, Jerry, 116, 135, 168
folk / commonsense: psychology, 28; theories, 28–30. *See also* commonsense

For and Against Method (Feyerabend/Lakatos), 110, 227 n. 44
formalism (in literature), 56
formulaic fiction, 91
found / made distinction, 106, 115, 120
Franklin, Sarah, 128
Frayn, Michael, 209 n. 14
Frazer, James, 52–53, 93
free will, 182–83, 188, 205. *See also* determinism
French literary theory, 139
Freud, Sigmund, 91–92, 100, 176–77, 179–80, 194, 202
Freudian(ism): theories, 13, 28; conceptual revolution, 176, 177
Frye, Northrop, 37, 40, 42–48, 51–53, 56, 60, 62, 65, 68–69, 93, 123–24, 152, 162, 166–69, 177, 193–97, 205
functionalism: in art, 204; as philosophy, 32, 137, 148; theory of mind, 212 n. 41
fundamental particles, 210 n. 23

Gaia theory, 100
Galileo, 109–10, 118
games, 231 n. 99
Geertz, Clifford, 78, 81, 83
generalism, 21. *See also* specialization
genetics: constraints, 78; inheritance, 30; legacy of, 202; ontological status of, 30, 211 n. 29; theory of, 55
genre fiction, 51, 66, 91, 169
genres, literary: seasonal correlates, 195. *See also* Theory of Genres
geocentric universe, 205. *See also* Ptolemaic
geology, 17, 174; deep time, 181, 243 n. 67
geometric: explanations, 32–33, 191, 213 n. 62, 230 n. 81; and literature, 44
geophysics, 17
Gestalt, 87
God, 128, 172, 180, 182, 190; as meme, 88, 223 n. 60
Gödel, Kurt, 19
Goethe, Johann Wolfgang von, 47, 50
Golden Bough, The, 52
Goodwin, Brian, 135, 235 n. 39
Gould, Stephen Jay, 37, 81–82, 99, 173, 176, 180–81, 189, 191–92
Gozzi, Carlo, 47, 48
Graham, Ron, 139

grammatology, 121
"Grasshopper, The" (Xlebnikov), 61
Graves, Robert, 60
gravity: laws of, 142, 156, 172; metaphorical, 184
Gray's Anatomy, 79
Greeks (ancient), 50
"Greensleeves," 88
Gribbin, John, 133, 143
Gross, Paul R., 85
Gutenberg Elegies, The (Birketts), 69

Hacking, Ian, 146
Haraway, Donna, 104–6
hard science, 35
hardware / software distinction, 94
Hardy, Alistair, 221 n. 21
Hardy, G. H., 140
Harris, Wendell, 53
Harrison, Jane, 52
Hartman, Geoffrey, 124
Hawking, Stephen, 143–44
Hayles, N. Katherine, 104–9, 111–13, 130–31, 222 n. 28
Haywain (Constable), 8
Hegel, G. W. F., 121
Heisenberg, Werner, 18–19, 106, 140
Herrnstein, Richard J., 103–4
Hertzsprung-Russell (HR) diagram, 196, 245 n. 123
hierarchy: collapsed, 119; general principle of organization, 136; of methods, 110; ontological, 157, 190; taxonomy as, 44
high and low art, 57, 96
Hilbert, David, 41
Hirsch, E. D., 63–64
Hitler, Adolf, 241 n. 28
Hogan, Patrick Colm, 168, 223 n. 71
Holocaust (Shoah), 184, 186
holocaust, 187–88
Holton, Gerald, 101–2, 129
homeopathy, 101
Homo Aestheticus (Dissanayake), 86, 92
homocentrism, 192. *See* anthropocentrism
homunculus, 179, 184, 186
Hopi language, 151–52. *See also* Whorf
hostile takeovers, 133–34
How the Mind Works (Pinker), 95, 161, 208 n. 5

Hull, David, 89
human / non-human distinction, 105, 174
human agency, 176, 182, 193
human nature: universality, 49, 78, 80, 167; diversity, 79; and literature, 98. *See also* evolutionary psychology.
Huxley, Aldous, 20, 137- 38, 144
Huxley, Thomas H., 36
hygiene metaphors, 100

idealism, 118
"ideas" and "opinions" (Booth), 147–48
identifying poems, 159–60
identity theory (of mind), 28–29, 210n. 23
ideograms, 163
If Not Now, When? (Levi), 187
Illusion of Conscious Will, The (Wegner) 220n. 142
illustrations, scientific, 17
imperialism: scientific, 13–14, 75, 199
improvisation, 65
In Search of Schrödinger's Cat (Gribbin), 143
incompleteness theorem, 19
indifference of nature, 173
individualism: and the novel, 194, 202
inexhaustibility of literature, 45, 170, 218n. 117
influence of the unconscious, 179
Information, The (Amis), 16, 141, 190, 193–94
International Encyclopedia of Unified Sciences, 26
Innumeracy (Paulos), 141
Intellectual Impostures (Sokal and Bricmont), 142
intellectuals demands of sciences and humanities: contrasted, 143
intentionality: authorial 61, 169 (*See also* meanings); in literature 123, 204; in science 166, 170, 172–73; stance 36, 213n. 60, 226n. 19
interdisciplinarity: difficulties with, 20–21; pessimism, 149–50, 158, 238n. 113
interference patterns, 15
IQ (intelligence quotient), 104
irrationality: contra science, 137; of literary criticism, 126–27

irreducibility of literary works, 51. *See* reductionism

Jackson, Tony, 161–62
Jakobson, Roman. 13, 41 58–66, 68–69, 74–75, 159, 164, 204
James, Henry, 96, 98
James, William, 13, 117, 126, 208 n. 5, 227 n. 52
Jastrow, Robert, 180
Jencks, Charles, 163, 240 n. 16
Jenkins, Simon, 146–47, 154
Johnson, Samuel, 85, 118
Joyce, James, 42, 95, 140, 163, 165
Jung, Carl Gustav, 41, 53–54, 86, 90–91, 93; collective unconscious, 92; memes, 89
"just-so stories," 81

Kafka, Franz, 42, 95
Kant, Immanuel, 63, 122
Kasparov, Gary, 72
Keats, John, 54, 63
Kekulé, August, 107, 110
Kelvin's Dictum, 219n. 130
Kernan, Alvin, 69, 70, 124, 206
Khlebnikov, 217 n. 90. *See* Xlebnikov
Kimura, Motoo, 154
King Lear, 51
Kipling, Rudyard, 81
Kline, Stephen Jay, 128, 134–36, 150, 153, 155, 168
"knowing that" / "knowing what," 148
Koba the Dread (Amis), 205
Kripke, Saul, 33, 137
Kuhn: incommensurability thesis, 126, 138, 150–53; on history of art, 225 n. 3
Kuhnian science, 172

Lakatos, Imre 110
Lamarck, Jean-Baptiste, 216 n. 65
Lamarckian inheritance, 54, 216 n. 65
Lange, Robert, 103
language instinct, 45, 84
Language Instinct, The (Pinker), 79
Language Thought and Reality (Whorf), 151
Laplace, Pierre-Simon, 135–36
Laplacean determinism, 134, 188
launch windows, 64

INDEX

Laws of Literary Invention, The (Polti), 48, 50
law(s): discipline specific, 26; inviolable, 78, 174; of physics, 24, 77, 86 (*See also* gravity, laws of; Second Law of Thermodynamics); science in legal courts, 15
Leavis, Frank Raymond, 36, 124, 140, 149
Lederberg, Joshua, 25
Lennon, Kathleen, 24, 28
Levi, Primo, 184, 187
Levine, George, 97, 113
Lévi-Strauss, Claude, 46, 59, 74- 76, 93, 200–202
Lewontin, Richard, 81, 82, 99
Limon, John, 18
linguistic(s): analogy with literary study, 75; analyses, flaws in, 67; formulas, resisted 224 n. 98; determinism, 151; as discipline 12, 13, 37; limits of, 206; method of 58, 59, 60, 61, 65, 66, 74, 165, 164; rejection of Whorf, 153; relativism, 151, 153; as science, 39, 40, 57, 76, 164, 208 n. 4; and scientific texts, 18; "turn," 205
Linnaean Taxonomy, 19, 43, 47, 51
literariness (Jakobson), 58, 66, 159
literary: criticism as science, 41; distinct from subliterary, 51, 66, 68–69, 159; empiricism in, 48; ignorance of, 139–40; irreducibility of, 51; politics, 160; science, 18; as structured whole, 42, 48; taxonomies, 43, 48, 49 (*See also* Polti, Georges); value claims for, 51, 160, 164
Literature Lost (Ellis), 45, 56, 124
logical positivism. *See* positivism
London Review of Books, The, 117
long-range sciences, 174
Lovelock, James, 100
Luddites, 138, 236 n. 58
Lycidas (Milton), 159
Lysenko, Trofim, 102

magic, 112
Malin, Irving, 122
maps, 17
marginalizing author, 72
Margulis, Lynn, 35
Marshack, Alexander, 86

Marx, Karl, 176
Marxism, 45–46, 56, 68. *See also* external attitudes
materialism: as theory of mind, 24, 28, 37, 78; as worldview, 31, 39, 56, 134, 189, 197
mathematics: as art, 41; and education, 139; explanatory force of, 146; as language, 146, 152; limited understanding of, 21; realism / formalism, 152, 214 n. 14; non-mathematical sciences, 114; strong, 73, 94. *See also* reductionism
Maxwell, James Clerk, 186
Mazlish, Bruce, 180, 192, 197
McEwan, Ian, 139
meanings: "attended," / "unattended," 64; imposed, 169; unintended, 61, 63–65
medicine, 15
memes, 87–89, 223 n. 60, 239–40 n. 13
Mendel, Gregor, 30, 172
Mendeleyev, Dmitri, 172–73
Menke, Richard, 186
Merquior, José, 200–201
metalanguage: of poets, 62
metaphor in science, 16, 17
metaphysics, 11, 27, 98; Hopi, 151
methodology: of sciences, 15; of non-sciences, 27, 125; monism, 13, 110, 112, 134, 137
Midgely, Mary, 20, 34
Mill, John Stuart, 32
Miller, Geoffrey, 165
Mimesis and the Human Animal (Storey), 161
modern synthesis, 179
Modernism, 49
modular theory of mind, 13, 83–84, 93
Mondrian, Piet, 163
Moore, G. E., 103
moralistic fallacy 103, 120. *See also* naturalistic fallacy
morality: as objective knowledge, 115; and science, 102–3, 129
Morgan, Elaine, 221 n. 21
morphic resonance, 100, 102
Mozart, Wolfgang Amadeus, 146
multidisciplinarity, 21, 153
Murray, Charles, 103, 104
Murray, Gilbert, 52. *See also* Cambridge Ritualists

music: as art, 41; analogous with science, 146, 149
mythology, 44, 90

Naess, Arne, 201
Nagel, Thomas, 103, 175, 189, 190
narrative: regularities across, 53, 92–93; sequence, 50; style, 50
natural kinds, 43, 157
naturalistic fallacy, 103. *See also* moralistic fallacy
Nazis, 115, 129
Necker cube, 87
neo-Lamarckism, 102
neo-pragmatism, 21, 35; continuities with pragmatism, 229 n. 68. *See also* pragmatism
neurosciences: as disciplines, 28–29; neurochemistry, 90, 155; neurology, 135
neutral theory of evolution, 154
New Age movement, 101, 145, 225 n. 2
New Criticism, 170, 177
New Journalism, 125
New Scientist, 145
Newton, Isaac, 18, 162, 172
Newton's Sleep (Tallis), 139, 141, 143
Newtonian universe, 19, 114
Nineteen Eighty-Four (Orwell), 137
Nobel Prize, 144
non-adaptive structures, 82. *See also* spandrels
non-human perspectives, 175
non-scientists, 19
Norris, Christopher, 75, 131, 145, 152
Notes from Underground (Dostoevsky), 137

objectivity: competing senses, 203; as consensus, 113, 227–28 n. 52; in literary study, 56, 207; as prestigious, 115; in science, 106
observation: theory-laden, 106–7, 226 n. 24
Odyssey, The (Homer), 88
O'Hear, Anthony, 106, 138, 173
On Human Nature (Wilson), 98
ontology: of science, 26; of theories, 27
"opinions and ideas" (Booth), 147–48
Oppenheim, Paul, 25–27, 31, 135, 149, 157
Oppenheimer, J. Robert, 140

order of nature, 43. *See also* order of words
order of words, 46
Orr, H. Allen, 154, 239 n. 13
Orwell, George, 137–38, 246 n. 16
over-interpretation, 60
oxidization, 29

paleolithic rock art, 86
painting: analogy with literature, 44, 58
paleontology, 119, 180–81
Panglossian paradigm, 222 n. 29
paracetamol, 155. *See also* acetaminophen
paradigms, 151–52
Paradiso (Dante), 62
parascience, 12
parasite: critic as, 62, 169–70; senses distinguished, 245 n. 2
past tense, 183
Pasteur, Louis, 227 n. 43
pathetic fallacy, 209 n. 12
patterns, 167–70, 215 n. 23
Paulos, John Allen, 141
penicillin, 110
pharmaceutical companies, 101
phenomenological criticism, 45, 46
philistine, 236 n. 58. *See also* Luddite
philology, 41
philosophy as literary genre, 126
philosophy: versus science, 27, 30, 132, 154
phlogiston, 29
photorealism, 19
phrenology, 41
phylogenic tree, 85
physicalism, 24, 28
physics, 63, 112, 115, 136; imperialism, 75, 199
physics envy, 35
Picasso, Pablo, 18–19, 232 n. 114
pidgin, 93, 222 n. 41. *See also* Creole
Pinker, Steven, 39, 45, 72, 79, 81, 85, 93–96, 139–41, 161, 164–65, 173, 192, 208 n. 5
plate tectonics, 17, 19
Plato, 63
playfulness, 121–22
Pleistocene hominids, 80, 81, 162; environment, 220 n. 13
plots: commonalities across geography, 52, 53; and emotions (correlation), 48,

49; numerical limits of, 47, 50, 215 n. 45; as taxa, 44. *See also* Polti, Georges
plumbers, 158
pluralism, 36
poet: as critic, 62–63; as herd animal, 169
poetics, 51, 58, 67
politics: external to criticism, 46, 49; and science, 102–6. *See also* external attitudes
Pollock, Jackson, 240 n. 16
Polti, Georges, 47–51, 53, 56–57, 88, 93, 167
Pomorska, Krystyna, 74
popular fiction, 21, 51, 90, 92. *See also* genre fiction
popularizations of science, 14, 19–20, 22, 138, 143, 148; inadequacy of 144, 149, 154; and popular literary criticism, 208 n. 9; and specialization, 237 n. 85
pornography, 91, 95
positivism, 24, 35, 40, 114, 135; and quantum physics, 234 n. 27
postmodern philosophers, 144
poststructuralism, 94, 96–98, 160, 162, 163
Pound, Ezra Loomis, 42
Powers, Richard, 148–49
pragmatics (linguistic), 12–13
pragmatism: continuities with neo-pragmatism, 229 n. 68; Jamesian, 117–18, 227 n. 52, 228 n. 54; Rortean (contrasted), 127, 228 n. 54
Prague Linguistic Circle, 74
Prandtl, Ludwig, 129
prepared learning, 78, 83
prescriptive grammar, 84–85
Primate Visions (Haraway), 104
primatology, 104–5
primitive formulas of literature, 44
print media: obsolescence of, 69
Professional Correctness (Fish), 157
professionalism: disciplinary, 158, 166
programming language, 36
propositional attitudes, 28–29, 211 n. 26
prosody, 41, 59
Proust, Marcel, 122, 170
pseudoscience, 41, 100–101
psychoanalyis, 12, 68, 177
psycholinguistics, 12, 208 n. 4
psychology: behaviorism, 177, 204; as discipline, 12, 13, 52; interest in fiction, 92; as objective science, 115, 208 n. 4
Ptolemaic cosmology, 196–97, 205
public understanding of science, 149
Putnam, Hilary, 14, 25–27, 31–34, 36, 116, 135, 149, 157, 191

quantum formula of literature, 169
quantum mechanics, 18–19, 131, 228 n. 62
Quine, W. V. O., 125–26

"race memory," 53, 55. *See also* collective unconscious; Jung
race and science, 104
Rachels, James, 171, 174–76, 201–2
racism, 160, 201
ranking disciplines. *See* disciplines, hierarchy
rationalism, 202
Reader's Digest Medical Guide, 144
Red Queen, The (Ridley), 79, 179
reductio ad absurdum, 34
reductionism: hierarchical, 25–29, 31, 94; linguistic, 58–59; literary criticism as, 123; physics, 24; possible "in principle," 235 n. 42; problems with, 32, 34, 211 n. 33; radical, 13, 134, 205–6; smooth, 29, 30, 133, 208 n. 4, 211 n. 26. *See also* conceptual integration; consilience
Reed, Lou, 95
relativism, 12, 56, 94, 204, 207
relativists, 99, 130, 157, 206
relativity: of descriptions to purposes, 124, 157; Einstein's theory of, 18, 197–98
religion, 49, 52, 129
replacement vocabulary, 38
res cogitans, 24–25, 55
rhesus macaques, 104–5, 225 n. 18
rhetoric of science, 17
rhetorical tricks, 132
Richards, Graham, 86
Richards, I. A., 37, 69
Riding, Laura, 60
Ridley, Matt, 79, 177, 179
Rise of the Novel, The (Watt), 194
Robey, David, 75
Roman roads, 184
romanticism: conception of creativity,

56, 57, 69, 74, 152; criticism of, 124–25; incompatibility with science, 180
Rorty, Richard, 14, 30, 35, 36, 40, 94, 97, 113–23, 126–28, 130–32, 137, 151–54, 157–58, 173, 189, 203, 205
Roses, Hilary and Steven, 138
Ross, Andrew, 101–2, 104
Ryder, Richard, 175, 201
Ryle, Gilbert, 148

Saussure, Ferdinand de, 58, 74, 217 n. 77
Scheherazade, 158
Schopenhauer, Arthur, 178–79, 200
Schrödinger, Erwin, 140, 143
science: analogy with music, 146, 238 n. 111; authority, 100; contrasted with religion, 109; contrasted with tradition, 101; of creativity, 72; credibility, 37; and democracy, 109–10, 227 n. 33; disinterest, 68–69; displacing humanities, 194; epistemological superiority of, 22; history of, 225 n. 3; ideology and, 102–3; ignorance of, 22, 139–41; image, 114; language of, 16, 145; learning, 127; of literary criticism, 37, 38, 46; materialism, 12, 199, 202, 205, 207; method, 109–12, 132, 227 n. 37; neologisms in, 16; neutrality of, 103; in painting, 18; in poetry, 216 n. 72; realism, 130; of sportsmen, 64–65, 73; story of, 149; worldview of, 129–30, 132, 151
science fiction, 145
Science Wars (Ross), 104
Scientific American, 145
Searle, John, 71, 221 n. 22
seasonal tropes (generic correlates), 194–195
Second Law of Thermodynamics: as exemplary law, 141–43, 156; inviolability of, 174; in fiction, 186. *See also* Amis
self-deception, 178
Selfish Gene, The (Dawkins), 87, 144, 178
selfish gene, 19
Seligman, Martin, 78, 83
semantic / syntactic analysis, 60
semiology / semitotics, 74
Serres, Michel, 97
sexism, 201
sexual selection, 165

Shakespeare, William, 58–61, 63, 65, 68, 73, 95, 107, 142, 186
Sheldrake Rupert, 100, 102
Shelley, Percy Bysshe, 96, 98–99
side effects, 222 n. 28
Simon, Herbert, 239 n. 8
simulations (computer), 70–72
Sinfield, Alan, 205
skyhooks, 82, 173
Slaughterhouse-Five (Vonnegut), 16, 181, 183
Smith, Peter, 30
Snow, Charles Percy, 14, 23–25, 27, 114, 127, 138–40, 142–43, 145–48, 156, 186, 203
soap operas, 93
Sober, Elliott, 33
Sociobiology (Wilson), 23–24, 199
sociobiology, 23, 80, 98, 103; contrasted with evolutionary psychology, 221 n. 13
Sociobiology Study Group, 103
sociology: consistency with anthropology, 77
soft / hard disciplines, 35, 40
software / hardware language, 73, 213 n. 65
Sokal, Alan, 109, 112, 142–45, 149, 154, 156
"Sonnet 129" (Shakespeare), 59–60
Sontag, Susan, 91, 96, 200
sophistry, 14
Sorrell, Tom, 233 n. 14
spandrels, 82, 221 n. 26
specialization, 21, 25; as educational problem, 25; vocabularies, 59, 131, 150, 153, 157
speciesism, 175, 201
Speigelman, Sol, 89
spiritualism, 122
sports (analogy with poetry), 64–65, 73
square-peg-round-hole, 32- 33, 116–17, 191, 213 n. 62, 230 n. 81. *See also* geometric explanations
SSK (sociology of scientific knowledge), 104, 106, 108, 128, 132, 137
SSSM (standard social science model), 78, 83, 220 n. 2
Stalin, Josef, 102
stances, 36, 213 n. 60
statistical claims (versus axioms), 164

Steiner, George, 103, 183
Stone-Age man, 13. *See also* Pleistocene
Storey, Robert, 161
storylines. *See* plots
structural biology, 235 n. 39
structuralism, 41, 56–57, 74–76
Structure of Scientific Revolutions (Kuhn), 150
stylistics, 64, 67
sub-literary fiction, 92, 96. *See also* genre fiction,
subroutines (computer behavior), 171
supervenience, 20, 116, 135–37, 155, 168
Surrealism, 125
Swiss Army knife theory of mind, 84

Tallis, Raymond, 40, 138–40, 142–43, 145–46, 148–49, 156, 176, 181
Tattersall, Ian, 35, 40
taxonomies: alphabet as, 50; and authorial intention, 167, 169–70; literary, 40, 45–47, 56; reality of, 49
technical vocabulary of criticism (weakness of), 47
technology: contrasted with science, 14, 128–29, 154, 156
territorialism, 149
tessellation, 203
textbooks, 148
textualists, 123, 205
theoretical physics, 145
Theory of Genres, 43
Theory of Modes, 43, 193
Theory of Myths, 43
theory of optics, 162
Theory of Symbols, 16, 43
thermodynamics. *See* Second Law of
Thirty-Six Dramatic Situations (Polti), 47, 50
thirty-six dramatic situations, 49, 89, 167
Time's Arrow (Amis), 180, 183, 185–88
Todorov, Tzvetan, 58, 67–68, 76, 199, 245 n. 1
Tolstoy, Leo, 98
Tooby, John, 77–78, 80–81, 83–84, 97–98, 208 n. 5
traditional culture, 139
transferability of methods, 77
transubstantiation rites, 52, 216 n. 55
Tristes Tropiques (Lévi-Strauss), 200
Trivers, Robert, 177

trivia, 145, 148, 156
tropism, 169, 171–72
truth: as domain relative, 147; and happiness, 119–20. *See also* coherence theory; consensus theory; vocabularies
Turgenev, Ivan, 65, 218 n. 112
Twin Earth (Putnam), 229–30 n. 74
two cultures, 15, 21, 37, 96, 99, 207
Two Cultures (Snow), 14, 23, 139–40, 186, 203

Ulysses (Joyce), 164
Uncertainty Principle, 18–19
unification of disciplines, 34. *See also* reduction, hierarchical; consilience
unity of knowledge: challenged, 108 (*See also* relativism; constructivism); grounds for, 23–24, 35, 75, 77. *See also* consilience
Universal Grammar (UG), 39, 40, 45, 84
un-translatability: of mathematics, 146, 150–51; of great poems, 152
utility: of literary study, 159; of science, 141, 146–48, 154, 156

value judgments, 38, 51, 219 n. 119
van Fraassen, Bas C., 11, 114
Vermeer, Johannes, 19
vestigial features, 80
Vienna Circle, 24, 26
view from nowhere, 103, 175
View From Nowhere, The (Nagel), 189
vocabularies: constitutive, 113, 121; discipline specific, 32, distinctiveness of, 159; specialist, 20, 21, 108
von Neumann, John, 231 n. 99
Vonnegut, Kurt, 16, 181–82, 184, 188–89

Wallace, David Foster, 21
Waste Land, The (Eliot), 163–64
Watson, James, 42, 172–173
Watt, Ian, 190, 194
We (Zamyatin), 137
Wegner, Daniel, 220 n. 142
Weinberg, Steven, 31–32, 129–33, 137, 153, 173, 189
Westermarck effect (incest avoidance), 164
Western Canon, The (Bloom), 69, 124

Whorf, Benjamin Lee, 150–53
Williams, Bernard, 122
Wilson, Edward O., 14, 23–35, 37–39, 49, 58, 73-78, 82, 85, 89–90, 94–96, 98, 100, 113, 134–35, 157, 163, 190, 199, 202
Wimsatt, William K., 60
Wittgenstein, Ludwig, 27
Wolpert, Lewis, 132, 141–43, 145, 156
Wordsworth, William, 57, 65, 72, 96, 98, 99
wormholes, 145

Wuthering Heights (Brontë), 164

Xlebnikov, Velimir, 61, 62, 63

Yale School, 123
Yeats, W. B., 90, 122
Young, Thomas, 15

Zamyatin, Yevgeny, 137, 138
Zeitgeist, 19; and memes, 89
Zeno of Elea, 71
zoology, 114, 149, 166, 175, 228 n. 61